Passage to Modernity

Passage

To

Modernity

An Essay in the Hermeneutics of Nature and Culture

Louis Dupré

Yale University Press

New Haven and London   1993

Published with assistance from the Louis
Stern Memorial Fund

Designed by Deborah Dutton.
Set in Trump Mediaeval and Syntax types by
DEKR Corp., Woburn, Massachusetts.
Printed in the United States of America by
BookCrafters, Inc., Chelsea, Michigan.

Library of Congress Cataloging-in-Publication
Data

Dupré, Louis K.
    Passage to modernity : an essay in the
hermeneutics of nature and culture / Louis
Dupré.
        p. cm.
    Includes bibliographical references and
index.
    ISBN 0-300-05531-5 (cloth: alk. paper)
        0-300-06501-9 (pbk.: alk. paper)
    1. Philosophy, Modern.   2. Philosophy,
Renaissance.   3. Nominalism.   4. Humanism,   5. Self (Philosophy)   6. Nature.
7. Culture.   I. Title.   II. Title: Modernity.
B791.D86   1993
190—dc20   93-2940

A catalogue record for this book is available
from the British Library.

10 9 8 7 6 5 4 3 2

For Edith
who graces nature

Contents

Preface

The subtitle of this work is to be taken quite literally. My
book purports to be no more than an essay, despite the dis-
tressing number of footnotes. Much in the argument must
remain undeveloped and a good deal of its claims less than
fully supported. On each topic more qualified scholars have written specialized studies. If I have nevertheless presumed to write generally on a
subject that has challenged so many specialists, it is because the subject
has proven to be of vital significance for the understanding of our time.
That understanding begins not with the Enlightenment, but with a complex intellectual revolution that occurred toward the end of the Middle
Ages.

Despite the modesty of its present achievement, this work is indebted
to many: first, my students at Yale in a course presumptuously called
"The Shape of Modernity"; next, my hosts at the Higher Institute of
Philosophy of Leuven, University College of Dublin, the Istituto degli
Studi Filosofici at Naples, the Colloquio Castelli in Rome, the Vrije
Universiteit in Amsterdam, and the Royal Academy of Belgium, all of
which honored me with invitations to lecture on some aspect of this
topic; finally and most sincerely, those who were kind enough to read
parts of my text and by their criticisms prevented at least some rash

conclusions, unwarranted generalizations, and incorrect interpretations from finding their way to print. Among them I mention with particular gratitude Marjorie O'Rourke Boyle, Jacques De Visscher, Ernan McMullin, James Murphy, Cyril O'Regan, Edward and Rebecca Papa, Hilmar Pavel, and Kathryn Tanner. Michael Buckley and Thomas P. McTighe wrote incisive critical comments on the entire manuscript. So did Charles Trinkaus, a scholar as generous as learned, to whose comments and writings I owe a great debt. Finally, special thanks to Hans-Georg Gadamer who some years ago encouraged me to undertake this project. Susan Lucibelli has, once again, competently and patiently transferred constantly revised manuscripts into a coherent text.

Passage to Modernity

Introduction

The idea of modernity has long attracted critical attention. Many hold its principles responsible for various ills that threaten to drain our culture of meaning and purpose. Those charges presuppose that we know how to distinguish the *modern* from the *premodern*. Most critics, however, finding it unnecessary to be precise on this issue, remain satisfied with reversing the praise that earlier generations showered upon an allegedly modern mode of thinking and acting. While they exalted rational objectivity, moral tolerance, and individual choice as cultural absolutes, we now regard these principles with some suspicion. Undoubtedly there are good reasons to distrust the equation of the real with the objectifiable, progress with technological advances, and liberty of thought and action with detachment from tradition and social bonds. But should we attribute all such excesses to the original principles of modern culture? At the very least an assessment of modernity requires that we establish what the original revolution implied and what may have been unnecessary developments or even deviations from it. Much thereby depends on where we place the borderstones marking the beginning of the epoch.

If we plant these borderstones at the onset of the Enlightenment, the critique will continue to have an easy target, for neither the theories nor the practices of that optimistically progressive and narrowly rationalist period enjoy much support today. But is such an equation fair? The Enlightenment isolated certain principles from their original context and simplified complex principles and theories it inherited from the preceding two centuries. Its originality has been singularly overrated. The epoch of Galileo, Descartes, and Newton, on the contrary, excelled in innovative thinking. Whitehead called the seventeenth century the century of genius, and leading European cultures have referred to it as their classic age in art and literature. But the success of its most outstanding achievement has brought to the scientific project a disproportionate significance in evaluating the rise of modern culture. The Renaissance, which preceded it, contributed other, theoretically no less influential principles of modern culture. Such contemporary critics as Stephen Toulmin and Alasdair McIntyre have rightly objected to the unwarranted equation of the modern project with the scientific conceptions of the seventeenth century. Indeed, the very heterogeneity of the originating principles forces us to look for a more primitive cultural layer.

That archaic phase, beginning in the late fourteenth century and mostly completed before the end of the fifteenth, brought to a conclusion arguments that were initiated in medieval theology yet also gave rise to an early humanism. That humanism, though thoroughly innovative, preserved, as Paul Kristeller has shown, a strong link with medieval Italian culture. "Italy had a narrow but persistent tradition of her own which went back to ancient Roman times and which found its expression in certain branches of the arts and of poetry, in lay education and in legal customs, and in the study of grammar and rhetoric."[1] Early Italian humanism developed quite naturally out of a native rhetorical tradition of the Italian Middle Ages. Dante and Petrarch, while proudly aware of their creative originality, remain fully loyal to a medieval worldview. Indeed, so much so that later humanists in northern Europe thought of Petrarch exclusively as a medieval figure.[2] The term *phase* may be inappropriate to refer to a variety of currents dispersed over separate movements—some literary or artistic, others philosophical or theological—frequently in conflict with one another. Nor is there a straight continuity with the later stages of modern culture, as if this archaic layer constituted the simple core of all subsequent developments. In some way the principles of early humanism, however seminal, stand in clear opposition with those developments. They introduced an alternative position.

Only when the early humanist notion of human creativity came to form a combustive mixture with the negative conclusions of nominalist theology did it cause the cultural explosion that we refer to as modernity. Its impact shattered the organic unity of the Western view of the real. The earliest Ionian concept of *physis* had combined a physical (in the modern sense!) with an anthropic and a divine component. The classical Greek notion of *kosmos* (used by Plato and Aristotle), as well as the Roman *natura*, had preserved the idea of the real as an harmonious, all-inclusive whole. Its organic unity had been threatened by the Hebrew-Christian conception of a Creator who remained outside the cosmos. Yet, through his wisdom, support, and grace, he continued to be present in this world. At the end of the Middle Ages, however, nominalist theology effectively removed God from creation. Ineffable in being and inscrutable in his designs, God withdrew from the original synthesis altogether. The divine became relegated to a supernatural sphere separate from nature, with which it retained no more than causal, external link. This removal of transcendence fundamentally affected the conveyance of meaning. Whereas previously meaning had been established in the very act of creation by a wise God, it now fell upon the human mind to interpret a cosmos, the structure of which had ceased to be given as intelligible. Instead of being an integral part of the cosmos, the person became its source of meaning. Mental life separated from cosmic being: as meaning-giving "subject," the mind became the spiritual substratum of all reality. Only what it objectively constituted would count as real. Thus reality split into two separate spheres: that of the mind, which contained all intellectual determinations, and that of all other being, which received them.

In this book I intend to investigate the origins, the process, and the effects of this double breakup: the one between the transcendent constituent and its cosmic-human counterpart, and the one between the person and cosmos (now understood in the narrower sense of physical nature). The two combined caused the ontotheological synthesis that had guided Western thought to break down. Only recently have we become fully aware of the momentous impact of the abandonment of that theoretical ideal, defined more than two millennia ago. The critique of modern culture began in the nineteenth century, but its early forms focused on the problematic condition of one of the isolated components—the cosmos or the self—rather than on the break-up of the original unity. Thus Hegel in his *Phenomenology* describes cultural alienation as inherent in culture itself, even though he illustrates his thesis by a particularly modern instance of it: the artificial civilization of the seventeenth-century court, resulting in the revolutionary tensions between a "base" and a "noble" consciousness. Dissatisfied with such a purely ideological argument, Marx linked those tensions to a specific social-economic development of the modern age: the rise of industrial capitalism. But that critique remains within the parameters of a culture conceived as a process of self-directed transformation. It fails to question the definition. As a result, Marx's attempt to restore the person to a premodern wholeness merely succeeded in constraining the human model to one of the more questionable con- sequences of the modern fragmentation, namely, that of the *homo faber* opposed to nature, without any transcendent mediation between them.

Similarly, when Freud took our civilization to task for its repressive character (especially in *Civilization and Its Discontents*), he pointed out that the erotic (*Eros*) and the aggressive (*Thanatos*) drives had increasingly jeopardized the human potential for happiness. But he never explained why Eros has become an obstacle in the formation of modern society and, particularly, why Thanatos has grown into such a menacing threat. Freud remained keenly aware of the historical nature of the cultural repression, but he raised no questions about the particular cause that started the process in a specific time period. Like Marx, he remained within the modern premises: the physical world appears as an independent, often antagonistic reality, and religion as an illusion, temporarily useful but eventually to be overcome. Nietzsche went further in his critique. He questioned the ontotheological conception that has dominated Western thought from the beginning. Since Socrates our culture has given an absolute priority to the Logos, and it has justified its one-sidedly intellec- tualist orientation by founding it on the idea of a spiritual God. The nihilism inherent in this idea has increasingly undermined the ontotheo- logical foundation of Western thought. In Nietzsche's critique the modern epoch merely intensified and completed a process that had begun in the fifth century B.C. Nietzsche attributes no particular significance to the early modern epoch: the seeds of nihilism have been present since Socrates.

Without unduly oversimplifying, we can, I think, conclude that each of the three great critics focused on one of the components of the onto- theological synthesis. Marx denounced the distorted relation of the person to the natural world, which has resulted in alienation from both the natural and the social environment. Freud focused on the predicament of the modern self. Nietzsche both denounced the Platonic-Christian idea of transcendence and feared its departure. All three described our condition as having now become problematic, yet none identified the problem with modern culture as such.

Although, generally speaking, contemporary critics have come to question principles specific to the modern epoch, several continue to follow Nietzsche in viewing the entire process of Western thought as a continuous tradition headed from the start for the problematic rationalism of today's culture. Not only the modern phase of this development, but the ontotheological synthesis that stands at the origin of Western thought, led to our present predicament. Heidegger and, in our own day, Derrida and Rorty share this view with Nietzsche. Others detect a deep *caesura* between the modern outlook as it finally settled in its definitive form (not before the seventeenth century) and the premodern period. Rather than holding ontotheology responsible for present woes, they attribute them to its break-up. Stressing the difference, they deny that the modern conclusions follow from the ancient premises, even though the Greek-Christian theoretical orientation created the possibility of the later development. Thus, the modern primacy of the subject, while inconceivable outside a theoretically oriented culture, nevertheless cannot be derived from ancient *theoria* or medieval contemplation. This second group includes defenders as well as outspoken critics of modernity. Among them are Hans Blumenberg and John H. Randall, Eric Voegelin and Alasdair McIntyre.

This book also separates the modern period from the preceding one on the basis of an essential distinction. But it further distinguishes the early humanist conception that transformed the nature of the interaction among the components of the traditional synthesis from the later idea of a subject conceived as sole source of meaning and value. Although the former changed the relations within the synthesis, it did not destroy the synthesis itself. The extraordinary creativity that introduced modern culture, even while the old synthesis was breaking up, held, in fact, the promise of a new cultural integration. The latter was a far more radical revolution, partly induced by the disintegrating effect of older late medieval factors. Since the formation of modern culture consists of a number of quite heterogeneous factors and cannot be reduced to a single set of principles, it requires a hermeneutic before admitting a critique. My essay remains principally on the level of the former. I felt that the very complexity of the elements involved in the making of modern culture left no choice but to be modest in criticizing it.

Moreover, we are still living in the modern age and, however critical we may be of the principles established at its beginning, we continue to share many of them. Critics of modernity implicitly accept more of its assumptions than they are able to discard. Even those who globally reject its theoretical principles continue to build on them. Post-modern critics are unambiguous enough, it seems, in repudiating the primacy of the subject, the reduction of the real to the objective, as well as the logocentric emphasis on epistemological issues. Yet does the self-referential nature of thought and language assumed by several post-modern authors not return speech to the central position from which the theory had expelled the speaking subject? Has the post-modernist critique gone beyond de-sublimating modernity while still remaining part of it? Whatever the answer to these questions may be, I trace the problematic features of modern thought to a more recent epoch than Nietzsche's followers usually do. Its seeds lie buried not in the sands of ancient or early medieval rationalism but in a set of assumptions newly formulated at the closing of the Middle Ages.

The fact that I attribute modern problems to modern principles does not imply that I expect their solution from a return to premodern principles. Cultural changes, such as the one that gave birth to the modern age, have a definitive and irreversible impact that transforms the very essence of reality. Not merely our thinking about the real changes: reality itself changes as we think about it differently. History carries an ontic significance that excludes any reversal of the present. Nor is it possible to capture that changing reality in an ahistorical system. Indeed, if the argument advanced in the following pages concerning the fragmentation of what once constituted an integrated synthesis of thinking, being, and acting is at all valid, then no all-comprehensive, timeless metaphysical reflection in the classical style can come to grips with our present existence. The disintegration of what once used to be integral components of a single reality deprives such a reflection of its object. Individual thinkers and entire schools of thought critical of the modern fragmentation have attempted to reverse its effects by returning to premodern premises. We have witnessed the birth of neo-Aristotelians, neo-Platonists (in both senses of the term), neo-Thomists, and, most recently, neo-nominalists. Those who, by updating past thoughts, hoped to neutralize such baneful features of modern thought as the opposition between subject and object or the loss of a transcendent component underestimated the radical nature of the modern revolution. Its problems cannot be treated as errors to be corrected by a simple return to an earlier truth. That truth is no longer available; it has vanished forever. Undoubtedly, as I shall argue, the past possesses a permanent meaning, and philosophical reflection in particular never loses its timeliness. Plato and Aristotle still have more to say to us than any of our contemporaries. But past thought cannot solve modern problems. Though eternal in its own way, it does not address conditions that are exclusively our own—such as the fragmentation of our world picture. It may assist us in sorting out modern issues, but it does not provide ready answers. Modern culture has introduced a totally new way of confronting the real. A proper method for dealing with it requires first and foremost that we critically recognize that difference. We have only recently begun to do so. As T. S. Eliot wrote, "We had the experience but missed the meaning."

A genuinely new synthesis, if ever to come, will have to rest on newly established principles. Meanwhile, the philosophical explorations made by major thinkers, particularly those of the modern age, can assist us in preparing it—as they, with increasing clarity, have formulated the issues that are at stake. In our own century such philosophers as Bergson, Whitehead, and Heidegger have emphasized the ontological significance of change and historicity and have thereby made it possible to recognize at least the possibility of a genuine novelty of being. That a new synthesis nevertheless continues to elude us does not justify abandoning the search for it. Our present task may well be the humble one of exploring how the fragments we are left with may serve as building blocks for a future synthesis.

But the claim made in this book concerns not only, and not even primarily, the future. If significant cultural changes affect the very heart of the real, the past retains a permanent meaning in the present. Though an introduction hardly presents an opportunity for providing the needed philosophical support, it must nevertheless lay out, in a summary way, the basic presupposition of this claim. Unless we assume that the cultural revolution of the modern age was an event of ontological significance that changed the nature of Being itself, much of what is discussed in the following chapters would bear little meaning to the present. The argument underlying this essay was guided by the idea that change has a significance that goes well beyond the contingent historical conditions in which it occurred. It marks a new epoch in being.

Does the historically transient ever acquire permanent significance? On the basis of a long-held view that the ultimately real is essentially unchangeable, most thinkers of the past have answered this question in the negative. Why should what begins in time and is destined to disappear with time not be as transient in meaning as in appearance? Metaphysics has generally continued to accept Parmenides' early disjunction: Being is or it is not—thus allowing no room for ontological novelty. Yet from the beginning philosophers have had afterthoughts about the principle. Already Plato (in this respect following Heraclitus) broke through Parmenides' static position when he elevated motion (kinēsis) to a rank equal to rest (stasis) as one of the two super-ideas in which all others participate. Generally speaking, however, identity continued to prevail, as witnessed by the eternal motion of the Greek kosmos, the unchanging God of medieval theology who creates in accordance with eternal ideas, and the mathematical model of rationalist philosophy. Only recently have philosophers begun to adopt a more dynamic ontology in which becoming presents the real face of Being.

If Being reveals itself only through time, the successiveness of its disclosure must possess a permanent significance. For that reason, cultural symbols of the past continue to illuminate present existence. One of philosophy's tasks consists in showing the permanent truth of those transient expressions. Karl Jaspers wrote: "If history is the disclosure of Being, then truth is present at each stage—never completed but always in movement."[3] Where there is truth, there is permanent, though not necessarily static, meaning. One of the first thinkers to seek the permanent meaning of the transient historical processes, Ernst Cassirer, declared it to be his intention to "accomplish for the totality of cultural forms what [Kant's] transcendent critique has done for pure cognition."[4] But what is the source that conveys this ideal permanence to the transient forms of culture? Is it merely the reflecting mind itself, as Cassirer thought? Heidegger denied it. Only if Being itself is intrinsically temporal, are we justified in attributing a permanent meaning to cultural processes. That Being is indeed temporal and that it discloses itself through history, is, of course, Heidegger's well-known thesis. Yet the same Heidegger pronounced all Western philosophy since Socrates a prolonged misunderstanding! Obviously, our contemporaries continue to struggle with the problem of ontological novelty.[5]

One particular difficulty inherent in any search for such a permanent meaning is that it must probe beyond the more or less coherent but always provisional conceptions through which a particular epoch understands itself in order to find its lasting significance. The fact that medieval thinkers supported their worldview by a now abandoned cosmology does not render the philosophical systems of Aquinas, Scotus, or Ockham obsolete. But how shall we decide what in the transient course of history possesses permanent meaning without exposing ourselves to all the prejudices of the present? If all truth has an historical dimension, then the truth about history is itself historical, and we must be prepared to accept that further reflection may judge the past differently from the way we do. We may concede this without being unduly disturbed by it. Each generation has a task to understand how the fundamental shifts in being and thinking are reflected in the present. Specifically in this work, my question is the hermeneutic one: How is the shift that occurred at the dawn of the modern age to be seen in the light of our thinking, feeling, and valuing today? Future generations may make different appraisals, but they will not invalidate ours now. Precisely by its hermeneutic approach our project differs from that of the history of ideas on which it so heavily relies. The historian of ideas considers ideas under their formal aspect— as expressions of the mental life of a particular epoch. As ideal conceptions the historian may rank them all equal, without attaching a decisive significance to their lasting truth or lack thereof. Indeed, for the Kantian founders of that intellectual branch of history, metaphysical issues counted for little more than other historical phenomena. Cultural epochs come and go, introducing forms, concepts, and structures, which in due time will make room for others. In their wake they leave historical monuments, works of art, intellectual and technical achievements, as well as a sizable amount of cultural flotsam. Ideas may play a guiding role in structuring the form of an epoch. Yet once they cease to capture attention, they appear as ideologies destined to take their place in the museum of past beliefs. Nothing leaves a more discouraging impression of the futility of human convictions than a mere history of their succession. A reflection on past thought that is not a search for permanent meaning leaves us defenseless against cultural nihilism.

An even more fundamental distinction separates a philosophical reflection on past culture from a social one. Philosophers omit economic, social, or technical factors from their consideration. It cannot be doubted, however, that those factors have created conditions indispensable for the emergence of the ideal structures that philosophy is concerned with. Yet by themselves such contingent elements fail to account for the coherence of a worldview that integrates wide-ranging philosophical, religious, scientific, social, and aesthetic elements. The early capitalist, town-based economy undoubtedly transformed the models of thinking and feeling of a previously rural society,[6] but neither economic nor social changes explain the inner cohesiveness of ideal forms. To take account of nonideal factors in a search for the ideal meaning of culture is necessary; to treat them as causes, deceptive. Causal explanations hold true only within the same order of reality in which their alleged effects appear. Beyond that, they function at most as conditions. No causal interpretation could ever explain why a cultural complex gradually loses its intrinsic meaning, nor how a new one succeeds in disengaging itself from the subsequent cultural chaos. As one social historian wrote at the end of a distinguished career: "The more one penetrates into an epoch of historical development and comes to study its processes as well as its individual shapes, the more such [sociological] interpretations become questionable. The 'rational' appears ever more helpless, and the historical becomes ever darker and deeper. Incomprehensible powers—but are they powers?—exercise their impact and our interpretation turns more and more into a mere description and a pious guessing of ultimate enigmas."[7]

Historical explanations of the appearance of new patterns of culture and thought should start from an awareness that deducing them from earlier factors will never suffice for justifying their historical novelty. Thus, to present the intellectual gestalt of modern thought as a secularization of Christian theology (as Karl Loewith did in *Meaning in History* [1949]) is to miss an essential feature of modernity, namely, that it marked a departure from what came before. As Hans Blumenberg pointed out in his classic *The Legitimacy of Modern Age*, there is something irreducibly original about the modern age.

Any interpretation of the past aims at understanding the present. Yet in the process of doing so it affects the future as well and thereby the very development of the real itself. Those who in a particular epoch impose a new pattern of meaning on the life and thought of their time do more than apply a different film of thought to an indifferent reality. They transform the nature of reality itself. If the preceding carries any metaphysical weight, it would be contained in the unoriginal thesis that Being must not be conceived as a substance unmoved by thought. Cultural changes leave a different reality in their wake. Applied to the present subject, this means that nature became "nature" only within a human vision and that any fundamental change in that vision effects a change in nature itself. That such a thesis must not be dismissed as subjective idealism appears in the dialectic between nature and mind as developed by recent philosophers such as Maurice Merleau-Ponty. Even contemporary scientists and theoreticians of science, however reticent to discuss ultimate essences, do not hesitate to speak of the nature of the universe as if it contained an ideal component. Mathematical equations, artificial intelligence, principles of determinacy or indeterminacy—all assume a real relation between the mental and the physical. Indeed, is not the most remarkable quality of the real, the one that supports our ability to discourse about it, that it includes an ideal element without which it would never have given birth to mental life? As Karl Popper wrote: "I would even suggest that the greatest riddle of cosmology may well be neither the original big bang, nor the problem why there is something rather than nothing—but that the universe is, in a sense, creative: that it created life, and from it mind—our consciousness—which illuminates the universe and which is creation in its turn.[8]

Culture, then, consists not in what humans add to the real, so to speak. It is the active component of the real itself transforming the passive one.[9] Yet culture performs its active function inadequately if it does not adopt a listening as well as a speaking role with regard to a given nature. Ideally it displays the creative give-and-take of a good conversation: we allow our ideas, values, and customs to be shaped by a given order, in the very process of transforming that order. Contrary to the ancients, the moderns have come to regard culture rather exclusively as an autonomous human creation. This change in the attitude toward nature forms a central theme in the following argument.

Due to its particular focus—the fragmentation of the ontotheological synthesis—this study places much emphasis on the religious factor. Indeed, religion, at first in the form of theology, later in spiritual life and aesthetic expression, did play a major part in the transforming process. The fragmentation was set in motion by nominalist theology while the temporary reunification was accomplished by the cultural-religious movement of the Baroque. But all chapters between the first and the last show a concern to reintegrate the elusive transcendent component on which the synthesis had rested. This focus may also explain—if not fully justify—the historical bounds set to this book. Few of the principles determining modern culture were established before the end of the fourteenth century and even fewer after the first half of the seventeenth. Moreover, the 1648 peace that concluded thirty years of almost universal European warfare froze into a definitive political and spiritual condition what until then had appeared a reversible process. Its cultural, religious, and political division of a common heritage has continued to define the spiritual outlook as well as the political attitudes of European nations. The French historian Henri Daniel-Rops rightly considered it the date that concluded the formation of the modern age.

> The Treaties of Westphalia finally sealed the relinquishment by statesmen of a noble and ancient concept, a concept which had dominated the Middle Ages: that there existed among the baptized people of Europe a bond stronger than all their motives for wrangling—a spiritual bond, the concept of Christendom. Since the fourteenth century, and especially during the fifteenth, this concept had been steadily disintegrating. . . . The Thirty Years' War proved beyond a shadow of a doubt that the last states to defend the ideal of a united Christian Europe were invoking that principle while in fact they aimed at maintaining or imposing their own supremacy. It was at Münster and Osnabrück that Christendom was buried. The tragedy was that nothing could replace it; and twentieth-century Europe is still bleeding in consequence.[10]

The cultural conditions that made this development possible were created long before. Uncovering them will require the long prolepsis into the past of chapter 1. Weighing the full impact of the early modern revolution demands occasional explorations into the present or the recent past; they occur mostly in the final chapters.

Part I

From Cosmos

to Nature

This great grandmother of all creatures bred,

Great Nature—ever young yet full of eld,

Still moving, yet unmoved from her stead,

Unseen of any, yet of all beheld.

—Edmund Spenser, *Mutability Canto* VII, 13

Chapter 1

Classical and Medieval Antecedents

Nature as Form

Leslie Stephen described the term *nature* as contrived to introduce the maximum number of equivocations into any theory it enters.[1] The semantic disintegration of what once functioned as a single, though complex, concept into a multiplicity of meanings began when *physis* became *natura* and was completed when, early in the modern age, nature lost two of its three original components.

In Greek myths as well as in early philosophy, *physis* appears simultaneously as a primordial, formative event and as the all-inclusive, informed reality that results from this event. *To be* consists in partaking in an aboriginal act of expression. Nothing precedes that expression. As ontological ultimate it provides the definitive answer to the question how things came about.[2] Indeed, the eruption from the chaos of non-being remains itself beyond the reach of rational discourse. Cosmogonic myths, as they survive in the poetically polished and coherently ordered versions found in Homer's and Hesiod's poems and possibly in Plato's description of the Demiurge in the *Timaeus*, articulate this timeless yet time-constituting event. One version known only from late Gnostic sources, but probably more ancient in origin, personalizes the original void in the couple *Bythos* (abyss) and *Sigē* (silence). From this formless, speechless emptiness springs forth a universe of meaning and form.

The first Greek thinker known to have presented *physis* as an all-comprehensive, creative principle was Thales of Milete (ca. 625–545 B.C.) A millennium later Proclus (410–483) still considered that same one principle of nature the source of all beings. "The one Nature has the many natures dependent from it, and, conversely, these are derived from one Nature, that of the whole."[3] In this one sentence the last great Greek philosopher encapsulates the lengthy process by which classical thought made the transition from an only partially unified *physis* to a single but complex *kosmos*, that is, an ordered totality of being. The Ionian sources of Greek reflection conceived of nature as dynamic and extended in time. A different, South Italian strain of thought, possibly of Pythagorean origin, presented reality as unchangeable in essence. According to Parmenides (ca. 504–456 B.C.) the *physis* of the Ionians, which started with one principle yet then broke into a multiplicity, did not properly describe the true nature of things. The first principle remains unique, incorruptible, and indivisible. The realm of appearances, object of Ionian speculation, yields no genuine knowledge but only opinion. Parmenides himself presented a cosmology of the appearing world in the second part of his famous poem, which he cautiously entitled "The Way of Opinion." While this South Italian thinker excluded movement from being, Heraclitus in Asia Minor identified nature with strife and change.

Plato influenced Greek speculation on nature in two important ways. Gradually the notion of *physis* had become normative. Some Sophists had used it for construing a purely naturalist code of behavior. The model of nature, they argued, justified what instinct induces humans (like other animals) to do. In response to the threat of moral relativism implied by such an interpretation of nature, Plato (if not Socrates before him) specified the normative quality of *physis* in accordance with the particular nature of each being. Nature, then, prescribes a different conduct to beings animated by a spiritual soul. This moral specification was to play a decisive part in future ethical theory.

Plato's other contribution, though less recognized, may have had even greater consequences. In Book X of *The Laws* he followed a different line of attack, denying that *physis* could ever function as ultimate norm of conduct. *Physis* itself depends on an ulterior principle, he argued, and it is one that definitively deprives naturalism from any support. As a principle of movement, the mysterious Athenian of *The Laws* reasons, nature must be subordinated to a higher principle that moves itself as well as other beings. Since self-movement belongs exclusively to living beings, soul, the principle of life, must be regarded to be more primitive than nature. But if soul comes first, then nature depends upon a higher, spiritual order, and "it is the existence of the soul which is most eminently natural" (892 c). Plato thus distinguishes in the original concept of nature two distinct principles: a transcendent one that functions as the cause of motion, and one that depends on it as its effect. This distinction laid the philosophical basis for later attempts to integrate the classical concept of nature with that of a Hebrew-Christian Creator beyond nature.

Aristotle limits his use of *physis* to a principle of motion (*Physics* II, 1) in beings capable of self-induced motion and rest, which, for him, surprisingly included the four elements. He defined it as "a source or cause of being moved and of being at rest in that to which it belongs primarily, in virtue of itself," thereby opposing "natural" beings to artifacts.[4] Nature teleologically directs organic processes to their destined perfection. It establishes the norms that things developing in time must follow if they are to attain their projected end. The more comprehensive term *kosmos* constitutes the ordered totality of being that coordinates those processes as well as the laws that rule them. *Kosmos* includes, next to the *physis* of organic being, the *ethos* of personal conduct and social structures, the *nomos* of normative custom and law, and the *logos*, the rational foundation that normatively rules all aspects of the cosmic development. It thus appears obvious that the narrowing of the content of *physis* in Plato and Aristotle disqualifies it from being regarded as the single predecessor of the modern concept of nature. We have two concepts to consider: one that has shrunk its original meaning and another that has extended its own, or at least made it far more precise—*physis* and *kosmos*.

What did the Greeks of the classical era understand by *kosmos*? Clearly, its meaning of ordered totality exceeded that of the physical universe we now call cosmos. Moral and aesthetic values were as much a part of it as physical (in the modern sense) processes. When Philo later refers to the realm of ideas as a cosmos in its own right, he does not so much add a spiritual dimension as he separates the original cosmos into two parts. That separation may have been prepared by Plato's myth of the cosmos as the work of a divine Demiurge. Nonetheless, classical thought preserved the original, all-comprehensiveness of the *kosmos* that included the gods and was considered divine by Greek thinkers down to the sixth century A.D. In equating the Greek *kosmos* with the physical world, we project a later, narrower concept upon the more comprehensive Greek one. The modern translation of *kosmos* as "physical nature" is quite misleading since originally *kosmos* included theological and anthropic as well as physical meanings. The loss of the former two reflects the disintegration of the ancient ontotheological synthesis.

What induced the Greeks of the classical age to refer to the comprehensive structure of the real as *kosmos,* a term that originally meant "order"? It was, I believe, not so much a philosophical idea as a primitive intuition that determined the entire development of classical thought. If there is one belief Greek thinkers shared, it must be the conviction that both the essence of the real and our knowledge of it consists ultimately of *form.* Basically this means that it belongs to the essence of the real to *appear,* rather than to hide, and to appear in an orderly way. By envisioning the real as such as harmonious appearance, the Greek view displays a uniquely aesthetic quality, expressed as much in architecture and sculpture as in philosophy. That appearance, however, derives not from our subjective perception of the real; it is the form itself that shines forth. Indeed, Plato was to raise the form principle to an intellectual level inaccessible to sense perception.

Like all reflective civilizations, the Greek one experienced the need to justify the simultaneous presence of unity and multiplicity, of order and chaos, of harmony and strife. A similar concern dominated Indian sagas of the Vedantic age in their attempt to overcome all duality. Buddhism also strove to resolve the tension responsible for all suffering by reducing the multiple to an ultimate simplicity. But what distinguishes the Greek solution is its particular mode of holding these opposite principles in balance. Parmenides' initial attempt to reduce the real to a unity without multiplicity was not followed by later thinkers, who found the essence of the real in the complexity of harmonious form. The greater its formal quality, the more a thing deserves to be called real. Hence the surprising reference to the supremely real as the beautiful, that is, the perfect form.

Form operates thereby as the principle that reconciles discordant forces of conflict and disorder. Tragedy, in which the Greeks most directly articulated their existential concerns, dramatically asserts this ultimate rule of balance through form. Only in the creation of formal harmony does the mind resist the assaults of chaos and disintegration that constantly threaten the *kosmos.* The horrors of inherited guilt, parricide, incest, and infanticide presented by classical drama end up being subdued by the serene indifference of the eternal, cosmic order. On the human level that order, so easily disturbable by unbridled passion, succeeds in imposing its rule only after much conflict and strife.[5] Through resignation and that unique enlightenment acquired by suffering, humans learn to submit to the cosmic law and to discover that "deeper harmony" which Heraclitus deemed superior to a conflictless one. Everywhere—in mythical and philosophical reflection, as well as in architecture and sculpture— we encounter a fascination with form.

As mythical intuition developed into philosophical reflection, form moved even closer to the center of Greek thought. In diverse ways it came to constitute the very essence of being. Already Anaximander's metaphysical speculation on the origin of things concludes with the moral axiom that things which in their particularity threaten the primeval order eventually must "pay penalty and retribution to each other for their injustice according to the assessment of time."[6] Where the ultimately real consists more in the formal order of things than in their actual existence, the maintenance of the cosmic equilibrium becomes a crucial ontological issue. For the early physicists, nothing can be fully real without being in a state of harmony. Thales' water and Anaximenes' air, rather than functioning as substantial principles, present states of balance. The Pythagorean position differs from the Ionian one in that it locates the proportion of forms in a rational pattern that lies beyond appearances. It thereby seems to introduce a fundamental change in the nature of form as the appearing of the absolute. In fact, however, the change does not shake the original principle. Form continues to appear, though not immediately in sense perception but in an intellectual intuition. Thus it found its way to Plato's and all subsequent philosophy. Without denying the material quality of nature, the Pythagoreans judged the mathematical form to be more significant than the sensory appearance. To know the form required that the mind turn in upon itself.

The ideas of form and cosmic balance received a full ontological foundation in the metaphysical speculations of Parmenides and Heraclitus. For Heraclitus, the essence of the real consists quite literally in a dynamic harmony of opposites. Parmenides, though he relegated multiplicity and opposition to another, less substantial realm, nevertheless prepared Plato's view of spiritual form as separate from the physical appearance. The appearing world is real only to the extent that it partakes in this pure form. To know (*eidenai*) consists essentially in communing with the forms (*eidē*). It is a seeing (the aorist form *eidon* is derived from the same root) in the light that, radiating from the forms themselves "like a blaze kindled by a leaping spark," is generated in the soul.[7] How firm a grip the form principle had on Plato appears in his attempt to extend it to the invisible, intelligible realm, and even to its hidden origin—the good. As form consists in being well proportioned and shining with its own inner light, the beautiful (*to kalon*) becomes equated with goodness, to occupy the highest rank in the order of the real. Earthly imitations of the ideal forms—society and physical nature—reflect this celestial harmony. The good state, itself a supreme work of art, must educate its citizens in achieving harmony within their souls as well as with each other.

The concept of harmonious form dominates all of Plato's thinking about the physical universe. In the early dialogue *Gorgias* he writes: "Wise men, Callicles, say that the heavens and the earth, gods and men, are bound together by fellowship and friendship, and order and temperance and justice, and for this reason they call the sum of things the 'ordered' universe (*kosmos*), my friend, not the world of disorder and riot."[8] The later *Timaeus* is one long rhapsodic hymn on the beauty and harmony of that *kosmos*. Fashioned by a kindly and generous architect who "kept his gaze fixed on the Eternal" (29A), the world reflects its divine paradigm by the perfection of its form. The terms *symmetry* and *proportion* constantly return in the description. The Demiurge made the *kosmos* "in the shape of a sphere, equidistant in all directions from the center of the extremities, which of all shapes is the most perfect and the most self-similar, since He deemed that the similar is infinitely fairer than the dissimilar" (33B). The divine architect chooses the perfect motion for his work—one that allows it to spin around its axis at a uniform speed while remaining in the same spot. Endowed with a soul—the *anima mundi*, destined for a glorious career in the Middle Ages and Renaissance—the cosmos participates in the perfection of the eternal ideas and, even like them, serves as a model for ordering human life. The divine quality of the cosmos lies not in its spiritual being as such—being is only one of the ingredients in the mixture that composes it (35b)—but in its harmonious proportions, that is, in its form. With the emphasis on form begins an aesthetic vision of nature that dominated most of Greek antiquity, much of the Renaissance, and some of the romantic philosophies of Germany and England.

Aristotle abandoned Plato's theory of independent, immaterial forms. Forms reside within, rather than above things. But this change in no way lowers the central importance of form in his conception of the real. Rather than being immutable, form for Aristotle develops, and matter functions as that passive potential which allows it to do so. But the true reality of nature resides in the form. "The form indeed is 'nature,' rather than the matter; for a thing is more properly said to be what it is, when it has attained fulfillment than where it exists potentially" (*Physics* II, 1, 193b). Nor should we conceive of the Aristotelian form as a mere essence, in the later sense that opposes the intelligible aspect of substance to its existence. For Aristotle, the essence is the substance and requires no further ontological principle.

In early Greek thought the idea of form had always implied definiteness, that is, limitation. The unlimited was considered a negative category. In Pythagoras' table of opposites it appears on the side of evil, and for the Ionian physicists the ordered *kosmos* had emerged from the indefinite chaos. Even Plato and Aristotle preserved this idea though they qualified it somewhat. Infinite possibility, according to Plato's *Philebus*, constitutes a necessary moment of the process toward being. The aversion of the unlimited did, however, not extend to the duration of the *kosmos:* all conceived it as everlasting though limited. In view of this axiomatic finitude the idea of form may seem to dissolve in Plotinus's thought. Did the Alexandrian thinker not introduce what the Greek mind most abhorred when he posited the One above all determinate, knowable forms? Quite the contrary! First of all, Plotinus also regarded the *kosmos* as finite and by its formal beauty distinct from the indefinite prime matter. Indeed, Plotinus's faithfulness to the Greek primacy of form enabled him to produce what may be considered the first philosophy of aesthetics. Form constitutes the very principle of coherence of the cosmos. In one instance, Plotinus even refers to matter itself as a form. "All this universe is held fast by forms from beginning to end: matter first of all by the forms of the elements, and then other forms upon these, and then again others; so that it is difficult to find the matter hidden under so many forms. Then matter, too, is a sort of ultimate form; so this universe is all form, and all things in it are forms; for its archetype is form."[9] Even that highest principle which stands above definition Plotinus does not hesitate to call form, thereby extending the concept even beyond the limits of discourse.

The One, "not a particular form, but the form of all" (*Enneads* V, 5, 6), eminently possesses the perfection of form, namely, that beauty "which is also the Good" (*Enn.* I, 6, 6). "The Good is That which is beyond [the *Nous:* the intelligible sphere], the 'spring and origin' of beauty" (*Enn.* I, 6, 9). Precisely as principle of unity it conveys to a complex multiplicity its formal quality. If the material world or any objects in it—natural or artificial—possess beauty, they do so to the extent that they participate in the spiritual form (*Enn.* V, 8, 1). Unified by a single soul that transmits to it the formal presence of the One, the *kosmos* is a divine work of art, the perfect reflection of the good. Plotinus profoundly admired "the vastness and beauty and order" of that world in its eternal motion (*Enn.* V, 1, 4). Nor did that world originate as the effect of a fall, as the Gnostics claimed. Its soul is as eternal as the intelligible realm it reflects and as the One in which it participates. All things in this world are beautiful by sharing in intelligible form. Far from abandoning the Greek equation of form with reality, Plotinus extends it by applying it to the very foundation of reality.

In sum, for the Greeks, the principle of form contains the definitive justification of the real. The decisive question was not why something existed, but how it could exist meaningfully, that is, in orderly form. Real being begins with intelligible form, with a multiplicity rendered harmonious through unity. In this respect the fundamental question of Greek metaphysics differed from the Christian one. Having deprived the form of its intrinsic necessity, the Christian doctrine of creation evoked the further question: Why does form exist? Even if the Greeks had raised that question, their gods would not have provided the answer. The gods' own being had to be justified by the form principle. Their archetypal being consisted of nothing more than perfect, incorruptible form, and their main attribute was immortal beauty. When thinkers and poets of the classical age equated the divine with perfect form, they formalized what had lain dormant for centuries in the Greek perception of nature in the nymphs of springs, the satyrs of woods, the mysterious silence of noonday—and what had been pursued as ideal expressiveness in statues and temples. Form was divine and the divine was form.

Nature as Law and as Logos

Even as *physis* moves all living things toward their immanent telos according to Aristotle, so does the *kosmos* define each being's goal and limits within the totality. Even the gods, representative figures of the eternal order (Walter Otto called them *Seinsgestalten*), remain subject to the irrevocable law of this order. *Dikē* (justice), who guards the gates of

truth governing the cosmic order in Parmenides' poem, rules the conduct
of gods as well as of mortals. A primeval hierarchy distinguishes gods
from men while uniting them in the same *kosmos*, as Pindar states in
the exordium of the sixth Nemean ode: "There is one race of men, one
race of gods; but we both have breath of life from a single mother. But
sundered power holds us divided."[10] The natural order also sets the norm
of human conduct, which it conveys through custom and tradition. *Nomos*, which we now tend to translate as "law," included both law and
convention in the eternal cosmic order. Only a spiritual revolution could,
in the fifth century, reduce the meaning of *nomos*, once the voice of the
eternal order, to that of "mere" convention and oppose it to the unchanging reality of *physis*. Originally one had been the permanent expression
of the other. Convention follows the same eternal order as nature itself.

Equally eternal and divine was that ideal quality of the *kosmos* that
renders its rule intrinsically intelligible—the *logos*. From its beginning
Western thought has assumed that reality possesses the manifest clarity
of coherent discourse. For Greek thinkers of the classical age, nature is
saturated with mind, and this, as Collingwood pointed out in his classic
The Idea of Nature, is what made a science of nature possible in the first
place.[11] Reason promises the kind of regularity and predictability that
alone warrants reflection. Contrary to later rationalism, however, that
logical quality did not have its origin in the human mind: it constituted
the very core of the real itself. The modern question—whether intelligibility is grounded in the structure of the real or imposed by the mind—
could not occur to early Greek thinkers, since both mind and reality
participated in the same intelligibility. Thus, when Pythagoras and his
followers in the sixth century B.C. declared number to be the essence of
reality, they intended to define the real as it is in itself, not merely as a
mental representation. The pitch on a stringed instrument does correspond to the length of the string. The movements of the planets do follow
an invariable order.

The early mathematization of knowledge did, however, drive a permanent wedge between the rationality of the real-in-itself and our immediate experience of it. Thus Parmenides, taught by a Pythagorean
teacher, came to distinguish "true" being, conceived in consistent
thought, from the unreliable opinion conveyed by the senses. In this
equation of essential with ideal reality, thinking and being coincide. But
contrary to later idealism, intelligibility resides primarily in the *kosmos*;
the mind only participates in it. Other thinkers never performed the kind

of radical abstraction on the concept of the *logos* characteristic of the South Italians. Heraclitus' *logos*, still identified with fire, remains closer to the concrete Ionian principles of balance. Nonetheless, that fire remains as remote from ordinary experience as Parmenides' true being: "For though all things come to pass in accordance with this Word (*logos*), men seem as if they had no experience of them, when they make trial of words and deeds such as I set forth, dividing each thing according to its kind and showing how it truly is."[12] Heraclitus' *logos* determines the order of things as well as the correct manner of thinking that order and of acting in accordance with it. The link between the inner law of nature, symbolized by fire, and rational discourse integrates the social with the cosmic order. That *eucosmia* entails *eunomia*, that the laws of the *kosmos* run parallel with the laws of the mind and of the city, constitutes one of the central insights of early Greek thought.[13] It rests on an unwavering belief in the basic unity of the three different aspects of nature: the physical, the theonomic, and the anthropic. It is also the point on which modern thought most radically differs from ancient.

Another aspect, however, of early Greek philosophy has remained consistently present in Western thought up to the present, though recently it has come under attack. It concerns what Derrida has called a "logocentric" orientation of metaphysics that results, he rightly claims, in a view of Being as presence and in the primacy of spoken language. Indeed, the equation of discourse with Being cannot but imply a presence of Being within language, whether spoken or written, and this immanence gives logical discourse direct access to Being. It renders metaphysics logocentric from the start, while eclipsing the mysterious ineffability of Being. Logocentric thinking did indeed develop into rationalist philosophy but not until additional factors, introduced at the end of the Middle Ages, separated that logos from the very being within which Greek thought had first located it. The real problem, then, as I see it, began not with the original linking of being and *logos*, but with the impoverished interpretation of *logos* as residing exclusively in the human subject and depriving all other being of its inherent meaning.

It must be conceded, however, that the danger of a rationalist interpretation of the aboriginal logos threatened Western thought long before the epistemologies of the early modern age. Even by the fifth-century, opposition between *physis* and *nomos* tended to make human law, and by implication the *logos* present in it, subjective. As teachers of rhetoric, keenly aware of the practical significance of language, the Sophists detected in the persuasive word an effective instrument for turning any situation to the speaker's advantage. In different ways they disjoined the order of nature from that of culture and convention. Isolating *logos* as an exclusively human prerogative, they deprived the natural course of things from its own *logos*. Thus *physis* and *nomos*, nature and human convention, originally united, became separated from and often opposed to one another. The ethical significance of this separation has, under the influence of Plato's strong critique of it, often been interpreted as a lapse into moral relativism. But although it creates the possibility for such a relativism, it need not actually result in one.[14] Most Sophists continued to consider nature the basis and ultimate norm of things. Disagreements begin with their attempts to sort out how custom and law, by free human decisions, relate to nature.

How complicated the relation was appears in Plato's dialogue *Gorgias*. Callicles anticipates Nietzsche's position that human law was invented by the weak as a protection against the law of nature that favors the strong: "But I imagine that these men act in accordance with the true nature of right, yes, and by heaven, according to nature's own law, though not perhaps by the law we frame. We mold the best and strongest among ourselves, catching them young like lion cubs, and by spells and incantations we make slaves of them, saying that they must be content with equality and that this is what is right and fair."[15] Callicles, then, agrees that there is a law of nature but complains that human law has emasculated it. Also Thrasymachus, in Plato's *Republic*, defends the thesis that nature favors the strong while conventional law tries to protect the weak against nature's law. The positions of Callicles and Thrasymachus may have been caricatured by Plato, but Protagoras, generally respected for his learning, also sharply distinguished *physis* from *nomos*, albeit in a less oppositional way. Protagoras regarded nature as the precivilized state of human life that law and convention enable us to surpass.[16] Clearly, the opposition between *physis* and *nomos* forced Greek thinkers to reexamine a fundamental thesis of their intellectual tradition.[17]

Plato may well have started writing in order to restore the normative quality to the traditional concept of nature. Far from begin opposed to law, the *physis* of a thing defines what it is supposed to be, thus setting its fundamental norm. In such later dialogues as *Timaeus* and *Laws*, Plato expanded the norm of nature by subordinating the entire social order to the cosmic totality. No human enterprise can ultimately succeed without profiting the whole: the whole person and, beyond that, the whole of

society and of the *kosmos*. Aristotle supported the normative conception
of nature by a well-defined teleology. A thing's essence is "what it *was*
for it to be" (*to ti en einai*)—an expression that has preserved some of the
flavor of the ancient emergence of nature. It determines nature as a process
that is intrinsically goal-directed. The purposes that men set for themselves in establishing customs and laws, products of human "art," must
conform to the end immanent in human nature. "When a thing is produced by nature, the earlier stages in every case lead up to the formal
development in the same way as in the operation of art and *vice*
versa. . . . We may therefore say that the earlier stages are for the sake of
the later and, generally speaking, art partly completes nature, partly it
imitates nature" (*Physics* II, 8, 199a8). Nature remains the guiding principle of development, even for free beings. Their teleological orientation
ought to determine both private conduct and social conventions.

The more virtuous (that is, "excellent") we grow, the more we allow
ourselves to be guided by nature and the more aptly we discern the course
of action appropriate in each particular instance. Ultimately what ought
to be coincides with what a person or any organic being is according to
its true, fully developed nature. Though the teleology of nature rules all
things in the *kosmos*, only in the human person does this entelechy attain
the level of purpose. Humans alone must choose among their inclinations
in order to attain their natural goal. Thus to call humans by nature
political means not that a biological urge drives them to associate with
their fellows, but that they reach perfection only in a self-chosen community. Nature thereby functions more as a final cause that lures its
subjects in a particular direction than as an efficient one that irresistibly
drives them.

Aristotle's concept of nature includes three distinctive strands of
meaning: (1) a potential for development, the *energeia* for growth to
perfection (as in *Metaphysics* 4.4, 1015a7); (2) the essence of the developing thing (as in *Met.* 3.4, 1030a3); (3) the goal or perfection of the thing
once it attains the end of its development (as in *Politics* I, 2, 1252b). Later
generations elaborated these meanings without preserving their original
coherence. The idea of nature as perfective norm came to dominate Stoic
philosophy and, through that channel, the Scholastic theory of natural
law. Modern thought from the Renaissance through the nineteenth century developed the idea of nature as potential into an ideology of progress
unrestricted by such limits as Aristotle had set to any natural potency.
Nature as essence emerged in isolated form, detached from its normative

meaning, in the eighteenth-century theory of natural rights. Taken together, the three characteristics of Aristotle's concept of nature constituted a teleological conception that none of the later developments of each of them taken singularly ever attained. Only by being simultaneously potential and norm is nature able to achieve the goals it pursues.

From this "naturalist" perspective it becomes understandable why, for Aristotle, phenomena as they present themselves may essentially be trusted, and why theories that fail to follow the appearances or that dismiss inherited beliefs about them may not. Aristotle thereby rejects a major trend in Greek thought, one initiated by Parmenides and completed in Plato's theory of the forms, that sharply opposes truth to appearance. But his position differs even more sharply from the modern one that, for different reasons, also started with a basic distrust of appearances in order to seek truth in the "foundation" that caused them to "appear." While the Parmenidian dismissal of appearances originated in the mind's confidence of having access to a transcendent truth, the modern one stems from a loss of faith, not only in the trustworthiness of appearances but even in the very powers of knowledge. Rather than doubt them, Aristotle justifies appearances through themselves. He is a thorough empiricist, but his empiricism, unlike that of seventeenth-century philosophers, rather than being derived from doubt, is rooted in a total trust of the order of nature.

Martha Nussbaum has shown how essential this trust in appearances is in Aristotle's thought. "Returning us, in each case, to the appearances, he reminds us that our language and our ways of life are richer and more complex than much of philosophy acknowledges."[18] The reference to language is particularly appropriate, for in his discussion of language Aristotle presents a clear instance of the axiomatic quality of his belief in the rightness of nature. Surprisingly the critical thinker who changed so many inherited opinions claims that even the most archaic utterances must contain truth because nature cannot allow human wisdom to go astray over a prolonged period of time.[19]

On what ground does Aristotle base his confidence? I have no doubt that it was on an ontotheological vision of the real. No less than Plato, he supports his metaphysics by the assumption that beings owe their intrinsic meaningfulness to the divine quality of the *kosmos*. It would be incorrect to understand this divine quality as a foundation since that assumes a distance between nature and its divine ground, whereas Aristotle's natural world, unlike that of modern philosophy, is itself divine.

Both the gods (if they exist) and the Prime Mover form parts of the *kosmos*. Precisely this all-inclusive divine quality enables all processes in the natural world, from the lowest organism to the human endowment of speech, to attain their end.

The assumption of a cosmic harmony and of a natural teleology also dominates Stoic thinking. But while Aristotle's normative concept of nature combines the essence of the natural thing with its potential for growth (the *energeia*) and with the goal or perfection at which its development aims, Stoic thought stresses nature's normative quality without allowing much to its development. Its static, more deontological interpretation influenced the theory of natural law in Christian theology and in modern political theory. It remains an abstract morality of intention that in some ways anticipates Kant's ethical theory. But the Stoics insisted all the more on the unity of all things within a single nature, as the Presocratics had done in their concept of *physis*. A divine Logos at the core of the *kosmos* sanctified nature's norm into divine law. Ethics never appeared more integrated with cosmology than in Chrysippus's well-known statement: "Living in accordance with virtue is equivalent to living in accordance with experience of what happens by nature—for our natures are parts of the whole."[20] Nature has endowed human beings with reason in order to enable them to explore what nature truly demands. For humans passively to follow their natural inclinations without the intermediacy of reason must count as vice rather than as virtue. The Stoic ethical concept of nature with its clear distinction between is and ought marked the final victory over the naturalist interpretations of the Sophists. *Physis* has entirely become *nomos*.

The Roman concept of nature owes much to Stoic thought. Yet it contains a twist that would prove deeply influential at a later epoch. In the Roman view all humans share the attribute of reason and thereby surpass any social inequality that Aristotle could still regard as natural. Moreover, Roman Stoicism insisted strongly on the person's social responsibility within the totality of nature. It called for equitable legislation, even in dealing with non-Roman powers. Thus it provided the first justification for a jus gentium, an international law. Its political character transformed Stoic ethics from one of intention into one of political action.[21] Nature requires human intervention in order to attain its own end, while at the same time it grants humans the means to realize its intervention. Robert Spaemann captures the teleological circle in the relation between humans and nature. "The natural as such is what men have not made. Yet all that is man-made is in a further determinable way also 'natural.' For all making can change only what already is."[22] The *ingenium* by which the person creatively surpasses his given nature is itself a given, natural potential for development. Nature, then, defines the person's task, while *ingenium* enables him to respond to its summons.[23] Clearly, for Cicero as well as for other writers of the late Roman republic and the early empire, the human person plays a more active part in governing nature than he had in either the Aristotelian or the Greek Stoic conceptions. The teleology of nature here comes close to being a teleology by and for the human person. Nevertheless, Roman writers continue to regard this active human role as consisting essentially in cultivating a naturally given potential. Cicero, the first Roman to use the term *cultura animi* (in the sense of personal education), keeps its meaning closely tied to its agricultural root—*colere,* to foster what nature grants. In this respect he, together with all other ancient thinkers, still differs from the modern ones for whom culture is a creation independent of nature's own intentionality.

Tensions and Resolutions in the Christian View of Nature

The quality of a civilization may be measured both by the complexity of its ingredients and by the harmony of their order. The more diverse elements it succeeds in integrating within a harmonious and unified balance, the greater its potential and, usually, its achievements are. Judged on that scale the culture of the Middle Ages after 1200 ranks very high indeed. It succeeded in effectively uniting squarely opposed elements and strongly diverging tendencies within a single coherent vision. It neither resolved conflicting tensions nor simplified intricate realities, yet it proved sufficiently comprehensive and flexible to accommodate unlimited additions and ramifications. Its adoption of the ancient concept of nature within a doctrine of creation that was in several ways uncongenial with it exemplifies this all-embracing openness. Through its assimilation medieval thought succeeded in conveying new depth to the ancient concept and in bringing it to a new flowering.

An all-inclusive concept of *kosmos* such as the Greeks knew did and could not exist in Israel. The whole of creation manifested Yahweh's power and presence, but it never attained the kind of self-sufficient unity that the Greek *kosmos* possessed. Moreover, the later Christian idea of a world created "from nothing" (*ex nihilo*) and hence devoid of intrinsic necessity would have conflicted with the divine character of Greek nature. Indeed, because they considered Plato's preexisting matter (the *chora*, from which the Demiurge in the *Timaeus* fashioned the *kosmos*) incompatible with God's all-inclusive creative act, Christian thinkers stressed that all of creation originated through a free decision of God. For the Greeks, however, a freely creating God would have destroyed nature's divine sufficiency. If nature for the Greeks emerged, for Christians it was brought to emerge. "So soon as nature is conceived to be created by God, the contingent becomes more than an imperfection in the embodiment of form; it is precisely what constitutes a natural object more than an embodiment, namely a creature."[24] Nevertheless, since the creative act transfers a form aboriginal in God to an extra-divine existence, a divine presence somehow continues to dwell in creation. Divine causality is formally immanent as well as effectively transcendent. Ex-pressing in time what from all eternity resides in God, nature retains an intrinsically normative character. In a well-known passage of his Letter to the Romans, Paul ascribes to nature a religious and moral authority: "When Gentiles who do not possess the law carry out its precepts by the light of nature, then, although they have no law, they are their own law, for they display the effect of the law inscribed in their hearts" (Rom. 2:14).

During the early decades of their faith, however, Christians, knowing that "the figure of this world was to pass away," felt disinclined to expect much ethical guidance from nature or even, at first, to consider the world an object of serious religious contemplation. Yet as the second coming was delayed, they developed a more positive attitude and assimilated more and more theories current in late antiquity. The cosmos, now limited to the physical universe and no longer divine in itself, still contained the marks of God's presence. In the end Christian culture succeeded to a surprising degree in integrating the ancient concept of nature with its doctrine of creation. Thus a real continuity links the Christian conception of nature with ideas current in Rome at the end of the republic. Among them the Stoic ones dominated. They had already made their impact upon such Deuterocanonic writings as Sirach (Ecclesiasticus) and The Book of Wisdom, which presented the world as created by measure, number, and rule and as reflecting the wisdom of its divine maker. The essential difference consisted, of course, in the fact that nature depended on God both for its essence and existence. The idea that only the existence of the world had to be created while its essence, as pure possibility, preceded God's creative act would have made as little sense to Christians before the twelfth century as the identification of being with mere existence would have to the Greeks. The emphasis on existence in the theology of creation may have had biblical origins,[25] but it never excluded essence from God's creative act in the High Middle Ages. Even for Aquinas, who considered the distinction between essence and existence a real one, the essence of a thing is the principle according to which it exists. The two cannot be separated. Leibniz's theory of possible worlds, to one of which God conveys actual existence, deviates from the original idea of creation and marks, in fact, a return to a more essentialist Greek conception.

The doctrine of creation redefined the teleology of the Greek *physis* by rendering the course of nature intrinsically dependent on a transcendent principle. But it did not reduce nature to a mechanism that was moved from without, as the later theory of creation as efficient causality was to do.[26] Indeed, the idea of God's immanent presence in creation soon drove Christian theologians, especially in the Greek-speaking world, to Neoplatonic philosophy. In Plotinus's and Proclus's theologies the One—which Christians identified with God—remains present in its emanations while nevertheless transcending them. Nature itself *re-presented* God and this representation laid the basis for a theology of the image and for an original Christian mysticism. Already the Epistle to the Colossians (1:16) had referred to Christ as "the image of the invisible God, the first-born of all creatures." The creature, archetypically present in the Son, is an image of that uncreated image. For the fourth-century Cappadocians Gregory of Nyssa and his brother Basil, human *physis* bears the image of its divine archetype, the Logos, image of the Father. The soul recognizes the divine image in itself and in the cosmos and returns both it to their divine archetype.[27]

Still, the Christian conception of form, though in essence continuous with the Greek one, went through some severe crises. How could a cosmic symbolism prefigured in and centered around one individual—the Christ—conform to the universal Greek idea of form? Moreover, if God had definitively revealed himself in the "man of sorrows," how could one continue to regard the splendor of the universe as the image of a God who had appeared "in the form of a slave"?

It took centuries before the Christian mind realized the full extent of the contrast. When it did, it provoked two major crises, one in the East and one in the West. The Eastern one directly centered on the question of form. After a period of unproblematic adoption of the Hellenistic modes of form-giving, Byzantine religious artists felt the need to abandon the

naturalism they had inherited from Hellenistic and Roman pictorial traditions. Gradually they eliminated all contingent details, erased all
strictly personal traits, minimized spatial perspective, and, in order to
symbolize the celestial origin of their sacred figures, emphasized their
unchanging, eternal status, placing them against a background of golden
divine light. Thus they attempted to express the mystery of God revealed
in human nature by means of an abstract, spiritualized form. Yet when
Nestorians claimed that in Christ coexisted not only two natures but also
two persons—a divine and a human—any representation of his human
form threatened to render his divine status ambiguous. In order to safeguard the purity of Christ's divine personhood, iconoclastic movements
prohibited all bodily representations of Christ. Underneath the Nestorian
controversy the iconoclasts rightly perceived a universal problem: How
could one appropriately represent the divine at all?[28] This may seem a
strange problem to arise in a religion based on God's visible appearance.
But the narrow concreteness of the divine manifestation in one individual
severely restricted and, according to the iconoclastic emperors, precluded
the legitimacy of any other representation. For any artistic representation
would inevitably deviate from the form God had chosen for his manifestation. In the end, however, the sacramental universality of the incarnated
Word whose presence in the world had consecrated all forms proved to
be a stronger argument than the uniqueness of its particular appearance.[29]

The Western crisis resulted from an increasing doubt concerning a
fallen nature's ability to incorporate the divine form. Early Latin theologians had consistently been less daring than the Greek ones and, in true
Roman fashion, had preferred to concentrate on practical—moral and
judicial—issues. To be sure Augustine as the Neoplatonic thinker he was,
especially in the *Confessions*, envisioned creation, and in particular the
soul, as an image of God even as Cappadocian fathers Gregory and Basil
had done. Yet when he later concretely applied his theory to the triune
God of the Christian revelation, he offered little more than external
analogies between God and the creature. Instead of showing the intrinsic
participation of the image within its divine archetype, he stressed its
extrinsic analogy. Only through knowing and loving its divine archetype
does the soul's external similarity grow into an inner presence. Thus in
the process of knowing God, the soul becomes reunited with that divine
image in which it has its origin. With all ancient and medieval thinkers,
Augustine assumes that the act of knowing consists essentially in partaking in the known.[30] Although Augustine's theology displays a strong

mystical elan, it is unmistakably moving away from the Greek concept of a divine information.

Whereas for Eastern theologians salvation meant *deification* (union with God), Westerners tended to view redemption as a healing of human nature. This may appear to be a matter of theological preference inspired by the more practical outlook of Latin thinkers. But the increasing emphasis on healing hid, below theoretical differences, a growing moral pessimism as Rome and its Occidental empire were disintegrating. To its inhabitants that meant, more than a political change, the end of civilization: the disappearance of the familiar orderly way of life and of all values, moral and aesthetic. This moral pessimism surfaces in Augustine's anti-Pelagian writings. Followers of Pelagius, an Irish monk, had, in a theology that reflected an equally dim view of human nature, insisted on the need for a harshly ascetic regimen of penance, prayer, and hard work for those anxious to be saved. Each person was responsible for his own redemption or at least, as semi-Pelagians later qualified, had to make the first move toward it. To this conception the older Augustine opposed his own somber view of human corruption. Sinful nature remains totally incapable of attaining its natural end and even of regaining, by its own powers, the disposition required to receive God's healing grace. The battle gradually intensified and even after Augustine's death the anti-naturalist polemics were constantly refueled by ever new ammunition taken from the saint's inexhaustible arsenal. Except for a short Carolingian spring, a profound loss of confidence in human nature darkened the European mind for half a millennium.

The darkness suddenly lifted toward the end of the eleventh century when a fresh awareness of the Incarnation as a cosmically transforming event suddenly dawned upon the entire civilization and spawned a new trust in nature. The mood lightened, the vision concentrated, and for the first time a genuine Christian naturalism emerged. Anticipating the Renaissance, the period that initiated the High Middle Ages reclaimed the classical heritage. Its access to ancient sources remained limited and its interpretation of them dubious. Nonetheless, this truncated legacy inspired an openness toward nature. The twelfth-century Neoplatonic School of Chartres granted nature creative powers comparable only to those once reserved to the Creator. Even the ancient astronomy returned. In Bernardus Sylvestris's famous *Cosmographia*, the stars play as decisive a part in human destiny as they ever had in pagan antiquity. "The firmament is inscribed with stars, and prefigures all that may come to pass through decrees of fate. It foretells through signs by what means and to what end the movement of the stars determines the course of the ages. For that sequence of events which ages to come and the measured course of time will wholly unfold has a prior existence in the stars."[31]

Now, if human destiny had merely played out a scenario written in the stars, such astral speculations would have buried human freedom under an oppressive fatalism. But the intentions of Bernardus and of his fellow thinkers went in the opposite direction. The human microcosmos resides at the center of the macrocosmos, thus giving physical nature its definitive meaning. The ultimate dominion over the universe rests with us. Through our knowledge of the stars we escape being determined by them. Foreknowledge of their motions enables us to circumvent otherwise inevitable effects.

The parallelism between the macrocosmos and the human microcosmos induced writers of the High Middle Ages to draw ever more elaborate analogies between the individual and the cosmos. In *De planctu naturae* Alain de Lille compares reason to the fixed stars, sensibility to the planets, and the soul to God. Later, Saint Bonaventure was to relate the entire structure of the universe to its microcosmic center. The warm heart and the cool, moist brain above it correspond to the radiating sun and stars below the cool, crystalline heaven. The dispensation of grace matches the arrangement of the seven planets: seven sacraments, seven gifts of the Holy Spirit, seven virtues, and seven deadly sins.[32] Currents hostile to the new naturalism survived, but on the whole the tide flowed in the opposite direction. Christians once again came to trust the impulses of nature, and they began to pay attention to the subtler feelings and emotions of the soul. The romance of Abelard and Heloise, including Abelard's sad epilogue to it as told in his *History of My Misfortunes*, clearly announces the dawn of a new age. Jacob Burckhardt credited the Italian Renaissance with the invention of the subject. But the twelfth century could with more right lay claim to that. A new self-consciousness marks the entire culture.

What gave the initial impulse to the new mentality? Was it courtly love as has been claimed? Not likely. Provençal poetry undoubtedly prepared a new sensitivity. But it began to express that love only after the courtly tradition had already declined.[33] Poets of the thirteenth century, such as the authors of the *Roman de la rose*, pretended to recapture feelings of an era that no longer existed. Realist painting and sculpture soon followed poetry in a conveying a new sense of nature—both cosmic and human. Amazingly, this naturalism caused no break with the theological vision that had nurtured it. "La nature médievale n'envie rien à la grace," Gilson wrote.[34] Indeed, the new experience of nature enhanced its sacramental function. A *verbum materiale* (the cosmos) more generously endowed conveyed richer content to the *verbum divinum* read in Scripture and heard in church. A wider horizontal base linked the cosmos more firmly to its vertical axis.

The sacramental attitude toward nature strengthened the interest in countryside, plants, and animals, as well as emotions and feelings. Only an observing eye could read nature as the twelfth-century poet Alain de Lille invited in his well-known verses:

Omnis mundi creatura
Quasi liber et pictura
Nobis est et speculum.

Medieval symbolism referred to the divine word as its primary analogate. God had revealed himself as Word—both in person and in Scripture. The written revelation received its ultimate meaning from God having become Word. Scripture in turn became the model of all other words and books, which expanded its primary speech.[35] Nature appears as yet a further stage in that process of revelation, one charged with the task of visibly manifesting what the Word communicates to the mind. Like Scripture, which conceals as much as it reveals, nature confronts us with the task of decoding a revelatory text—"the book in which the creative Trinity shines, is thought, and read."[36] Understanding its meaning requires the key of Scripture; yet nature, in turn, conveys physical content to Scriptural symbol.

Love assumed a new significance in religious life. What contemplation had been for earlier mystics, love was in the new age. Indeed, contemplation came to be identified with love. Bernard of Clairvaux declared St. Gregory's axiom, *amor ipse notitia est* (love itself is a knowledge) to be the guiding principle of contemplative life. Suddenly the idea of love appears everywhere.[37] On love mysticism it is Bernard, however, whom we best remember. It is difficult to overestimate the impact that Bernard, clearly the most influential person of the twelfth century, had not only on the religious attitude of his time, but on its entire cultural outlook. It is one of the paradoxes of history that this exceedingly ascetic figure was a major force toward a more positive valuation of the created world.

Bernard's doctrine in *De diligendo Deo* and his *Sermons on the Song of Songs* must have impressed his contemporaries as an amazingly new sound. Ever since Origen, the *Song of Songs* had served as the favorite biblical vehicle for mystical commentary. But what the Greeks had cautiously spiritualized, the austere Bernard, in other respects so intolerant of concessions to the flesh, applied in its full erotic power to the relation between God and the soul. "No sweeter names can be found to embody that sweet interflow of affections between the Word and the soul, than bridegroom and bride." Bernard's bridal mysticism not only communes with God through love, it ends up identifying God with that love. "The bridegroom is not only loving, he is love." Through the divine nature of love, human love assumes a sacred quality. Even when directed toward Christ's human nature, love is divine "because our hearts are attracted most toward the humanity of Christ and what he did or commanded while in the flesh."

And yet, in the development toward that mystical naturalism Bernard remains a transitional figure. The essential object of his love was the divine Word, even though that Word had to be reached through Christ's humanity. For Francis of Assisi and his followers, however, Jesus the human individual became the object of the devotion. This turn to the individual removed whatever hesitations Western Christians might once have felt about expressing the God-bearing form. God's incarnation in an individual human nature religiously legitimated the uninhibited representation of the physical features of Christ and of those whose lives had been touched by him. It also granted individual form a definitiveness which it had not possessed before. Thus began a daring cosmic symbolism that endowed each facet of nature with inexhaustible expressiveness. Far from being added to nature, this symbolic potential constituted its very essence. To the medieval mind, nature appeared intrinsically symbolic. A merely literal reading of nature would have fallen far short of a full understanding. This symbolic naturalism gave birth to a new aesthetics: the one that formed Cimabue, Duccio, Giotto, and such early humanists as Dante, Petrarch, and Boccaccio. Spiritual meaning resided in the cosmos itself and, as such, allowed a multitude of human interpretations. The interpreter could feel free to specify its content according to the spiritual needs of the occasion. Meaning was given, but no particular meaning was given exclusively. Hence, unlike the precisely conceived metaphors of modern symbolism, symbols display a much looser and less definitive character. What may appear to us arbitrary metaphorization is, in fact, an attempt, never complete, to explore one facet or another of a semantically inexhaustible cosmos.

The same freedom of interpretation that had ruled biblical exegesis also determined the understanding of nature as visible image of the invisible. As figures in a poetic text refer to one another in a play of continually transformed analogies and affinities, so does the symbolic vision of nature constantly shift its perspectives. Knowledge came to consist chiefly in commentary on the two books, Scripture and nature, which, both being endowed with multiple meanings, allowed endless cross-references. What Foucault wrote about the sixteenth century applies far more directly to the High Middle Ages: "Knowledge consisted in relating one form of language to another form of language; in restoring the great, unbroken plain of words and things; in making everything speak. That is, in bringing into being, at a level above that of all marks, the secondary discourse of commentary."[38] The epistemic *apriori* imposed no categorical structure upon the real, but a perspective for reading what was directly, but never simply or exhaustively, given.

Though achievements in architecture, sculpture, and painting matched and even surpassed the literary ones, language defined the limits of meaning and set the standards of expression. The sacred authority of the word gradually extended to all literature. Thus the pagan classics could be read as containing the *integumenta fidei* (William of Conches), the cryptic anticipations of Christian mysteries yet to be revealed. The word as such was sacred and, in all its forms, implicitly revealing. It was an awareness of the word's active participation in God's expressiveness that enabled early Italian humanism to articulate the aspirations of a new age. As God created from nothing through his divine Word, the poetic metaphor, according to Dante, calls a previously nonexisting entity into being. Linguistic symbolization viewed as a divinely creative act presaged the modern conception of meaning as conveyed by the human mind.

The new, more concrete vision of the Incarnation raised the significance of the individual. It contrasted with the primacy of the universal that had ruled earlier thought. Today we find it hard to imagine a scale of being in which the individual does not occupy the highest echelon. Yet by far the longer and arguably the most consequential part of our tradition did not grant the individual the ultimate importance we do. Since Plato and Aristotle, if not before, Greek thought had posited the universal as intellectually prior. Greek sculpture of the classical age, although it later served as a model for expressing individual personhood, represented universal types. Even the realistic portraits created during the Hellenistic and Roman epochs aimed at displaying universal virtues and vices.

Christian doctrine, however, conflicted with this axiomatic primacy of the universal on one essential point. In the Incarnation God had assumed human nature in one single individual. Remarkably enough, Christians began to challenge the primacy of the universal only after having supported it for centuries. Even then it was not logical consistency but the pressure of a nonphilosophical religious movement that forced speculative thinkers to reconsider it. The major challenge came from a barely educated religious genius—Francis of Assisi. His devotion to Jesus of Nazareth, the individual, opened a new perspective on the unique particularity of the person. Francis upset an intellectual tradition which he hardly understood and which he certainly had no intention of challenging. If the Image of all images is an individual, then the primary significance of individual form no longer consists in disclosing a universal reality beyond itself. Indeed, the universal itself ultimately refers to the singular. It would take thinkers, mostly Franciscans, over a century to draw the philosophical and theological conclusions inherent in Francis's mystical vision. But in the end, the religious revolution begun in the twelfth century succeeded in overthrowing the ontological priority of the universal.

Inspired by Francis's vision, Bonaventure (1221–74), his spiritual son, reformulated the relation between Creator and creature. Bonaventure preserved the traditional *rationes aeternae* (the universal Platonic forms) within God but placed them in the incarnated individual Word as in their divine archetype. In the contemplative love of Christ, then, the mind assimilates the forms in a way that surpasses the truth of abstract knowledge. True cognition consists in uniting a created image with its personal archetype, Christ, the synthesis of all ideas.[39] If the essence of all ideas resides in an individual, the weight of knowledge shifts from the abstract universal to the singular.

But it was the younger Franciscan John Duns Scotus who developed the primacy of the individual into a wholly new philosophy. The awesome complexity of his system reveals the seriousness of the obstacles he encountered in attempting to avoid a complete break with the tradition. Scotus understood that he had to revise the traditional philosophy of form more fundamentally than Bonaventure had done. What distinguishes one being from another of the same kind and makes it this rather than another—the *forma individualis*—is itself a form, rather than being a mere quantification of a universal *species* singularized by the principle of indeterminacy (*materia signata quantitate*) as Aquinas had proclaimed. The singularity of the individual adds a *formal* characteristic to the universal forms of genus and species. Individuality, then, far from being a mere sign of contingency, constitutes the supreme form, and perfect knowledge consists in knowing this individual form. Scotus understood that a theology based on the primacy of love must appraise the individual differently than one based on the ancient priority of universal cognition. With Scotus's *forma individualis*, later condensed to *haecceitas*, a centuries' old rule of the universal concept of form came to an end. The primacy of the universal continued to dominate some schools of thought—specifically, the Neoplatonic one to which some of the greatest thinkers of the early modern age belong, including Cusanus, Ficino, and Bruno. But the decisive Neoplatonic hold on Western thought was broken.

With Ockham (ca. 1290–1349/50), the entire ontotheological synthesis began to disintegrate. The Franciscan thinker perceived with characteristic sharpness how inconsistent the new philosophy of the individual had become with the fundamental epistemic principles inherited from Plato and Aristotle. According to those principles, knowledge rested on the assumption that the real is intrinsically intelligible and hence that the mind merely actualizes what is already potentially cognizable. Ockham no longer takes such a built-in harmony between mind and nature for granted, which subjects God's ways of creation to human norms. Even the assumption that in knowledge the mind shares a universal form with the real, however deeply entrenched in the tradition, is abandoned. Ockham does not question the need for universals in the process of human cognition. But they exist neither in an independent realm outside the mind as Plato was believed to have held, nor even inside the singular reality as Aristotle had taught. Our only access to the real consists in an intuition normally conveyed through the senses. To know by means of a contact with physical reality, however, is essentially a process of efficient causality, wherein no form is transferred from that reality to the mind. Indeed, God may directly infuse an intuition without sense impression.

Nowhere does the distance between mind and reality appear more clearly than in the nominalist rejection of the so-called impressed *species*. For Aquinas and subsequent realist metaphysicians, the *species* had constituted the link between intellect and reality. Through it the mind gains access to the rational core of its object. It does so by "abstracting" the intelligible element from the sensuous *phantasm*, but even more by "illuminating" this *phantasm* with its own intellectual light. "[The active intellect] throws light on the phantasm, because . . . by the power of the active intellect the phantasms are made fit for the abstraction therefrom of intelligible intentions" (*Summa theologiae* I, 85, 1). In the *species* the real is united with the mind, and turns its potential intelligibility into actual understanding. Being the very union of the mind with its object, it is neither a copy nor a representative of the known object. Indeed, it is not known in itself at all, since no independent reality mediates between knower and object. "The intelligible species is not what is actually understood, but that by which the intellect understands . . . because the things we understand are the objects of science; therefore if what we understand is merely the intelligible species in the soul, it would follow that every science would not be concerned with objects outside the soul, but only with intelligible species within the soul" (*Summa theologiae* I, 85, 2).

The argument against the theory of the *species*, first formulated by the Dominican Durandus and later adopted by Ockham and the nominalists, discloses the different assumption that underlies the modern conception of knowledge. How could the *species* mediate, thus goes Durandus's objection, between the knower and the unknown when it remains itself unknown? It would require a second *species* to know the first one, and so on in an infinite process.[40] This line of reasoning presupposes that the *species* functions as a separate reality that mediates between two wholly opposite elements. For Thomas, on the contrary, the *species* actually identifies what is already potentially united. No new bridge is thrown; the *species* only enables the mind to walk across the existing one.

Obviously, the trust in the essentially rational quality of nature that had supported traditional epistemology, has collapsed. Henceforth ideality belongs exclusively to the mind. By the same token, the transcendent factor ceases to function as an active constituent of the ontotheological synthesis. For it had been precisely through the form that the finite participated in the infinite. Christian theologians had always succeeded in maintaining the link between the forms and the realm of the divine through God's eternal image, the divine archetype of all created reality. In late nominalist theology, the form lost this function and the link with the divine became a more external one. Modern thought increasingly defined the relation between finite and infinite being in terms of efficient causality. If form was no more than a construction of the human mind, it could no longer secure the intrinsic union between the finite and the infinite.

The subversion of the ancient meaning of form did not mark the end of its use in Western thought. Quite the contrary, once emptied of its divinely given real content, it appeared ready to start upon a wholly new career. Both in humanism and the Renaissance, form developed into the very essence of expression. Nominalist philosophy had, at least negatively, prepared this change. As meaning became detached from the given structure of the real, words and forms became independent symbols of expression. This cleared the road toward the unrestrained creativity of humanism and the Renaissance. But nominalism also prepared the scientific revolution. By conveying to concepts and terms an exclusively mental status, it allowed the mind to build them into systems of bare signifiers. As pure signs they could serve as the flexible tools the new, empirical study of nature required. Thus form, the central concept of Greco-Christian thought, stood ready to assume yet another function in defining the nature of the real. More versatile than ever because unhampered by apriori restrictions, form became the symbol of the mind's expressive independence. As the next chapter will show, the transition to free expressiveness did not occur at once. In early humanism, the creative self continued to be embedded within a cosmic and transcendent totality. Not before the Renaissance and the later phase of humanism did form become fully detached from its ontotheological context.

Chapter 2

Nature and Form

Form in Humanist Letters and Renaissance Art

Any periodization of the early modern age remains controversial. The similarities that link its culture with what we assume to be a previous epoch are as many as the differences that separate them. Moreover, the lines of similarity and difference in one area of culture do not run parallel with those in another. Art and literature may develop differently than theology. The problem is particularly acute with respect to the complex idea or cluster of ideas of nature. While artists, humanists, and spiritual theologians of the fifteenth century stressed a divine presence in nature, school theology actually widened the distance between God and nature. In some respects the former continued a view of nature that was already present in the twelfth century. Saint Francis and his followers as well as philosophers and poets of the Chartres School had in different ways begun to regard nature as in some manner divine. The "immanentists" neither denied nor minimized the createdness of nature, but instead of the total dependence of nature they emphasized its created creativity. Nature came to be viewed more as a self-moving organism.

Philosophy rarely reflects the origins of changes in cultural perception. It seldom registers them before they reach the stage of full maturity.

When Marsilio Ficino developed the first philosophy of modern culture, its basic principles had already been accepted, albeit implicitly, by many artists and humanists. If I preface a discussion of the modern view of nature with a reference to Ficino, I do so without suggesting that he stood at the beginning of it. But he formulated some of the theoretical principles others had accepted yet never fully articulated. In his symposium on Plato's *Symposium,* one of the participants presents nature as the all-comprehensive organ through which the universal soul transmits the seeds from which all natural things will sprout. Being the generative power of the self-moving world soul, nature operates through that soul and depends upon it. Ficino, or rather his spokesman Antonius, bishop of Fiesole, supports this basically Neoplatonic theory by the mysterious reference to "second" and "third things" in Plato's (apocryphal) second letter (312 E). He interprets the third things as the realm of the soul and the second as that of the ideas. Both derive from "the king of all" whom he identifies as God. Nature, then, the generative power, in Ficino's view, reflects the divine beauty through the mind and the soul.[1]

Now, the early humanists knew nothing of Plato's second letter and were only indirectly acquainted with Plotinus's theory. Nevertheless, Ficino supplied a coherent theoretical frame for humanist thought when he subsumed the idea of nature under a spiritual form. Formal beauty thereby became a primary quality of nature. A fundamental assumption, present among humanists from the beginning, here found at least an indirect justification: namely, that beauty results from the spiritual perfection of form, a perfection that may be attained through rhetoric (which includes poetry). In declaring spiritual form the source of beauty, Neoplatonic philosophy revived by Ficino made it into the essence of the truly real. The nature of beauty and the beauty of nature had been a constant topic of discussion among poets and humanists and was to remain so all through the sixteenth century. Few, however, had succeeded in bringing theoretical clarity to what had remained obscure in medieval aesthetics, namely, what comprised the essence of beauty. For Plotinus and his followers, there was no doubt. Beauty consists in the triumph of form over matter. Things in the world are beautiful "by participating in form," that is, "by sharing in a formative power which comes from the divine forms" (*Enneads* I, 6, 2). Since these divine forms are spiritual, a corporeal form will be more perfect as it is more spiritual. It also follows that beauty is an essential quality of nature—its very core—rather than the outcome of a contingent arrangement of bodily parts. Whatever is, is beautiful to the extent that it truly is, in other words, to the extent that it partakes in spiritual form.

Ficino's Neoplatonism justified the assumption shared by poets and artists of the early modern age that aesthetic form perfection had an ontological significance. It also indirectly legitimated the humanist conviction that perfect form could best be attained through rhetoric. If form is spiritual, language, being the most spiritual expression of the embodied mind, supplies the ideal medium for the achievement of formal perfection. Of course, Renaissance painters and sculptors later claimed the same privilege for their medium—in some instances, such as that of the young Michelangelo, on the same grounds derived from the same Ficinian source.

It requires some justification to single out the humanist concern with form, for in some way such a concern has marked every stage of our culture. Hegel states a typically Western principle in declaring that all content attains its truth in form and in describing form as so essential to reality as reality's essence is to itself.[2] The singular significance of the humanist movement, however, consists in having introduced a different notion of form. Contrary to the ancient view that conceived form as given with the real, form for the humanists was an ideal to be achieved. To be sure, they continued to consider nature the model of formal perfection. But nature came to be viewed as a work of art created in accordance with aesthetic rules. Artistic achievement, then, far from being a pale imitation of nature, became the very norm by which to measure nature. Huizinga was right: humanism was a form before being an inspiration.[3] Its conception of form was shaped by rhetorical interest: in language the mind imposes its own form on the real.

The foundations of this ontological theory of language must be found in the Jewish and Christian theology of the Word. Form and language are born with and in the aboriginal utterance of God's eternal Word. In that Word all forms preexist and through it all things have been created. The humanist movement forcefully reasserted the link between God's primordial expression in the eternal Logos and the rhetorical pursuit of linguistic perfection. Mainly influenced by Augustine's thought, the earliest humanists had from the beginning given a spiritual meaning to their rhetorical ideal. In their endeavor to revive the art of rhetoric, they stood, in fact, closer to the medieval theological tradition than to the classical culture from which they derived their models. Their interest in antiquity, at least in the beginning, remained highly selective and was mostly restricted to rhetoricians such as Cicero and Quintilian.[4] But to a higher degree than medieval or ancient rhetoricians the humanist regarded himself a creator of form. As Dante had written, through metaphor the poet creates "from nothing" in the order of language as God through his Word creates *ex nihilo* in the order of nature. Form became an ideal, partly realized through divine creation and partly to be realized through the human word.

The humanist ideal of form, combined with an interest in nature that since the twelfth century had been growing more direct, awakened an aesthetic sensitivity for cosmic harmony. Of course, humanists did not discover scenic beauty. Anyone who has read Virgil and Horace, and, before them, the Hellenistic pastoral poets knows better. Their aesthetic perception of nature had persisted throughout late antiquity—we find vestiges of it in Boethius, Cassiodorus, and Augustine—and some of it had been transmitted to the Middle Ages. But medieval writers saw the cosmos more as a universal symbol of a higher order. Dante shifted the focus from the universal to the singular appearance and the individual expression. Burckhardt credits Dante with a new sensitivity for the physical detail. "Not only does he awaken in us by a few vigorous lines the sense of the morning airs and the trembling light on the distant ocean, or of the grandeur of the storm-beaten forest, but he makes the ascent of lofty peaks, with the only possible object of enjoying the view—the first man, perhaps, since the days of antiquity to do so."[5]

Yes, indeed, but nature still serves mainly as a backdrop for human drama. Dante became first and foremost the great poet of the individual. Even Petrarch, though more self-consciously aware of nature as an independent entity, never allows it to occupy center stage. Modern readers have made altogether too much of his famous ascent of Mont Ventoux: they tend to fill the gaps in his narrative with their own aesthetic anticipations. When the poet fails to describe the spectacular view from the top, this is not due, as Burckhardt writes, to an overwhelming experience that left the poet speechless but to the totally alien character of the rugged mountain scenery, which urges him to seek refuge in himself. "I was completely satisfied with what I had seen of the mountain and turned my inner eye toward myself."[6] Petrarch experiences nature as strange to the mind's inner life. His actual experience of nature, then, appears to have consisted in little more than horror at the sight of the huge, formless space below. His curiosity to venture out and explore nature held an aesthetic promise for the future but, like Noah's dove, found no resting place.[7]

One of the first writers to express genuine delight in an independent and purely aesthetic contemplation of nature was the Renaissance Pope Pius II, Aeneas Silvius Piccolomini. His *Commentaries* bring to sensitive, elegant wording what ancient poetry had merely suggested. Thus the pope describes an excursion to the neighborhood of his hometown:

> All the hills about Siena were smiling in their vesture of foliage and flowers, and luxuriant crops were growing up in the fields. The Sienese country immediately around the city is indescribably lovely with its gently sloping hills planted with cultivated trees and vines or plowed for grain, overlooking delightful valleys green with pastureland or sown fields, and watered by never-failing streams. There are also thick forests planted by nature or man where birds sing most sweetly and on every hill the citizens of Siena have built splendid country seats.[8]

The *Commentaries* abound with such poetic descriptions of landscapes suffused with the gentle light of the Tuscan and the Alban hills, painted in the idyllic pastoral hues of Pinturicchio's frescoes—with little depth but great charm. Leonardo, an innovator here as in so many other instances, added complexity to the aesthetics of nature. To him nature appeared awesome, mysterious, and inscrutable as well as beautiful. While peering into the dark entrance of a cave he feels "fear and desire: fear of the threatening, obscure cave, and desire to see whether there would be some strange object inside" (paura e desiderio: paura per la minacciosa e oscura spilonca e desiderio per vedere se là entro fusse alcuna miracolosa cosa).[9] Precisely this sense of wonder stimulates in him the desire to explore the secrets of nature.

Painters had preceded poets in pursuing individual form. Cimabue and Giotto replaced the golden background, with its universal Neoplatonic light symbolism, by particular sceneries of fields, trees, and gardens. Especially in the portrait the shift toward the singular became manifest. Flemish painters of the fifteenth century, the first great masters of the genre, display a detailed interest in individual rather than typical traits. Since these painters never directly underwent the influence of classical models, their naturalism has been described as "one of the ultimate forms of development of the medieval mind."[10] Wrongly, it seems. Van Eyck's meticulous analysis of personal features, Van der Weyden's relentless scrutiny of inner emotions, and Memlinc's self-conscious search for a pure aesthetics of the human face announce a new pursuit of form.

An expanded sense of space accompanied the new conception of form. For the Flemish as well as for Italian artists of the early Renaissance, space, rather than being part of the represented object, assumes an independent, homogeneous quality that detaches the figures from their environment. Nor does the viewer share that represented space. The artist projects his subject at a distance, into a sphere of its own, removed from the ordinary world. The new mode of representation forced the artist to keep two independent forces in balance—the figures and their spatial environment. To prevent one from absorbing the other he must endow the former with an inner spatiality that enables them to maintain a dynamic independence with respect to the latter. Figures become weightier and acquire a tactile quality. A heightened sense of form renders aesthetic representation ever more independent. In another sense the painted scene now comes to depend entirely on the viewer's perspective: one-point perspective places it within the subject's own angle of vision. This subjective quality, typical of Italian painters since Ambrogio Lorenzetti, distinguishes them from Byzantine and medieval paintings. Yet it does not constitute the most distinctive feature of the new spatial vision. The great Flemish artists Van Eyck, Van der Weyden, and Memlinc never adopted it. With them also the eye follows the objects into a distance of vanishing clarity, but it does so by means of multiple lines of perspective meeting in a sacred focus beyond the subjective field of vision. At least for Van Eyck, the lines of perspective point toward a spiritual center, and the represented space becomes a symbolic setting for a transcendent sanctuary.[11] Though depicting nature to its last realistic detail, Van Eyck and Van der Weyden invite the viewer to a more inward contemplation.

Considering the central position of the human subject in much early modern art, we may be surprised at the growing reassertion of the ancient principle that art ought to imitate nature. Indeed, the Renaissance vigorously reinstated the *imitatione del vero*, and Leonardo praises the realist Masaccio for having shown in his art that painters who were not taking their models from nature were laboring in vain.[12] The early humanists had come to look upon nature as a divine work of art. Yet as the fifteenth- and sixteenth-century view of nature as an organic, creative entity further transformed the meaning of imitation, nature instead of being a model to be copied by the artist became a standard of aesthetic creativity. Thus Leon-Battista Alberti exhorts the artist to emulate nature rather than to copy her. "It seems to me that there is no more certain and fitting way for one who wishes to pursue this [the attainment of grace and beauty] than to take them from nature, keeping in mind what way nature, marvellous artificer of things, has composed the planes in beautiful bodies."[13]

While transforming nature through his own form-giving creativity the artist imitates her most. When the painter treats a two-dimensional object as if it were a window through which a three-dimensional scene appears, as Alberti invites him to do, then, in fact, he reshapes nature, though in accordance with nature's own rule. The new emphasis on the artist's creative impulse confirms Walter Pater's thesis that the early Renaissance should be esteemed more for its projects than for its accomplishments. The formative project more than the finished product attracted artists of the early Renaissance. Even artists of the High Renaissance display an amazing readiness to abandon one fully mastered mode of expression for experimenting with a new one. For Leonardo, Bramante, and Verrocchio, as for many others, the aesthetic fulfillment found in a variety of expressions surpassed that of achieving paramount excellence in any single one. Michelangelo in his later years left unfinished what the creative impulse had ceased to inspire.

Besides imitating nature as a divine work of art and, more fundamentally, as a model of creativity, art in its early modern conception also fulfills a complementary role with respect to nature. Though perfect on its own level, nature appears imperfect when compared with the formal perfection of mind. The artist's challenge consists in transforming nature in accordance with this higher beauty. A widely accepted Neoplatonic theory justified such a move. The mind enhances nature's perfection by imposing its own spiritual form upon the imperfect, corporeal one presented by nature. As Marsilio Ficino put it: "The human person imitates all the works of divine nature; those of inferior nature he brings to perfection, corrects, and improves" (Homo omnia divinae naturae opera imitatur et naturae inferioris opera perficit, corrigit et emendat).[14] Even when portraying a real land- or seascape, aesthetic representation does not so much refer to a reality beyond itself as create an original expressive form inspired by an existing one. Landscapes ought to be invented, Cennini teaches in Il libro dell'arte.[15] Leonardo straightforwardly proclaims the human mind "il modello del mondo," destined to raise nature to that higher standard of reason which the mind possesses. Painting presents not only natural creations, "but countless others that have never been created by nature"[16] —a weighty statement coming from the man who proclaims that artists ought to take their models from nature.

Still, artists of the early Renaissance continued to view themselves as creating in unison with nature: mind and nature relate harmoniously to one another. As a microcosmos, the person occupies a central position within nature. According to Leonardo, the mind recognizes itself in the natural form upon which it then bestows its own formal perfection. Yet before acting upon nature the mind must submit to the "reason" immanent in the given form. In perfecting nature's forms, the artist creates with nature. Observation of nature's forms must conspire with creative imagination to realize the truth of nature. Because of the aesthetic importance of observation, Leonardo still considers science and art united. Thus he surprisingly concludes that painting is a science, indeed the higher one, since it intuitively reveals the unique, internal structure of its object, which cannot be learned as other sciences can.

> The sciences that may be imitated are such that a discipline can equal the founder . . . : they are less perfect than those that cannot be inherited. Among those, painting must count as the most important. It cannot be learned by a person devoid of natural talent. The opposite happens in mathematics where the pupil learns as much as the teacher. [Painting] does not allow itself to be copied as is the case with writings where the copy is worth as much as the original.[17]

The beauty of the cosmos and the human ability to improve it through art found their definitive meaning in Ficino's Neoplatonic philosophy of universal love. Beauty, being the radiance of the divine form, incites a cosmic love that unites all creatures in their return to the divine One. This harmony of all forms inspires the human mind to a contemplation of God's beauty. (Ficino's commentaries on Plato's *Phaedrus* and *Symposium* are based on this idea.) The theory of a divine Eros had, of course, never disappeared since Plato first formulated it. Yet contrary to Plato and, even more, to such of his Christian followers as Augustine, for the moderns the earthly form holds a definitive significance. Rather than being a way station to the eternal, the form invites an exploration within itself. The worldly reality itself is spiritual in its core. Instead of being an ascent beyond creation, the ecstasy of the modern artist and poet is rather

a descent from the sensuous surface into its spiritual form, which participates in an intra-divine expression. The creative impulse of the Renaissance changed the relation to nature. The artist complemented and
corrected nature, yet he never ceased to consider himself an integral part
of it. His attitude, unlike that of later thought, was not that of a subject
opposed to a cosmos to which it conveys its entire meaning and value. If
matters had remained at that point, modern culture would merely have
marked a new phase, not a break, in a continuous tradition. A break did
occur, however, once the human subject assumed the part of sole form-
giving principle while reducing nature's given meaning to a subordinate,
increasingly instrumental, position. What for early humanists and Renaissance artists had been a constructive dialectical tension turned into an
opposition between mind and nature. This reversal occurred in the philosophy of the seventeenth century when mind alone become the source
of meaning. Yet other, less radical reconceptualizations of nature preceded
those of the classical age.

Toward a New Knowledge of Nature

Galileo and Descartes may have been the pioneers of modern physics. Yet
alternatives to the traditional world picture had begun to emerge well
before them. Humanists and thinkers of the early Renaissance showed
little interest in rethinking the nature of the universe. Compared with
such fourteenth-century Scholastics as Nicholas Oresme or John Buridan,
they were clearly inferior. Humanism never showed a serious interest in
cosmology. For Coluccio Salutati, knowledge of nature consisted in comparing diverse passages in classical authors on a given subject and in
attempting to render them coherent despite glaring contradictions. Ermolao Barbaro, who in his *Castigationes plinianae* attacked the heretofore
unquestioned authority of Pliny's *Natural History*, merely criticized Plin-
y's use of literary sources without questioning their content.

Even the revival of Platonic and Pythagorean mathematical theories
bore little fruit among the humanists.[18] Before Copernicus's *Revolutiones*
and Galileo's *Dialoghi* and *Discorsi*, few thinkers of the Renaissance
considered combining mathematical methods with empirical observation.
Nicholas of Cusa and Leonardo were exceptions. Cusanus claims that the
mind possesses *certain* knowledge only of numbers. Since reason is ex-
plicated in mathematics, it holds the key to understanding nature. Unlike
Galileo and Descartes, however, Cusanus assumes no mathematical struc-

ture in nature itself. Nor does he regard mathematics in any way as an intuitive science. Precisely its wholly nonintuitive quality constitutes its unique appropriateness for the mind's ascent to an unknowable God.[19]

While for Cusanus mathematics had remained a theoretical *apriori*, Leonardo combined it with actual observation. Yet he makes no absolute distinction between the mathematical qualities of nature and our perception of it, as if the former were more true than the latter (as Galileo and Descartes were to claim). His concept of form integrates subjective aesthesis with objective intuition. Even as the humanists had elaborated a different ideal of form in language and rhetoric, so Leonardo articulated a new concept of form in the visual arts on the basis of a changed perception of nature. The actual practice of painters and sculptors had, of course, preceded his theory, as Masaccio's and Mino da Fiesole's works testify, but Leonardo justified what they did. The permanent, unchangeable *ragioni* inherent in nature must guide the artist as well as the thinker.[20] In Leonardo's notebooks we find the ideal, familiar from literary humanism, of art completing and perfecting what nature initiates. But he insists that artistic form must be discovered in and extracted from nature. Observation of nature precedes artistic expression. Being the one who most intensely experiences nature, the artist penetrates its inner secrets. Still, if observation reveals the forms of nature, experience alone does not convey its essence. That essence the mind must find in itself. Experience is to be assumed by reason, *maestra e tutatrice della natura*. Only when passing from direct observation to rational reflection does the mind penetrate to the essence of nature beneath its phenomena. In joining aesthetic theory with the systematic study of nature Leonardo remains a transitional figure. Galileo expressed the idea of natural form predominantly in geometrical or mathematical terms, thereby loosening the union between physical essence and artistic ideal. The natural models that guide the artist are now assumed to be taken from the more superficial realm of experience while the essence of nature lies hidden in its mathematical core.

Some of Leonardo's aesthetic attitude toward nature survives in Galileo's *Dialogue on the Two Systems*. He praises the great artists, poets, architects, musicians, and inventors who unlock the divine wisdom present in nature and, more intimately, in the mind, but Galileo initiated a systematic study of nature that was no longer restricted to or primarily determined by direct observation. The idea that nature is to be known by means of mathematical methods has become so familiar that we hardly understand the opposition to it at the beginning of the modern age. Yet Francis Bacon, the "great instaurator" of modern science, strongly objected to those who mixed mathematics with the study of nature. Nor did Bacon stand alone with his aversion. The great chemist Jan Baptist van Helmont also supported a pure observation of nature, uncontaminated by mathematical deductions. Even George Berkeley, who had already witnessed the triumph of the natural sciences (to which his own optical theory contributed), considered "the nobler visions" of direct experience more revealing: "In perusing the volume of nature methinks it is beneath the dignity of the mind to affect an exactness in reducing each particular phenomenon to general rules, or showing how it follows from them. We should propose to ourselves nobler visions, namely to recreate and exalt the mind with a prospect of the beauty, order, extent, and variety of natural things: hence by proper inferences to enlarge our notions of the grandeur, wisdom, and beneficence of the Creator."[21]

Those who stood closer to the origins of modern science felt less inclined to consider such "nobler visions" as merely subjective impressions irrelevant to the knowledge of nature proper. William James still preserved the awareness that a mathematical science of the world is only one among several possible systems chosen for the purpose of casting chaos into order. "The most promising of these ideal systems at first were of course the richer ones, the sentimental ones. The baldest and least promising were the mathematical ones; but the history of the latter's application is a history of steadily advancing successes, whilst that of the sentimentally richer systems is one of relative sterility and failure."[22] Such "richer" systems were the ones inspired by the Renaissance ideal of form. They assumed a nature endowed with an inner teleology, rather than being the outcome of mechanical causes in an indifferent, mathematically homogeneous universe. Foremost among them were various alchemical theories which all, in one way or another, presented nature as an organic, self-sufficient, teleological entity.

Too often the cosmology of the early modern age continues to be viewed as a prehistory of the scientific revolution, as if there had been nothing between the Aristotelian world picture and the mechanistic one.[23] Such a view overlooks a prolonged attempt to understand the universe through chemistry rather than through the laws of mechanics. Until the end of the seventeenth century alchemy developed side by side with mechanical physics as an alternative science. Both shared the axiom that all parts of the cosmos are connected, but they envisioned this relatedness in different ways. The basis for alchemy was provided not by the homogeneity of nature that results from mathematical reduction but by an internal harmony underlying all things. Alchemy reappropriated the ancient idea of an initially perfect cosmos and transformed it into what was to become one of the root metaphors of modern cosmology, namely, that of an ontic fullness in which no gaps separated one part from another.

Established since time immemorial in China, India, and Egypt,[24] alchemy may have begun as a sort of initiation rite that enabled a person fully to participate in the life of nature and to master its secrets. The alchemist assists nature by accelerating natural processes, thus allowing them more rapidly and more effectively to follow their inherent teleology. Since the human body contains all the ingredients and proportions distributed over the totality of nature, the alchemist who unveils the overall teleology of nature is also able to cure the body. At the basis of the alchemical enterprise lies the concept of a microcosmos perfectly attuned to the macrocosmos of nature.

In his seminal study *The Great Chain of Being,* Arthur Lovejoy has shown how this idea, at least in the West, relies on two Neoplatonic assumptions.[25] One states that any being that is not absolute has to be less than perfect; the other that a universe derived from and reflecting the radiation of the absolute must nevertheless bear the mark of divine perfection and hence be as perfect as possible. A created universe is, by its very nature, imperfect. But it attains its highest perfection possible within its own limits by including an uninterrupted series of beings, from the lowest to the highest degree, without gaps between its various kinds and species. Despite this unsurpassable fullness of Being, the universe remains ontologically imperfect. Its fullness is made up of a multiplicity of forms none of which is totally perfect. Christians had always assumed that the universe in some way reflected the perfection of its Creator. In late medieval theology, however, this idea of perfection lost its persuasive quality: a God eminently free was not bound to create any particular world at all. The Renaissance revival of Neoplatonism brought needed support to the *principium plenitudinis,* which a voluntarist theology of creation had undermined. Without the principle of fullness strongly reasserted by Neoplatonic theology, alchemy would have lacked the philosophical basis for upholding the uninterrupted contiguity of all elements, which was the very condition for combining them with one another.

Both the theory of fullness and that of general restoration of the cosmos claimed an earlier ancestry in an ancient wisdom, reputedly lost but partially preserved in hermetic writings.[26] Belief in a *prisca theologia* was widespread during the Renaissance. Bacon himself viewed his efforts at establishing a new science as a "restauration"—meaning both an innovation and a recovery[27] —that would revive the ancient magic lost by later ages. According to Paracelsus, a most original thinker and the foremost alchemist of the Renaissance period, alchemy would recreate the cosmos to its pristine state. While doing so, it would also heal humans from inner tensions and disharmonies which cause physical disease. The alchemist transforms nature's distorted state into one of balance and harmony. The idea of forcefully redeeming nature guides Paracelsus's entire speculation. Once initiated through secret ancient wisdom into the hidden correspondences that link the various components of nature, the mind becomes capable of reshaping parasitical growth into organic order. The alchemist does so by liberating that *quinta essentia* which lies buried in all things in the form of gold. A cryptic alchemical principle states: "Unless the order of nature be disturbed, you will not engender gold, unless it shall previously have been silver."[28]

Though the alchemist assumption of a basic unity of all elements of the universe runs counter to the atomistic principles that stood at the beginning of the modern science of chemistry, the theories of Paracelsus and other Renaissance alchemists nevertheless prepared the later acceptance of the science. Newton was driven to the study of alchemy (on which he left thousands of pages in manuscript) in order to explain the active forces of life within the general passivity of matter in mechanical philosophy. Creation with all the life it contains must have been a chemical process in which light, the first-born of God's creatures, animated dead matter into living agents.[29] Paracelsus's theory that all bodies consist of three primary substances (sulphur, mercury, and salt) replaced the Aristotelian concept of matter as a universal substratum, on the basis of which bodies could change into one another, by substantial elements that remained unchanged but were capable of entering into unlimited combinations.[30] With respect to the later science of mechanics, Paracelsus's primeval harmony of all parts of the cosmos presented an alternative to the concept of a physically homogeneous universe ruled by identical laws. The alchemists strike a particularly modern chord in requiring human interference with natural processes as a condition for achieving cosmic harmony. The ancient idea of the microcosmos in which all things converge now becomes an active agent of transformation. Rather than serving as nature's assistant, the person now becomes its controller. Paracelsus's ultimate objective remains, even by today's norms, one of unsurpassed ambition: to create an artificial, humanlike creature—the *homunculus*—who appears in Goethe's dramatic version of the legend of Faust (for which Paracelsus himself may have stood as original model).

A comparably ambitious desire to scrutinize the secrets of nature in order to control them underlies much of the astrological movement at the beginning of the modern epoch. Astrological speculation had, of course, formed a substantial though somewhat eccentric part of medieval cosmology. But the idea of Providence had kept the influence of the stars within rather restrictive boundaries. No secondary cause, least of all one that would influence human destiny, was allowed to escape direct divine supervision. Yet as nature came to be regarded as a relatively autonomous creative system, the determining power of the celestial spheres regained some of its ancient credibility. The fact that their impact remained at best conjectural proved no decisive obstacle. The rhetorical tradition felt no qualms in applying what seemed certain in one area to another where there was no evidence for it. The principle of a universal harmony of nature rendered sufficiently plausible what experience could not confirm. The Neapolitan humanist Giovanni Pontano uninhibitedly appealed to this dubious principle.

> Since the mind itself relies much on likenesses and among those
> especially on those that are or certainly appear to be identities . . . ,
> it compares them at the same time, and if this comparison in all
> respects agrees, an approbation and consensus is born which has
> in itself a marvellous power for conjecturing and reaching a
> conclusion. . . . These conjectures, though not entirely certain and
> necessary, nevertheless prove most of the time to be correct and
> usually conform to this line. Thus our knowledge of the heavens
> and of the stars partly rests on reason and partly on conjecture.
> Established by reason is what we call astronomy. . . . What is called
> astrology is in part rational since it deviates in no way from nature
> and its course. . . . But in part it is conjectural.[31]

Within the arena of astrology two opposite forces of modern culture fought a major battle. On one side stood the almost divine power of nature, Spenser's "great grandmother of all creatures bred." The more one stressed God's immanence in the cosmos, the more reasonable it appeared that all parts of this cosmos influenced one another. This principle favored astrology as long as the stars were held to belong to a higher sphere. On the other side stood the newly asserted lordship of the person, master over all of nature.

Marsilio Ficino felt torn between two theories both of which he embraced: the mystical presence of God to the individual soul, and the communication of the cosmic spheres united by a single world soul. How can the individual soul destined for personal salvation be part of a totality ruled by the world soul without ceasing to be an autonomous spiritual center? Ficino pondered this question at length and in his *De vita triplici*, a strange medical text intended to cure "the disease of the learned," he concluded that stars do influence human affairs, astrological knowledge enables us to control their impact and thus all the more firmly to rule over the cosmos.[32]

Even the rationalist Pomponazzi granted the celestial spheres a limited impact on the will. The very coherence of the cosmos required that spiritual forces be integrated with the basic rhythm of the universe. God does not influence the lower world directly, not even in the order of revelation, but through intermediate, cosmic causes.[33] Even those who repudiated astrology, like Pico della Mirandola, did not do so on the basis of rational arguments. Their rejection resulted from a moral consideration: for the person not to be fully free conflicted with his supreme dignity. Cassirer is right: "The pathos that inspires his [Pico's] work against astrology is not so much an intellectual as an ethical pathos. . . . To accept astrology means to invert not so much the order of being as the order of *value*—it means making of matter the master of spirit."[34] The same argument of human autonomy that had led Pico to deny astral influences had made Ficino conclude that we control and manipulate them. But both rejected an attitude of passive submission to the influence of the stars in favor of an unwavering assertion of human dominion over the cosmos. The person is viewed as self-determining even where the early astrological tradition continued to hold sway.

Even after the acceptance of the heliocentric theory had seriously begun to undermine the vertical world structure from which the impact of the planets drew much of its plausibility—power had to be supplied "from above"—astrological speculation showed no signs of abating. Nor did the Reformation's clear theological distinction between a divine realm and the created world terminate astrological interest. By means of the stars the learned Melanchton attempted to determine the year of Luther's birth, which Luther had forgotten.[35] In the sixteenth century Bruno appears to have been among the few to realize that Copernicus's revolution spelled the end of planetary power: "the planets you see above and below the canopy of heaven . . . are only bodies, creations similar to our earth in which the divinity is present neither more nor less than it is present in this body which is our earth as well as in our very selves."[36] Henceforth, the heaven of the soul must reign over the cosmic heavens.[37] Nevertheless, the same Bruno appears to have supplemented his income by astrological readings.

In the chaotic beginnings of a cultural revolution ideas tend to spin off in various, frequently opposite directions and unleash competing forces. Which ideas triumph often depends less on inner logic than on the rhetorical power and ideological simplicity of those who defend them. At the advent of modern culture the conception of freedom eventually weakened the belief in astrology because it obtained a more powerful grip on the imagination. Astrological speculations, as indigenous to the period as the rise of the modern concept of freedom, eventually yielded to what was becoming the stronger idea. The disappearance of alchemy—itself a typically modern phenomenon, at least in Paracelsus's version—is harder to explain. For a long time it continued to coexist with the budding sciences of physics and chemistry (sometimes in the same person, as in Van Helmont and Newton!). So we may presume that what pioneers of modern science continued to believe in did not vanish for purely rational arguments. Pseudo-sciences appear to obey the same principles (formulated by Kuhn and Blumenberg) for explaining the success or decline of scientific theories: they are determined not by pure rationality, but either by an increasing dissatisfaction with the anomaly of relevant facts left unexplained in an existing theory or by the greater or lesser compatibility of a different explanation with the dominant total worldview.[38] In the early modern period that view was largely one of cosmic order. Alchemy and astronomy supported the aesthetic ideal of a harmoniously coherent universe. Their appeal decreased as the mechanistic theory presented a conception of a homogeneous universe that explained more phenomena and explained them better.

The Infinite Universe

After late medieval theology weakened the direct link between the Creator and a predictable world order, two possibilities presented themselves for restoring the multiple natural phenomena to the coherence of a rational cosmos. According to one, the human mind assumed the part which earlier generations had attributed to God or to nature. When theology ceased to guarantee that meaning and value would be given with the world, it fell upon the mind to define or invent them. Such a move inevitably resulted in a separation between a meaning-giving mental subject and a physically given but meaning-dependent world. This was the option actually chosen by modern philosophy and science. Characteristic of it was that it dispensed with theology altogether: philosophy became secular. The other option, which we shall now consider, consisted in filling the theological vacuum by retheologizing nature in a manner that would be unassailable by the earlier objections. This conception, rooted in Platonic and Neoplatonic sources, differed from earlier theories (including the nominalist ones) in that it conceived of God's immanence in a more intimate way than later Scholasticism had done by stressing a formal rather than an efficient divine causality.

In Aristotelian cosmology causality descended from above (*sursum est unde motus*) and reached the world via a chain of mediations. In the panentheistic systems of the Renaissance, divine causality affected all levels of reality directly and simultaneously.[39] These systems differed even more sharply from the mechanistic ones of the seventeenth century in which motion came entirely from without. Two major thinkers—Cusanus and Bruno—presented theories in which the finite depended on the infinite in a relation of formal causality. Cusanus defended the total immanence of divine power against the traditional conception of a hierarchy of spheres transmitting God's power to the "natural center" of the universe. In a moving cosmos, he argued, there can be no fixed center—the sun no more than the earth. An observer in motion always perceives his own position as central with respect to changing surroundings. Now, according to Cusanus, motion is inherent in all finite things, including the earth itself, for all change and hence move. Thus, long before Galileo the German cardinal overthrew a cosmic system in which energy had to come, via a series of mediations, from the periphery of the universe. If nature is "the unfolding of things in motion," the notion of a natural center loses all meaning.[40] From the point of view of a moving subject, center and periphery of other moving objects necessarily remain perspectival. Only a being that remains in absolute rest can ever constitute a natural center. Reviving the metaphor of the unlimited circle with the ubiquitous center (*DI*, I, 23), Cusanus argues that God, who remains equally close to all points in the universe, alone deserves to be called its center.

But Cusanus goes further. Since time and space do not exist beyond this moving universe, nothing limits it from the outside, and the cosmos must be at least privatively infinite. Cusanus does not base this infinity of the universe upon empirical evidence. Nor does he simply transfer the hermetic metaphor of God—the circle whose center is everywhere—to the physical cosmos.[41] He bases his conclusion upon the idea of God's total immanence in creation. In his thought, that divine immanence, implied in the very concept of creation, made a different cosmology not only theologically acceptable but necessary. For a theology of total presence is ultimately incompatible with a divine power that enters the universe at one single point rather than at all points at once.[42]

The idea of God's total presence in the universe, however, did not simply reinstate a pre-Christian cosmology. The difference between Cusanus's idea of divine immanence and the one in which Neoplatonic philosophy had articulated God's cosmic presence appears clearly in the cardinal's rejection of the world soul. The fifth-century Greek philosopher Anaxagoras had first introduced the idea of a cosmic mind (*Nous*). In Plato's *Timaeus* the divine Demiurge animated his cosmos with a universal soul. Not until Plotinus, however, did this soul become an ontic component in the structure of reality. In its creative function the universal soul rivaled the Hebrew-Christian Creator (see especially *Enneads* V, 1, 2); so its chance of entering the body of a Christian theology would have seemed exceedingly small. Yet it succeeded in doing so to a surprising extent.[43] It owed its acceptance mainly to the fact that Neoplatonism had lowered the world soul to a level below what Christians considered the divine sphere proper, namely, that of the One and the Mind. It thus appeared to be sufficiently far removed from God to be adoptable without any risk of pantheism. Yet the world soul showed an ineradicable tendency to reclaim its divine status. Some twelfth-century theologians equated it with the Holy Spirit, of whom the Pentecost liturgy sings that he has filled the universe (*replevit orbem terrarum*). In 1121 Abelard's thesis "Quod Spiritus Sanctus sit anima mundi" was condemned. That and the advance of Aristotelian philosophy (which had no need for a world soul) arrested its progress.

During the Renaissance it regained full strength, gathering the united support from such traditional adversaries as Platonists, hermeticists, and even quite a few Aristotelians. For Telesio, Cardano, Bruno, and Campanella, all of nature possesses psychic qualities of motion and life, perhaps even sensation. The revival of a hermetic tradition that linked all things in an organic harmony animated by a single life spirit rendered the idea of a world soul more credible. In Cardanus's *De subtilitate*, for instance, we learn that metals grow like seeds in the earth. Stones are animated and procreate through "stone semen."[44] Even the learned Marsilio Ficino considered planets "ensouled." How else could they move continuously in regular circles without ever leaving their "natural place"?[45] Now, this universal ensoulment by no means entails a pantheistic immanence of God in all beings. As Cusanus perceived, precisely because God is not directly immanent in a Neoplatonic cosmology, a mediating realm between the One and the many is required in which intellectual forms exist "subsequent to God but prior to things."[46] Cusanus had no use for such a mediation, however, because, for him, God is directly immanent in each and every part of the cosmos and needs no realm of forms independent of their individualized existence in time. Cusanus, then, rejects the world soul not because it makes God immanent in the world but because it does not sufficiently do so.

Bruno's case is different. Having decided for an even more intimate union between God and the cosmos, he rejects the idea of creation altogether. Yet still needing a principle for distinguishing God and his cosmic manifestation, he sees himself forced to reintroduce the world soul. Being the necessary link between the divine nature as it is in itself and its equally necessary "emanation," the world soul, for him, unites God with the world more intimately than a dependence conceived in terms of efficient causality. At the same time it distinguishes him from that world. More consistent than most Christian Neoplatonists, he understood that the world soul was a substitute for creation and could not function as a complement to it. An early convert to Copernicus's theory, Bruno regarded it as his special mission to propagate the heliocentric world system. But he soon realized that Copernicus's reversal had left the essential principle in the traditional world structure unchanged. The Polish astronomer had merely replaced the center of the universe from the earth to the sun. Thus the most resistant of the Aristotelian notions survived the Copernican revolution, namely, that all things have their "natural place" (*locus naturalis*). The resilience of the *locus naturalis* may be attributed to the role which it had played in representing God's ordinary presence in traditional cosmology. Though not essential to the Christian doctrine of creation, the idea that things have a naturally assigned place was never-

theless deeply enough entrenched in the tradition to survive all cosmological innovations until (and including) Galileo's. The concept of a
natural place depended directly on the idea of a centered universe. Bruno
perceived that once the earth had been removed from its central position,
any ground for considering the universe centered at all disappeared. Copernicus had inconsistently continued to grant the solar system a central
position, even while undermining its spiritual basis. Moreover, if the
universe is infinite, then, as Cusanus had shown, the idea of a fixed center
had itself become meaningless.

Bruno possessed neither the empirical evidence nor the philosophical
arguments to support the existence of an actually infinite universe, that
is, one stretched out beyond any calculation of space and time. Nevertheless he understood that once we abandon the ancient idea of a circular
motion of the heavens, the need for considering the cosmos finite disap-
pears. With remarkable foresight and without any of the later evidence
Bruno rejected such a motion. Instead of a scientific theory, the Dominican visionary fabricated a mythical representation with fragments of
ancient and medieval theories. In his infinite universe, the world soul
would guarantee the order and coherence that the theory of the *locus
naturalis* had once secured in a centered cosmos. It was Bruno, then, not
Copernicus, who first envisioned a totally open cosmology. With the full
force of a powerful imagination he poetically articulated, rather than
intellectually conceived (as Cusanus had done), what it is like to inhabit
a universe without center or periphery. In his didactic poems and philosophical dialogues we hear the cry of wonder when suddenly the boundaries of the cosmos collapse and men confront not the unexpected but
the inconceivable: *infiniti mondi,* uncountable beacons of light alternat-
ing with oceans of darkness, disparate fires in unending stretches of
primeval cold, myriads of solar systems, each one revolving around its
own center and occasionally colliding with others in limitless space.
Beyond the struggle of worlds Bruno imagined the elements, each one
striving to gain a supremacy which an impartial universe continues to
deny them. This vision of a boundless universe animated by a divine
spirit filled the former Dominican with a mystical intoxication expres-
sible only in poetic language.

The Italian dialogue *De l'infinito* begins with the question: "How
could the universe be possibly infinite?" to which Bruno replies with the
counter question: "How could the universe be possibly finite?" A perfect
God must reveal himself in an infinite number of worlds, for no single

one could ever express the fullness of the divine Being. "There should be an infinite image of the inaccessible divine countenance and there should be in this image, as infinite members thereof, innumerable worlds."[47] To withhold any possible manifestation would be "invidious" on God's part and hence incompatible with divine perfection. Precisely because his expression is total and necessary, God is as entirely immanent in the unfolded being of the universe as he is in himself. "Nature is either nothing or the divine power itself that animates nature."[48]

Bruno's daring theory profoundly disturbed the cosmic picture of traditional Christian theology, which hinged on a universe limited in space and time, in the center of which God's incarnation had occurred. His conception of an infinite universe surpassed that of Cusanus's unlimited one. For the cardinal, the boundless universe does not rival God's positive infinity and remains therefore intrinsically finite. Even though God created the universe as perfect as it could be in actuality, he could never exhaust his creative power. Unlike Cusanus's Creator, Bruno's God necessarily actualizes all his possibilities in cosmic self-expression. Bruno's notion of infinity possesses a qualitative density that renders his cosmic system absolutely perfect: nothing could be added to it and no aspect of the divine remains hidden behind it. The world is grounded in God's essence, not in his will. In it he manifests himself so totally that no further revelation is needed or possible, for a revelation still presupposes that God is able to conceal things whose manifestation depends on his discretion. Where Cusanus's theology culminates in a *docta ignorantia*, Bruno's concludes in an exhaustive knowledge of God through the infinite cosmos.

God's unity keeps the infinite world in which he has expressed himself from disintegrating into an incoherent multiplicity. Insofar as he is one, God transcends the manifold universe. Bruno significantly concludes each one of his three poems on the infinity of the cosmos with a hymn to divine unity. The universe reflects all of God, yet the reflection differs from the reflected. Nor does the infinity of the universe coincide with God's infinity, even though both of them are divine. God unfolds himself in the universe, and yet the unfolding continues to differ from his enfolded nature.[49] Through the world soul God mediates his transcendent unity with the endless multiplicity of the cosmos. "The World Soul is the formal constitutive principle of the universe and of that which is contained in it. I declare that if life is found in all things, this Soul emerges as the form of all things. . . . According to the diversity of the disposition of matter, and a reordering to the power of material principles, active and passive, [it] comes to produce diverse configurations, and to effect different powers."[50] The dynamic quality of Bruno's world soul which moves all things from within renders the idea of a Prime Mover altogether superfluous. Because of the intimacy of God's immanence in nature, Bruno refers to the world soul that makes this immanence possible as *primo principio* rather than *causa*. "Principle is that which intrinsically concurs toward the constitution of a thing and what remains within the effect."[51] Even as the intellectual soul in Aristotle's psychology penetrates and moves the body while transcending it, the world soul rules and directs all things from within while surpassing each one of them.

Matter possesses a divine status in Bruno's theory. Far from being the lowest rung on the ladder of being, matter functions as that active co-principle of soul that secures each part of the universe its specific power and thus accounts for the variety of forms and degrees in creation. Uncreated and creative, it must be regarded as no less divine than the world soul itself. As Bruno describes it in a terminology borrowed mostly from the ancient atomists, matter ceases to be a metaphysical principle and is well on its way toward becoming the independent substance it will be in the materialist systems of the eighteenth and nineteenth centuries. Reversing the Aristotelian conception of matter as the immutable, passive basis that underlies constantly changing forms, Bruno turns it into an active principle through which the *natura naturata* unfolds itself into innumerable individual substances, spiritual as well as corporeal. "That therefore which unfolds (*esplica*) what is enfolded (*implicato*) must be called a thing divine and an optimal parent, bearer, and mother of natural things, indeed nature itself in substance."[52] Matter then ultimately coincides with nature as principle of generation. This creative function of matter was, surprisingly, made possible by the Christian dogma that God had directly created matter as well as form, while in Greek thought matter owed its reality entirely to form.

Since the twelfth century nature had become ever more autonomous and creative. Yet few writers had raised nature to what Calvin was to call "a substitute of God" (*Institutes* I, 5). Earlier naturalism had derived nature's creative powers from the transcendent source of God's creative act.[53] Bruno redivinized nature, considering a voluntary creation by an inscrutable God wholly inadequate to account for the intimate divine presence in all things. His noncreationist panentheism found few direct followers (Spinoza being the most significant). Yet eventually his idea of an immanent causality entered the very mechanistic science of nature that had, from Descartes to Newton, considered God's creative act as indispensable for bringing the physical mechanism into being as well as for setting it in motion. But since the physical world required no further divine assistance, later mechanist philosophers, beginning with Diderot, came to regard nature as altogether self-supporting and self-moving. At that point nature attained a transcendence of its own, and philosophers, often unwittingly, began to reintroduce Bruno's theories. French materialists were heavily influenced by Spinoza who himself had rationally developed Bruno's intuition of a self-supporting cosmos. German idealism, also under the influence of Spinoza, revived interest in the Italian "pantheist." Schelling wrote a philosophical dialogue entitled *Bruno*, and Hegel devoted many pages to him. But German philosophers, unlike the French, fully acknowledged the religious quality of Bruno's thought.

Bruno was not the only nor the earliest thinker of the Renaissance to challenge the traditional view of a power transmitted from a single point through several intermediate spheres. (In his encyclopedic *De rerum natura*, begun in 1565, Bernardino Telesio presented the cosmos as a single, homogeneous, and organic system ruled by a balancing internal principle.) Yet none possessed the expressive power of the man from Nola and few exercised a greater (albeit an indirect) influence on later modern thought.

Chapter 3

The Emergence of Objectivity

The New Meaning of Method

The lively cosmological speculations of the fifteenth and sixteenth centuries discussed in the previous chapter lacked, for
the most part, the method and scientific discipline of such
late-medieval thinkers as Buridan, Oresme, and Autrecourt. But they may
have influenced the scientific movement in a substantial albeit indirect
way. Platonic speculation on the sun as symbol of the mind may seem
unrelated to the development of a scientific cosmology. Yet as Hans
Blumenberg has shown, it removed the principal philosophical obstacle
that barred the way toward the acceptance of a heliocentric system.
Indeed, such extra-scientific considerations may have spurred Copernicus
to begin and continue his daring investigation. The dedication of the
Revolutiones to Pope Paul III with its reference to the Pope's favoring of
the Platonic sun symbolism shows how well the Polish scientist was
aware of the role such speculations could play in rendering the new world
system adoptable.[1]

The revolutionary quality of Copernicus's theory did not fully appear
until, through Galileo's discoveries, the stars ceased to function as fixed
boundaries of a cosmos centered around our solar system. Even those who

did not openly subscribe to the new cosmology eventually came to accept that the laws of physics apply universally to all parts of the cosmos, and that the mathematical methods used in formulating them are not restricted to astronomy. The eminent French intellectual historian Robert Lenoble distinguishes the seventeenth from the sixteenth century by the new relation between art and science and by the impact that relation had on the entire culture. In the earlier period the aesthetic concept of form had remained united with the scientific one. Leonardo had not hesitated to classify painting as a science. Even Bruno and the young Galileo had, in the Neoplatonic tradition, allowed aesthetic considerations a part in formulating cosmological theories. In the course of the seventeenth century, however, the weight shifted heavily toward science and scientific philosophy; aesthetic theories were forced to conform to mathematical norms. The engineer replaced the artist as model of the age. To understand nature no longer meant to describe its outward appearance but to penetrate its inner secrets. One "knows" only what one has built up from within. In Lenoble's pithy expression: "Connaître c'est fabriquer."[2] Or as the British physicist Robert Hooke claimed in the dedication of his work to Charles II, to discover the truth of nature means "to begin to build anew upon a sure foundation of experiments."[3] The idea of an independent nature with its own teleology makes room for a mechanical one, mathematically constructed and subject to human purposes.

Galileo played a pivotal part in this metamorphosis. With many humanists he had originally shared the Platonic idea that the essence of reality must be ideal. Yet while Plato (and his followers) had separated the essential form from its nonessential participation in the physical world, Galileo assumed the ideal form to reside within the physical. The ideal predicates constitute the essence of the observable phenomenon. Galileo postulated a mathematical core at the root of physical being. To know a phenomenon, then, requires that we first break it down into its quantifiable elements in the metodo resolutivo. What remains may be discarded as ontologically irrelevant. But this means that what Galileo reconstrues with these elements is, in fact, not the original reality but one reduced to fit the mathematical grid. Here begins the common thread that holds all aspects of science together in the seventeenth century.[4]

The mathematical proportions of various parts of the cosmos had fascinated inquisitive minds from the beginning of Western culture. For the Assyrians and Egyptians, as well as for Pythagorean and Platonic philosophers (the late and the early ones), numerical proportions had constituted the rule and perfection of the cosmos. For Plato geometry described the enduring, ideal normative structures of form within an ever-shifting nature. In the *Timaeus* and the *Laws* social union as well as astronomical motion were subject to mathematical laws. Yet those laws did not account for the accelerated or decelerated movements observed in the physical world. They served as ideal models that nature as we actually observe it could only approximate. The celestial spheres alone belonged to an ideal order capable of achieving the perfect patterns outlined in geometrical models. Thus astronomers since Plato felt justified in simply assuming that the orbit of celestial bodies must describe the perfect form of a circle. In his early years Galileo accepted much of this mathematical idealism; yet his later use of mathematics had a very different purpose—namely, to capture the nature of motion as actually observed in increasing or decreasing movements. The ideal mathematical pattern Galileo used in calculating those movements was not an escape from the intractable irregularity of the physical world into an ideal order but an attempt to use that order to grasp the essence of the real world. Mathematics constitutes the ideal core of the physical universe, not an independent ideal realm imitated but distorted by that universe. In this respect Galileo sides with Aristotle rather than with Plato! True, his spokesman Salviati concedes to Simplicio in *Two Chief World Systems* that we must "allow for the impediments of matter."[5] Yet these material impediments do not prevent the world from being geometrically intelligible in principle, provided the discrepancy is inconsiderable or we account for it in our subsequent calculations. Galileo assumes that the physical world is perfectly regular and unchangeable solely for the purpose of simplifying a matter too complex to be grasped in its entirety.

When Galileo applied geometry to the general theory of motion, he set out to measure an indifferent succession of moments regardless of the more or less ideal quality of the outcome. Celestial bodies, previously reputed to belong to a different, more perfect order, now became subject to the same general law of motion. Henceforth uniformity not harmony counted as the determining factor. The mathematical method used universally for measuring motion would, in principle, abolish the traditional distinction between celestial and terrestrial mechanics. One method applied to both, and its purpose was to discover "a mechanics which would unite the different types of motion, celestial and terrestrial, either in a single set of descriptive quantitative 'laws' or, even more ambitiously, in a single explanatory theory."[6] If the method proved successful, the entire cosmos would become subject to one and the same ideal rule. We may regard this homogenization of the cosmos by universal mathematical laws Galileo's most revolutionary achievement. Theologians, already disturbed by the scriptural problems provoked by the new cosmology, understandably felt reluctant to abandon a theory on which the transmission of divine causality hitherto had rested.

As historians have repeatedly pointed out, the controversy turned not, or at least not primarily, around the change in the world picture. Pope Paul III himself had welcomed Copernicus's theory and the Jesuit astronomers of the Roman College—the famous Father Clavius foremost among them—were quite willing to consider a heliocentric alternative. The main issue was causality. One revolutionary conclusion of Galileo's new system was that power need not continuously flow from God once nature became endowed with a uniform intrinsic necessity of its own. The communication of motion, which had played such an important role in the ancient worldview and on which major arguments for the existence of God had rested,[7] lost its significance in a mechanistic order where bodies, once they moved, would continue to do so until stopped by an external cause. It needed no further assistance after it had received its initial impulse. The new science of mechanics did not dispense with a Creator who would initiate motion, but it appeared to withdraw God from nature after his creative act. Only the availability of an alternative interpretation of Scripture would justify the acceptance of Galileo's "hypothesis," Cardinal Bellarmine concluded. But none was available. There was another, aesthetic reason why many felt reluctant to abandon a system rich in spiritual meaning and intricate harmony for a law of flat uniformity. Hans Jonas has drawn attention to it. "For the modern idea of understanding nature, the least intelligent has become the most intelligible, the least reasonable the most rational. At the bottom of all rationality or 'mathematics' in nature's order lies the mere fact of their being quantitative constants in the behavior of matter, or 'the principle of uniformity' as such, which found its first statement in the law of inertia—surely no mark of immanent reason."[8]

Nonetheless, Galileo's attitude remains in some respects traditional. His outlook is still theoretical in the ancient sense of "contemplative." He assumes that nature itself is intrinsically geometrical and hence that the scientist, in uncovering mathematical proportions, reads what nature contains. This view would eventually make place for a purely constructionist use of mathematics whereby the mind imposes its own patterns of intelligibility on nature.[9] In the traditional worldview mathematics had been part of the rational-aesthetic order of a cosmos that was either divine by nature or the creation of an all-wise God. It followed, so to speak, from the world's divine quality or origin. For later empiricist thinkers, the mathematical nature of physics had a quite different meaning. To nominalists, as most of them were, the world order offered no divinely guaranteed predictability. No theological principles supported the claim that the cosmos had to follow geometrical patterns. To serve as principles of interpretation, mathematical equations or geometrical patterns must emerge from or at least be confirmed by observation. Galileo's view cannot be reduced to either tradition, but he transformed both. The mathematical apriori introduced an element of universality in empiricist thought that observation alone could never supply and yet one that was needed to provide the order of nature with an intrinsic stability. Bacon overlooked this when, on the one hand, he promised induction as the revolutionary principle for the future science and, on the other hand, considered mathematics irrelevant for it.

One of the most problematic features of the new science from a theological point of view was its self-sufficiency. Osiander had prefaced Copernicus's *Revolutiones* by presenting it as a hypothesis, and Galileo's theory also was acceptable as long as he did not claim that it was the definitive word about the world order. That final word had always belonged to theology, that is, to Scripture as interpreted by the Church. The mere fact that the new science required no higher authority whatever, that it could do perfectly what it did by itself and, by all appearances, reach a definitive truth caused a major crisis. When Church authorities eventually, with great reluctance, had to retreat before the evidence of the new "hypothesis," the basic problem remained unsolved. As a result, theology gradually withdrew from its millennial task of defining the fundamentals of the worldview. The withdrawal went slowly. Theocosmological speculation continued all through the seventeenth century. As late as the nineteenth century theology still provided the beginning and the end of the cosmological story. But scientists could devote their attention exclusively to what occurred in between these two poles without worrying about the ultimates. Metaphysics also became detached from scientific cosmology, though in a less dramatic way. Philosophy became reduced to a metascience that articulated the presuppositions of what science actually did without itself being actively engaged in the study of nature.[10] The methods of science became normative for thinking as such.

Thus, amazingly, the science of physical nature severed itself from the philosophy that had given birth to it and whose main subject had once been cosmology.

Thinkers in our time have forcefully reacted against this neglect. Whitehead described his great work in metaphysics as an essay in cosmology. But the fact that he had to gather the categories for his philosophical cosmology from past philosophies (Plato, Aristotle, Locke, Hume) rather than from modern science reveals how far philosophy and natural science had grown apart. The cosmology of the modern worldview has cast off the specifically human as well as the theological components. As such it provides no more than a "world picture," a mere representation of the world.

Bacon embraced principles almost exactly opposite to Galileo's. His knowledge of mathematics was limited and his need for it in the scientific interpretation of nature even more so.[11] He distrusted any apriori assumption of a preestablished harmony between the mind and the world. The world owes its origin to a divine decree, and it is unwarranted to project human reason upon God's mind. Since Copernicus's system rested on apriori conceptions, Bacon remained profoundly skeptical about its validity. For him, the scientist must follow the humble method of experiment and induction, not the presumptuous one of Aristotelian demonstration, which anticipates inquiry and is abstracted from the facts sooner than is fit.[12] Such statements have the pleasant ring of scientific modesty, as Basil Willey once observed in an elegant lecture entitled "Bacon and the Rehabilitation of Nature."[13] But is it really, as he claims, an observation of God's work as a supplement to his word?

That Bacon's project was more than a study of observed "facts" appears clearly enough in the *Novum Organum* where he describes his purpose as a metaphysical investigation of "forms which are . . . eternal and immutable" (II, 9). These forms, to be sure, are not Platonic ideas or epistemic aprioris. He defines them as "fixed laws," established by divine decree and hence discoverable only by empirical methods or "axioms" to be "educed" from experience (II, 17 and II, 10). He refers to this process of discovery as one of "legitimate induction" (II, 10), and it is under the name of that method that history has remembered him. But seldom do his "eternal forms" emerge from generalized observation: they mostly result from hypotheses "verified" by a number of (questionable) methods.[14] Indeed, these forms, by Bacon's own account, "for the most part" escape the senses (II, 6), since they usually appear in clusters in composite bodies. Bacon postulates their existence on the basis of observations that he interprets as being their effects. His "metaphysics" aims at approximating as closely as possible the indivisibly simple, which at one point he equates with mathematical simplicity. Hence his puzzling statement: "Inquiries into nature have the best result when they begin with physics and end with mathematics" (II, 8). One can hardly claim that he actively pursued this mathematical ideal!

If the alleged modesty of Bacon's observational method is somewhat deceptive, so is his submissiveness to a divinely established order. Undoubtedly, Bacon's attitude was religiously inspired. In the past, he claims, men have neglected the "oracles" of God's works in order to follow "idols" of their own making. Now the time has come for a "voluntary submission to the divine oracles" and thereby to cleanse the world of all idols. But that submission turns out to be extremely ambiguous. Its entire purpose consists in acquiring control of nature. Bacon commends humility only "to extend more widely the limits of the power and greatness of man." In *The New Organum* he criticizes past (Catholic) centuries for having neglected our God-given right to know and thereby to conquer. Now the moment has arrived to recover that right and to exercise the full power over nature granted us by divine bequest. The theme of power constantly returns in Bacon's writings, and he concludes the preface to *The Great Instauration* with an admonition to avoid pursuing knowledge for any but practical purposes. In a posthumous fragment, *Valerius Terminus* (written around 1603, published in 1743), he insists: "the true end, scope, or office of knowledge, which I have set down to consist not in any plausible, delectable, reverend or admired discourse, or any satisfactory arguments, but in effecting and working, and in discovery of particulars not revealed before, for the better endowment and help of man's life."[15] If a desire for power that conflicted with their contemplative vocation caused the downfall of the rebellious angels, man fell through an opposite desire for pure (as opposed to practical) knowledge that interfered with his calling to dominate nature. Paradise may yet be regained by following our true vocation. It may well be this religious inspiration that secured Bacon's writings their surprising influence, even at a time when science had begun to turn away from his methods. The Puritans rediscovered his work, which confirmed their own opposition to a disinterested (and therefore morally "vain") concept of knowledge in favor of a practical, utilitarian one.

The ship sailing through the Pillars of Hercules that embellishes the title page of the *Novum Organum* symbolizes modern science's intent to remove all the obstacles former ages set to the desire to know. Since the voyages of Columbus, Magellan, Drake, and others, the metaphor had lost its original geographical meaning. But Bacon applied it to science: that also must break through its former barriers. What started with a journey of discovery must now turn into one of conquest. In science a benevolent Providence has granted a *magia naturalis* for our benefit. Though Bacon rejected alchemy and magical practices, the goal of his project derived from a similar ambition. His theory meant to provide the alchemical and magic aspirations with a scientific basis. In his late *Silva Silvarum* (between 1620 and 1626) he advances a theory of elective affinities not unlike the one of alchemy. "It is certain that all bodies whatsoever, though they have no sense, yet they have perception: for when one body is applied to another, there is a kind of election to embrace that which is agreeable, and to exclude or expel that which is ingrate."[16]

Bacon's call for unlimited control over nature rested on the assumption that nature possessed no purpose of its own. Well before mechanistic philosophy, he eliminated final causality from scientific investigation, comparing it to a consecrated virgin who bears no offspring. His opposition to teleological interpretations and concomitant belief in unrestricted human power over nature originated in the voluntarist view of creation. What is, is as it is, merely because God willed it so. This placed the entire responsibility for conveying meaning and purpose to the world entirely on the human person, the only creature endowed with purposiveness. Such a conception of the cosmos contrasted, of course, with the traditional one in which a rational, divine order ruled nature, to which man owed respect and obedience. Bacon tends to transfer the theoretical question: In what does a thing's nature consist? to the functional one: How does it work? and ultimately to the one: What human purpose does it serve? We should avoid, however, attributing to Bacon the later positions that he may have inspired. He certainly was not an instrumentalist. For him the light still precedes the power. He remains more devoted to the traditional ideal of *theoria* than his later followers.

Puritan physicists enthusiastically received Bacon's theories and, by the middle of the seventeenth century, almost universally interpreted them in a pragmatist way. Whereas for Plato, Aristotle, and the Stoics, as well as the church fathers and the Scholastics, knowledge (provided it did not turn into *hybris* or "vain curiosity") had been an end in itself, the culmination of the good life, Bacon's followers transformed it into a means to a practical rather than a theoretical end. Philosophical investigation thereby changed into a practical, problem-solving activity accomplished for the purpose of forcing nature to respond to the "vexation of art." Robert Boyle, the founder of the new science of chemistry and a fervent admirer of Bacon, came close to dismissing disinterested knowledge as an immoral pursuit of vainglory. "There are two very distinct Ends that Men may propound to them selves in studying Natural Philosophy. For some Men care only to know Nature, others desire to command Her: or to express it otherwise, some there are who but desire to please themselves by the Discovery of the Causes of the known Phaenomena, and others would be able to produce new ones, and bring Nature to be serviceable to their particular Ends."[17] Boyle preferred an experimental method of investigation which, unlike the more speculative mathematical one, aims at practical results. With many of his learned British contemporaries, he regarded the mostly theoretical French natural philosophy as merely protracting the infertile, verbal knowledge of the past. In contrast, the British, practical approach dealt with "things."[18]

When the motive of knowledge becomes practical, the epistemic process tends to become restricted by the boundaries of what is conducive to productive action. Method acquires a meaning it never had before. To be sure, systematic knowledge has been methodic since Greek philosophy, but Aristotle had clearly stated that the discipline of methodic thinking required conforming the mind to the nature of the subject. With Bacon and most seventeenth-century philosophers, method turns into a screen imposed upon the subject matter that restricts the investigation to what will most effectively and most speedily yield reliable results. The mind systematically selects what it desires to learn while discarding those elements it considers irrelevant to its investigation. Of course, any science—defined as specialized field of knowledge—requires a pattern of selection. But the one Bacon introduces differs from the ancient *theoria* which, expecting nature to disclose itself, did not set up any apriori method of screening independent of the subject matter. Even Galileo did not separate method from content, as Bacon proposed.

More than any other factor, the new emphasis on method gave birth to the *idea* of science that, in the seventeenth and eighteenth centuries, assumed an importance greater than science itself. An ideal before being an actual achievement, it directed anticipated results toward their proper place within a preestablished schema. As such it gave rise to a characteristically modern belief in the unlimited human ability to conquer nature by rational methods combined with an unshakable confidence in a state of universal happiness that would follow from this conquest.

The Idea of Science and the Rise of Technology

The term *ideology* normally refers to those common, unexamined assumptions that unify the beliefs and values of a community. Applied to science it includes the presuppositions implicitly accepted by professional investigators as conditions for having the results of their work admitted for discussion by their peers. These conditions, as historians of science have repeatedly shown, rarely derive from scientific evidence but more often from prescientific stipulations. The two trends discussed in the previous section—Bacon's pragmatism and Galileo's quantification— which to a great extent determined the scientific revolution, were not themselves the outcome of incontrovertible evidence.

Bacon's practical orientation was inspired by noble motives: to develop knowledge that would benefit the entire human race rather than providing contemplative satisfaction to privileged individuals. The objectives of overcoming sickness, prolonging life, lightening labor, facilitating exchange and communication require no apology. Science for Bacon offered the most practical as well as the least expensive solutions to basic human problems. But without a common teleology that integrates humanity with nature, the mastery of nature becomes its own end, and the purposes originally pursued by it end up becoming secondary. For Bacon knowledge still preceded its practical application. But once his followers implemented their utilitarian principles by means of a mechanistic physics, science was destined to give birth to the most comprehensive feature of modern life—namely, technology.[19] By shifting from a given, preestablished order of nature to one determined by individually or communally experienced needs, they fundamentally transformed the attitude toward the cosmos that had prevailed since the Greek classical age. More than applying the conclusions of a theoretical science to the solving of practical problems, technology construes an alternative order of reality.

One might object that it was the Greek idea of form that made the technological attitude possible since that idea implied a view of the real as having been shaped according to a model. Had not Plato's theory of the forms and perhaps even Pythagoras's doctrine of numbers implied a constructive concept of reality? Aristotle, although he rejected the theory of the forms, nevertheless compared the function of the four causes that constitute reality to the elements instrumental in creating a statue. Moreover, a practical mechanics emerged in Hellenistic Alexandria with Archimedes. Yet in spite of those precedents, the general outlook of the Greeks, which was rarely rejected in subsequent ages, fundamentally differed from the one introduced by Bacon and his followers. *Praxis* in Greek thought remained close to *theoria;* indeed, the supreme form of *praxis* consisted in a life devoted to *theoria.* Even the term *technē* was closely related to theoretical activity. Whereas in the process of knowing the form enters the mind from without, in *technē* it leaves the mind in order to enter into matter. As Aristotle puts it in the *Metaphysics:* "From art [*technē*] proceed those things of which the form [*eidos*] is in the soul of the artist. . . . The active principle then and the starting point of the process of becoming healthy [the objective of the medical *technē*] is, if it happens by art [*technē*], the form [*logos*] in the soul." Similarly, the house as built by the architect comes from the house that preexists as pure form. The same interpretation and even the same example reappear in Augustine: "the house [in reality] proceeds from the house [in the mind]."[20]

The modern idea of science was not the outcome of a single factor. It rested on a practical, voluntarist view of nature as well as on a theoretical, mechanistic one that related all parts of nature to each other. The two combined resulted in an instrumentalism that was fundamentally at variance with the ancient conceptions of *cosmos* and *technē.* From the new perspective, the meaning of form lies entirely in the function it fulfills. This became evident in eighteenth-century mechanistic comparisons of nature to a machine. A machine tolerates no superfluous features: all parts serve the functioning of the whole. Yet the whole is not determined by an inner teleology but by an external agent, by a divine or by a human mind.[21] Natural processes, then, are exclusively determined by efficient causality. Purpose and means become relative concepts in the functioning of this closed system. The technical imperative summons the goal-defining person as much as he summons nature. The instrumental attitude allows no definitive distinction between ends and means, nor between contemplation and action. Within the closed circuit of instrumental thought the very idea of final end becomes meaningless. Each moment serves as a signal referring to another signal. Technique and theory serve one another.

The universal homogeneity of nature presupposes a common measure that, according to Galileo and Descartes, consisted in a common quantifiability. Still, it would be simplistic to trace the progress of science entirely to this factor. Physics in seventeenth-century Britain owed much of its success to its steadfast refusal to follow the Cartesians in equating its laws with those of mathematics. Newton carefully distinguished the mathematical investigation of "the quantities of forces with their proportions consequent upon any conditions supposed" from the physical one that compares those proportions "with the phenomena of Nature."[22] Even Descartes, it should be mentioned, did not simply reduce nature to "extension" when he declared extension to be the essential attribute of material bodies. His well-known statement in *Le monde*—"Give me extension *and motion* and I will construct a world"—testifies to that. Without motion the extended substance would remain inert forever. Nor did he claim that mathematics alone yields certainty, but that the knowledge of nature (and of the self) must attain a degree of certainty equal to that of mathematics. In the *Rules for the Direction of the Mind* (Rule # IV) he describes his universal mathematics as a science that by means of the deductive method used in mathematics proper reaches conclusions of equal reliability. Still, if the primary qualities of nature may all be reduced to the one attribute of extension (including motion once the Creator has initiated it), then reliable cognition of nature becomes limited to the quantifiable.[23]

Theoretical knowledge of nature needs to isolate those phenomena it analyzes from the total experience. Such an abstraction is, of course, indispensable in any theoretical investigation. At the beginning of the modern age, however, ordinary experience and scientific theory came to stand in opposition to one another. The distinction between primary and secondary qualities, initiated by Galileo, tended to equate true physical reality with those qualities of bodies that can be given a precise quantitative formulation, while it lowered secondary ones to the order of "appearance" (though caused by physical reality). When Descartes posited extension as the one essential characteristic that all known bodies share, and Newton (in his third rule) extended this as a characteristic (though not the only one) to all bodies—even those beyond the range of perception[24]—the gap between ordinary experience and science became unbridgeable. In the words of the British philosopher F. H. Bradley: "Nature is, on the one hand, that show whose reality lies bare(ly) in primary qualities. It is, on the other hand, that endless world of sensible life which appeals to our sympathy and extorts our wonder. It is the object lived in by the poet and the observing naturalist."[25] Already Copernicus's cosmological theory had conflicted with a direct sensory experience of space. Bruno's idea of an infinitely extended universe and Galileo's conclusions about the motions of stars previously considered to be fixed removed the scientific concept of space ever further from its ordinary representation.

The absolutization of space became the nucleus of the abstraction performed by early modern students of nature. For Bruno, infinite space constitutes the very essence of physical reality. "If someone who accepts an infinite universe wonders where the universe is, I answer: In infinite space. But where is infinite space? Nowhere where there is limit: everywhere where there is none."[26] He empties this space of such bodily qualities as "transparence, color, humidity, and sortlike things."[27] Space is an absolute, and only those qualities that coincide with space—namely, its quantitative dimensions (an anticipation of Galileo's distinction between primary and secondary qualities)—count as absolute. The idea of reducing the essence of nature to a small set of properties that must account for all other qualities goes back to Democritus, but in modern thought this reduction lead directly to the opposition between subject and object. Secondary qualities are entirely conditioned by subjective perception, even though they may have an objective foundation.

To discount any but the primary qualities in defining what is real in our knowledge of nature favors spatial intuition over all others. Undoubtedly, spatial qualities are the ones that lent themselves to the kind of mathematical analysis that the new concept of science required. But this provides no ground for granting these qualities an ontological priority over the so-called secondary ones, as if they alone defined the essence of the natural world. By regarding some properties as inherent in nature itself and others as attributable to nature only as the cause of subjective sensations that do not correspond to the original substance, we detach the observer from nature in such a way that he ceases to remain an integral part of it. The restriction of scientific knowledge of nature to extension and motion (in Newton also mass), separates this particular kind of being in an irreducible way from *res cogitans*. It then becomes an independent substance, defined by permanence in space and void of those qualities that characterize the life of the mind. While past philosophy had consistently endowed the physical world with an internal teleology, Descartes deprived it of what to him was a purely ideal predicate reserved to the *res cogitans*. At the same time, by declaring extension the essence of

physical substance, he conveyed to it an unprecedented bodily concreteness. Yet, as Whitehead has pointed out, this concreteness, consisting of
one component detached from a complex totality, is misplaced. Its spatial
homogeneity rules out development: the laws of the natural world thereby
attain the fixed character that, paradoxically, once had been the exclusive
privilege of the ideal realm of ideas.[28]

The point of this discussion concerns, of course, not the abstract
nature of modern science, but rather an idea of science that effectively
limits knowledge of nature to what is accessible to the method of mechanical physics. At the root of the scientific philosophy that eventually
was to replace the metaphysics of nature lies the metaphysical assumption that physical nature is a substance in its own right. Descartes quite
consistently ranked metaphysics at the basis of physics, as a preambulum
that defines its concepts and justifies its basis.[29] Which states we consider
"effects," and hence require a causal explanation, and which ones we take
to be ultimate depends indeed on principles not given with immediate
experience.[30] In fact, the experience that supports and justifies the theory
has been selectively restricted by the nature of the investigation. How
much this is the case appears from Descartes's answer to Beeckman's
objection that careful observation conflicted with his theory of pendulum
acceleration: "Even if he [Beeckman] were able to devise a thousand
experiments to define it more exactly, I do not have to bother trying those
myself, if they cannot be explained by reason."[31] Practical and even theoretical considerations may have motivated Descartes's dismissal of the
objection. Each fact, for him, needs to be incorporated into some system
to make scientific sense and a single observation to the contrary should
not suffice to give up an otherwise coherent theory as long as no alternative is available. But the cavalier tone of Descartes's remark suggests
that the idea of a rationally coherent system had a priority over the
possibility of explaining each single phenomenon.

Before Newton physicists show little concern about the epistemic
restrictions metaphysical assumptions may impose upon our knowledge
of nature. Newton, more critically aware of their impact, questioned what
Copernicus and Kepler certainly and Galileo probably presupposed—
namely, nature's inclination toward a perfect geometrical order. But more
important, in the General Scholium of the *Principia* he rejected the metaphysical assumption accepted by the earlier philosophers that science
defines the essence of its object. Indeed, he intended to avoid metaphysical
principles altogether, although his metaphysical scholium on absolute

space and time shows that he was not entirely consistent in this effort! As a result of the enormous impact of the *idea* of science, philosophy increasingly came to be reduced to a critique of scientific epistemology.[32]

Nature as Representation

The distance that separates immediate experience from reflective knowledge has always elicited the philosophers' concern. Already Parmenides distinguished appearance from reality. But the problem took on a new urgency after the conveyance of meaning had become the exclusive task of the knowing subject, for it required the subject to transfer the thing experienced to a representational mode of being. Only within the mental immanence of representation does the mind acquire the kind of control needed to apply its rules for what it accepts as true. Spinoza brought the implications of the modern conception of knowing to a consistent conclusion when he transferred the locus of truth from correspondence with reality to internal coherence of the mind's own idea.

In *Philosophy and the Mirror of Nature*, Richard Rorty has appropriately compared such knowing through representation to reflecting reality in the mirror of the mind. Plato had first applied the mirror metaphor to the process of knowing but in the opposite sense: the mind understands itself only by contemplating its image as reflected by the true reality of the ideas. In the twelfth century nature begins to appear as the glass in which the human mind sees God and occasionally also itself reflected. Montaigne still uses it in that sense: "This great world . . . is the mirror in which we must look at ourselves to recognize ourselves from the proper angle."[33] The smallness of the human person—"as a dot made with a very fine brush"—makes such a study of oneself on an enlarged scale necessary. Modern thought, Rorty points out, has reversed the metaphor: the mind mirrors nature. Thus Bacon writes: "God has framed the mind of man as a glass capable of the image of the universal world, joying to receive the signature thereof as the eye is of light."[34] The truthfulness of the image depends on the mirror's ability to reflect the original. Therefore Bacon cautions against distorted reflections in a mind that "is rather an enchanted glass, full of superstition and imposture, if it be not delivered and reduced." The source of truth for Bacon continues to lie outside the mind, although the emphasis placed on the need for the right "perspective" suggests that the mind's role has gained in importance.

For Descartes the truth of nature becomes established in the mind's reconstruction of it. The mind thereby functions as the mirror in whose reflection truth originates. But if so, how can it know itself, Gassendi wondered.[35] The physical eye, incapable of seeing itself directly, nevertheless is able to see itself in the mirror, yet for Descartes there is no mirror beyond the mind. If we do not know the nature of the mirror, however, how can we evaluate its capacity for reflecting the true nature of things? In this objection lies the entire problem of knowledge as representation. Unless the eye know itself, how could it know how (and, in the end, what) it reflects? What allows the mind to refer the mirrored image to an original if it ignores *how* it reflects the original? Descartes felt that the objection went to the heart of his theory and responded that the mind's mirror also reflects itself. Yet the mind possesses no more than an awareness of its existence. Does that suffice for justifying the knowledge of things in themselves through an act of representation? Locke perceived the difficulty and stated that the mind knows only its own ideas. Of the reality beyond these ideas we have certain knowledge only in the cases of the self and of God. The Scholastic position had, of course, been that the ideal *species* through which we know is itself not an object of knowledge but merely an instrument for knowing the real— *hoc quo cognoscitur* (that through which we know).

This Scholastic distinction had already considerably removed itself from the position of ancient and early medieval philosophy, according to which to know consists in becoming in some way what one knows. For Aristotle, the mind is potentially the intelligible and becomes it actually through the cognitive process. That Aristotelian realism stands clearly formulated in Alexander of Aphrodisias's commentary on *De anima:* "Any intellect that knows this [highest, divine] intellect somehow becomes it itself, if indeed to know is to take and receive the known form and to become like it."[36] Saint Thomas freely invoked Aristotle's authority in such phrases as *cognoscere est fieri quodammodo omnia* or *intelligibile in actu est intellectus in actu*, but his theory of the *species* deviates from the earlier epistemic realism. A second, more fundamental separation between knower and known occurred at the end of the Middle Ages. Without a radical rethinking of the theory of signification by the nominalists, doubt concerning the possibility of knowing reality as it is in itself might never have arisen. When John Duns Scotus granted the universal forms of knowledge an ideal reality of their own (in his "formal distinction on the side of the object"), he raised concepts to a status of relative independence with respect to the reality they represent. Ideas possess, in his terminology, an "objective being" (*esse objectivum*) that is more than the mind's intentional presence to the real. Ockham rejected this ultra-realist interpretation of concepts, but he adopted and radicalized the independent nature of the cognitive act with respect to the real in itself. For him, all true knowledge must be intuitive. But intuitive knowledge does not necessarily depend upon the presence of an external object.[37] God may cause the mind to know intuitively what neither is nor has ever been. Ockham's theory carries the immanence of conceptual forms to a point where intuitive knowledge becomes entirely established within the mind. Descartes echoes Ockham's theological reservations about linking intuitive knowledge to extramental reality: "For there is no doubt that God possesses the power to produce everything that I am capable of perceiving with distinctness."[38]

Although a wholly immanent concept of truth need not necessarily result in skepticism, it did so very soon. The fourteenth-century nominalist Nicholas d'Autrecourt had already formulated what would become the core of Descartes's doubt as well as the principle supporting his strategy for overcoming it: "Nothing that is known is known with a certitude of its existence, except knowledge itself."[39] There was, to be sure, the reassuring assumption that in the divinely established order things run parallel with ideas. Descartes appropriated this assumption when asserting that whatever may be conceived clearly and distinctly must exist in reality (in his letter to Gibieuf of January 19, 1642). Moreover, for Descartes a representation was not merely an intermediate sign, as it had been for some nominalists. For him representation displays the immediate presence of the object. (He uses the terms *repraesentat* and *exhibet mihi* interchangeably.) The question remains, however, how he supports, after the radical doubt (overcome only for the existence of a "thinking thing"), the certainty that a true idea corresponds with the real. Indeed, the very criterion of distinctness he exhibits as a measure of truth would seem to jeopardize the certainty of such a correspondence. If it really suffices for the mind "clearly and distinctly [to] understand one thing apart from another in order to be certain that the two things are distinct,"[40] does that not cast a permanent doubt on the full cognitive coincidence of one reality with a totally different one?

The nominalist origins of Descartes's separation between idea and reality are well known. Nowhere does their impact upon representational thinking make itself more felt than in Descartes's theory of the "objective" being of ideas. In a well-known passage of the third Meditation he declares: "But in order for a given idea to contain such and such *objective* reality [in other words, ideal reality as a mode of thought], it must surely derive it from some cause which contains at least as much *formal* reality [in other words, the reality of actual existence] as there is objective reality in the idea."[41] In this argument for the existence of God, "objective" stands for "representational," and, significantly, representation is conceived as being so independent of whatever it represents that no extramental reality may correspond to it at all—only a real cause of the idea is required. At that point the question how the world we know in our ideas relates to the real world becomes a critical one. Already Nicholas d'Autrecourt had taught that ideas may be true independently of any reference to real things, even if real things were created in disagreement with them. Descartes's masters, the Jesuits of La Flèche, had adopted this strange doctrine in their teaching. Their pupil went beyond this claim when he took ideal reality to be normative for the nature of real.

Descartes must, of course, not be held responsible for a skepticism that, by the time he wrote, had affected the entire intellectual atmosphere in France. Others had either evaded the issue or been satisfied with a probability of which they could not justify the reliability. Montaigne wrote: "When reason fools us, we make use of experience."[42] But the nature of experience had become exactly the question. When evidence loses its ultimate trustworthiness as a criterion of truth, then truth needs a foundation beyond itself. Descartes attempted to find it by drawing the ultimate conclusions from the one inner datum unassailable by doubt, namely, doubt itself.[43] Doubt, then, stands not only at the origin of his questioning: it guides his entire search for certainty. (In the next chapter I shall reflect on the moral sources of a doubt that in the early modern age had become existential as well as epistemological.) In turning to his own doubt Descartes interiorized the question of truth to a point where the mind no longer had to rely on questionable evidence for reforging the bond with the real.

But is that sufficient? We know how in the indubitable reality of consciousness itself—the *cogito ergo sum*—Descartes found the point where certainty and truth totally coincide. The problem is, however, how to extend this privileged moment to the knowledge of the world beyond consciousness.[44] Can a theory that reduces knowledge to representation be more reliable than the representational function itself? No sooner has Descartes reached the bedrock certainty of the *cogito* than he succumbs to new doubts. Can I extend that certainty beyond the moment I experienced it? Does a remembrance of past evidence continue to grant irrefutable evidence in the present, or does it, once again, fall subject to the ultimate doubt that envelops all other knowledge? So Descartes feels the need to establish what Anthony Kenny has called a second order indubitability, by protecting the mind's internal criteria of clarity and distinctness—evident yet not beyond ultimate doubt—against a transcendent deception. I shall have to say more about the foundational idea of a veracious, good God, Descartes's decisive weapon in the struggle to protect the trustworthiness of clear and distinct ideas, and to relink the ideal order to the real one. But for now I turn from his controversial attempt to achieve through a transcendent foundation what truth cannot accomplish through itself to its expected benefits.

Even if the mind is in principle capable of reaching certain and reliable knowledge, the question remains how this may be achieved in the particular case of the physical world. How can the mind in the endless complexity of natural phenomena acquire the kind of intuitive certainty that Descartes is willing to consider true? He appears to have believed that simple units of consciousness—that is, clear and distinct ideas— would grant the mind purchase upon the simple natures of which, he assumed, physical as well as spiritual reality consisted. In the *Rules for the Direction of the Mind* Descartes describes simple natures (some of which "exist only in bodies," such as figure, extension, motion) as known through themselves (per se) by a knowledge that allows no error.[45] But how can the mind be certain that what it represents clearly and distinctly as simple natures are really such in reality? No appeal to divine guarantees will secure such a certitude as long as the specific criteria for attaining the truth in those matters have not been established beyond doubt. That Descartes's criteria failed to satisfy his opponents appears clearly enough in their objections: "Everyone thinks that he clearly and distinctly perceives the truth which he champions."[46] But how should this provide more than a psychological need to assent? One of his critics, Bourdin, perceptively noted that the immanentization of knowledge had jeopardized the union between objective truth and subjective certainty. "Other systems have formal logic, syllogisms and reliable patterns of argument, which they use like Ariadne's thread to guide them out of the labyrinth; with these instruments they can safely and easily unravel the most complicated problems. But your new method denigrates the traditional forms of argument, and instead grows pale with a new terror, the imaginary fear of the demon which it has conjured up. It fears it may be dreaming, it has doubts about whether it is mad."[47]

Descartes's opponents willingly concede that in the instance of the mind's existence the clarity and distinctness of the perception provides an adequate criterion of its correspondence to the real. But nowhere else does evidence attain the same degree of certainty, and so they feel reluctant to carry it beyond the *cogito*. While attempting to secure indubitable certainty, Descartes has transformed the concept of knowledge itself. For Plato and Aristotle, truth and certainty had remained inseparable. Certainty inevitably accompanies true knowledge where such knowledge bears the mark of necessity. Yet once nature may no longer be presumed to conform to reason, the mind's link with reality becomes thoroughly questionable and even the awareness of evidence ceases to shield it from doubt. The very possibility of truth, then, must first be safeguarded against the chance that the mind's apparatus for attaining truth may be irremediably vitiated. But while thus attempting to secure reliable knowledge, Descartes has replaced the central issue of truth with what is supposed to ground it. He avoids a dualism between truth and its foundation by positing as the universal norm of knowledge that one form of truth of which the grounding act itself constitutes the essence—namely, mathematical truth.[48] The demand of an unshakable foundation together with the mathematical model that followed from it gave the "idea of science" introduced in the preceding section its definitive orientation in the modern age: the truth of science lies in the fact that it can be grounded.[49]

From the early *Rules* (1628) to the mature *Principia philosophiae* (1644) Descartes remained unshaken in his confidence that his metaphysics would yield an indubitable foundation for all the sciences. In the preface to the French edition of the *Principia* he maintains that from the metaphysical principles those of physics can be deduced and from the latter "the knowledge of all the other things which are in the world." It might take centuries to complete the deduction, but at some time our knowledge of the physical world would be exhaustive and certain.[50] Yet the quest for absolute certainty has driven a wedge between immediate evidence and the rational foundation of evidence. It has weakened the bond that links the mind to the outside world, from perception to the thought of perceiving. No inner evidence about the world, however, can substitute for the primary certainty conveyed by that world as it impinges upon the senses. To exchange one for the other is, in Maurice Merleau-Ponty's words, "to take out an insurance against doubt of which the premiums are heavier than the loss for which it is to indemnify it—for then we move to a type of certitude that will never restore the *there is* of the world."[51] The point is not that perception provides absolute certainty—Descartes is, of course, right in asserting that it never does—but that it provides the only available way of contact with the physical world.

To devise norms of certainty inappropriate to the mind's contact with its object is to set up impossible standards for truth. In doing so we break Aristotle's rule for a prudential judgment, namely, that the degree of certainty must be proportionate to the nature of the object. Descartes's epistemic conditions can be met only by the mind's own constructions, such as mathematics and logic. Possessing no method for crediting nondemonstrative evidence with a theoretical legitimacy Descartes had to dismiss it as inadequate, though he was willing to accept less than total certainty in the practical area—as his rules for a "provisional" morality show. When truth is indissolubly connected with indubitability, no amount of probability can satisfy Descartes's requirement of absolute certainty. The probability argument may relent the moral demands imposed on the mind in search of truth, but it provides no theoretical justification for accepting any idea as true.

Precisely on this issue rests the difference with Pascal who, through his discovery of probability calculus, was able to establish the theoretical legitimacy of nondemonstrative evidence.[52] A well-known entry of *Pensées* marks a return to Aristotle's principle: "One must know *when* it is right to doubt, to affirm, to submit. Anyone who does otherwise does not understand the force of reason. Some men run counter to those three principles, either affirming that everything can be proved, because they know nothing about proof, or doubting everything, because they do not know when to submit, or always submitting because they do not know when judgment is called for."[53] If we accept that probability may have a genuine claim to truth, then demands for proof cease to be rational (and truthful!) once they exceed the limits set by the conditions inherent in the case itself. In his attempt to justify the move from a condition of objective uncertainty to the acceptance of religious faith, Pascal abandons the self-enclosed sphere of epistemic evidence altogether. Jeffrey Stout has drawn attention to it: the famous "wager" argument has nothing to do with the probability of God's existence but all with our stake in accepting it.[54] Over the centuries critics have remarked on the inadequacy of such a hypothetical form of reasoning with respect to the kind of total surrender faith requires. Indeed, if taken as the ground of faith, the wager argument would undermine faith's absolute commitment. But at the root of this theoretically inadequate justification lies the idea that faith requires abandoning the search for intellectual certainty altogether and morally committing oneself to the very reality concerning which the intellect remains uncertain. "It is the heart which perceives God and not the reason" (# 424). In faith one must see with "les yeux de la foi" if one is to see at all.

Pascal's critique brings a fundamental problem in Descartes's philosophy to the surface. No rational argument can securely relink the mind to reality after we have defined it as an isolated entity. To be sure, it belongs to the very essence of truth to be justified. But arguments carried a different meaning in the older tradition, a difference that clearly appears in the so-called proofs for the existence of God. Premodern theologians could be brief and quite cavalier about them. Yet for the moderns these proofs assumed a crucial importance: they were more carefully crafted, and still in the end they remained unconvincing (Descartes's own effort possesses both these qualities). In the earlier tradition they served to justify the acceptance of a transcendent dimension from the beginning considered to be present in the nature of the real. Modern thinkers, on the contrary, began by positing nature as in some way self-sufficient and neutral with respect to transcendence, thus charging the argument with the impossible task of converting an independent reality into a dependent one. This reversal parallels the one whereby rationalists first isolate the mind from all other reality and then expect to acquire inner certainty concerning its nature. The current battle against foundationalism signals a belated awakening from the Cartesian dream, yet combatants all too often remain within the intra-mental premises that started the dream and are thus forced to adopt a skeptical attitude with respect to the epistemological enterprise in its entirety.

Descartes's theory of ideas marks the watershed where the tide of cognition ceased to flow from the real to the known and turned from the ideal representation toward the extra-mental reality.[55] Threatened by the loss of certainty that had originated in late medieval thought, Descartes tried to regain a sure foothold by sacrificing the ancient concept of truth as participation in being and instead concentrated on the nature of representation and its internal criteria. Philosophy has mostly remained on this epistemological track ever since.[56] In a fundamental sense knowledge has always been known to represent. Differences begin with the manner in which the representation refers to the represented. In the realist conception that dominated thinking from antiquity to the beginning of the modern age, mental representation was directly united with the reality which it presented. Even when representation ceased to consist in an immediate presence of the real object to the mind, their union remained solid enough to allow no doubts about the mind's ability to comprehend the real in itself. To know continued to mean, albeit through a mediating idea, *fieri quodammodo omnia*—for the mind to attain the self-same reality of the known. But when nominalist thought began to question the link between thinking and reality, a wholly new epistemological problem arose. In the end Descartes's attempt to solve it took refuge in the fundamental principles of classical metaphysics—God and the soul—but only after having thoroughly revised their meaning and function.

In a succession of brilliant studies Jean-Luc Marion has shown how the father of modern thought began by transforming philosophy from a science of first things into an epistemological investigation of the first principles of knowledge. The search for epistemic foundations, however, required a metaphysical basis, and this, Marion argues, led to a new kind of *ontotheology*—that is, an ontological dependence of all things on a single principle.[57] Such modern thinkers as Galileo and Kepler still considered first principles of mathematics and logic "eternal truths" that required no further justification than their internal evidence. But since the entire cognitive system in which they appeared could be subjected to hyperbolic doubt, Descartes felt that they demanded an ulterior foundation. We have seen how in the thinking self the transition occurred from a purely ideal sphere to the bedrock of reality. But as Descartes conceives of the thinking self as a *substance*, the ideal process of knowing reenters the sphere of *being* and of metaphysics. As a result, all being, insofar as it must be represented by the mind, comes to depend on a single metaphysical principle—the thinking substance. Thus a new kind of *ontotheology* originates—one not grounded in God but in the self. In Marion's words: "A complete ontotheological structure follows: being-as-thought (*cogitatum*) grounds the being-par-excellence [the thinking substance] which in turn produces the thinking of each thought."[58]

Now, Descartes never lost sight of the fact that the thinking substance supports the real only to the extent that it is represented—the *res objecta intellectui*.[59] He never identified the real with the objective, as some later thinkers did, but sought the foundation of all being *qua being* in a transcendent ground. That ground, which Descartes identifies with God, supports the being of the thinking substance as well as that of all other reality. Descartes establishes this dependence by means of the comprehensive principle of causality. In the very consciousness of doubt with which the *cogito* started, the *res cogitans* experiences itself unable to account for its own nature. In the arguments for the existence of God in the third Meditation he shows that the presence of the idea of an infinite being, the origin of which surpasses the finite mind's creative ability, proves that in its intellectual operation the mind causally depends on a transcendent reality. Since this being is not causally dependent on any other, Descartes refers to it by the neologism *causa sui*.

At this point metaphysics, the science of first principles, has become fully reestablished, albeit on a very different footing. Seeking a foundation for the order of cognition, Descartes has redefined the ultimate ontological principles in function of the epistemic order. The foundation both of the mind and of the world is conceived in accordance with the conditions and needs of knowledge. Being thereby becomes *causare* or *esse causatum*. While Greek philosophy of the classical age had defined being in terms of form and its dependence primarily (though never exclusively) in terms of participation, modern thought conceived of nature as a causal interaction of forces and of transcendence as a supremely powerful divine will which created and ruled all things by means of efficient causality.

A God defined under the primary attribute of "incomprehensible power" (*puissance incompréhensible*) excludes any motive beyond the exercise of that power. If he creates, his creative act does not bestow upon his creatures the kind of intrinsic intelligibility a theory of participative analogy between Creator and creature would grant them. The voluntarist conception initiated by John Duns Scotus offered, once radically thought through by nominalist theologians, no apriori guarantee of any teleology. It defined nature in terms of submission to a system of invariable forces causally imposed at the beginning. Descartes interpreted the principle of efficient causality so universally and univocally that it became the sustaining source of God's own being: "God's power is so great that it is plainly the cause of his continuing existence."[60] Hence the new name for God: *causa sui*.

Whatever divine attributes Descartes adds to the primary one of unlimited power do not weaken the rule of efficient causality. If anything, they rather strengthen it. Thus in the fifth part of the *Discourse*, Descartes makes the surprising claim that if God were to create matter to form a new universe, leaving the whole in a state of chaos "as confused as the poets can imagine" yet submitting it to the same mechanical laws, that

indeterminate matter would order itself into a world not basically different from the one we know. Nor could the new laws have been different
from the old ones, since God's immutability would prevent him from
imposing other laws than the ones he devised for the present world. This
implies that even an evolution from chaos to order requires no inner
teleology. Once God creates "we may believe, without impugning the
miracle of creation, that by this means alone all purely material things
could in the course of time have come to be just as we now see them."[61]
Organic as well as inorganic matter loses its intrinsic intelligibility to a
mechanistic system divinely imposed on the world.

Of course, artists, poets, and even some philosophers continued to
relate to nature, as earlier generations had done. For them the mind was
an integral part of a single all-encompassing reality. But increasingly the
assumption that the human mind alone conveyed meaning and purpose
began to dominate modern thought. The first discomfort with the mechanistic view of nature surfaced when the concepts of extension and
mechanical force were applied to organic nature. Descartes had been
satisfied to interpret animal life as a segment of the *res extensa*. Few
shared his judgment, least of all poets such as La Fontaine, whose talking
animals protested against being reduced to unfeeling entities. Naturalists,
among them the Dutch zoologist Jan Swammerdam and the English John
Ray whom he influenced, reintroduced the teleology that had been exiled
from a strictly mechanistic science. Swammerdam everywhere finds "the
finger of God"—as he curiously expresses in the dedication of one of his
works: "Illustrious Sir, I hereby present to you the almighty finger of God
in the anatomy of a louse." Or in the discussion of the snail, "an impure
and slimy little animal but significant for those who investigate the Lord's
works."

But the mechanistic model proved to be too firmly entrenched in
science to be easily dislodged, especially in Descartes's home country.
Even the French pioneer of zoology George-Louis Buffon (1707–88) continued to use mechanistic language. In the magisterial "Vue de la Nature"
that introduces volume 12 of his *Histoire naturelle* he discusses life in
terms of forces, although he attempts to expand their range so as to
include *forces vives*. The very purpose of the mechanistic universe is to
serve those living forces: "Space and time are means, the universe its
object, motion and life its scope."[62] Concerned to preserve the self-enclosed system of nature Buffon links these living forces to the laws of
mechanics. A single system ruled by the law of gravity includes both

mechanical forces and powers of life. But life obeys those mechanical rules in a more complex play of attraction and repulsion. Despite these efforts to fit his organic system within the mechanistic world picture (particularly evident in the second "Vue de la Nature" in volume 13), Buffon is forced to admit: "La Nature n'est pas une chose . . . la Nature n'est point un être" but "une puissance vive immense qui entraine tout, qui anime tout."[63] Buffon continues to defend even this reversal of mechanism within the static premises of a mechanistic view of nature. Yet the tensions and ambiguities, particularly those caused by a time factor that forces him to "move back to the different ages of nature," unmistakably announce the approach of a different vision of life. The great zoologist returns to the Renaissance conception of nature as an organic, self-moving whole. For Descartes, the metaphor for nature had been the automaton. The automaton also seems to move from within, but its motion is, in fact, entirely determined by external causes. Buffon's organic theory revives some elements present in Bruno, giving them a more precise scope and a scientific foundation. But a discussion of this later development falls beyond a reflection on the beginnings of the modern idea of nature.

At the end of this first part we cannot but be surprised how far current cosmology has moved away from Galileo, Bacon, and Descartes, even from Newton. What then appeared most new now seems most antiquated. As the theoretical chemist Prigogine recently observed, we are ever more abandoning the description of the world as a machine and returning to the Greek paradigm of the cosmos as a divine work of art. Yet despite innovative physical theories and the protests of poets and artists against the reduction of nature to object, the imagination of our culture is still groping for a viable alternative model. Our continuing failure to "think" the new, despite our growing dissatisfaction with the old, appears all too visibly in the unprecedented ecological disasters of our time, in the increasing hazards of a yet uncontrolled technology, and in the dismaying lack of aesthetic harmony in our human-made environment.

Part II

From Microcosmos
to Subject

Deus igitur hominem factum, velut alterum

quemdam mundum, in brevi magnum, atque

exiguo totum, in terris statuit.

—Walter Raleigh

Tu es seul maintenant malgré ces étoiles,

Le centre est près de toi et loin de toi,

Tu as marché, tu peux marcher, plus rien ne change,

Toujours la même nuit qui ne s'achève pas.

—Yves Bonnefoy, *Hier régnant désert*

Chapter 4

The Nature of the Subject and the Subject of Nature

The Discovery of Humanitas

In part 1 I followed the slow conversion of nature into an object. In part 2 I will reflect on the transformation the self underwent after it became separated from the other constituents of the original synthesis, specifically, how it gradually turned into a mere function of the objectifying process.

The Czech philosopher Jan Patocka once described our culture as distinguished by "a care for the soul." Certainly when Socrates shifted speculation from cosmology to reflection on the moral life he opened up a new realm of being. Plato developed this moral concern into a metaphysics of the soul as spiritual substance. Christian writers accepted his view but almost from the beginning started transforming it. That they differ is obvious; less clear is how. Is it true that the discovery of the spiritual for the Greeks was unrelated to what for Christians became the interior life, that the moral sources are not within but, as Charles Taylor claims, outside the soul in the good? "It is hardly an exaggeration to say that it was Augustine who introduced the inwardness of radical reflexivity and bequeathed it to the Western tradition of thought."[1] Such an evaluation of the Greek notion of the spiritual as lying beyond the mind will not survive an attentive reading of Neoplatonic texts from Plotinus to

Proclus and, I suspect, even of Plato. Plato's theory of remembrance, beyond providing an epistemological method, points to the inner life as to the very locus of the spirit. Surpassing the temporal realm requires that the soul turn inward to a selfhood that partakes of the eternal. If in his later dialogues Plato spends less time defending the doctrine of recollection, it is because he can assume it to be known, not because he abandons it.

Precisely upon those mature writings Neoplatonists based their theory of the soul and of the absolute. At the same time they unanimously held that only the inward turn leads the soul to the spirit (*nous*), which constitutes its inner essence. It was by reading Neoplatonic writings that Augustine became converted to the life within. The ontological levels of soul, spirit, and absolute for Neoplatonists as for Neoplatonic Christians are not hierarchically stratified above one another—forcing the soul to gaze upward—but within one another. It is true that a major difference separates Christian thinkers (including Christian Neoplatonists) from the ancients, but the distinction lies in the fact that Greek philosophers held a less clearly individualized view of the soul's identity. Christians stressed the infinite value and independence of each single soul. Greek thinkers from Plato to Proclus, granted individual souls a certain separateness but insisted more on the universal soul-ness in which they participated. In Plato's *Timaeus*, as well as in Plotinus's and Proclus's commentaries on it, this universal character takes the form of a world soul and a universal soul. Along the same lines Aristotle suggests, according to his Arab interpreters, that although the single mind is strictly individual in its receptive potential, it becomes activated by a common universal agent intellect in which all individual minds participate.

This brings us to the main point. If a spiritual and interior self appears in the classical phase of our culture, its clearly delineated individuality does not. Even thinkers of late antiquity held fast to what could be called the concept of an "extensive self,"[2] which allowed the individual a distinct field of action subject to a code of ethics yet prevented it from being the philosophical and moral ultimate it was to become later. Human beings first and foremost belonged to a universal order. The *kosmos* included humans as an integral though unique part of itself. For Aristotle the soul had been primarily a biological concept, the *entelechy* of the body, and as such part of the *Physics*. Though the mind enters the individual soul, after death it returns to its own universality. Even in Plato the soul had been intermediate between the world and the realm of

idea. Their link with the cosmic order incorporated individuals in a particular social structure. Those who were not fully integrated into that
social totality—foreigners and slaves—held no title to full humanhood.[3]
Not until the social crisis of the *polis* when the cities became submerged
in the enormous Hellenistic (and later Roman) empires, did the ties with
the community weaken and a sharp idea of individual selfhood began to
emerge. Stoic and Epicurean views of human existence reflect the impact
of this privatization, but they remained mostly restricted to an intellectual elite.

The Christian doctrine of individual salvation further detached the
person from the cosmic context insofar as it made each individual personally responsible to God. Each person stood in a direct relation to God
rather than to the cosmos. This intimate relation to a divine archetype of
which each individual was a unique image constituted the very essence
of personhood. For Augustine the self was the sanctuary of a divine
presence. "I entered into my own depths, with You as guide; and I was
able to do it because You were my helper. I entered and with the eye of
my soul, such as it was, I saw Your unchangeable Light shining over that
same eye of my soul, over my mind."[4] This exalting of the individual
self, however, did not transform the person into an atomic entity. The
Church constituted a new community on which the individual depended
as much for the attainment of his destiny as he had previously depended
on the state, albeit in a different manner. But more fundamentally, the
Christian community as well as its individual members shared in the
dignity of the mystical body of Christ. At the same time, Christians ceased
to identify with a political and often hostile state based on an incompatible religious foundation. Once the Church became the religion of the
empire, however, and especially after it inherited the responsibility for
public order, it fell upon its members to build and maintain political
structures. As former institutions disintegrated, the social significance of
the Church increased and Christians came to view themselves more as
members of a body of redemption than as chosen individuals. The Renaissance ideal of creative individuality did not destroy the person's social
linkage, although it may have weakened the bond with the Church. Early
humanists in the northern Italian cities revived the ancient idea of citizenship.[5] Nor must we think of the Renaissance as having discovered the
individual as Burckhardt claimed; the discovery of a new type of individuality began in the twelfth century.

Despite these qualifications, the Roman ideal of *humanitas* that inspired the early humanists radically transformed the way men and women came to see themselves as individuals. For Cicero and Quintilian, *humanitas* had consisted in what we would translate as "culture" or "education" understood as the fullest integration with one's political, moral, and rhetorical tradition. Aulus Gellius explicitly identifies *humanitas* with the Greek *paideia*. For early humanists, it referred to the study and assimilation of the ancient rhetorical models. Thus the concept assumed a universal, albeit socially elitist meaning. Humanism would remain primarily a rhetorical movement even after it broadened its ideal into a more comprehensive moral one. In a person's rhetorical-poetic ability—that is, the unique potential for using language in a creative, metaphorical way—Dante and Petrarch had seen the most distinctively human quality. That potential had been granted by nature, but its realization remained an ideal to be achieved by culture. Gradually the ideal of *humanitas* came to include social style, intellectual openness, even Christian piety, and ended up being an all-inclusive ideal of human development. Charles Trinkaus describes the transition from the narrowly rhetorical to the broadly moral meaning. "*Humanitas* was likewise perceived as a broad yet well-identifiable conception of the person, characterized by a lively interest in individual well-being and in the civilization or culture that lies at the basis of the common life. . . . Deeply inserted in *humanitas* was the idea that the linguistic disciplines fulfilled essential functions, moral and social, for the life of humanity."[6]

Throughout these variations, however, the humanist movement constantly preserved its aesthetic concern with form—literary and artistic first, yet also political and personal—and its confidence in the human power to create it. In its original state human nature fell far short of approaching the ideal. The then-popular eulogies on the dignity of the person were matched by complaints about the primitive nakedness in which nature has left us in this world. Most humanists felt ambiguous about the human condition and some, such as Poggio and occasionally Alberti, believed that even culture was not capable of bringing relief for human misery. But more, with Gianozzo Manetti, regarded the *studia humanitatis* at least as a comfort in our woes, or, with Valla, saw in man's creative powers a divine gift for improving his lot. The arts must provide in needs which nature itself has failed to fulfill.[7]

With the idea of the human responsibility for bringing all creation to its destined perfection returns the ancient concept of the person as microcosmos. In the fourth century Gregory of Nazianze had described man as recapitulating (*anakefalaiosis*) the entire creation. Human nature "enfolds all intellectual and sensible nature and encloses all things within itself, so that the Ancients were right in calling it a *microcosmos*."[8] Nicholas of Cusa, no humanist himself yet a thinker well acquainted with the movement, articulated the modern meaning of the old metaphor in his panentheistic philosophy when he called the person a contraction of God's all-comprehensive nature. As the human person "contracts" God in himself, so does all other creation contract the person's spiritual universality. Human nature includes everything within itself and attains all things by the power of its sense, intellect, and will. "The human person is a god, yet not absolutely, because he is human; a human god, then. Person is also the world, but not in the world's contracted existence, because he is human. Hence the person is a *microcosmos* or a human world."[9] In his all-enfolding being the human person determines the meaning and value of the cosmos. By his spiritual nature the person stands in the center of the universe. Cusanus's vision of an infinite universe emptied the idea of a physical center of its meaning. Though accepting the possibility of intelligent life on other planets, he nevertheless held that none surpasses our planet whose inhabitants possess a nature that includes all things. Thus the German cardinal, anticipating Copernicus's refutation of a geocentric universe, assigned the person a place at its spiritual center.

Partaking in all parts of the cosmos the person bears a unique responsibility for maintaining and furthering its order. He impresses his own form upon nature and, through this form-giving activity, he conveys to the universe a unity it would otherwise lack. While giving form to the world the person also realizes his own humanitas. In the humanist view, the various activities of rhetoric, art, and political and social structuring define the very idea of personhood. As Cassirer has noted, here *operari* precedes *esse*.[10] Yet the early modern ideal derives its creative norms from a universal nature. Nature, without whose consent "nihil egregie aut bene fieri potest" (Guarino), guides the entire process of human development.[11] The humanist ideal is one of mutual harmony between cosmic and human nature.

Some early humanists do display an inclination toward solitude and introspection. Petrarch's report of his ascent of Mont Ventoux typically concludes with the poet withdrawing from the mountain scene and, with the aid of Augustine's *Confessions*, reverting to himself. That self appears obviously far more worth exploring than the wild surroundings. In *De vita solitaria* the poet defends the cult of the inner life independently of its traditional religious setting. His *solitarius* follows the rhythm of the liturgical hours yet, unlike a cloistered monk or hermit, walks and reads at his own leisure. The retreat in which he seeks *tranquillitas animi* resembles more that of a Roman dignitary temporarily out of office than the monastery of his day. More revealing of a new type of introspectiveness is Petrarch's searching self-examination in his unpublished *Secretum*. Augustine, the writer of the *Confessions*, here appears as Petrarch's moral conscience. The saint chastises him for having fallen short of realizing the ideals that he as a humanist and a Christian had embraced. In a searing critique of the poet's love for Laura, he cools his ardent feelings by the picture of an indifferent woman who has distracted him from his vocation. Petrarch's stratagem to view his inner life through the penetrating eyes of Augustine conveys an objective quality as well as a transcendent perspective to his introspection. Through them this thoroughly modern exploration of the soul's hidden recesses avoids the subjectivism of later introspective attitudes.

The tension between inner life and outward appearance becomes more obvious in sixteenth-century epic poetry. While depicting extroverted heroes, the epic turns into a vehicle for the exploration of emotions and feelings. *Gerusalemme liberata* as well as *The Fairie Queene* introduce previously unknown habits of introspection and modulations of the human heart as worthy of intense interest. Comparing these epics to Virgil's, their common model, we realize how much they belong to a different age. For the modern poets, tenderness and intimacy no longer originate in an objective, even cosmic reality from where they resonate in the poet's feelings (*sunt lacrimae rerum*), but in a private reflection that sets the poet apart from that reality. Having expressed his inner feelings, the poet once again compares them with the outer realm. He recognizes truth as residing only in the secret inwardness while the appearances of external reality constantly turn into illusions.

The truth of Tasso's characters, to stay with my chosen example, constantly conflicts with the outward impressions they convey. Even the uncomplex warrior Clorinda belies her appearance. When she suddenly reveals her lovely face and long hair hidden under the helmet, the contrast instantly transforms the feelings of Tancredi, who was pursuing her as a male enemy. Yet the newly revealed truth remains subject to deception. When Erminia dons Clorinda's mantle and helmet, Tancredi is once again misled, this time in what appeared to be the object of his love. Before Tasso and in a more radical way, Ariosto had questioned the truth of appearances through the content of his *Orlando furioso* as well as through its form. The madness of his love deprives its hero, Orlando, from any discernment between reality and illusion. Also, in the central symbol of Alcina's enchanted island (Canto VI) nothing is what it seems. The sorceress robs her visitors of any criterion for distinguishing truth from falsity. But more fundamentally, the very form of the epic challenges its content. Ariosto's irony casts doubt not only on the events of his narrative but on the truth of poetic reflection itself. The poem constantly examines itself and by means of illusion exposes delusion.[12] Renaissance theatre with its intricate plots of mistaken identity gave yet another twist to this subtle dialectic of appearance and reality. Shakespeare's comedies, the accomplished masterpieces of this playful oscillation, leave the viewer utterly confused about what must count as real and what as illusion. The theatre here parodies a real-life fear of deception concerning the true nature of the outside world. The constantly shifting appearances of that world irresistibly drives the reflective mind inwardly.[13]

Sixteenth-century painting likewise reveals a growing distance between the person and the cosmic environment. One-point perspective had placed the painted scene in an objective space of its own, removed from the viewer's immediate field of vision. Landscape painting—a new genre in itself—increased that distance by allowing the scenery to assume a life of its own. Nature dwarfs the persons who forelornly wander in it, as in Breugel's dramatic *Fall of Icarus* or in Patinir's biblical scenes. Such a reduction of the human presence may seem to argue against the increased significance of the individual, but the overall effect of this drowning of humans in the vastness of nature is that it throws them back on their solitude and awakens them to their own subjectivity.[14] By evoking a sense of distance early Renaissance art accomplishes what later styles will attempt by more distinctly subjective means. Simultaneously with the depersonalization of the landscape originated the direct exploration of the human psyche in the portrait. At first portraits were equally cool and detached. Holbein's and Moro's studies scrutinize their subjects from a distance without empathizing with them as Rembrandt and his followers were to do. Indeed, detachment with respect to the human subject characterizes most art of the early Renaissance. Lyrical poetry, however personal and soul-searching, symbolizes its most private experiences in complexly articulated formal poems. The highly stylized sonnet becomes the favorite form for articulating intensely personal feelings.

That isolated self, once solidly anchored in a cosmic and religious security, ceased to offer a safe shelter against the uncertainties of outer reality. Within themselves thinkers, poets, and artists confronted the same insecurity that made them question the world around them. Hamlet has become such a familiar figure that we may forget how thoroughly modern a creation he is. After having pursued the self's endless shifts of mood and perspective, Montaigne felt forced to conclude that no solid basis existed upon which to build a universal science of selfhood. Unlike his later reader Descartes, the author of the *Essais* never found a bedrock certainty in the self. What is totally unique yields no universal truth— even about its own nature. True, "chaque homme porte la forme entière de l'humaine condition" (Each person carries the entire form of the human condition) (*Essais* III, 2). But that *forme entière* does not warrant universal statements, for universal in the self is only a total openness with respect to the nature of one's life, which varies from one individual to another. Montaigne found the living self too complex for general theories and preferred to go "the humbler and less dignified way of personal experience and introspection" without making universal claims. Nevertheless, introspection discloses a different kind of truth that, though not universalizable, may still be communicable. Indeed, precisely in and through expression does the truth concerning the self disclose itself. Words alone shed light on the inner life, even though in the course of expressing it they change it. "Painting myself for others, I represent myself in a better colouring than my own natural complexion. I have no more made my book than my book has made me: 'tis a book consubstantial with the author" (II, 18).[15] The self defines itself in the very process through which it expressively transforms itself. In the form-giving act more than in its objective achievement, Renaissance artists sought to achieve full selfhood. For Montaigne, this meant following life in all its unpredictable, illogical ramifications and developing "a full soul" rather than only one part of it. "I have made it my whole business to frame my life: this has been my trade and my work" (II, 37). Sainte-Beuve understood him well: "Etre homme, voilà sa profession; il n'a d'autre métier, n'approfondissant rien de trop particulier, de peur de se perdre, de s'expatrier hors de cette profession humaine et générale." (To be a man, that was his profession. He has no other and refuses to go deeply into anything too particular, lest he lose himself and become exiled from this human, general profession.)[16]

The need to rely on one's inventive wits in a world that held neither inner nor outer security found an appropriate form in the new literary genre of the novel. Rabelais and Cervantes created heroes who, shaking the trust in traditional certainties, left little choice but to steer one's life by the wobbling beacon of a self unenlightened by philosophy or theology. Rabelais's rambunctious Panurge dismisses even the flickering light of skeptical philosophy, in which Montaigne still sought a tenuous justification for his doubt, as needlessly "confusing."[17] But the undisputed master of the genre was Cervantes. Much of *Don Quixote* turns around the question: What is real, what illusion? By means of a panoply of mirrors reflecting reflections in other mirrors, the author succeeds in thoroughly confusing the reader about the answer. At first the lines of distinction appear drawn clearly enough. The Don suffers from a delusion that ridiculously distorts his perception of reality. But as the story proceeds, the question grows more subtle. We see Pancho falling victim to his own scheme to deceive his master with fabulations of an enchanted Dulcinea. The duchess whom they visit bluntly confronts him with the self-deception resulting from his ruse. "You my good Sancho, though you fancy yourself the deceiver, are the one who is deceived" (II, 33). Don Quixote solidifies the illusion into reality when he perceives Dulcinea in the very dress described in Sancho's tale. When later he admits that he may not have actually seen her, the firm wall that separates image from reality crumbles altogether. "God knows whether Dulcinea exists on earth or not, or whether she is phantastical or not. These are not matters whose verification can be carried out to the full" (II, 32). The second part (published later) adds complexity to confusion when the narrator applies a historical critique to the factual correctness of the earlier book, comparing it with the new, more rigorous standards of the later one, as well as with the wholly inadequate ones of a competing writer. Finally, Cervantes with growing insistency raises disquieting questions about his hero's state of mind: Who is wise and who insane? He who shows superior wisdom in all matters but one, or he who, endowed with ordinary perception, lacks insight in the fundamental issues of life?

When meaning is no longer given with existence, existence itself becomes a quest for meaning. The novel symbolizes this quest. But the same conception of life as project motivated poets, artists, statesmen, chieftains, and even the *cortegiano*—the man of stylish leisure—in their pursuit of humanitas. Indeed, to present "humanity" as an ideal assumes that the purpose of life must be conquered rather than accepted. The idea of truth through creative expression inspired the major poets of the six-teenth century—Shakespeare, Spenser, Cervantes, Tasso, Ariosto, Ron-sard—as it inspired many artists and explorers. But the pursuit of a total presence in the very act of form-giving animates even artificial works with an original spiritual vitality.

The Creative Word

The heightened awareness of the person's expressive, form-giving ability, I have suggested, originated in the early humanists' sense of the creative power of language. Christian culture had inherited a veritable cult of the word from its Hebrew ancestry. That cult turned into adoration at the beginning of John's Gospel: *In principio erat Verbum.* Had God not cre-ated the world by his Word? And had he not revealed himself through that same Word? Scripture and cosmos supported each other in giving meaning to reality. Nature also can be read as a book, but only by means of a code provided in *the* book. The Bible alone, Emile Mâle wrote, discloses the harmony that God has established between the soul and the universe.[18] "Some people read books in order to find God. Yet there is a great book, the very appearance of created things. Look above you; look below you! Note it; read it! God, whom you wish to find, never wrote that book with ink. Instead, He set before your eyes the things He had made."[19] Thus wrote Augustine. The metaphor was resumed in the twelfth century and resulted in Alain de Lille's well-known verse:

> Omnis mundi creatura
> Quasi liber et scriptura.

Language provided the model for the interpretation of nature. The words of Scripture illuminate the meaning of the created world, itself an image of the uncreated Word. On the other side, nature was never far from the Bible reader's mind, as the floral and faunal illustrations of the illuminated manuscripts constantly remind us. Thus a single symbolic complex of meaning united word and cosmos. Each in a different way expressed God's eternal Word, and, while one shed light on the other, together they conveyed the fullness of divine truth. Human words pro-vided commentary on this divinely revealed truth. This, however, must not be understood in an uncritical way, as if each spoken or written word were sacred and true. Only the core of human speech, the human capacity to express meaning through language, partakes of God's Word. As for the precise relation between actual words and the reality they attempt to express, there had been a variety of interpretations. Early in the twelfth century the relation between *verbum* and *res* became looser than it had been. While knowledge once had been thought to interiorize the known in an internal word, the *verbum internum* that was subsequently externalized in spoken or written language, the later theory separates the *verbum* (both internal and external) from the *res*. The difference appears clearly in Abelard, who writes: "Words primarily establish understanding of things, not of themselves; through the intermediary signs we use, words direct the mind of the listener to the likeness or image of a thing so that in the likeness it may contemplate not the likeness itself but the thing for which it stands."[20]

The medieval dialectician here declares words to be about things, rather than directly expressing their internalized reality. They point beyond themselves toward a reality that they in no way incarnate. Saint Thomas's position differs. In one sense one might claim that his *verbum mentis*, his word of the intellect, internalizes the real itself—and that is the thrust of his doctrine of intellectual being. But from a more realist perspective this is not the case. The word originates through the so-called *species*, which separates the natural being as much from the ideal one as it unites them. "An external thing does not exist in our intellect according to its own nature, rather, it is necessary that its *species* be in our intellect, and through this species the intellect comes to be in act" (*Summa contra Gentiles*, I, 53). That *species* is, of course, not a mere copy of the thing— if it were, how would we ever know how it resembles the original?—but neither is it the thing itself as passively imprinted on the mind. It rather consists in the mind actively impressing its own mark upon the thing or illuminating it. After due qualifications the same is true of the outcome of this illumination, the *verbum mentis*. Here Bernard Lonergan has captured Aquinas's position with characteristic precision: "The intelligibility of the procession of an inner word is not passive nor potential; it is active and actual; it is intelligible because it is the activity of intelligence in act."[21] On the relation between concepts (inner words) and spoken or written words, Boethius, commenting on Aristotle's *On Interpretation*, had written that only concepts directly signify things while words do not.[22] Most Scholastics repeated this—with the clear exception of Scotus ("that which is properly signified by the word [*vox*] is the thing [*res*]") and the possible one of Saint Thomas. But they had done so without depriving words of the intimate link with the real that the eternal Word, expressed in the language of Scripture, had established with all of creation. Language is a natural endowment given to humans, which enables them to return creation to the primeval intelligibility of their divine origin: words possess a sacramental value. Moreover, with language the human race has in Scripture received the model and code of its proper use.

This intimate link with a given reality broke down in fourteenth-century theories of signification. At the beginning of his *Summa totius logicae* Ockham distinguishes words (spoken or written) from concepts as being natural signs insofar as they refer to something else (in this case, mental concepts), but not in the sense that they are able to stand for other things (*pro illo supponere*).[23] A word, then, is merely a sign in the general sense—a conventional signal (today called a "symbol" in logical or mathematical theories) that externally refers to another reality without participating in it. A real symbol, instead, re-presents the signified reality. The opposition between word and reality became considerably sharper when true nominalists, like Nicholas d'Autrecourt, questioned the relation between concepts and reality as well as the presence of an immanent reason that formerly had been assumed to rule nature. In such a view, language ceased to give expression to a *logos* immanent within the real. Its task was restricted to referring, extrinsically and often indirectly, to the real. Jacques Derrida has pointed out how a systematic and historical link exists between a theology of the Logos and the intrinsic meaningfulness of language. Only when spoken words partake in that divine Word through which the Creator secures the essential intelligibility of his creation can we safely presume that they intrinsically correspond to the very nature of the real. "The intelligible face of the sign remains turned toward the word and the face of God. . . . The sign and divinity have the same place and time of birth."[24] This theological interpretation goes to the heart of medieval realism. But the separation of sign from signified did not occur as a result of the secularism of the Enlightenment as Derrida claims: already the nominalist crisis had severed the bond between human words and the divine Logos. If we can no longer take for granted that God's decrees follow an intelligible pattern, then we also cease to trust that the eternal Logos secures the basic veracity of human speech. Henceforth words were to be used at man's risk and discretion without carrying the traditional guarantee that, if properly used, they touch the real as it is in itself.

This dissolution of the medieval bond with reality essentially changed the nature of language but at the same time allowed it a greater independence with respect to a given reality. By detaching words from things it provided an indispensable condition, albeit a negative one, for language to develop freely beyond its function of naming the real. Language had, of course, never been purely referential, otherwise poetry could not have existed; yet a full awareness of the independence of the *verbum* with respect to the *res* hardly existed before nominalist philosophy. Unintentionally it created a wider space for metaphorical creativity. Such a creativity formed an essential part of the early humanist program. There is little evidence that nominalist philosophy directly influenced the early humanists. None of the poets who initiated the literary humanism of the fourteenth century—Dante, Petrarch, Boccaccio—shows traces of nominalist thought.[25] Dante still stood in the older realist tradition while neither Petrarch nor Boccaccio felt any sympathy for Scholastic philosophy, least of all for the subtleties of the nominalist school. Also, Italian universities in the fourteenth century had by no means turned as universally to the *via moderna* as the French had. We might add that nominalism, though it spurred an interest in linguistic theory, can hardly claim credit for having promoted the poetic or literal use of language. It consistently harbored a suspicion of the verbal screen hung between the mind and the actual observation through which we have direct access to reality. The empirically minded nominalists tended to grant final authority only to the word of Scripture. Their contempt for verbal knowledge survives in Bacon's critique of the four "idols"—all of them created by linguistic deception—that block the road to scientific knowledge. Nevertheless, it would be hard to deny that the nominalist theory by making language more independent created at least the negative conditions that allowed the humanist cult of the word to develop and flourish.

The positive impulse of the humanist view of language came from a more remote past, namely, from a medieval rhetorical tradition turning to Roman models. For the Romans, rhetoric had been an art not a philosophy. Theory served no other purpose but to justify practical rules. Cicero, Quintilian, and Seneca believed as firmly in the basic function of language to express the nature of things as the Stoic and Epicurean philosophers whom they followed. Its task for Cicero consisted in transmitting a truth inherent in the very nature of the real. Yet because word and reality remained united, this transmission in rhetoric granted the word a catalyzing role in the emergence of truth.[26] The fact that for Christians truth preexisted in a divine Word enhanced the significance of rhetoric even more.[27] Eventually this led to the conclusion that the mind can think the truth only through language. Their concern with language drew all the early humanists to the ancient rhetorical models. But while one group sought to achieve linguistic perfection foremost through the richness of the living vernacular, another preferred the controlled and unchangeable dignity of ancient Latin. Despite these differences, all shared a fundamental respect for the word.[28] Erasmus's combination of verbal fireworks and stylistic discipline, Rabelais's catalogues of names, Cervantes's discussions of the meaning of terms, Montaigne's search for ever subtler verbal nuances, Shakespeare's exuberance of language—all originated in the cult of the word.

But humanism did more than return to the earlier rhetorical tradition. It redefined culture. Giovanni Pontano's *De sermone* is one long argument for the essentially linguistic nature of culture.

> Even as reason itself guides us and teaches us to which actions we should turn, so does speech serve to bring those things which the mind conceives through reasoning into the public realm, as we are social beings and born to live in groups. Hence where speech is nobler and more abundant, there also is there a greater supply of those goods which life requires, for need is given to men as a companion at their birth. Through it [speech] life itself becomes better equipped to acquire virtue as well as happiness.[29]

Reversing the traditional order of reference from nature to language, humanists viewed nature through the mirror of language. Whereas previously symbolic meaning had come from Scripture, the humanists considered all poetic discourse capable of disclosing new levels of meaning. The early ones extended what once had been the privilege of the revealed word to all poetic language. Fifteenth-century humanists treated classical texts as authorities equal to Scripture because all metaphorical language creates new meaning. Coluccio Salutati defines the poet's task as "si qua gesta fuerint vel quasi gesta narraverint ad significandum aliud ordinare" (to order deeds or what they present in such a manner that they mean something else).[30] A poem, he explicates in a letter, exhibits one meaning while signifying another—its very essence is symbolic. Precisely this metaphorical quality enables language, both in Scripture and in poetry, to name the sacred. For human language can speak of God only in words *creaturae convenientibus*.[31] Under the veil of mythological images poets reveal a sacred truth, complementary to the word of Scripture.

Albertino Musato, the poet laureate of Padua (1315), showed how far poets were prepared to carry their vatic authority. Having been charged with writing obscene verse, he replied in his defense that all metaphorical use of language, regardless of the subject, possesses a theological character.[32] Similarly Boccaccio ascribes a hidden meaning to his libertine stories in the *Decamerone*. The poet's *figmenta* transfer the reader beyond the veil (*velamen*) of ordinary appearance toward the hidden reality.[33] Indeed, the theological interpretation of poetic language prepared the later acceptance of the aesthetic theology of the Renaissance Neoplatonists.[34] According to Tasso, the poet not only represents the things of this world but also symbolizes those invisible forms that, according to Platonists, constitute the true reality. He creates *idoli*, sacred images, that powerfully refer to a mysterious, invisible reality.[35]

A dead language like Latin lacked the flexibility needed for attaining this poetic ideal. Only the living vernacular remains theologically creative. Such was Dante's thesis in *De vulgari eloquentia*. In the metaphorical use of language the poet wields a divine power that calls forth meaning from nothingness. By what Dante called "l'infinito eccesso del Verbo" (*Paradiso* XIX), poetic language evokes meanings that lie beyond the reach of perception. In a crucial passage of *Paradiso* Dante describes his paradoxical strategy with words: "Transhumanizing—its meaning to convey in words cannot be done; but *let the example suffice* [l'esemplo basti] to whom grace grants experience " (*Paradiso* I, 70–72; emphasis added). The metaphor evokes what words in their literal meaning cannot convey.[36] Metaphor has, of course, always proven indispensable to thought. How else could humans have referred to those invisble realities that form the object of religion and philosophy? But before Dante and the early humanists poets had not been as aware of their creative potential. As a human god the poet creates another world; while describing nature he surpasses it. In Sidney's words: "Nature never set foorth the earth in so rich Tapestry as diverse Poets have done, neither with so pleasant rivers, fruitfull trees, sweete smelling flowers, nor whatsoever els may make the too much loved earth more lovely: her world is brasen, the Poets only deliver a golden."[37]

Somewhat in contrast with this conception of a symbolic, hidden truth, classicists considered language a work of art, a man-made *artificium*[38] that had reached perfection long ago and possessed aesthetic meaning independently of the truth of its message. Their claims of Roman support for such an aesthetic formalism were dubious. Cicero in *De oratore,* the work that enjoyed the highest authority among the Latinists, had declared that oratorical prose must serve primarily a practical purpose. By isolating the aesthetic quality of language from its truth-creating function, Latin classicists hastened the decline of language from being a channel of truth to becoming a mere tool of expression. Lorenzo de Medici, though surrounded by such stylish Latinists as Poliziano and Landino, perceived the artificiality of using a dead language for expressing living passions and preferred the Tuscan dialect.[39] Around 1500, when the French invasions and the internal turmoil in the cities of northern Italy threatened their cultural unity, the tide turned decisively in favor of the vernacular as cultural idiom. Dante's treatise *De vulgari eloquentia,* reissued in 1524 by the Italian humanist Trissino, ignited the quarrel of the ancients and the moderns.

The new polemics about language, however, differed from the older ones. Sperone Speroni, in his influential *Dialogo delle lingue* (1542), largely plagiarized in du Bellay's *Défense et illustration de la langue française* (1549), no longer bases his defense of the vernacular on its unique qualifications for disclosing a higher—that is, a symbolic—truth as Dante had done, but on the exactly opposite argument. Any language possesses the ability to express any idea since it consists entirely of conventional signs. For a scientist, the time spent on learning an artificial language like Latin is wasted. Language originally must have been one, the sixteenth-century French theosophist Guillaume Postel concluded, since a plurality of tongues would have been redundant.[40] This indifference toward the particular semantic structure of a language announces the univocal technical expression of the future. It stood in stark contrast to the attitude of such humanists as Valla and Erasmus who valued the unique genius that distinguishes one language from another.

Renaissance philosophers, intent on reviving ancient thought, detected underneath the classicist attacks on Scholasticism an aversion to philosophy itself. Their separation of philosophical content from linguistic form opened a gulf between them and the humanists that would widen over the years. Marsilio Ficino remains friendly in the dedication of his great *Theologia Platonica* to Angelo Poliziano, yet he forewarns him that his work does not aim at being a display of classical Latin. Where content counts, Scotus's barbaric expression surpasses that of the most accomplished classicist. The youthful Pico was blunter. Expert in both classical languages, he censured the classicists for confusing the particular expressiveness of the Latin language with the universal truth expressed in it.

"Aut enim nomina rerum arbitrio constant, aut natura" (Names of things are established by convention or by nature). If words mean by nature, the philosopher, not the rhetorician, is to explain how; if they mean by convention only, no language deserves preference over others.[41] Pico turns the distinction between philosophy and rhetoric into an opposition. His letter to the eminent classicist Ermolao Barbaro betrays more than a touch of contempt:

> "There is such a contrast between the task of an orator and that of a philosopher that none greater can be imagined. For what does the rhetorician do but seek to lie, to deceive, to be circuitous, and to insinuate? You take pride in maintaining that it is your business to influence the will, to make black appear white, and white, black; and you can, with words, elevate, destroy, support, or annul anything that you wish; finally, it is your claim that with the near magical lure of eloquence, you can transform at will things themselves in appearance and character. . . . Can such a one have any affinity with the philosopher whose sole purpose is to know, and to demonstrate the truth to others? No philosopher could serve the truth who sought merely to create impressions and to seduce with language."[42]

Yet in reducing the word to a purely instrumental function, Pico, Sperone, and those who followed them disregarded the specific part the nature of each language plays in the disclosure of meaning. In the physical sciences that specific character of the expression had to take second place to its accuracy. Eventually that required more univocal symbols than any ordinary language, Latin or vernacular, had at its disposal. Galileo saw far into the future when he described nature as a book written in mathematical symbols that demanded a mathematical language to decode. "Philosophy is written in this grand book—I mean the universe—which stands continuously open to our gaze—but it cannot be understood unless one first learns to comprehend the language and interpret the characters in which it is written. It is written in the language of mathematics, and its characters are triangles, circles, and other geometrical figures."[43] Ordinary language suffices only for articulating those subjective impressions caused by the more objective primary qualities.

The semantic changes that accompanied the birth of modern science sealed the division between ordinary experience and scientific interpretation, which a common language had previously united in a single life world. Galileo expected science and art to meet at the top because for him—as for Plato—poetic forms as well as various artistic idioms consist as much of mathematical proportions as the science of nature. (Galileo held poetry and the arts in high esteem, as appears from the beginning of *Two Systems* and several other passages.) In fact, the two grew ever further apart. In scientific prose a *mathesis universalis* gradually took the place of the *universale concretum* of the metaphor that had dominated the naturalist writings of Bruno and other sixteenth-century authors. The need for accurate formulation inverted the traditional use of language. The pioneers of the vernacular—Dante and Petrarch—would have found it hard to imagine a philosophical treatise on any subject (including a defense of the vernacular) written in a language other than Latin. However outspoken their preference for the *vulgare nobile* in poetic utterance, scientific truth, because it was unchanging, had better be expressed in a language that was both traditional and definitive. The conception of truth that was making its way in the emerging scientific movement changed this view. Together with old methods and obsolete principles, the new learning abandoned much of the terminology used in expressing the old. The tentative, flexible shape of languages still in the process of receiving their definitive form suited the experimental approach of the budding sciences.

Francis Bacon openly flouted the "cult of words," which he linked to a reactionary reverence for the authority of the past. In attacking "the idols of the marketplace" the former lord chancellor denounced what humanists had regarded as the particular strength of language—namely, that words may attempt to disclose what observation withholds. Truth must be learned from the observation of nature not from books. If science was to avoid the verbal pitfalls of the past, its theories must be couched in words that remain as close as possible to an exact description of experience. This scientific sobriety appeared to call for the kind of simple, colorless, and exsanguine prose of so many treatises across which the great chancellor's spirit, "rising like a genie from [his] tomb, . . . casts its shadow."[44] But scientific writing did not turn bland until long afterwards. Early seventeenth-century philosophers wrote better than their predecessors. Descartes and Malebranche became masters of French prose; Bacon and Hobbes continue to be regarded as models of English style, and Galileo of Italian.[45] All of them occupy distinguished places in the history of their national literatures. They brought to scientific vernacular the care for correct and elegant wording conveyed by a classical training. The efforts of the despised cultists of words who had educated them had not been spent in vain!

Eventually the humanist cult of language took refuge in the schools. European education adopted the ideals of the Jesuit *ratio studiorum* as universal principles of learning. Grammar schools and colleges built their curricula on the axiom that access to truth and civility depends on linguistic ability. Polished speech and stylish writing emerged as the distinctive mark of the civilized class. The more the vernacular became refined, the more it tended to separate a nation's social classes. Especially in seventeenth-century France, cultured expression served as a barrier that allowed members of the higher classes to retain their distance from the masses. Language was as much a device for dividing social enclaves from one another as a means for uniting those within them. But linguistic exclusiveness also enabled different sections within the same class to define their identity by means of sublanguages. Thus religious groups in seventeenth-century France, Italy, and Spain succeeded in creating their own isolated spiritual universe by means of a specialized devotional vocabulary. In France this became the area inhabited by "les dévots" or "les spirituels," eventually "les mystiques"—substantives which had never before existed in the French tongue. The language they wrote and spoke created a semantically closed circuit that provided spiritual autonomy but did so at the price of a reduced system of communication.

In summary, for a brief period early humanism united the various strands of an emerging era in a comprehensive cultural ideal that wedded the pursuit of verbal perfection with a Christian theology of the Logos. The flourishing time of humanism, though short, was long enough to leave at the threshold of modernity the memory of an alternative to what Heidegger has denounced as the *Sprachvergessenheit*, the linguistic forgetfulness of the modern age.[46] What caused this early humanism to be so soon and so definitively abandoned? Conceived primarily as an ideal of rhetoric and mostly indifferent—if not hostile—to philosophy, it remained defenseless against its rationalist opponents. Among them were the heirs of the nominalist scholarship humanists had bitterly attacked. But more than from their blows, humanism died because of its all-too-exclusive literary interests. It was unprepared to incorporate or even to legitimate the principles of what was to become the most significant intellectual development of the early modern age—science. From the beginning it had opposed Scholastic thought for its indifference to language, life, and feeling. In the end, the descendants of that condemned School philosophy won the day.

Literary humanism was to regain some of its former vitality in the German neoclassical ideal of *Bildung,* but by that time scientific specialization and democratic leveling had progressed too far to allow it to be more than a small, elitist movement. Its last remnants died in the trenches of the Great War. Today the idea of language again stands at the center of our intellectual interest. Linguistic theories dominate philosophy and literary theory in French formalism (structuralist and deconstructionist) and Anglo-American analysis. These trends, however, trace their origins not to the humanist tradition but to the nominalist forces that defeated it. Indeed, this neo-nominalism signals what George Steiner has called the crisis of the word in which the traditional link between word and world breaks down. For the Greeks of the classical age the Logos had dwelled within the real, and for Christians language had participated in the aboriginal divine Word, the archetype of all created being. With the humanists the word had assumed a creative power of its own, but only within a given reality destined to be completed in verbal perfection. That tradition died as language became increasingly self-referential.

The Self as a Subject

The most decisive change in the way the self came to envision its role within the total order of being is symbolized in a strange reversal in the meaning of the term *subject.* Subject, the translation of *hypokeimenon* (what lies under something), had once named the most elementary level of being. In the course of the modern age it surprisingly came to stand for the ultimate source of meaning and value previously attributed to God or to a divine nature.[47] The story begins with Scotus. He attributed a distinct mental reality to the known, referring to it as an *esse objectivum* in the mind.[48] "Objective" being, then, was ideal, in contrast to extra-mental real or "subjective" being. This distinction between real and mental being widened in nominalist philosophy. Still, the subject continued to refer to the *suppositum* of being and its qualities. One substantial subject, however, was distinct by the ideal nature of its activity: the human mind. Once this mental subject came to be regarded as the source of the ideal qualities previously considered inherent in all other *supposita,* it bound them to itself as objects, that is, as being for-the-subject. It thereby took on the Promethean task of reconstructing the entire order of reality in ideal terms.[49] Paradoxically, in the process of doing so the self increasingly lost its own substantial content to the all-absorbing cognitive and volitive functions it exercised.

In at least one way humanism had prepared for this shift by presenting the second nature humans create for themselves through culture as raising them above the rest of nature. Still, for the early humanists the person remained the creative power *within* the substantiality of Being—at its cutting edge, so to speak. Renaissance philosophers carried the difference further to a point where the person as an independent power began to compete with nature or the Creator in constituting meaning and value. Tomasso Campanella declared that by thought and artistic achievement persons so totally surpass nature that they cease to be part of it.[50] Even more drastically, Bruno assigned to the person the task both to shape himself and to convey meaning and form to the universe, thus inverting the position of nature from norm to object of human manipulation. Rather than perfecting nature in accordance with nature's internal teleology, the person now submits it to exclusively human purposes. Bacon, as we saw, advocates obedience to nature only as a means to control her: "Natura nonnisi parendo vincitur" (We conquer nature only by obeying her).

The new attitude transforms the idea of culture from cultivating what nature gives freely to yoking it forcefully to human wants. Plato in the *Protagoras* had cautioned against the risks involved in any attempt to conquer nature. When Prometheus brought humans the fire required for civilization, he failed to equip them with the virtues indispensable for protecting civilized life against self-destruction, namely *aidos* (reverence) and *dike* (right, justice). For the Greeks and even for the more pragmatic Romans, Hercules, the plodding but reliable servant reputed only for having accomplished such humble but useful chores as cleaning stables and ridding the land of monsters, had, more than the rebellious Prometheus, appeared a trustworthy model in the project of cultivating nature.[51] At the dawn of the modern age that tradition retained its authority. Coluccio Salutati still elevated the dull-witted Hercules to the rank of patron of poetry, the foremost expression of cultural creativity. Boccaccio, however, proclaimed Prometheus the hero of culture. He continued to hold that position throughout the modern age. Only Gianbattista Vico, returning to the earlier humanist tradition, restored Hercules to his ancient place of honor.

Still, the move toward the subject was not inspired by Promethean pride: it had become inevitable in the wake of late medieval thought.

After the traditional source of meaning dried up, the self had no choice but to function as a "subject." The role of meaning-giver was inflicted on it in the wake of a profound spiritual crisis. The incertitudes of nominalist theology, intensified by the exposure to the non-Christian cultures of classical antiquity as well as by the discovery of new continents, had deeply shaken the traditional worldview and raised fundamental questions. Existential crises of this nature always elicit religious responses, but in this case religion itself formed part of the problem; indeed, its central core. Sixteenth-century religious humanists and reformers were torn by a spiritual anxiety that their theological answers never fully allayed. Luther remained subject to returning attacks of doubt. Calvin never felt fully confident that he had found the theological and rational support his position required. In his remarkable portrait, William Bouwsma describes the French reformer as ridden with intellectual and emotional insecurity.[52] The entire epoch suffered from anxiety. When faith split into opposing confessions and religious wars devastated large parts of Europe, it appeared that religion, rather than solving the spiritual crisis, was at the heart of the turmoil.

In that total disarray, inner as well as outer, the rediscovery and study of the ancient skeptics convinced the educated that one could lead a morally respectable life without possessing certainty concerning matters that had never been uncertain before. The doctrine of the Greek Pyrrho (365–270 B.C.) attracted a great deal of attention. Gian Francesco Pico della Mirandola, the nephew of the great Renaissance thinker, enrolled Pyrrho's theory in the service of his attack on worldly learning, *Examen Vanitatis Doctrinae Gentium* (1520). Pico harbored no libertine intentions. Quite the opposite. Since philosophy supplies no certainty, he concluded that the mind should turn to divine prophecy. Stimulated by Pico's argument, Montaigne began to read a Latin translation of the Greek skeptic Sextus Empiricus, a reading that resulted in his famous *Apology for Raymond Sebond*. This text, no more than Pico's, reflects religious agnosticism but, as Richard H. Popkin has shown, was inspired by a search for a less vulnerable support of religious faith. With many of his educated contemporaries, Montaigne thought that a deflating of philosophical theories might bring an end to the religious controversies that were tearing French society apart.[53] If all human learning remains unreliable, it serves little purpose to challenge the Church's authority in the name of Scripture since the sacred text, as all others, is open to multiple interpretations. Moreover, the authority of biblical texts depends itself upon the Church for their inclusion in the canon. Thus, Montaigne promoted religious tolerance on the basis of fideism, yet his skepticism extended well beyond theological matters. It sprang from a fundamental doubt about the mind's capacity for certainty in any area. "Unless we find one thing of which we can be *completely* certain, we can be certain about nothing," he wrote in the *Apology*. But precisely that one thing was not available. External appearances deceive the mind everywhere, but more alarmingly, the mind deceives itself. Rather than providing a ground for certitude as it later did for Descartes, the nature of the self is for Montaigne the source of all uncertainty.

Descartes's strategy is particularly instructive for assessing the depth of the epistemological crisis. He hoped to restore the foundations of human knowledge by converting moral uncertainty into philosophical doubt and doubt itself into a method for attaining certainty. Throughout the *Discourse on Method* we detect echoes of ancient and modern skeptics. As first rule of the new method Descartes restates the fideist Charron's proposal not to accept as true what can be doubted.[54] Given his confident conclusions, we tend to dismiss his doubt as purely methodical, symptomatic of a supreme trust in the mind's ability to reach certain knowledge against all odds. But such an appraisal conflicts with the picture Descartes himself paints of the moral condition in which he started his philosophical quest: "a man who walks alone in darkness," who left his homeland to live in a country whose language he never properly learned to speak "as in the remotest desert."

There are good reasons for taking the existential and moral depth of Descartes's *crise pyrrhonienne* quite seriously.[55] Converting doubt into a method was not the bravura act of an acrobat performing without a safety net but a last ditch effort toward spiritual survival on the part of one who, with many of his learned contemporaries, felt he had no intellectual security left beyond that of his own doubt. His argument displays the scars of this initial loss of faith in the mind's basic ability for truth. The very persistence of doubt, after Descartes has reached the rock bottom certainty of the *cogito ergo sum* and established the reliability of clear and distinct ideas, indicates that more than an epistemic issue is at stake. Much has been made of the "circle" that forces the philosopher by means of clear and distinct ideas to prove the existence of God in order to render clear and distinct ideas trustworthy. Our concern here is not with the presence or absence of a logical fallacy in the argument, but rather with its logical use. Once an idea is evident, no additional evidence can be gained by such a proof. As Descartes's contemporary Pierre-Sylvain Régis had observed: "Toute évidence est également évidence, et partant toute évidence est également la règle de la vérité" (All evidence is equally evidence and hence all evidence is equally rule of truth).[56] At the same epistemic level there can be no hierarchy of evidence. Once evidence is established, the conditions of reliable knowledge have been met.

Even if we grant that certainty about one's own thinking and about God's existence yields more solid evidence than mathematical principles and a methodically acquired knowledge of the material world, the latter ought to be sufficiently secure from insurmountable doubt after the former has established the possibility of attaining genuine knowledge. When Descartes nonetheless persists in questioning, we suspect that he is exorcizing ghosts of an altogether different nature. The possibility of an evil genius that may still interfere with thinking truly suggests that a deep-seated moral pessimism lies at the bottom of the epistemological problem. Far from apriori removing all doubts about the availability of truth, God may be a cause of error. The hypothesis of a deceiving God can be regarded as part of the hyperbolic doubt, but at its heart lies a more fundamental uncertainty. If God is defined primarily through his infinite, incomprehensible power (as happens in Meditation I), then we may legitimately wonder how much epistemic safety one can expect from an inscrutable deity. To render the idea of God serviceable to his argument, Descartes had to overcome the problem created by late nominalist theology— namely, that of a totally unpredictable God. This he eventually does, though without much philosophical justification, by limiting God's omnipotence by a moral attribute. God is not merely infinite and omnipotent, he is also perfect in a way that prevents him from ever deceiving his creatures because the will to deceive always derives from a "defect" (Meditation III). Hence, though God has the power to deceive, he cannot *will* to deceive us. Yet Descartes's appeal to a good and truthful God does not imply that we share a common knowledge with him, as we learn from his letter to Arnauld: "I dare not even say that God could not make a mountain without a valley, or that one plus two might not be three."[57] What we perceive as true may still not be divine truth, but such a difference in perspective casts no fundamental doubt on our own pursuit of truth.[58]

The symptoms of Descartes's moral insecurity appear in other instances as well. His guidelines for a "provisional morality," never to be converted into more definitive rules, point at a difficulty he experienced in establishing standards of conduct on the basis of reason alone. To us this may not seem a defect, but by Descartes's rationalist standards it certainly was. At times he even appears to raise questions about the universal applicability of his critical method. He insists on the strictly autobiographical character of his writing and cautions that what has worked for him may not do so for others. How surprising to read in a text entitled *Discourse on Method*:

> My present aim, then, is not to teach the method which everyone must follow in order to direct his reason correctly, but only to reveal how I have tried to direct my own. . . . But I am presenting this only as a history, or, if you prefer, a fable in which, among certain examples worthy of imitation, you will perhaps also find many others that it would be right not to follow; and so I hope that it will be useful to some without being harmful to any, and that everyone will be grateful to me for my frankness.

Even here the fear of deception persists. "Yet I may be wrong: perhaps what I take for gold and diamonds is nothing but a bit of copper and glass."[59]

Yet the moral quality of Descartes's doubt also reveals an existential dimension of his thought in which some of his contemporaries detected an Augustinian trait. Cardinal de Bérulle, Descartes's ecclesiastical patron, and Malebranche, his philosophical follower, regarded his philosophy as a new foundation for a spiritual theology. Certainly the way he conceives of the self discloses its openness to transcendence. The third Meditation, which lays the foundation of the self's cognitive ability, concludes with an unexpected religious passage: "[Before I pass on to other truths] I should like to pause here and spend some time in the contemplation of God; to reflect on his attributes, and to gaze with wonder and adoration on the beauty of this immense light, so far as the eye of my darkened intellect can bear it."[60]

For a moment the French philosopher reminds us of Augustine's self-examination before God.[61] But only for a moment, because Descartes's introspection reverses the traditional order from God to the soul.[62] All ideas—including the idea of God—have their formal basis in the mind, which envisions all beings as *cogitata*. At least in that sense the self forms the foundation for the idea of God, and without that foundation the second ontological one, laid by God's causal activity, would play no role in the self's reflection. God has to be proven, and to be proven on the basis of the prior certainty of the self. The thinking self, then, remains the ground—though not the cause—of the idea of God.

Descartes has identified self with mental substance—"moi, c'est-à-dire mon esprit."[63] But does this mental substance possess any content of its own? Descartes describes it by its opposition to bodily substance—"une chose qui pense, et non-étendue . . . , et qui ne participe à rien de ce qui appartient au corps" (a thinking thing, and not extended . . . , not participating in anything pertaining to the body)[64] —but he fails to define what positively distinguishes mental from bodily substance. He never progresses much beyond showing that consciousness exists as an irreducible mode of being and hence that it must be attributed to a different substance. When later thinkers in the Cartesian tradition attempted to make a science of this mental substance, not surprisingly they turned—both for method and content—to the far more developed notion of substance as extension. Thus French thinkers of the eighteenth century ended up with a materialist theory of the person.

The absence of any ontological content in the very being that grounds all others has intrigued readers of Descartes since Heidegger first drew attention to it. "If the *ego sum, ego existo*, determines the entire sense of *esse*, why is this richness of ontic determinations of the *ego* accompanied by a massive, ontological silence on the mode of being of the *sum?*"[65] This disconcerting emptiness of the foundational self announces its primarily functional future in modern thought. Mind is what defines (and soon will constitute) the real in ideal categories and controls it through *praxis*. The modern self possesses little content of its own, and this poverty contrasts with Augustine's conception of the soul, which to him was the richest of all concepts. While Descartes's self occasionally reveals glimpses of this former richness, he has set the notion of selfhood on a course where it was to become a functional one, namely, the source of meaning and value. Typical in this respect is the statement with which the famous reduction of the piece of wax to the category of extension concludes: "I must therefore admit that the nature of this piece of wax is in no way revealed by my imagination but is perceived by the mind alone."[66] "Perceived by the mind alone" means that a true understanding requires us to make abstraction from all passively received (through sense or imagination) qualities and ideally to reconstitute its nature through an active intellectual grasp. Here begins a development that reached its final conclusion in Fichte's conception of the self as a creative act.[67] Goethe's variant on the beginning of the Fourth Gospel goes to the very heart of the modern project: *Im Anfang war die Tat* (In the beginning was the deed). Even as Faust, the subject produces its own identity. Some later thinkers declared the notion of a self to be no more than a function of its own activity. Already for Marx, the idea of a subject was a meaningless remnant of romanticism.

In one sense the idea of self-making through self-expression may be traced back to early humanism. Yet the humanists mediated the self's expressive power through its integration with nature and through its intrinsic dependence on a transcendent reality. The self of rationalist philosophy, however, serves a foundational purpose: the existence of the world and of God have to be established and defined by the thinking subject. In becoming pure project, the modern self has become severed from those sources that once provided its content. The metaphysics of the ego isolates the self. It narrows selfhood to individual solitude and reduces the other to the status of object.[68] In the next chapter we shall see how this theoretical egocentrism inevitably leads to a moral one. The "care for the soul" with which this chapter began can be compared with Nietzsche's dark saying that modern man has "a small soul."[69] It seems an amazing charge to make after four centuries of unparalleled self-eman-cipation, and yet a justified one. In the course of assuming control over everything else the self has, as Kierkegaard put it, lost sight of its own identity. Separated from that totality which once nurtured it and largely deprived of the interiority which once defined it, it has become an indigent self.

Chapter 5

The New Meaning of Freedom

Voluntarism and Its Consequences

The modern concept of subjectivity rests solidly on the idea of freedom, so much so that many consider autonomy *the* characteristic of the new age. But a concern with freedom already marks the earliest period of our culture. The ideal of self-governing citizenship guided the development of the Greek city and survived its decline. That early ideal, however, had been political rather than individual. It aimed at enabling a select group of citizens to live in conditions of communal equality and *autarkeia*. Neither in theory nor in practice did those allowed to pursue it trouble themselves much about individual rights. Political freedom tolerated, and often required, a great deal of restraint in private areas. Socrates's unwavering insistence on the individual's moral responsibility undoubtedly prepared a more personal concept of freedom, yet even his battle with moral relativism was primarily motivated by the spiritual well-being of the whole social body. Aristotle, who wrote after the city-states had lost much of their independence, considered freedom rooted in society. Throughout he assumes that the community possesses a reality that exceeds the sum and importance of its individual members and that conditions their ability to attain virtue and freedom. Those who do not participate in governing the political community—such as children, women, and slaves—hold no full title to freedom. For those of us in the twentieth century who tend to regard freedom as primarily a personal quality, the classical notion remains hard to understand.

The idea of personal freedom independent of the state, however, also originated in antiquity. Greek philosophers of the classical period had not always unambiguously extolled public virtue over private perfection. Plato's report of his failed Sicilian experiment in the seventh *Letter* testifies to that. Aristotle, who set the standard for a politically oriented ethics in his *Politics*, presents in the tenth book of his *Nicomachean Ethics* a very different contemplative ideal. In the huge Hellenistic and Roman empires with their distant centers of government, the sense of political community weakened if it did not vanish altogether. In that climate the Stoa presented a new ideal of freedom that, while not avoiding political or social duties, consisted in an inner attitude, independent of external circumstances. The art of living well, according to the slave Epictetus, begins with distinguishing the world over which we have no power from the self for which we are responsible. This distinction between the internal realm of freedom and the external world of compulsion will later find its way into Kant's ethics. Still, Stoic and Epicurean conceptions of freedom differ substantially from modern ones. They foster attitudes of withdrawal rather than of dominance, of disengagement rather than of conquest.[1] Christianity eventually gave the idea of personal freedom a wholly new content. The "glorious freedom of the children of God" (Rom. 8:21), unlike the Stoic *autarkeia*, was unattainable by human effort alone. Oriented toward individual salvation, the Christian ideal remained at first indifferent to political structures. Yet no sooner had Christianity become the official religion of the empire than Christians felt compelled to extend an ideal that had been initially individual, or at least limited to a particular community, to the entire political order. Thus freedom regained much of its previous social and political scope. If nothing else, man's fallen condition had made external structures indispensable.

Despite these accommodations, a tension persisted in the Christian view that eventually surfaced in two opposite (and never reconciled) tendencies in the modern conception of freedom. Augustine formulated both of them in the course of two polemical campaigns he launched, first against the Manicheans, then against the Pelagians. The definitive, insurmountable nature of evil in Mani's theology (a Gnostic reformulation of the dualistic old Persian religion) resulted in a pessimism incompatible with the Christian doctrine of redemption. So Augustine, the converted Manichean, strenuously defended the ultimate supremacy of the good. In a controversy of his later years, however, the same Augustine displayed considerable pessimism concerning human nature's capacity for good after the fall. Against the ascetic teachings of Western monks, according to which at least the beginning of the redemptive process depends on the practice of moral virtue, the African bishop declared human effort powerless at every step of the road to salvation. The restauration of fallen nature wholly surpasses the power of human freedom. Augustine's two positions were not incompatible since the freedom of the redeemed is itself a grace God grants to his elect. Yet in this election God's sovereign will predestines some to freedom, others to permanent bondage. The very idea of freedom became thereby heavily mortgaged in its effective power. The ambiguity persisted all through the Middle Ages and at the dawn of the modern period, the tension exploded in a fundamental religious crisis (see chapter 8).

This early strain notwithstanding, medieval thought succeeded in elaborating a theological synthesis that maintained a surprising balance between corruption and redemption, individual and society, voluntarism and intellectualism. Toward the end of the epoch, however, this symmetry came to be disturbed by a top-heavy voluntarism. When in 1277 Etienne Tempier, the archbishop of Paris, condemned a number of Aristotelian theses alleged to be held by various theologians (including Aquinas), his gesture signaled the end of the Greek idea of freedom that in its highest instance coincides with rational necessity. God's perfect freedom had, in Aristotle's unmoved mover as well as in the Neoplatonic One, excluded choice from divine activity. Moreover, that divine necessity remained utterly indifferent to all lower levels of being. The finite world had not come into existence through a voluntary act of the Creator but either had existed through an intrinsic necessity of its own or had resulted from a necessary divine emanation. How much Christian thinkers had absorbed of this conception appears in the Scholastic denial that any real relation exists between God and the world, an astonishing position to take for a religion that placed divine love at the center of its doctrine. Nevertheless, Scholastics succeeded to a remarkable degree in integrating the idea of a free creation with that of divine necessity by means of an exemplarist theology that conveyed to all creatures an ideal preexistence in the divine mind and that reinterpreted the Neoplatonic emanation as a free outflow of the divine attribute of love.

Franciscans, whose order had been founded on the experience of God's concrete love for each creature, found this solution less than satisfactory. Already Thomas's contemporary Bonaventure had considered love God's supreme attribute and placed human beatitude in the loving union with— rather than the contemplation of—God. Scotus was the last great theologian to attempt to reconcile the Greek idea of divine sufficiency with the existence of a contingent world order dependent on a divine decision. He presented that entire order with all it implied as the effect of a single divine decision made in the beginning, thus dispensing God from ever having to react to creaturely actions as they developed in time since such a reaction would have rendered God dependent upon his creation. Even the Incarnation, traditionally interpreted as a divine response to the contingent event of the fall, Scotus held to be foreordained irrespective of human sin or innocence. The solution, however ingenious, implied an uneasy compromise. Although Scotus's God does not immediately interfere in the actual development of his creation, he nevertheless creates in the beginning without inner necessity and, hence, measured against the Greek concept of freedom, contingently.

Ockham overcame the inconsistency by substituting for the idea of a divine necessity detached from the contingent world one of absolute power. A free creation to him meant that God had set the world on its course by choice and that he preserved it by his continuous support in such a manner that creation in all its developments—including those caused by free human decisions—depends at each successive moment entirely on divine power. That power remains entirely God's own even while he is constantly reacting to human actions in time. Ockham does not question that God's omnipotence preserves the order of things set up at the beginning, but he stresses that that order depends at each moment on God's resolution to abide by it. God's sovereign power is not intrinsically bound by any necessity other than that of its absolute freedom, nor is that freedom subject to what we consider ultimate rationality. Total unconditionedness characterizes divine power in the sense that no act or event in creation necessitates its freedom. Divine power remains absolute at any moment, supporting the ordained—that is, the actually chosen order—yet exceeding by its infinite possibility the scope of that actuality.[2]

It is difficult to overestimate the impact of this momentous reversal of one of the leading concepts of Western thought. Its theological effects will be considered later. Here I am concerned only with its effect on the conception of human freedom. As much as Aristotle's freedom had fol-

lowed a divine model of rationality, the voluntarist conception was mod-
eled after the archetype of an open-ended, indefinite, and hence potentially
infinite power. One of the immediate consequences was that the will of
the lawgiver, rather than the intrinsic rationality of the law, determined
the legal order.[3] Even thinkers who claimed to be following the Aristo-
telian-Thomist tradition, such as Suarez in his influential *De legibus*,
embraced the voluntarist position.

A second, more significant though less direct, consequence was the
vacuum of indeterminacy left by the fact that the course of the universe
could no longer be assumed to reflect the qualities of reason, goodness,
and so on traditionally attributed to its Creator. God's ineffability combined with the unrestrictedness of his absolute power invalidated Greek
speculations about what a world ought to look like. The argument implied
that no predictable order ruled the world and hence that only empirical
observation could establish the nature of that order. The new voluntarism
even affected the intellect's own activity. Truth was not simply given
with insight; it required an assent of the will. The knower assumed full
responsibility for what he or she affirmed.

The voluntarism of late medieval and early modern thought cannot
simply be explained by nominalist theology. Its seeds had been planted
in Augustine's theology of love, which had been accepted both before and
outside the *via moderna* by such decidedly anti-nominalist humanists as
Petrarch and Salutati (especially in *De fato, fortuna, et casu*). Nor do
voluntarist theologies account for the outburst of creative activity in the
early modern age, although more than any other factor this awareness of
creative power contributed to the new perception of freedom. Freedom
henceforth became a self-choice, more than a choice that selects among
given alternatives. It refused to be restricted by the given.

Nicholas of Cusa saw in this creative freedom a godlike endowment
whereby the human person surpasses and dominates all other creatures.
We know the cardinal's daring statement: "Man is a god, but not absolutely, since he is [only] man. Man is the world, but he is not everything
in a contracted way, since he is man. Man then is a *microcosm* or a
human world."[4] This conception changes the person's role in the cosmos.
That role consists not in accomplishing a task within a preestablished
order, but in conforming that order to self-chosen goals. Marsilio Ficino
also speaks of the godlike quality of freedom. "The power of the human
person almost resembles that of God's nature." (Similis ergo ferme vis
hominis est naturae divinae.) These words define the essence of the new

freedom: "non servi naturae, sed aemuli" (not servants of nature but its competitors).[5] When Pico's Creator denies Adam a fixed place in nature and orders him to define himself by his own free will, freedom becomes self-creation. "We have not made you either celestial or terrestial, mortal or immortal, in order that you may, as it were, *become your own maker and former, and shape yourself in whatever form* you like best."[6]

Renaissance writing abounds in discussions of free will of which the famous exchange between Erasmus and Luther is the best remembered. The literature of the time reflects the power and complexity of self-creative freedom, but also its unprecedented dangers. In Shakespeare's great tragedies—Macbeth, Julius Caesar, Hamlet—the modern conception of freedom redefines the very essence of the drama. Its protagonists no longer struggle with fate or supernatural powers but with the awesome responsibility of having to shape their own lives without being able to predict the consequences. Once again, Prometheus reemerges as the mythical hero of culture. Earlier Christians had regarded this rebel with suspicion and had either domesticated him into a bringer of benefits not stolen but divinely granted (Lactantius), or they had replaced him by the more submissive Hercules (Salutati).[7]

The actualization of a freedom conceived in this manner requires a certain indeterminacy of its external environment. A totally predefined and predictable universe severely restricts self-determination. The more open the universe, the more creative freedom is allowed to be. Giordano Bruno concluded that an infinite universe infinitely expanded the realm of human freedom. Within a condition of total cosmic indeterminacy, inherent in a universe unlimited in space and time, the *infinito interiore* of the free agent is given unrestricted possibilities for expressing itself. In *The Expulsion of the Triumphant Beast* Bruno, reinterpreting Aristotle's well-known statement that the gods in granting man intelligence and hands have placed him in a position equal to their own, concludes that action is the purpose of all theory.[8] Elsewhere, however, Bruno with characteristic inconsistency declares supreme freedom to coincide with total necessity. "Necessity and freedom are one. Hence we should not fear that who acts by the necessity of nature, does not act freely. Rather would he not act freely if he acted in any way different from what necessity and nature, indeed, the necessity *of* nature, requires." (Necessitas et libertas sunt unum, unde non est formidandum quod, cum agat necessitate naturae, non libere agat: sed potius immo omnino non libere ageret aliter agendo quam necessitas et natura, immo naturae necessitas requirit.)[9] But how can a nature that necessarily emanates from such a "necessary" divine freedom allow unlimited choice? Obviously here two opposite models of freedom confront one another: a late medieval one stressing total indeterminacy, and a Stoic one that ultimately coincides with total necessity. Bruno failed to harmonize them and left them standing independently. Spinoza opted for the Stoic model and, for the last time, consistently developed its consequences. Renaissance thinkers continue to hesitate, frequently adopting elements from both at the cost of considerable inconsistency.

By and large, however, the ideal of open-ended self-determination prevailed. Life itself increasingly came to be viewed as a project through which the person shapes his or her own selfhood. The emerging novel explored these new possibilities. In this respect, the Russian critic Bakhtin has pointed out, it differs from its predecessor, the epic. While the epic unfolds in an unchangeable, remote past, the time of the novel remains incomplete, open toward the future. "From the very beginning the novel was structured not in the distanced image of the absolute past but in the zone of direct contact with inconclusive present-day reality."[10] The novel moves in the now of freedom: its heroes—such as Don Quixote and Pantagruel—go out to impress their vision on the world. A particular interest of Cervantes's work lies in the fact that it not only represents the new concept of freedom, but that it does so with critical irony. Don Quixote, blissfully unaware of the limits the world sets to human projects, walks straight into disaster. Cervantes's hero symbolizes the defeat of a nation that had come to envision its very existence as a vocation: to liberate Spain from the infidels, to vanquish the Islam in all of Europe, to eradicate the Northern heresies, to conquer and convert the New World.[11] By the time he wrote, all of these undertakings had either floundered or resulted in conditions more undesirable than the ones they purported to remedy. Especially the disaster of the Armada, the expedition of which King Philip II had assured his doubting admiral that God himself would command and in which Cervantes had participated, undermined the confident faith of the nation in its own destiny. Cervantes, wisened by the mishaps in his own life and by the painful lesson learned by his country, had become sharply critical of any attempt to restructure existence according to preconceived schemes,[12] yet his critical attitude with respect to life conceived as a preestablished project was by no means universally shared. It was far more common to question any authority whose pedigree could not be traced back to autonomous reason. Even a divine authority would first have to be accepted on the strength of its rational support. A claim of authority as being immediately derived from a divine source, such as the theory of the divine right of kings advanced, was challenged from the moment of its appearance. This different attitude appears most clearly in the transformation of the concept of natural law.

A primary problem in any discussion of morality and moral change lies in the difficulty of grasping what previous generations considered normative. Although the terminology used to express moral convictions often remains the same, its meaning may have undergone a fundamental change. Concepts such as law, obligation, and the like made their way into the modern age along very circuitous trails. Chapter 1 disclosed some of the deceptive shifts of meaning in the term *nature*. The transformation of "freedom" in the modern age introduced further ambiguities. These changes in meaning in turn influenced the assessment of what counts as a moral norm. Nature continued to play a prominent role in defining moral standards, but it did so in a considerably different manner. In his *Politics* Aristotle wrote: "There are those things which make men good and excellent; these are nature (*physis*), habit (*ethos*), and reason (*logos*)."[13] Striking in this description is that, unlike in modern theories of morality, habit receives as much weight as reason. Each of the three sources of morality results, so to speak, from the pattern of life. Goodness consists in following the internal guidance of community, tradition, and nature that constitute the fabric of ordinary existence. Even the Stoics, who articulated the idea of normative nature in their concept of natural law, did not interpret law as an ordinance promulgated by an external authority and enforced by sanctions. Nor does reason function as an independent norm; it merely presents nature itself as being intrinsically normative, as appears in Cicero's succinct formula: "Lex est ratio summa insita in natura, quae iubet ea quae facienda sunt." (Law is the supreme reason inherent in nature, which commands what is to be done.)[14]

The Hebrew and Christian conception of God as universal Creator and omnipotent lawgiver subjected morality to a transcendent authority in a way unknown to Greek thinkers of the classical and Hellenistic periods. A transcendent sanction of morality was obviously not unknown to the ancients, especially the Stoics, but it was distinguished from that of the Jews and the Christians by one decisive difference: nature itself was divine. Jews and Christians derived morality's normative quality from an authority beyond nature. Nevertheless, the norms of the moral law remain within nature: reason and divine authority concur in defining the content of the law. Once, however, the order of nature came to be viewed as proceeding from an inscrutable sovereign Creator, nature lost its decisive normative authority. Henceforth the moral imperative must receive its formal sanction from a divine decision rather than from nature and right reason. Ockham and some late nominalist theologians extended God's authority to the point where he may command and regard as meritorious an act that goes against the norms of human nature (such as adultery) and even hatred of God. Thus detached from the inner teleology of nature, morality comes to depend exclusively on divine commands. The determining criterion of the moral act shifts from its natural appropriateness to the authority of the lawgiver.[15] While the authority of the law for Aquinas had resided in right reason, the new conception of law grounded it primarily in the divine will. This voluntarism characteristic of nominalist theology heralded the end of a long ethical tradition in which rational and legal authority had held each other in balance. It prepared the modern concept of moral autonomy in presenting the divine lawgiver as a model for the human one. Even as God's essence consists in unrestricted, self-sustaining power, so is the person a self-sufficient center in his own right.

Neither humanist nor Renaissance attitudes can be derived from nominalist theology, yet they could hardly have developed as they did without the cultural conditions created by late medieval thought. In any case, by the time of the Renaissance the moral weight had shifted from nature understood as an all-comprehensive principle of order to the individual. The person alone is held responsible for the course of his or her life and for mastering the power to realize self-chosen objectives. This ideal of self-realization gradually transformed the concept of moral perfection from living one's life as an integral part of community and cosmos into an active pursuit of personal excellence. Indirectly this voluntarism prepared an ethics of obligation in contrast to one of virtue.[16]

Private Morality and Public Virtue

Among the ethical traditions of classical antiquity Epicureanism alone had isolated morality from its social context, yet until Valla the prevailing Christian attitude toward it had been thoroughly negative. (Dante had Epicurus and his followers buried in a cemetery of heretics in hell because they "make the soul die when the body dies" [*Inferno* X, 15].) But thinkers of the high Renaissance, while appealing to Stoic models, had begun to detach moral perfection from the social and natural context that had been essential in Stoic ethics. Stoic writings had been popular all through the fifteenth century, but more for style than for content. In the sixteeenth century, however, Stoic philosophy suddenly began to be taken seriously. Epictetus's *Enchiridion* and Seneca's *Letters* became manuals of conduct, while Cicero's writings, formerly models of stylistic elegance, were studied for moral guidance. The Stoa's moral ideal of living in conformity with nature (to which Cleanthes [310–233] had extended Zeno's original principle "living in harmony" [*homologoumenos zèn*]) appealed to the educated, particularly in areas plagued by political turmoil. They favorably contrasted the conception of human nature as essentially good and trustworthy with the late medieval theological pessimism.

Yet Christian Stoics faced a difficult task in attempting to reconcile the Stoic idea of an eternal cosmic order with that of personal responsibility before God, as well as with the Renaissance concept of freedom as self-assertion. How awkward such a reconciliation could become appears in the Flemish humanist Justus Lipsius. In his *De constantia*, he manfully tries to combine the theories of Seneca and Epictetus with the fundamental tenets of the Christian faith. The resulting hybrid is neither Stoic nor Christian nor modern. The ancient *fatum*, now equated with "Providence," determines the chain of earthly events toward its predestined end. Freedom hardly makes a difference in this eternally established order.[17] Such a determinism in the cosmic and social order evidently fell short of what had been part of the Christian's responsibility. It failed even more with respect to the modern ideal of freedom as a transformative creative power. Why, then, did Renaissance thinkers wish to gain the support of an ancient authority that seemed so singularly unattuned to their own views? Part of the answer lies in the need authors of the late Renaissance felt for reattaching their moral individualism to the ancient inclusive idea of nature. Their efforts to do so remained mostly unsuccessful: the very concept of freedom that motivated the enterprise lost its meaning in the attempt to justify it.

Frequently they sacrificed the spirit of Stoic philosophy to the letter of some isolated adages. Thus when Campanella appealed to the Stoic concept of nature in declaring preservation the supreme good for all things ("Conservatio summum bonum est rerum omnium"), he betrayed the ancient meaning. Cicero had indeed held that the general well-being of nature required an instinct of self-protection in the individuals ("a natura datur se ut conservet"). But Campanella's interpretation transformed what had been the goal of nature as a whole (regardless of the individuals) into an exclusively private goal.[18] Inverting the order, he inducted the ancient concept of nature to justify the individual's drive to self-preservation. Hobbes went even further in particularizing that universal goal of nature, as will appear in the next section. More fundamentally, both Hobbes and Campanella, in typically modern fashion, use a teleological concept of nature to support a notion of individual freedom defined by power. The nominalist theology in which this notion originated had declared unconditioned power God's main attribute. Such a view leaves no room for any presumption of teleology in nature as a whole, as it would shackle divine freedom to a goal beyond the self-determining, inscrutable exercise of its power. A radically voluntarist view invalidates the purposiveness held by ancient philosophers in general (with the exception of the Epicureans) and by the Stoics in particular.

Descartes continued to rate "incomprehensible power" as God's primary attribute, translating it in terms of efficient causality—God is *causa sui*. His definition of substance, "a thing that exists in such a way as to depend on no other thing for its existence" (*Principles* I, 52), applies only to one being, the one that bears the name *causa sui*. Descartes did not draw this radical conclusion. He considered mind and corporeal reality to be substances in their own right, albeit with a more limited independence. Spinoza, more consistently, concluded from Descartes's definition of a thing that depends on no other thing that there could be only one substance that, by its very nature, had to be totally independent: "Whatsoever perfection a substance possesses is due to no external cause."[19]

A discussion of Spinoza's conclusion falls beyond the scope of this book, so, let us return to Descartes, through whom the supremacy of the will entered the mainstream of modern thought. Voluntarism strongly influenced his epistemology. For Descartes, the assent is given by the will, and its impulse is, in the final analysis, what drives the mind to truth or prevents it from attaining truth. In a letter of February 9, 1645, Descartes stresses what he calls the *positiva facultas* of the will, which allows it to move not only without evident reasoning but even against reason.[20] Even as God determines his absolute power by a divine decision (*de potentia ordinata*), the will, image of God in its own infinite comprehensiveness, determines itself in the very act of choosing. In the *Meditations* Descartes explicitly compares the will to God's absolute power:

It is only the will or freedom of choice, which I experience within
me to be so great that the idea of any greater faculty is beyond my
grasp; so much so that it is above all in virtue of the will that I
understand myself to bear in some way the image and likeness of
God. For although God's will is incomparably greater than mine,
. . . nevertheless it does not seem any greater than mine when considered as will in the essential and strict sense.[21]

The freedom of the will directly expresses the fact that the mind is an
image of God: it presents the infinite within the finite.

The difficulties Descartes experienced in establishing rules for a
moral system are symptomatic of his predicament in attempting to submit it to any determination but the very act of choosing. That he never
succeeded in surpassing the practical guidelines of the *morale provisoire*
sketched in his early *Discourse on Method* (III)[22] should cause no surprise
in view of the total open-endedness of a will considered independent of
the intellect. Another difficulty arose when he distinguished the *res cogitans* from the *res extensa* as an independent substance. The traditional
rule of ethics—to live in conformity with the whole of nature—becomes
hard to follow when the body is assumed to be an independent substance
subject to the unchangeable laws of a mechanical universe. At that point
the mind has nowhere to turn but to that internal realm where it can
score none but "ideal victories."[23] Not until Kant was moral philosophy
able to detach this inner realm from the closed and fully determined
causal network of the physical universe. As we know, Kant succeeded in
doing so only by restricting the moral act to the intention. His withdrawal
of morality from the physical and social order to the inward domain of
consciousness completed what modern thought had prepared since its
beginning, namely, a privatization of freedom.[24] Once meaning and value
become constituted by a sovereign subject, the source from which morality draws its concrete content dries up. This moral privatization removes the ethical from what for the Greeks had been its center—namely,
political life—and reduces society to an inter-individual, contractual
structure.

Though the split between private morality and social structures did
not fully appear until the end of the eighteenth century, its origins lie in
earlier conceptions of society as a voluntary construction. Social institutions have always been targets for personal ambition. (One need only
think of the candidate emperors in the later Roman Empire and the

machinations at the Byzantine Court.) But political thinkers during Greece's classical age and Rome's republican era as well as during the Middle Ages had been unanimous in granting the community at least a theoretical priority over private interests. For Aristotle, virtue had consisted primarily in habits conducive "to achieve and preserve the good of the community," especially that of the *polis,* the perfect community (the *koinonia teleios*). The *polis* educates and trains individuals as well as morally fulfilling them: it functions both as end and as means. From that perspective, the good of human nature consists in the first place in a common good, and the virtuous life aims, above all, at building and maintaining a good society. "While it is desirable to secure what is good in the case of the individual, to do so in the case of a people or a state is nobler and more divine."[25] This primacy of the common good survived the individualizing tendencies of Hellenistic philosophies. For Stoic philosophy, living virtuously amounted to living in accordance with nature as a whole since "our own natures are parts of the whole" (Chrysippus).[26] A life in accordance with nature meant, for the Stoics, a life in accordance with universal reason, for as Cicero pointed out, reason requires that one measure one's actions by the universal plan of nature.[27]

The Christian doctrine of individual salvation did not substantially weaken the ancient communal ideal after Christianity became accepted as the state religion. In *The City of God* Augustine, turning the tables on those who held Christians responsible for the decay of the empire, attributed its collapse to their lack of civic virtue and concern for the common good. Only truly religious citizens scrupulously observe their obligations toward the political commonwealth. When the Christian society was fully established, a concern for the good of the community became an essential part of justice. Life in a community of virtue once again became the supreme ethical goal, at least in this world, for the commonwealth was subordinated to a higher (but still communal) end in the next one. For Aquinas, the individual ought to serve the community as the part serves the whole: the common good "surpasses the individual good of one person."[28] By applying Aristotle's ideal of the *polis* to society at large, Aquinas shifted the emphasis from participation in the civic affairs of a limited body politic to the maintenance of unity and coherence of the *res publica christiana.* That *res publica christiana,* represented, however imperfectly, a Christian ideal of universal brotherhood to which all particular political structures had to remain subservient. Thus a comprehensive social order ruled the political one. Only after the empire had begun to lose its power, did the cities (especially in Flanders and northern Italy) and later the emerging national states gain full political autonomy.

This reemergence of a genuinely political exchange formed the context in which the Florentine Dominican Remigio de'Girolami wrote the first treatise on the common good (*De bono communi*). He came closer than any medieval thinker before him to reinstating Aristotle's unqualified priority of the civil common good over all others. Christian virtue, according to him, required first and foremost that one be a good citizen. "Homo tenetur pre-amare commune sibi."[29] Only the *civitas* allows individuals to become full persons while the Christian *communitas* prepares the disposition in its members needed for a city to flourish. Fra Remigio's political ideal was revived (mostly without its Christian foundation) by some humanists of early fifteenth-century Florence. Patterning their theories on models of the Roman republic, they declared the good life incomplete as long as its ideals are not politically implemented.[30] Early humanists had revived the debate about the relative merits of public and private life initiated by Cicero when he withdrew from public office, but as the Renaissance progressed, that debate tended to develop into a dual code of ethics. Moral principles, which continued to rule the conduct of private life, gradually lost their authority in political relations. For more extreme thinkers, political virtue came to consist in securing the most effective government by any available means. Here again there was a shift from the law of reason to that of power.

The politics of power, although constantly invoking ancient authorities, undermined in fact the normative authority Greek and Roman political thought had attributed to nature. In the new public discourse civil law, even as divine law in nominalist theology, was assumed to be grounded in the lawgiver's will rather than in any natural order of things. Indeed, the entire political order rested on a positive decision. Legal theories of the fifteenth and sixteenth centuries reduce social structures to individual decisions, deriving the binding quality of law entirely from the authority of lawmaker. By the end of the sixteenth century the hypothesis of individual beings deciding to move into a social state had become widely accepted.[31] Neither the theory of the divine right of kings nor the opposing one of natural rights succeeded in restoring the normative teleology of a human nature conceived as intrinsically social. The former extended divine voluntarism to God's political representative on earth. The latter supported its normative claims by a theory of individual rights that was totally at odds with the earlier social concept of natural law. Modern political thought moved away from the apriori of a social *given* that previously had determined political concepts. The contrast glaringly appears in Machiavelli's idea of the state as a manmade project. But we shall see that even those who continued to uphold a traditional theory of natural law, such as the sixteenth-century Schoolmen Vitoria and Suarez, adopted a voluntarist interpretation of civil law.

A host of conflicting interpretations signals the difficulty of assessing the significance of Machiavelli's theoretical achievement. Part of the confusion stems from the fact that he wrote his two major works with different objectives in mind. The immediate purpose of remedying the political situation of northern Italy in the fifteenth century inspired him to writing *The Prince,* while *Discourses on the First Ten Books of Titus Livius* discloses a more general republican view of the modern state. *The Prince,* then, should be read as a *livre d'occasion,* perhaps an appeal to the Medici to restore public order and political unity in an Italy that had lost the very notion of political freedom and that, in the author's judgment, needed a government with unrestricted powers. Yet Machiavelli knew that drastic measures would not suffice unless the state could count on the devoted support of its citizens as only a genuine republic can. Machiavelli's definitive political message lies in the argument of the *Discourses* in favor of a Roman-style republican government. There can be no doubt, however, that both books establish a wholly new conception of politics. While for Aristotle ethics (of which individual morality formed part) had culminated in civic life, for Machiavelli politics occupied a territory of its own, divorced of morality and ruled by different, often conflicting principles. This disjunction between political power and other duties conflicted as much with Aristotle's ethical ideal as with medieval Christian principles.[32] It isolated political life as an independent realm, subject only to rules of practical efficiency.

More than a philosopher Machiavelli was a technician of statecraft who analyzed the functioning of the state on the basis of historical experience in order to find effective methods for strengthening its authority. Universal principles in his thought fulfill an exclusively instrumental function toward achieving pragmatically defined particular goals. One such principle is that human nature remains essentially identical at all times: ruled by the same passions, obeying the same reflexes, yielding to the same selfish instincts. The stratagems by which men attempt to attain their goals vary, but their inclinations never change. This fundamental stability enables us to learn from history. "Whoever considers the past and present will readily observe that all cities and all peoples are and ever have been animated by the same desires and the same passions; so that it is easy, by diligent study of the past, to foresee what is likely to happen in the future in any republic, and to apply those remedies that were used by the ancients."[33] Of course, different circumstances shape different attitudes.[34] But human nature, according to Machiavelli, has never altered its basic responses to similar circumstances.

Despite this deterministic apriori, Machiavelli proposes a political ideal that requires patriotic virtue in ordinary citizens and practical wisdom as well as unscrupulous determination in political leaders. His description of Cesare Borgia's cunning ruthlessness concludes with a morally disconcerting encomium: "Reviewing thus all the actions of the duke, I find nothing to blame; on the contrary, I feel bound, as I have done, to hold him up as an example to be imitated by all who by fortune and with the arms of others have risen to power."[35] Political leaders ought to avoid practicing Christian virtues: they weaken the strength of the state. The ancients held politically more apposite ideals. "Pagan religion deified only men who had achieved great glory, such as commanders of armies and chiefs of republics, whilst ours glorifies more the humble and contemplative men than the men of action. Our religion, moreover, places the supreme happiness in humility, lowliness, and a contempt for worldly objects. . . . Its principles seem to me to have made men feeble, and caused them to become an easy prey to evil-minded men."[36] Still, underneath Machiavelli's principles of realpolitik lies a concern that links them to Aristotle's ethical ideal. For the Florentine also, the good life is the one spent in a well-run state where qualified citizens participate in the handling of public affairs. Nor does he consider such an ideal unattainable within the limits of our egoist nature. For the selfishness with which humans pursue their private aspirations hides a more profound social instinct. The art of the statesman consists precisely in exploiting the former for the benefit of the latter. In doing that, he elevates his subjects to an ethical state that merits the sacrifice of private ideals.

From Natural Law to Natural Rights

Political philosophers in the sixteenth century were reluctant to embrace such radical principles. Instead they attempted to adjust the ancient theory of natural law to the new, more voluntarist model of society. The natural law doctrine became, in fact, the battleground on which modern

social philosophy struggled to assert its identity. It resulted in a fundamental reinterpretation of that doctrine. Scholastic philosophers claimed
to follow Aquinas's theory but shifted the determinative moment of
natural law from reason to the divine will, thereby changing its meaning.
Others, such as the French jurist Jean Bodin, used the concept of natural
law for justifying what people do naturally: grabbing power by force and
holding onto it by more power. Clearly a novel reality was emerging from
an old idea. That idea had passed through a long and checkered history
before arriving at this latest metamorphosis.

The Stoics had developed Aristotle's normative concept of nature
into an ethics of obligation. When presenting nature's norm as a law, they
stressed the religious sanction, which since Plato had adhered to the norm.
This law was the same in Athens and in Rome, today and tomorrow, for
one and the same divine legislator had issued it in accordance with right
reason.[37] At the basis of all human laws, Cicero writes, lies an eternal
one originating in God's rule of the universe. Roman writers at the end
of the republic distinguished this *lex naturalis* from the *lex civilis*, to
which lawyers later added the customary rules Romans observed in dealing with other nations (the *ius gentium*) as a subspecies either of natural
law or of civil law.[38] After multiple adjustments to Christian doctrine,
Aquinas still basically proposed the classical theory: through natural law
creatures participate in the eternal law by which Providence rules the
universe. Even positive law derives its authority from natural law, having
"just so much of the character of law as it is derived from the law of
nature."[39] The essence of law in this millennial tradition lies in the rule
of reason. Voluntarist theories of the later Middle Ages brought it to a
temporary halt when they transferred the determining factor of legal
authority from that rule of reason to the decision of the lawgiver. While
for Aquinas positive law had been a "determination" of the natural law,
for the voluntarists, positive law became its model. This shift appears in
Calvin all the more clearly since he defines the natural law in traditional
terms. "The law of God which we call the moral law, is no other than a
declaration of natural law, and that of conscience which has been engraven
by God on the minds of men."[40] The natural law remains the law of
reason, yet it is exclusively the divine command—not nature or reason—
that establishes its obligatory character and hence makes the law "law."
"Precisely because the *ordo naturae* has been posited by God, we must
heed it."[41] The "order of nature originally appointed by Him" (*Inst.* I, 16,

3) attracts our attention to God's law yet provides no sufficient motive for a person to lead a righteous life (*Opera*, 2, 203).

An impressive attempt to incorporate the voluntarist notion of natural law within the traditional one was made by Francisco Suarez. In his *De legibus ac Deo legislatore* he purports to follow Aquinas's doctrine and in a substantial way he does. For him also, the natural law is based on reason, insofar as an obligation can be attributed to the natural law only when reason can prove that it is essential to the demands of nature. Yet in the end the function of reason remains purely informative, not legislative. "Although the rational nature is the foundation of the objective goodness of the moral actions of human beings, it may not for that reason be termed law. For the intellect is able merely to point out a necessity existing in the object itself, and if such a necessity does not exist, the intellect cannot impart it; whereas the will endows the object with a necessity which did not formerly characterize it."[42]

Only the intervention of the promulgated *placet* of the lawgiver conveys to a law its obligatory quality. Judgment, for Suarez, "directs" the mind toward the necessity of law, but it does not sanction it as law. Only the lawgiver's decree does so. The Spanish Jesuit avoids the nominalist position according to which God rather than reason may promulgate law, yet the voluntarist element in his thought is undeniable. Both the spirit of his order and the political demands of his age supported it.

Contrary to medieval jurists who had resisted endowing any single political body or person with absolute authority (despite the strenuous efforts of such autocratic popes as Boniface VIII), the advocates of a strong central government in the new national state placed the formally determinative moment of legislation entirely in the sovereign's promulgative act. The obvious analogy between a royal edict and a decree of God's sovereign will is not coincidental: those who supported the latter in the spiritual order were also the ones to promote the former in the temporal one. In his struggle with the Avignon pope, John XXII, the German Emperor Lewis of Bavaria found theoretical support for his polity in an entourage of nominalist theologians. In Suarez's day, champions of the divine right of kings attempted to reassemble that old alliance of theologians and politicians. This time they were less successful. Despite its typically modern identification of the formal element of law with the decision of the lawgiver, the theory of divine right rested too much on a medieval hierarchical transfer of divine power to suit the new worldview.

Suarez attacked the doctrine in *A Defense of the Catholic and Apostolic Faith*, addressed to King James I, its most authoritative promotor. The Jesuit philosopher denied that monarchical decrees are unqualifiedly binding: they are so only on condition that they conform to reason and revelation. But Suarez went further: no person can claim a natural authority over another. Instead he argued that sovereignty, though unlimited within the limits of divine law, originates in the people: political authority derives from the human community. "All men are born free; so that, consequently, no person has political jurisdiction over another person, even as no person has dominion over another."[43] At the same time he insisted that the community becomes politically constituted only "by the will of all who were assembled therein." Before being formed into a political state, the community may be considered either "a kind of aggregation without any order" or a multitude gathered together in one political body by "individual volition or common consent."[44] Once it is in place, however, a political constitution functions like the institution of marriage: partners freely enter it, yet after the contract has been concluded, its binding power surpasses that of the consenting individuals. Similarly, the transfer of sovereignty, once accomplished, cannot be freely revoked by single citizens. Suarez thus strongly supported an absolute monarchy even while remaining the principal adversary of the divine right of kings. Yet he also upheld the right of resistance including, in the extreme case, tyrannicide against a ruler whose government substantially violates divine law. The Spanish philosopher consistently steered a middle course between a preestablished natural hierarchy of authority and a legal positivism. For him, the foundation of political structures lies in the social nature of human beings, though their concrete determination is left to a political contract.

Contrary to most seventeenth- and eighteenth-century theories, Suarez's contract assumes no prepolitical "state of nature" fully endowed with human rights and duties. That so-called natural or imperfect communities (families and private organizations) require the existence of a "perfect community" (the state) for their peaceful survival, does not imply that the imperfect ones precede political society in time as the theorists of the state of nature assumed. Nor are the rights inherent in human nature independent of the actual existence of a civil society. Humans do, indeed, constitute a natural community—Suarez calls it *unum corpus mysticum*—beyond any concrete political government. But for Suarez, this fundamental community does not exist before the state. It is merely what André de Muralt has felicitously called *une communauté de but.*[45] Because humankind is by its very nature oriented toward the realization of a common good, people conclude political contracts.

Though presenting an alternative to early modern political theories, Suarez's doctrine is not free of problems. He avoided the untenable distinction between a presocial state of nature and a subsequent social one, only to stumble into another one that led to the same results. By giving natural law a content independent of any political structure, he created a rift between a natural law based on abstract reason and the political tradition in which it had to find its concrete expression. This typically modern separation between an abstract idea of human nature and a concrete political realization of it opened a space for an area of "human rights" that existed before and independent of any social structure. The separation became far more obvious in those who supported a social contract. They eventually turned the same natural law, which for Suarez defines human life as essentially social, into a presocial moral principle. Suarez himself would never have accepted the individualist conclusions others drew from his abstract concept of nature. For him, human nature is intrinsically social from the start. Nonetheless, soon Suarez's abstract theory of natural law (also held by his confraters Molina and Mariana), came to play an increasingly significant role in the argument that individual human rights have priority over political structures, an argument dissenting French Calvinists, English Catholics, and Puritans used in their resistance to religious laws imposed by an absolute monarchy.[46]

Thomas Hobbes built the priority of the individual with respect to social structures into a consistent political theory. Since the state is based on a contract among individuals, it originates in a prepolitical condition. The question whether such a condition ever historically existed is, as Hobbes pointed out, not vital to the theory. But, historical reality or theoretical postulate, the prepolitical "state of nature" logically precedes and conditions any social institutions by which individuals bind themselves in a concrete choice. In this state of social indeterminacy the will possesses the same absolute right to exercise its freedom as God's absolute power before he determines it to a concrete act.[47] The fact that in the state of nature individuals have unconditioned rights (*jus omnium in omnia* [*Leviathan*, XIV]), shows how strong the voluntarist current runs in Hobbes's thinking. The remarkable thing is that he succeeded in incorporating it in a science of society based on the deductive-mathematical method used in Galilean physics. Rejecting Descartes's sharp separation between mental and physical substance, Hobbes conceived a mechanistic law of nature that included both. But a uniform system of nature cannot tolerate destabilizing drives that threaten to disturb the balance of mechanical forces. To prevent them from having a disruptive effect on his mechanistic universe, Hobbes introduced a stabilizing principle that forces individuals to reenter the system, namely, the fear of death. When self-created chaos becomes a menace to survival, the universal principle of preservation (mechanistically interpreted) takes over.

In Hobbes's theory self-assertion conflicts with self-preservation. Vainglory and unlimited greed endanger the individual's life. In the end the more fundamental drive prevails: the fear of death proves stronger than the strongest passion. Only through the desire to preserve life and the fear of losing it does the inexorable law of nature succeed in bringing divisive individual aspirations under its universal sway. Hobbes carefully avoids introducing any moral obligation into his law. Though he traditionally defines it as "a precept, a general rule, found out by reason" that forbids "to do what is destructive of life . . . and to omit that by which he thinketh it may be best preserved,"[48] he does not regard it as morally normative in the sense in which the natural law had formerly been understood. It imposes no restrictions on the *jus omnium in omnia*, except the biological ones implemented by the instinct of preservation. He thereby appears to have reduced the natural law to a law common to all living things, without the specifically moral quality that had traditionally distinguished the natural law. The will is no more than an integral part of the mechanism of appetite, one that animals share with humans: "the last appetite or aversion immediately adhering to the action, or to the omission thereof" (*Leviathan* I, 6, p. 189).

Notwithstanding his efforts to submit all of nature to uniform forces, Hobbes experienced major difficulty in trying to maintain his laws of nature within a mechanistic frame. This becomes evident in his second law of nature: "That a man be willing, when others are too—to lay down this right to all things; and be contented with so much liberty against other men, as he would allow other men against himself" (*Leviathan* I, 14, p. 190). At this point loopholes appear in the allegedly universal law. Some may be unwilling to abide by this rule. As the mechanistic system breaks down further, he is forced to introduce more moral elements. Since no juridical order exists to enforce the laws of nature, Hobbes declares them to oblige *in foro interno*, that means, "they bind to a desire that they should take place" (*Leviathan* I, 15, p. 215). He continues to insist that this second law and all following ones are not moral laws at all but "dictates of reason" entirely depending on the common instinct of self-preservation: "for they are but Conclusions, or Theoremes concerning what conduceth to the conservation and defence of themselves; whereas Law, properly is the word of him that by right hath command over others" (*Leviathan* I, 15, p. 217). In *De cive*, Hobbes more consistently acknowledged no natural law but only positive divine and human laws. Later British philosophers, beginning with John Locke, attempted to restore a normative, moral meaning to the notion of natural law: the "dictates of reason" may conflict with positive laws. But the more they stressed the norms inherent in an individualist concept of nature, the more they emptied their natural law of any concrete social content. Natural law thus comes to function as a rational basis of prepolitical, individual rights. Political structures remain subordinated to these rights and serve primarily to safeguard them.

In the classical tradition, rights had acquired a normative status only in and through the legal community. For the Romans, *jus* defined not an isolated abstract right but an order established in and through *lex*. Hence the very distinction between law and right on which Hobbes so heavily insists must be considered an innovation.[49] Unquestionably, during the early years of the Roman Empire the political protection of individual freedom had entered into the legal concept of *jus*. (Ulpian declares all men equal with respect to *jus naturale*.) But basically *jus* had remained what is *justum*, in other words, what defines a situation within an essentially social, legal totality. Far from pitting individual claims against a communal order, these claims received their entire support from that order. This tradition persisted through the high Middle Ages. Aquinas has little to say about natural rights as such, because right originates through law, and natural right through natural law. For him also, *jus* concretizes *justum*. "In human affairs a thing is said to be *just* from being right according to the rule of reason. But the first rule of reason is the law of nature."[50] In support of his view that humans exercise a natural right (*jus naturale*) in hunting wild animals he quotes Aristotle's *Politics* that such hunting is "just and natural."[51] He might also have referred to Cicero's Stoic philosophy and to Roman law for defining *jus naturale* in the concrete social conditions of law—civil and, ultimately, natural. Even Suarez and Grotius, who began to distinguish *jus* more clearly from law and often described it as individual right, nevertheless continued to define that right by means of law.[52] Nor did sixteenth-century French and English dissidents in their appeal to a superior justice intend to sever their alleged rights from the social order, but rather to have them incorporated in a less restrictive one based on universal divine principles.[53]

The Dutch jurist Hugo Grotius was among the first to understand the fundamental discrepancy between the idea of natural law and the prevailing voluntarist conceptions of law. Challenging dominant Calvinist theology, he defined it as a "law so unalterable that it cannot be changed by God Himself." Reason rather than the mere will of God had to determine its content. The problem was that reason had changed its meaning. It had lost the concrete social content that it had possessed in the past, as well as the transcendent component that had codefined it for the Stoics no less than for Aquinas.

Looking back at the complex development of political thought at the dawn of the modern age, we notice a shift in the function of law from constituting a realm of right to protecting rights that precede law. Although the right of nature appears limited by the law of nature ("liberty each man hath, to use his own power . . . *for the preservation of his own Life*"), it is left to the individual interpretation to decide what the law of nature demands. Hobbes's theory, then, marks the first major step toward an individualist concept of society. While sixteenth-century Scholastics (Vitoria, Molina, Suarez, Bellarmine) had left only the specifics of political life to a social covenant,[54] for Hobbes that life originates in a decision issued for the protection of individual rights.[55] Yet contrary to later theorists, Hobbes does not equate the common good with a mere convergence of individual interests. The total breach that separates the social state from the state of nature decisively distinguishes the social realm from the inter-individual one. Though the fear of death motivates individuals to enter it, society, once founded, transcends individualist intentions. Moreover, for Hobbes, that entrance remains not a matter of choice (as it is for Locke), but of survival, and hence is demanded by human nature itself. To be subject to such a practical necessity that nature must, at least in principle, be social. Thus via an individualist detour Hobbes rejoined the social interpretation of human nature. Those who later strongly stressed man's social condition, such as Hegel and Marx, found Hobbes's theory far more congenial to their own conception of society than subsequent seventeenth- and eighteenth-centuries theories.[56]

The modern turn to the individual has had equally significant moral consequences. Once the human self becomes detached from its cosmic and transcendent moorings, the good can hardly be more than what Hobbes calls it: "the object of any man's appetite or desire" (*Leviathan* I, 6, p. 120). What previously had given meaning to human life precisely because it surpassed individual aspirations, now came to be conceived in terms of personal need or fulfillment. Isolated from the totality from which it drew its very content, the self had nowhere to turn but to itself. Hobbes, conscious of the problems of such an isolation, attempted to incorporate that self within a single system of nature, but his mechanistic view deprived that system from the kind of teleology indispensable to any genuine morality.

It is difficult to avoid the conclusion that modern culture failed in morally justifying itself. Few of its representative thinkers succeeded in construing a coherent theory of responsible action. Bacon promised a moral system but never produced one. The same is true of Descartes. (Even that latter-day Cartesian Sartre in the end had to abandon the project of writing a philosophical ethics.) The problem directly followed from the disintegration of that all-comprehensive synthesis against which humans had been wont to measure their actions and choices. Once the bond with the whole was broken, the self became sundered from the source of moral content. This loss of content turned ethics into a subjective—though not necessarily a private—concern.

Plato had placed the Good beyond Being because only when perfected through goodness does Being attain completeness. Ontological completeness was the principal quality of the good, and its attainment the ultimate good of ethics, as Proclus had stated: "Completeness is a part of the Good, and the complete (*to teleion*) *qua* complete imitates the Good."[57] As science of the good, ethics had always been more than a concern about human perfection. Almost from the beginning it had occupied the center of an all-inclusive ontology. But when modern thought reduced the good to personal or social perfection, independently of and occasionally in opposition to the whole, it deprived it of ontological depth and marginalized morality with respect to the totality of Being. Few modern thinkers avoided the pitfall of severing the person as creative principle from the rest of nature. Spinoza stands out among those few. Fully accepting the responsibility modern culture had laid upon the person, he all the more stressed the need to maintain the bond with the totality of nature. Alone in modern philosophy, the Dutch thinker reintegrated ethics with ontology. For him, the *conatus* to the good was nature's own *conatus*. Unfortunately, the lack of a subjective dimension in his conception of nature prevented his *Ethics* from providing the moral synthesis demanded by modern culture. Yet his may well have been the most radical attempt to restore ethics to its central metaphysical position.

Chapter 6

The Birth of the Past

The Shaping of Destiny

The modern age was the first to distinguish itself from all others by a time indicator: *modo*—"now." Anxious to assert its superiority to past epochs, its culture exchanged the older claim of upholding a tradition for the one of surpassing it. A different sense of time directly followed the new sense of freedom. An unprecedented awareness grew that what humans accomplish in the transitoriness of time definitively changes the very nature of human life. History thereby suddenly acquired an existential significance that it had not possessed before. In a medieval cosmic play the human person clearly had the lead, but an all-knowing, unchanging God directed the play. The outcome remained predictable and hardly varied from one period to another. Once the temporal actor with limited foresight became director, however, the outcome ceased to be certain and the passage of time took on a far more dramatic character. The new role assumed a tragic character insofar as humans must shape their own future, however inadequately equipped and poorly enlightened they may be.

Paradoxically, the modern orientation toward the future created a more acute awareness of the past. Schelling clearly understood that: "The man who has not conquered himself has no past, or rather, never comes out of it, lives continually in it."[1] Formerly the past had principally functioned as a source of meaning to the present: unless the transient *now* could find a stable basis of permanence in the unchangeable past, it was considered to remain devoid of lasting sense. Hence the archaic need to attach each significant action in the present to a specific event or person in the past. (Thus Genesis [4:20–21] describes Jabal, Lamech's son, as "the ancestor of those who live in tents as shepherds" and his brother Jubal as "the ancestor of all who play the lyre and pipe.") In Plato's doctrine of recollection the remembered past is the entrance gate to the true, eternal present. Analogously the Church conveys a supernatural meaning to the present through a ritual reenactment of the past events of salvation. In modern thought the past serves a different purpose: to legitimate human efforts toward shaping the future. To achieve that purpose fully, the past had to be understood as irreversibly past,[2] rather than as a *magistra vitae* that instructs its pupils in the unchanging laws of life. While in the former view history appears infinitely repeatable, in the latter each period presents itself as irreducibly different. The great historian Troeltsch regarded such an awareness of the past the distinguishing mark of modern culture. Classical and medieval writers felt no need to contrast their age as radically to previous epochs as we "moderns" do.

The term *modern* had been current long before the epoch to which it gave its name. In Gelasius's *Epistulae Pontificum* (494/95) it refers to those who wrote after the church fathers. At the end of the Middle Ages it acquired a certain popularity in expressions as the *via moderna* in philosophy (referring to nominalist philosophy) or the *devotio moderna* (the religious life lived outside the monastery in common circumstances), but it never denoted an entire epoch. With the early humanists the terms *modernus* and *modernitas* assume a different meaning. Although they felt in many respects part of an unbroken tradition, they could not but become aware of the difference between the classical period and their own time. As they compared the qualities and deficiencies of their epoch with those of classical antiquity, a new historical consciousness broke through. Around 1400 Salutati refers to his own epoch as "modernitas" to distinguish it from antiquity. The historical awareness introduced by this particular distinction eventually resulted in a comprehensive understanding of the entire past as different. Not until the nineteenth century, however, did the present come to be regarded as a historical moment, as transient as all earlier ones.[3] We should, of course, beware of explaining the new attitude toward the past as a purely ideal phenomenon. There had been an experience of difference after the depopulation caused by the black plague and the disintegration of social structures, the decline of the empire and the emergence of the national states, the gradual rediscovery of ancient culture and the beginnings of a new science. But, at least for the humanists, the contrast between their own form-creative activity and what they considered a previous state of formlessness constituted a decisive factor of novelty.

Of course, systematic reflection on the past did not begin with the modern age. None of its historians equalled the intellectual stature of Thucydides. Even Herodotus, the "fabulator," states the intellectual seriousness of his intentions in the preface to his *Historiae:* "This is the record of an inquiry by Herodotus of Halicarnassus, set forth in order that what is remembered by men may not be obliterated by the lapse of time, that past and wonderful deeds performed by Hellenes and barbarians may not remain unrenowned, and in particular the reason why they made war against each other." His combination of dramatic encounters and spellbinding stories differs considerably from our critical investigations of the past. Nevertheless, a concern with causal explanation guided his narrative as it guided that of all ancient historians. The critical methods of Hellenistic and Roman historians were rarely surpassed before the eighteenth century. Nor did the so-called cyclical view of history prevent Greek and Roman historians from attaching a unique significance to the events they described. History may follow a returning pattern, but the memorable deeds accomplished in it were never to be repeated. They transcended the cycles within which they took place. That is why they needed to be preserved for posterity.[4]

Plato ranks the achievements of the human race on scales of progress and decline. Such ranking had existed since Hesiod, but the Greeks had been unable to agree on the direction history followed—forward or backward. In his story of Prometheus Hesiod appears to admit some progress through culture. But elsewhere he describes the decline from an age of gold to one of silver then further down to bronze and iron. Not until the Sophists do we find the kind of rectilinear progress, based on an increase in knowledge transmitted from one generation to the next, that was later resumed by the Enlightenment. Also, Stoic thought allowed for progress within the great cosmic year, the long period between the occurrence of identical astronomical conditions. Still, the cyclical view of time influenced the Greeks and Romans of the classical age in thinking that humans might learn from history when similar conditions would inevitably return.

For Christians, the totally unrepeatable event of the Incarnation decisively divided all cycles and successions of history. In principle the meridian line Christians drew between the periods B.C. and A.D. should have changed the direction of the course of history. The former were ages of darkness; the latter of light. Yet as we learn from *The City of God* as well as from St. Jerome's commentary on Daniel, a single providential destiny united all ages. The medieval mind may have had what Philip Ariès has called "a passionate concern for the past," but, at least in the beginning, a certain indifference toward past events not directly related to salvation blended out the specific distinctness of epochs and civilizations. Even Dante, who stands at the dawn of a new age, treated the classical past as if he had been contemporary to it. In the attitude of "temporal ease" typical of medieval culture, the succession of time played no critical part.[5]

With Petrarch the scene began to change, though in a somewhat surprising way. In his *Res memorandae* he asserts that he stands with one foot in one era and with the other in the next one, yet he does not refer to the Middle Ages on the one side and the new epoch on the other. He merely suggests that he is the last one to keep the memory of the ancients alive: after his death full darkness will fall over their culture. On the other hand, it was also Petrarch who reversed the traditional Christian distinction between "ages of darkness" and "ages of light." In a letter written in 1359 he refers to the centuries following the beginning of the Roman Empire as a period of *tenebrae*. From other writings (especially from his epic *Africa*) it appears that "darkness" here means decline. Occasionally he expresses a flickering hope that the darkness may be dispelled and our descendants regain the ancient realm of light. (Potuerunt discussis forte tenebris ad purum priscumque inbar remeare nepotes. *Africa* IX, 456–57.) This reversal breaks up the relatively homogeneous Christian view of history. Still, Thomas M. Greene cautions not to exaggerate the significance of this historical insight. "To say that Petrarch 'discovered' history means, in effect, that he was the first to notice that classical antiquity was very different from his own medieval world, and the first to consider antiquity more admirable. . . . [H]e recognized the possibility of a cultural alternative."[6] The present displeased him, and he would have preferred to live in the Roman republic. But at least the

dialogue with the ancients, through their works and through his letters
to them, enabled him to spend time in that alternative culture.

Nevertheless, Petrarch strongly reproved those fatalists who considered the decline of his own age irremediable. No invariable fate predestines one epoch to surpass another. As he writes to King Robert of Sicily
(*Fam.* IV, 7), he trusted to be able to emulate the ancients and if others
were to follow him, a new classical era might begin. According to Petrarch
each age may attain its own artistic greatness, endowed as it is with its
specific potential. At least in that respect all ages are equal, though their
creative powers differ. Later humanists, partly through Petrarch's example, were confident that they were restoring the continuity with the
classical age, but before Valla and Erasmus the awareness that the passage
of time from one epoch to another constitutes an irreversible, ontological
difference was virtually absent. As time went on, some became increasingly aware of specific differences between their humanist Christian culture and pagan antiquity, but even they failed to perceive each epoch as
unique and irreversible. Without contingent interferences culture would
have remained what it was for the Romans or the Greeks. Their wisdom
had never changed: it was eternal and only needed to be retrieved. Nothing
of deep concern to men and women of antiquity had lost its vitality: "no
language they have spoken, no oracle beside which they have hushed
their voices, no dream which has once been entertained by actual human
minds, nothing about which they have ever been passionate, or expended
time and zeal."[7]

When they turned to the history of their own time, fifteenth-century
humanists focused not so much on change and innovation as on finding
the right models for telling an essentially unchanging story. These were
obviously the ancient ones—as we see in the chancellors Bruni and Poggio
and later in Machiavelli and Guicciardini. Since human nature was assumed to remain unchanged, Renaissance interest in the past had rarely
moved beyond the ancient idea of history as *magistra vitae*. As Machiavelli puts it:

> The wise are wont to say, and not without reason or at random,
> that he who would forecast what is about to happen should look at
> what has been; since all human events, whether present or to
> come, have their exact counterpart in the past. And this, because
> these events are brought about by men, whose passions and disposi-
> tions remaining in all ages the same naturally give rise to the same

effects; although doubtless, the operation of these causes takes a higher form, now in one province now in another, according to the character of the training wherein the inhabitants of these provinces acquire their way of life (*Discourses* III, 43).

Moreover, for Machiavelli, as for some other writers of the Renaissance, events follow a sequence determined by invariable cosmic motions. In the preface to the *Discourses* he attributes the order and power of history to the planets and the elements. Some kind of invisible fate, which Machiavelli calls "Providence," watches over the cycles and secures their return to the point of departure. Even the development of religion follows the steady course of the cosmos.[8]

As the awareness of the self's creative power increased, the perception of history began to change. The new mode of writing history may well have contributed to this change. Once historiography became part of humanist rhetoric, the creative arrangement of events resulted in a sense of control over the subject matter.[9] Historians selected what they considered essential in a formless mass of events and ordered them in a pattern of their own making. Thus through the rhetoric of history the Renaissance chronicler discovered what Wilhelm von Humboldt later described as the creative art of the historian: "The manifestations of an event are scattered, disjointed, isolated . . . The truth of any event is predicated on the addition of that invisible part of every fact, and it is this part, therefore, which the historian has to add. Regarded in this way, he becomes active, even creative."[10] The Renaissance experience of writing history contributed toward the awareness that humans may, within the limits set by an unchanging nature and an invariable course of cosmic motions, affect history.

Obviously the process of historical form-giving alone would not have resulted in a different perception of the past and future had it not been accompanied by a more general awareness that humans shape their own destiny. Far more than their ancestors, prominent men and women of the Renaissance appear to have felt that freedom challenged them to shape their own lives in the short time granted them for doing so.[11] The classical ideal of fame regained its ancient status without being tempered by the Christian virtue of humility or by the ancient fear of defying the eternally established order of things. Politicians, artists, and poets of the high Renaissance acted, created, and wrote with a confidence in their own powers that shifted the direction of existence from the past to the future.

While pursuing their projects they also shaped their own lives. Destiny increasingly became what the free agent was able to accomplish in time. The *modo* of the moderns was not merely an epochal denominator: it also laid the accent on the now of this life. Though freedom experiences the full weight of responsibility in the present, it is the future that directs its exercise.

This orientation toward the future had been precedented by the eschatological movements of the late Middle Ages. On the basis of the apocalyptic theology of the twelfth-century abbot Joachim de Fiore they expected a third and final period in the history of this world dominated by the Holy Spirit after the reigns of the Father (before the Incarnation) and of the Son.[12] According to the spiritual Franciscans (especially the radical Fraticelli), the kingdom of God would be established within history (rather than beyond), and its coming would be accelerated by the observance of absolute poverty. What distinguished the future of the Renaissance was that it would be entirely the outcome of man's form-giving activity. Its eschatological hopes consisted of utopian projections of human power.

Thomas More's *Utopia* (1516), which gave the genre its name and continued to serve as general model, proposes a radical transformation of society by human fiat. More's ideal city, Habermas has noted, shares one major feature with Machiavelli's proposals—namely, that *we* must first establish the social conditions wherein citizens may realize their human potential and their moral ideals. "Virtue and happiness as such are here [in *Utopia*] conceived in the traditional manner; but what is modern is the thesis that the technically appropriate organization to meet the necessities of life, the correct institutional reproduction of society, is prior to the good life, without these in themselves representing the content and the goal of moral action."[13] In preparing the "correct" institutions, however, *Utopia* moves in the opposite direction of *The Prince*, namely, toward the removal (rather than the strengthening) of the social dominance of the few over the many. By abolishing the institution of private property the utopian kingdom seeks to prevent the unrestrained accumulation of goods, the basis of social privilege and power. More's utopians want to suppress "the conspiracy of the rich" who seek their own advantage under the name of the common good.[14]

Bacon's *New Atlantis* and Tommasso Campanella's *City of the Sun* (1623) turn this practical preparation of life in Utopia into a technical project. Bacon's *Atlantis* will be discussed in the next section. Campanella introduced a new functionary to society, one who was to stay and who would not gain full power until the political experiments of the twentieth century, namely, the social engineer. An enlightened despot, astrologist by profession, had to approve or reject public and private projects according to the position of the stars. He would assign people their place in society and, if necessary, reform them to fit preestablished rational patterns. Campanella's sun city rests on the principle (already implicit in More) that human beings must assume full control over their social destiny. Society functions as a technical-scientific artifact designed for achieving preconceived goals.[15] Unlike the religious visions of Joachim and the Fraticelli, Bacon's and Campanella's scientific world schemes require no successive stages for introducing the end of history. They bypass the period of extreme distress that in the apocalyptic literature preceded the final triumph. For them technical innovations would directly lead to a social paradise. The many utopias introduce a vision of history in which destiny would be controlled by human agents.

The Seeds of Progress

Whenever human action shapes the future, the idea of history as indefinite progress logically follows. But to render progress acceptable the new must justify itself before the authority of the past or invalidate that authority altogether. The early humanists viewed their work as a restoration of a remote past. As late as the seventeenth century European thinkers claimed to be returning to an older philosophy or theology. The justification of the new through the old had begun in the Proto-Renaissance of the twelfth century. The superiority of the achievements of the ancients was not to be questioned, yet younger generations, having inherited their achievements as well as all succeeding ones, enjoyed an additional advantage. Thus originated the famous analogy of the present dwarfs standing on the shoulders of the ancient giants. Although they were of lesser stature, the descendants received the entire wisdom of the classics while enriching it by their own experience. Posterity reaps what its ancestors sowed. *Quanto juniores, tanto perspicaciores.* The younger, the wiser! Similarly, the early humanists sought their own literary, aesthetic, and often their political models in a remote past. Renaissance hermeticists all reclaimed a *prisca theologia.* Even the iconoclastic Bruno invoked the support of a more ancient (that is, pre-Aristotelian) philosophy for his radically modern theories. Descartes himself called his revolutionary philosophy "omnium antiquissimam."[16] The superiority of the ancients might never have been questioned had it not been for the uniqueness of the Christian faith.

When the older Salutati had praised Petrarch as exceeding Seneca in style and Cicero in depth,[17] the "classicist" Poggio replied that no modern writer, least of all Petrarch, could approach, much less surpass, Cicero's literary qualities. In defending his position against Poggio's attack, Salutati invoked the superiority of Christian wisdom over ancient learning. "Not only Petrarch, but anyone else less than moderately learned, in our time surpasses the pagans Cicero, Varro, and all Romans, Aristotle, Plato, and literally all of Greece by the benefit and the doctrine of the Christian faith."[18] But then Salutati extended his argument beyond its theological limits: knowledge increases with time in a manner that would apply to the ancients themselves. All thinkers profit from the work of their predecessors! "Why do you and others, so enamored with Antiquity, estimate Plato and Aristotle more than those original, very ancient men? Do you not know that what they wrote or what they left us in writing, they had received from their predecessors? Little of what we praise in them could they claim as their own."[19] Thus the idea that by imitating and emulating ancient models we surpass them took root two hundred years before the famous *Querelle des anciens et des modernes*. The superiority of Christian doctrine, though not universally accepted (compare Machiavelli!), provided the original support for an ideology of historical progress.

It did not remain the only one. The justification of new political conditions would soon play an equally decisive role. Already the classicists Poggio and Bruni had selected their models in accordance with the conditions of their own time; they favored republican heroes (Brutus) over the imperial ones (Caesar and August) whom Dante's generation had preferred.[20] But after the national state emerged in France, Spain, and England, no appropriate ancient models were available. The new politics required rules other than those of the Greek city or the Roman Empire. That situation prompted a group of French jurists during the second half of the sixteenth century to abandon the search for historical precedents in antiquity and to justify their political government by contrasting it with all previous forms. The nationalist historians ridiculed the admiration of ancient and even biblical models.[21] Jean Bodin, the most influential among them, attacked the principle of historical decline both in its classical (Hesiod and Ovid) and its Hebrew (the declining empires in Dan. 2:36–40) versions. "In comparison with the present," he claims, "the so-called Golden Age may well appear to be an Iron Age." The Greeks, by the testimony of their own historians, were no more than savages, pirates, and brigands. "There you have your famous centuries of gold and silver. Men lived dispersed in the fields and forests like wild beasts, and had no private property except that which they could hang on to by force and crime: it has taken a long time to pull them away from this savage and barbarous way of life and to accustom them to civilized behavior and to a well-regulated society such as we now have everywhere."[22] Bodin's verdict on the patriarchs is equally severe. Behavior such as what the Bible reports of Cham, Lot, and Nimrod would simply not be tolerated today. Not only are our morals, customs, and laws superior to those of the ancients, but even our knowledge surpasses theirs. Ancient culture has nothing to measure with the mariner's compass, the discovery of the New World, the technology of modern crafts and warfare. Bodin admitted the existence of periods of decline, but for the new political structures of his time and, even more, for its science and technology, he felt only unqualified enthusiasm.

The assumption of an original state of harmony was too well established in classical and biblical sources, however, to be easily supplanted by the expectation of an uncertain future. The idea of unqualified progress required a more positive argument. Bacon provided it by projecting the past Golden Age into an anticipated future. According to the *Advancement of Learning,* true antiquity lies in the world to come—*Antiquitas saeculi juventus mundi.* The utopias that originally had carried a social message about the future were by the end of the sixteenth century interpreted as holding a scientific promise. Bacon explicitly supported his scientific utopianism by a prophecy of Daniel about the end of time:

> As all knowledge appears to be a plant of God's own planting, so it may seem the spreading and flourishing or at least the bearing and fructifying of this plant, by a providence of God, nay not only by a general providence but by a special prophecy, was appointed to this autumn of the world: for to my understanding it is not violent to the letter, and safe not after the event, so to interpret that place in the prophecy of Daniel where speaking of the latter times it is said, "Many shall pass to and fro, and science shall be increased" [Dan. 12:4]; as if the opening of the world by navigation and commerce and the further discovery of knowledge should meet in one time and age.[23]

In *The New Atlantis* Bacon builds his utopian predictions upon the recovery of a secret ancient knowledge—Egyptian and Chaldean—to which
the Bible cryptically alludes in the report of Solomon's wisdom.[24] In thus
leaping across history toward a more ancient past, Bacon uses the myth
of the Golden Age to justify its prophesy of the future. It was, of course,
an old strategy, known since Virgil's Fourth Eclogue, to transport the
aurea saecula toward the future as a restauration of the remote past.[25]

What distinguished Bacon's use of the restauration metaphor was his
attempt to give it a biblical foundation. This was considerably complicated by the fact that according to the Bible, and especially according to
Paul's interpretation of the fall, the world's condition had deteriorated in
the wake of an original sin. In view of the Reformation's increased emphasis on the corruption of nature, it is surprising that Bacon expects the
realization of his biblical prophecy to become possible through the purified religion of the Protestant age. As for the authority of classical antiquity, he follows the usual pattern: conceding the superior genius of the
ancients but neutralizing it by Bernard of Chartres's thesis of cumulative
experience. Progress requires that we acquaint ourselves with the classical
heritage, but having done so, we may consider ourselves the true ancients.
"For the old age of the world is to be accounted the true antiquity; and
this is the attribute of our own times, not of that earlier age of the world
in which the ancients lived; and which though in respect of us it was the
elder, yet in respect of the world it was the younger."[26] So, rather than
idolizing the ancients, as he felt the humanists had done, we should move
beyond them. The title page of Bacon's *Instauratio Magna* (1620) presents
Odysseus sailing past the Pillars of Hercules, the boundaries of ancient
venturesomeness. Those who had recently circumnavigated the earth had
passed the ne plus ultra of antiquity. "[T]hese times may justly bear in
their motto—*plus ultra*—further yet—in precedence of the ancient *non
ultra*—no further."[27]

Bacon's biblically founded theory of progress richly germinated in
Puritan soil, and by the middle of the seventeenth century his concept of
progress through applied science had become well established in England.
Thus Joseph Glanvill, an Anglican clergyman, in a work published under
the Baconian title *Plus ultra or the Progress and Advancement of Knowledge Since the Days of Aristotle* (1668), intensified Bodin's criticism of
the ancients and estimated the inventor of the compass worth "a thousand
Alexanders and Caesars or ten times the number of Aristotles."[28] A unique
combination of technical utilitarianism and biblical eschatology sup-

ported those surprising assessments. The contrast between the enthu-
siastic Puritan support for the scientific movement and Galileo's unhappy
experience with the ecclesiastical authorities reveals the presence of two
opposing currents in Christian thought. One, dominant in the Catholic
church and, to a lesser extent, in established Protestant churches, tended
to preserve the tradition. The other, mainly prevalent among nonesta-
blished groups and heir to some of the eschatological inspiration of the
late Middle Ages, supported a clearly progressive view of history based
on a scientific control of the natural world.

The concept of progress, which came with modern science and depended on it for its realization, is by its very nature unlimited. However
advanced we imagine scientific progress to be at any point in the future,
it remains always capable of further perfection. It directs its project toward
a concrete, historical goal attainable in time yet implicitly denies that it
can ever be reached. On this point the scientific ideal of progress differed
from the eschatology to which it owed much of its original inspiration.
We have seen how Bacon presented his vision of a scientific future as the
fulfillment of a biblical prophecy and thereby secured its success among British Puritans. In fact, however, the scientific movement and its concomitant idea of progress was also, and increasingly more, propelled by a quite
different factor that eventually replaced that original religious motivation.
The scientific-technical conception of the future essentially differed from
that of biblical eschatology. Unlike the apocalyptic future, which would
violently interrupt the passage of time and bring history to a close, the
modern future appeared as the endlessly postponed terminus of a continuing history. Biblical eschatology posited a beginning of time in creation and a transcendent irruption at the end. As the scientific future
gradually came to be viewed as entirely achievable by human endeavor,
it required an understanding of history from within time. The causes of
all phenomena lie in time and so do their results. In the Jewish and
Christian view, on the contrary, the origin of all temporal things lies
beyond time and all temporal causes function only as secondary ones.
History is enclosed within a transhistorical eternity at both its beginning
and its end. But where history becomes an autonomous human achievement in time, no such transcendent limits can be set. Its momentum
alone carries it into the future, albeit an indefinite future. As the idea of
progress became secularized (which did not occur until the second half of
the seventeenth century) the orientation toward the future became ever
more exclusive until it resulted in what Peter Berger has described as the

contemporary reversal of time. "Modernization everywhere means a powerful shift in attention from past and present to the future. What is more,
the temporality within which this future is conceived is of a very peculiar
kind—it is precise, measurable, and, at least in principle, subject to human
control. In short, it is time to be mastered."[29] The men and women of
the sixteenth century remained, of course, wholly unacquainted with the
"precise, measurable" time with which we are so familiar—though Campanella and Bacon might have surmised what Berger meant. But once the
priority of the future over the past and present became normative, the
distance that separated future realization from present anticipation assumed a crucial significance: it had to be counted and, wherever possible,
to be shortened.

The one-directional move toward the future required a constant reinterpretation of the past. Often the past merely served as a foil for justifying
the chosen course toward the future: either the past falls short of that
vision and thus invites change, or it already anticipates the future. A clear
case of legitimating the future are the early modern idealizations of the
Roman republic as a model for contemporary political objectives. The
idea that each period of history legitimates itself and must be judged on
its own merits, independently of its relation to others, is virtually absent
from early modern thought.[30] Not until Vico and Herder introduced the
organic concept of societies and civilizations did the interpretation of the
past through a projected future begin to wither. Before that time, period-
izations of history served hardly any other purpose than that of classifying
epochs according to their relation to a prospective future. In our own age
the idea of progress, however much qualified, still continues to deprive
past periods of their autonomy in such expressions as "premodern," "pre-
capitalist," or "prescientific" epochs.

But what, in light of this new historicism, are we to make of those
early seventeenth-century philosophers for whom historical time appears
to have counted very little? Intent on establishing a timeless and universal
truth they resisted wasting precious time on the study of a past which
had failed to attain that truth. In the *Discourse* Descartes cautions against
expecting much insight from the study of history. "For conversing with
those of past centuries is much the same as travelling. . . . One who
spends too much time travelling eventually becomes a stranger in his
own country; and when one is too curious about the practices of past
ages one usually remains quite ignorant about those of the present."[31] It
is tempting to attribute this remark to a personal prejudice in favor of

analytic and deductive knowledge, but Descartes's judgment is derived from his very notion of truth. If science consists of necessary knowledge, it can learn nothing from the contingent facts of history. This conclusion, stated in Descartes's third rule, induced his follower Nicholas Malebranche to separate genuine science from those "simples connaissances qui s'acquièrent sans aucun discours de raison, comme les langues, l'histoire."[32] This opposition between historical and scientific truth was the very thesis that Vico attacked as the fundamental error of Cartesian thought.

If such a prominent thinker as Descartes considered the historical factor negligible in the pursuit of scientific knowledge, what justifies us to speak of a more intense awareness of time as characteristic of the modern age? The paradox vanishes when we realize that such a dismissal of the tradition could only originate in a new attitude toward the past. Cartesian philosophy dispenses with the need for grounding doctrine on ancient authority. Except in moral matters, tradition ceases to be normative. Such a deliberate dismissal of the past presupposes a particular view of history. As David Lachterman accurately observed: "If Descartes lacked the 'historical sense' it is because he was busy inventing history in what becomes at least one of its primary modern senses: history namely as something of man's making, and thus potentially at his disposal."[33] The rationalist principles of knowledge eventually found their way to the study of history itself. The succession of events had to be interpreted exclusively by laws of efficient causality while teleological considerations ought to be discarded altogether. Hobbes first attempted to apply this principle consistently, but his pessimistic opinion of human nature forced him to admit that human beings behave more erratically than a mechanistic drive toward self-preservation allows. To render his description of the state of nature as one of perpetual warfare plausible, he had to introduce additional, less determinist principles. The great historians of the eighteenth century—Hume, Voltaire, Gibbon—fortunately for us, were to be even less consistent in applying the mechanistic dogma to which they occasionally paid lip service.

The atemporal rationalist view of the real did not succeed in slowing down the growth of an historical awareness. But the same cannot be said of its effect upon the inner time consciousness. Christian culture in fostering personal devotion had developed a sensitivity for the mind's inner duration. Nowhere does this appear more clearly than in Augustine's *Confessions*. If God's eternal Word was born in time, "secundum

tempus . . . natus est" (*Confessions* VII, 9, 14), the eternal human soul
has a duration of its own.[34] The famous voyage through memory in Book
X of the *Confessions* explores an inner time consciousness that relates a
succession of experiences to the spiritual soul's permanent core. Early
humanists revived this Augustinian idea for the self's duration. For Petrarch and Valla the self followed its own course, one that was not reduc-
ible to the objective events of history. Montaigne's introspection
spontaneously assumes the form of a narrative for describing what he
calls "l'histoire de ma vie" (*Essais* II, 9). This personal history follows
laws that remain independent of objective circumstances.

Descartes appears at first to have envisaged a similar road. In the
Discourse he describes his quest as "une histoire, ou si vous voulez mieux,
. . . une fable en laquelle, parmi quelques examples qu'on peut imiter, on
trouvera aussi plusieurs autres qu'on aura raison de ne pas suivre" (a
history, or, if you prefer, a fable in which, amongst certain things which
may be imitated, there are possibly others also which it would not be
right to follow).[35] In 1628 his friend Balzac had invited Descartes to write
"l'histoire de votre esprit, . . . le chemin que vous avez tenu,"[36] but as
the French philosopher came to draw more and more universal conclusions from his private history, he increasingly disregarded the self's particularity, moving closer to what Kant would later call a transcendental
subject—universal but devoid of a content of its own.

As modern thought turned this subject evermore into a meaning-
giving function, the sense of internal duration yielded to an objective time
consciousness. The self's outward orientation extenuated its sense of
inner identity, reducing it virtually to a connecting link among successive
and wholly contingent experiences. But precisely the inner time consciousness gives structure and meaning to existence. Its loss results in a
feeling of moral futility. Humans find it hard to live merely from one
moment to another without inner continuity, and they have consistently
tried to protect themselves against such a dissipation.[37] Reduced to a
stream that never pauses, the self becomes a flight from a vanishing
center, a ceaseless pursuit of an ever-escaping future. Only a strong sense
of identity accompanied by an awareness of inner duration can protect
the self against becoming dispersed in its extroverted, objectifying activity. Instead, that sense has constantly weakened, and the loss of an
interior life is one of the main factors responsible for modern man's "small
soul."

Time and Being: A General Conclusion

Moderns view reality through the prism of freedom and historicity. Since the beginning of systematic thinking in the West, mind had been a unique but integral component of Being. According to Plato's *Phaedrus*, all cosmic motion originates in self-movement, that is, in the soul's movement. Plotinus confirmed this metaphysical union of cosmos and soul when he defined both mind and soul as essential constituents of all reality. Astrology, alchemy, and magic, as well as the doctrine of a world soul, testify to the continued belief of later ages that soul and cosmos move in harmony. With the modern epoch their relation began to change. Viewed as a transforming agent, mind came to be conceived as a dividing principle that causes a rupture in Being. The idea was not entirely new. Some *Upanishads*, the sacred writings of India composed between the eighth and the sixth century B.C., had already suggested the existence of such a split. But in modern culture Being itself became a project for the mind. What previously had been the very substance of the real now provided merely the material to recreate it. With it came a shift in the meaning of time. Whereas the ontological center of gravity had once lain in the past— to be was what had been (still echoed in Hegel's *Wesen ist was gewesen ist*)—it was now transferred to the future: to be became what must and will be realized. The reversal was complete when the self came to view itself as a meaning-giving subject that constitutes the real as object.

After the momentous break-up of the original metaphysical unity, modern philosophy experienced major difficulties in defining the relation between mind and world. Occasionally monist systems replaced the original dualist ones, reducing one to the other: materialism equated mind with matter, idealism matter with mind. Until the nineteenth century, philosophy failed to address the fundamental ontological question raised by the self's new position with respect to other reality. Reflection continued to be guided by the ancient principle expressed in Parmenides's axiom: Being is and becoming is not. In conflict with a cultural *praxis* that focused entirely on what is not yet and, indeed, with its own idea of a meaning-giving subject, philosophy persisted in viewing the real fully established.

At the same time modern philosophy discarded the metaphysics from which it derived its own static presupposition. As it attributed the origin of meaning to the knowing subject, it replaced the ancient metaphysical question—Why is there Being at all?—with the epistemological one—

How do I know what is? Epistemology became a substitute for metaphysics. It failed to address the fundamental ontological questions raised by the new function of the subject: How does that subject's constitution of meaning and value affect the very nature of the real? Early modern philosophy failed to pose the questions that its own contributions (specifically, its definition of the self as subject) and that of the entire culture had made inevitable.

Before Kant, Fichte, Hegel, and Schopenhauer, the ontological significance of the new experience of creative subjectivity remained unattended. Freedom just appeared an odd fact among others. Most thinkers neglected to address even the immediate problem, how free choice is possible in a causally closed mechanistic universe. To do so would have forced them to confront the ontological question, how freedom succeeds in opening a space in the compactness of Being. Without addressing that question, philosophy could not hope to justify the unprecedented theoretical and practical significance it had granted to the subject. Yet rationalist as well as empiricist discussions of freedom persisted in ignoring the metaphysical issue implicit in their claims.

When Hegel later attempted to incorporate the modern experience of subjectivity within a classical style ontology, he found the traditional notion of Being no longer adequate. That notion had become too exclusively linked with the category of substance to continue designating reality in the process of being transformed by human thought and action. Hegel attempted to integrate subjectivity with substantiality by shifting ontological ultimacy from the idea of Being to that of Spirit. Critics have questioned whether an idea so closely associated with mental life was sufficiently comprehensive to include substance and subject without reducing the former to the latter. Others have wondered whether Hegel's Spirit preserves the transcendent dimension characteristic of ontotheology. A discussion of these objections falls beyond the scope of this book,[38] but the problem of transcendence remains a vital one to any metaphysical discussion of freedom. Not surprisingly, the static rationalist philosophy of the early modern age proved inadequate to present an ontological justification of history. It mostly regarded history as a tight web of causal connections similar to that of the natural world. To Spinoza, Leibniz and Lessing, historical events even as occurrences in the natural world possessed a factual, but not a metaphysical, necessary truth.[39] They played no part in the eternal order of the real. Empiricist historians, such as Voltaire, Hume, and Gibbon, drew the opposite conclusion: since history had obviously become the very face of modern culture, it was metaphysics (again, understood as the science of the unchangeable) that should be dismissed. In both cases an identical refusal to assign an ontological significance to historical change determined the argument. The weight of a history that remained unexplained and unjustified became an oppressive burden on the European mind. Nietzsche was right in seeing it as a cause of late modern nihilism.

Post-modern critics, aware of the inconsistency of a philosophy that continues to assume what it explicitly rejects—the ultimately static, unchanging quality of the real—have abandoned the epistemological project of modern philosophy altogether. Their critique has exposed the incoherence between two fundamental presuppositions of modern epistemology, namely, that the subject alone determines meaning and value yet the real remains ultimately static and identical. Most of them have rejected one as well as the other. While sharing their critique of the metaphysical assumptions of modern philosophy, I think nevertheless that the metaphysical question of the modern experience ought to be reopened. Contrary to school metaphysics, which has failed to account for the historical nature of the real, Whitehead and Heidegger, the two leading philosophers of our century, introduced creativity and historicity as fundamental categories in their quest for the ontological foundations of modern existence.

A major problem of a metaphysics that takes account of freedom and history concerns transcendence. Transcendence, understood in the most general sense as the distance between appearance and what justifies appearance, is basic to the metaphysical enterprise. If the ontologically ultimate (Being, Spirit, or whatever name it may bear) fails to surpass the mere givenness of things, any metaphysical quest for foundations becomes idle. Now, the justification of appearance has been conceived in various modes. The Platonic one is distinct from the Aristotelian, and both essentially differ from that of medieval metaphysics (which equates pure Being with a transcendent God). But all share the idea that our immediate experience of the world and of ourselves cannot be equated with the ultimately real. The nature of this distinction becomes problematic, however, when freedom functions as the source of meaning and value.

The idea of a first (efficient) cause, which thinkers until well into the eighteenth century postulated at the origin of the self, far from solving the problem, resulted in a contradiction. A transcendent foundation conceived exclusively in terms of efficient causality cannot possibly account for a free agent's creative activity. Indeed, it directly conflicts with the autonomy presupposed by the modern concept of freedom. The opposition between freedom and transcendent efficient cause first surfaced in the sixteenth-century disputes on freedom and predestination. Later, after Kant had laid out the implications of the two notions, it drove most major philosophies of freedom—from Hartmann and Nietzsche to Sartre and Merleau-Ponty—to reject any kind of transcendent dependence as being incompatible with the modern idea of freedom. At the same time, the very situatedness of freedom—its gratuitous contingency—requires the introduction of some principle of transcendence. Human agents are subject to an insurmountable contingency: they have to live within conditions they have not chosen, and they remain forever incapable of controlling the circumstances in which they are forced to operate. Finite freedom is locked in a never-ending combat with the "limit-situations" (Jaspers) created by a causally determined world on which it depends for the fulfillment of human needs and wants.

Without some kind of transcendence that conveys meaning to those efforts in the present, history turns into an aimless striving toward an elusive future. History becomes a heavy burden when existence in time, now identified with freedom, loses the grounding it once had in eternity. To replace the traditional notion of a transcendent God Nietzsche proposed a transcendence of time in and through (instead of beyond) time. In his theory of the eternal return time closes in upon itself and in the will to power overcomes its contingency. But for the will to power, freedom still exclusively controls history. So, I do not see how it provides the kind of transcendence that would solve the modern predicament. In the Buddhist philosopher Nishitani's words: "The Will to Power, Nietzsche's final standpoint, was still conceived as some 'thing' called 'will.' So long as it is regarded as an *entity* named will, it does not completely lose its connotation of being an *other* for us and thus cannot become something wherein we can truly become aware of ourselves at our elemental source."[40] But far more important than Nietzsche's failed solution is his incisive critique of the traditional idea of transcendence, conceived on the model of an efficient cause, when applied to the modern concept of freedom. Only recently have a few thinkers, foremost among them Maurice Blondel, Karl Jaspers, and Paul Ricoeur, begun to rethink the relation between freedom and transcendence in noncausal terms.[41]

To sum up, modern culture has detached personhood from the other two constituents of the original ontological synthesis. For Greek and medieval philosophers the person formed an integral part of a more comprehensive totality, yet ruled that totality in accordance with a teleology both immanent in its own nature and transcending it. The image of the person that emerged in the sixteenth century became increasingly more enclosed within itself. Eventually it narrowed its teleology to one of self-preservation or self-fulfillment, either social or individual.

Part III

From Deified Nature
to Supernatural Grace

Once we lived in what we saw; now the
rapaciousness of this new power, which
threatens to absorb all things, engages us.
Nature, art, persons, letters, religions, objects,
successively tumble in, and God is but one
of its ideas. . . . And yet is the God the
native of these bleak rocks. . . . We must
hold hard to this poverty, however
scandalous, and by more vigorous self-
recoveries, after the sallies of action, possess
our axis more firmly.

—R. W. Emerson, *Essays*

Chapter 7

The Fateful Separation

The Synthesis of Grace and Nature

Early Greek philosophy defined the terms in which Western thought was to formulate transcendence. The Ionian search for a ground of nature beyond its appearance as well as the Pythagorean distinction between a principle of intelligibility and the reality it renders intelligible made the relation from the more fundamental to the less fundamental an unavoidable issue. Classical Greek philosophy eventually resolved it by means of the form principle. The form resided within the appearing objects of which it constituted the intelligible essence, yet as determining factor it also surpassed them. In his dialogue *Parmenides* Plato presents the great metaphysician laying out the terms of a problem of well-nigh inextricable complexity. Forms can be neither only transcendent nor only immanent. They must be both, and Plato criticizes his own earlier attempts to meet that condition. His critical reflection set a dialectic in motion that, via Plotinus and Proclus, uninterruptedly continued for well over a millennium. One may think that Aristotle had disposed of Plato's solution when he placed the main principle of interpretation—the ideal forms—within the real while keeping only the ultimate justification of appearance—the unmoved mover—beyond the appearing reality. Yet the relation between reality and its transcendent foundation is far more intimate than the unmoved mover of the *Metaphysics* suggests. In his early dialogue *Peri Philosophias* Aristotle calls the world "the temple of the divine," and the order of the celestial spheres a sublime object of contemplation. Even in his mature writings he refers to a divine presence in nature. In *De anima* a divine agent intellect illuminates the mind by its active indwelling in the soul. It unites the soul with God in intellectual contemplation. According to W. D. Ross, Aristotle's God is immanent in the highest cognitive activity: "When Aristotle refers to the moments in which we can live a life like that of God, he will . . . be thinking of moments in which the partition between active and passive reason is broken down and we become aware of our oneness with the principle whose knowledge is always actual and always complete."[1]

At first sporadically but after the fourth century intensively, Christian writers began to use Platonic categories for articulating their own doctrine. At least initially they tended to downplay the fundamental divergence that separated the Christian conception of transcendence from that of Plotinus and Proclus. For Christians, nature owed its entire being to a free act of God, while in Platonic as in most Greek thought nature was divine through itself. There were other problems. The doctrine of creation had distinguished God from the world in a manner quite different from the Neoplatonic theory of emanation. While the latter presented the hypostases of Mind and Soul in a descending order, the former maintained the equality of the trinitarian hypostases—Father, Word, Spirit—within a single divine sphere. The decrees of Nicea (331) and Constantinople (381) defined the Son and the Spirit "consubstantial" with the Father. Moreover, in the Christian view God had created matter on a par with form, whereas for Platonists matter was a merely negative principle. Nevertheless, despite a Christian concern to safeguard creation's integrity, Platonism left a clear mark on its early formulations, insofar as it located the image of God (God's proper dwelling place) primarily in the mind. The body, though not deprived of traces of the divine, belonged to a lower level that often conflicted with the soul's aspirations. Indeed, it soon came to be held responsible for the inclination to evil. From there it was only one step to identify evil with bodiliness. Happily, in its earlier struggle with Gnosticism the Church had firmly ruled out such an equation by the mouth of one of its ablest theologians, Irenaeus (130–200), the Greek bishop of Lyon. Whatever came out of God's hands could not but be intrinsically good, Irenaeus taught, and it had remained so after the fall. God's image in the person survives, for that image consists in a dynamic unfolding of human freedom. Inevitably a gradual process of learning how to be free includes errors, but such errors educate the human race preparing it for a higher stage of redemption.[2]

Irenaeus's anti-Gnostic theology would not be forgotten when Platonism presented a subtler form of dualism. Meanwhile his conclusion that the fall has not severed the soul's union with God, appeared perfectly agreeable with Neoplatonic philosophy. Ever since its fourth-century beginnings, Neoplatonic theology consistently held that God's presence deifies the person and through him the entire cosmos. With Maximus Confessor (580–662) this theology of deification culminated in an exchange of nature between God and man: "man is, and is called God by grace," while "God is, and is called man by condescension."[3] In the cosmos God embodies himself. Greek-Christian theology insisted that neither person nor cosmos are divine by nature: their deification is given. But this gratuitous quality does not separate grace from nature, since nature itself is given and called to be deified. The idea of deification was never abandoned in the Christian East. "Eastern tradition knows nothing of 'pure nature' to which grace is added as a supernatural gift. For it, there is no natural or 'normal' state, since grace is implied in the act of creation itself. . . . The world, created in order that it might be deified,is dynamic, tending always toward its final end."[4] According to Vladimir Lossky who wrote these lines, nature and grace together constitute one image of God.

In the West, Neoplatonic theology was introduced by the converted rhetor Marius Victorinus (285–365). Augustine, its principal advocate, saw in it the answer to the Manichean dualism he had once embraced. Even as for the Greek Christians, God's image for Augustine consisted not in a copy but in a presence, yet while the Greek fathers construed the nature of the image in accordance with the divine archetype, Augustine built his idea of the archetype on the basis of its human image. This gave his and subsequent Western theology a more psychological character. No less than the Greeks, however, Augustine considered the same image to have been both created and redeemed. It comes as a surprise, then, to see Augustine laying the groundwork for the later separation between the order of nature and that of redemption. In part this was due to the more moral and medicinal view of grace that, from the beginning, had dominated the Latin tradition. But in Augustine's case an additional historical controversy played a part. Against the one-sided stress placed on the need of good works by the emerging Pelagians, Augustine reemphasized that the fall had wounded and incapacitated nature and hence that nature first had to be cured by the remedy of grace. Eventually this remedy will be viewed as a quasi-independent entity, rather than as the deification of human nature it had been for Greek Christians. Augustine cannot be held responsible for this later interpretation of his thought. But his anti-Pelagian writings unquestionably planted the seeds of two conflicting doctrines, neither one of which he would have accepted and both of which in their own way caused a break between nature and grace. With them begins our story.

According to one doctrine—the one that emerged in late medieval theology—grace superimposes a different reality upon nature. The other, which was prevalent in the Reformation and to some extent in Jansenism, reacted against the worldliness implied in a theory that conceived of nature as independent and self-sufficient. It stressed the corruption of nature to a point where grace, no longer able to transform it, merely covers its sinfulness or, as in Jansenius's theology, replaces it altogether. Thus grace in one case is added to nature; in the other, substituted for or extrinsically imputed to nature.

Some time during the thirteenth century the first signs of the theological dispute concerning the relation between nature and grace appear. The original context had been epistemological. Scholastics, following Aristotle, considered the order of nature independently of its destiny in grace an adequate object of rational investigation. While Albert and Aquinas incorporated this semi-independent but abstract field of thought into the undivided whole of a single theological vision, Averrhoist Aristotelians in various degrees began to detach the study of nature from that of revelation altogether. With the condemnation of the theory of "double truth" the powers of Averrhoism seemed roundly defeated, yet the more fundamental problem in combining Aristotle's philosophy with Christian theology remained, rooted as it was in a different concept of nature. In Latin theology the term nature had originally referred to human nature in the concrete context of a creation that itself was gratuitous. Thus Saint Augustine calls the original state of justice "natural"—an expression later to be adopted, but with a different meaning, by Baius and Jansenius. At the turn of the fourteenth century Duns Scotus still speaks of a "natural" desire toward a "supernatural" vision. But, viewed from an Aristotelian perspective, each nature is endowed with its own immanent teleology, the end of which had to be proportionate to the natural means for attaining it. If considered, then, independently of its revealed vocation, such a natural teleology might easily lead to a theological dualism.

Aquinas clearly perceived that an Aristotelian concept of nature was too restrictive for expressing the Christian meaning of *natura elevata*. He conceded that nature contained some immanently human teleology— Aristotle's ideal of virtue and contemplation in the good city—yet this end remained subordinated to the more fundamental one and was not attainable by human effort alone.[5] Clearly then, the Thomist concept of nature continues to be overdetermined by the category of grace. Independently of grace, nature may be a formal and abstract object of investigation, but it is not a concrete reality in its own right.

Saint Thomas recognizes a purely philosophical conception of nature as an object of a rational reflection independent of revelation, but in the concrete order of reality this is only an abstraction. A modern interpreter of Thomas's thought, Karl Rahner, called this separate nature a residual concept (*ein Restbegriff*) to be understood only through its dialectical counterpart—grace. It assumes a symbolic function in the Christian vision of the real.[6] At any rate, in Aquinas's thought, "nature" refers to human nature as it concretely exists, that is, as already integrated within the context of grace but as formally considered independently of what revelation teaches of that context. Viewed from that perspective, nature possesses a transcendent openness to grace and, some Thomists would claim, a *desiderium naturale* toward fulfillment in grace. Sixteenth-century theologians, however, tended to take the *natura pura* to be a full reality in its own right. On the basis of Aristotle's principle concerning the proportion of ends to means, they declared this nature incapable of any supernatural desire of God. Their theological dualism was complete but remained hidden behind a traditional terminology—"natural" and "supernatural"—whose meaning it subverted. In Aquinas, the term *supernatural* does not refer to a new order of being added to nature but to the means for attaining the one final end for which the power of nature alone does not suffice.[7] He calls God *agens supernaturalis* to distinguish the order of the Creator from that of creation (in which nature and grace appear together). Nature thereby becomes the effect of a supernatural agent.

The term *supernatural* did not begin to refer to a separate order until some sixteenth-century theologians clearly distinguished a natural human end from humankind's revealed destiny. Thus, Saint Thomas's sixteenth-century commentator Sylvester of Ferrara interprets his master's position

as disjoining the reality of nature from that of grace. If God were the
person's natural end yet that end could be attained only by supernatural
means, he argues, nature would fail to be proportionate to its own end.[8]
Aquinas never conceived of nature as an independent reality endowed
with a self-sufficient *finis naturalis*. It must be admitted, however, that
one feature of Saint Thomas's theological construction could, and eventually did, threaten the balance of its complex unity. It had nothing to do
with the acceptance of the Aristotelian apparatus but everything with the
Latin medicinal interpretation of grace. Rather than considering the Incarnation a decisive but by no means discontinuous moment in a process
of divine self-communication that had started with creation, as Scotus
(and later also Erasmus) was to do, Aquinas saw it essentially as a divine
response to the effects of the fall. Without the fall the Incarnation would
not have occurred.[9] Viewed from this perspective, redemption might be
interpreted as a supernatural cure for a natural disease and, as such, as
initiating a wholly different order of grace.

Another idea introduced with the Aristotelian categories did, in fact,
at a later stage become instrumental in separating nature from the divine.
It consisted in a particular interpretation of the causal relation between
God and creation. For the Greeks as well as for Jews and Christians, some
form of causality had always been the principal category for expressing
the link between God and the world. Yet a comparison between the
modern conception of this causal relation and the classical as well as the
medieval one discloses a major difference with respect to the immanence
of the cause in the effect. In Plato's *Parmenides* the psychic cause of
motion remains entirely within its effect. So do the combined causal
principles (the *synaitiai*) of the cosmos in *Timaeus*. True, Plato adds the
efficient causality of the Demiurge, but this mythical figure ought not to
be understood so literally as to reverse Plato's more fundamental doctrine
of participation. Even Aristotle's theology did not replace the theory of
participation by one of efficient causality as modern philosophy was to
understand that. Aristotle's notion of causality continued to reflect an
immanence of the cause in its effect. Natural substances contain the
source of motion and change within themselves and the concept of nature
(*physis*) is defined as the intrinsic source of substantial motion and rest.[10]

Early Christian theologians, understanding Plato's metaphysical principles as physical entities out of which the Demiurge would have fashioned the world, forcefully stressed that God created *ex nihilo*, a concept
unknown in ancient and biblical cosmology. In presenting the world as

an effect of God's efficient causality, they intended to refute what they assumed to be implied in Plato's theory, namely, that the Demiurge "created" out of preexisting matter. It was, of course, a literalist reply to a mythical story, but never never before the modern age did Christians consider a notion of extrinsic causality adequate to express the intimate, permanent presence of God to his creation. Even after Aristotle's philosophy became the chief conceptual instrument for articulating Christian theology and the category of efficient causality became the principal one for defining the entire relation of the Creator to his creation, it did not yet denote a purely extrinsic relation as in its modern usage.[11] Aquinas hesitated considerably between Plato's participation and Aristotle's efficient causality for conceptualizing the creature's dependence on God.[12] Even in the later *Summa Theologiae* when he had mainly opted for the latter, he wrote: "Being is innermost in each thing and most fundamentally present within all things, since it is formal in respect of everything found in a thing. . . . Hence it must be that God is in all things, and innermostly."[13]

Nonetheless, when proceeding to define the nature of this divine immanence, Thomas concludes that it must consist in a relation of causal dependency. Such an explication by means of Aristotle's efficient causality yields less than what the innermost presence promised, as the rest of the passage shows. "An agent must be joined to that wherein it acts immediately, and touch it by its power; hence it is proved in the *Physics* (VII, 2) that the thing moved and the mover must be together. Now since God is Being itself by his own essence, created being must be his proper effect; just as to ignite is the proper effect of fire." Thus we see how, even within an Aristotelian conceptualization, participation continues to balance efficient causality in Thomas's description of God's presence in his creation.

Saint Thomas's vision inspired poets and artists all through the next century. The majestic construction of cosmology and theology, of politics and philosophy, which Dante erects in *De Monarchia* and assumes throughout the *Comedia*, shows the creative and enduring power of a Christian Aristotelianism of which Aquinas had achieved the most balanced synthesis. Yet the very complexity of the synthesis made it vulnerable to being distorted in one direction or another. With the terms *nature* and *supernatural* Aquinas had differentiated two formally distinct aspects of one reality. More literal followers of Aristotle's philosophy, such as Siger of Brabant or Boethius of Dacia, separated nature, the object of philosophy, from the content of Christian revelation as if they were two different orders of being, thus preparing the later meanings of natural and supernatural. Aquinas regarded such extreme Aristotelians a serious threat to his synthesis. Rightly so, for though he emerged victorious from the battle with his antagonists, the trustworthiness of his project to reconcile Aristotelian philosophy with theology suffered a severe blow when, in 1277, Etienne Tempier, the archbishop of Paris, condemned some of his Aristotelian theses.

The Disintegration of the Medieval Synthesis

The adoption of Aristotle's philosophy was neither the immediate nor the principal cause of grace and nature becoming separated into two quasi-independent orders of reality. As Aquinas had proven, they could be kept in perfect harmony within an Aristotelian synthesis. Moreover, Aristotle's concept of nature possessed a flexibility and a potential for growth that made it adaptable to Christian theology. Since nature functioned essentially as a matrix of development and not as a fixed entity, it remained at least in principle receptive to the Christian theology of fall and redemption. How well Saint Thomas had realized that potential appears in his treatment of the theological virtues of faith, hope, and charity, which he, in the *Summa Theologiae,* succeeds in inserting into the Aristotelian theory of virtue. The disintegration of the synthesis into an order of pure nature separate from one of grace had been foreshadowed by Averrhoist philosophers yet in the end was mainly the work of those who had led the resistance against Aristotelianism, namely, the nominalists.

The concept of an unrestricted divine power in the nominalist theologies of the fourteenth and fifteenth centuries weakened the intelligibility of the relation between Creator and creature. Unconditioned divine power negatively affected any rational apriori for predicting the order of nature, and it had an equally unsettling effect on the theology of grace. Granted by an inscrutable divine decree, grace might be randomly dispensed or withheld regardless of the recipient's moral condition. This subversion of any mediation in the relation between God and the creature necessitated a new immediacy: "Alone in an ultimately unintelligible universe, and with the more fundamental conception of sin and the problems of its control opened up by the new anthropology, man could no longer count on the mediation either of reason or of other men in closer contact with the divine than himself. His salvation depended on an immediate and personal relation with God."[14] Mystical and devotional movements, stressing individual piety over school theology and ecclesiastical structures, responded to this need for religious immediacy. Union with God through experience had to bridge the theoretical gap opened between a wholly transcendent Creator and his creation. Direct spiritual experience partly restored a sense of divine immanence that was vanishing from theology.

Scotus in his critique of Aquinas's theory of the Incarnation planted the first milestone on the road that was to divide the supernatural order from the natural one. Traditional Christian doctrine as formulated in the Councils of Ephesus (431) and Chalcedon (451) had defined that in Christ one divine person unites two distinct natures—a divine and a human. Aquinas understood this to mean that at the moment of the Incarnation God's divine Word had assumed human nature in the unity of a single divine personhood. If the union had occurred at a later stage, it would have implied that an already existing person had subsequently been assumed into the divine nature—a thesis that had been condemned under the name "adoptionism." To avoid it, Aquinas posited that before the Incarnation no individual human nature had existed; for such a nature could only have existed in an actual person, and consequently "the human nature to be assumed by the Word would have preexisted in some person or hypostasis."[15] But how would a divine person assume a human nature without assuming its normal *suppositum,* namely, a human person? In Scotus's view, to define the concept *human nature* in a manner that applied only to Christ jeopardized its meaningfulness. He therefore argued that humanity as such, in all instances, is naturally endowed with the potential of being assumed by a divine person (or of being elevated in grace), although its actually doing so required a divine intervention.[16] Such an intervention, though special in its own way, avoided the equivocity of Aquinas's exception in the definition of human nature. But Scotus's solution came with a price, for it detached nature as such from what Christians regarded as its linkage to a divine destiny. Scotus's nature remains neutral with respect to this destiny: *either* it may be assumed into a hypostatic union with the divine Word or into an adoptive sonship of God in grace, *or* it may follow its normal course to the formation of a purely natural human personhood. Thus, in Scotus's artificial construction, intended to protect the concept of human nature from breaking under the weight of a theological exception, the actual person who bears that nature is no more than an indifferent, contingent addition to it![17] A theory, specifically devised for joining Christ more intrinsically to human nature, results in a quasi-independent abstraction of a pure nature. Scotus himself, however, was most anxious to avoid the theological dualism that he may unwittingly have provoked. This appears in yet another instance. Not satisfied to consider grace a meteoric element that invades an alien nature, he postulated that, in order to receive the infinite, human nature itself be endowed with an infinite receptivity and hence naturally disposed toward a union with a "supernatural" reality.

How ill Scotus's attempts were rewarded appeared in the fact that Ockham, who accepted Scotus's theologically neutral concept of human nature, was accused of adoptionism. Unfairly so, for the human nature Christ assumed had not previously existed in its normal basis (*in proprio supposito*) of an actual person.[18] But the charge, however unjustified, is understandable since in Ockham's thought human nature tends to become an independent entity, rather than being a relational concept as it had been for Aquinas and even for Scotus. Recent studies of Ockham's theory have shown how unjustified it is to call him the "father of theological nominalism," but there is no doubt that his position prepared the concept of nature as a self-sufficient reality. This conclusion follows from Ockham's reinterpretation of the traditional distinction between God's *potentia absoluta* (his sovereign power over all creation) and his *potentia ordinata* (the manner in which he actually exercises that power). The distinction, which originated in the eleventh century, had been merely an attempt to formulate the unconditional dependence of all created reality on God's sovereign power, in whatever manner he exercises that power. The *potentia ordinata* referred to the order God has actually chosen and to the restrictions it imposes on the concrete exercise of this power. Previously the two had not been distinct powers but the same one considered first generally, then specifically. The distinction also indicated how God's omnipotence always exceeds what he actually does.

Nominalist theology after Ockham transformed the concept of God's *potentia absoluta* in two ways. First, it extended the scope of the *potentia absoluta* beyond its previously assumed moral and rational limits. Thus God's absolute power came to include all that implies no logical contradiction. Ockham, who in other respects remained within the traditional interpretation, had already argued that God could illuminate the human mind so as to enable it to know intuitively without the presence of an object. He even could have created the will without directing it toward the good. Nor is God bound by any restrictions of good or evil in what he finds acceptable. A second change occurred when late nominalist theology separated the *potentia absoluta* from the *potentia ordinata*, as if they were two independent and successive moments in God's power rather than two distinct aspects of the one divine sovereignty.[19] According to this interpretation, God at a first time possesses absolute power, which he, in the second, entrusts to secondary causes. Thus notwithstanding an absolute power at any time capable of changing the order of nature, that order is perfectly trustworthy once God has ordained it. His decree to abide by secondary causes is practically (though not theoretically) irrevocable. The same consistency prevails in the order of grace. Although good deeds remain disproportionate to eternal salvation—which can only be gratuitous—God has chosen to consider them a necessary means to salvation. While the extreme voluntarism implicit in this interpretation of God's *potentia absoluta* would seem to undermine the intrinsic coherence of the order of nature, at least in Gabriel Biel, the last nominalist theologian of note, secondary causes obtain practical control both in the order of nature and of grace.[20]

God's general causality persists throughout, but late nominalism separated two moments that heretofore had remained united. In earlier Scholasticism, God did not surrender his sovereign power to secondary causes. His primary causality remained fully operative in the secondary causes. As Aquinas explains: "It is clear that the same effect is ascribed to a natural cause and to God, not as though part were effected by God and part by the natural agent; but the whole effect proceeds from each, yet in different ways, just as the whole of one and the same effect is ascribed to the instrument, and again the whole is ascribed to the principal agent."[21] The idea of an independent order of secondary causes gradually led to a conception of nature as fully equipped to act without special divine assistance. But if the actual order of nature functioned as an independent entity directed only by its own teleology, the elevation to grace had to be regarded as a divine addition to the realm of nature. Logic required that theology treat this additional order separately from that of nature.

Thirteenth-century Scholastics had always taken the term human *nature* as part of a concrete human condition determined by a supernatural destiny. Before the fall, they argued, that nature was harmoniously related to its higher vocation; after the fall it lost this harmony but not its vocation. The idea of natural law in Saint Thomas was based on the assumption of a theologically concrete—that is, wounded and transformed—nature. The much-debated natural desire (*desiderium naturale*) toward a vision of God in Scholastic thought had referred to nature's openness toward its transcendent vocation. The supernatural fulfillment of that desire presupposed a nature already animated by grace. Even when fifteenth-century theology began to distinguish two orders of being, it maintained a real continuity between them.[22]

Theologians did not begin to treat the concept of *pure nature* as a concrete independent reality until the sixteenth century. Despite its philosophical appearance, this concept was deeply rooted in late nominalist theology. It might have remained a theological abstraction if Renaissance naturalism had not given it an acceptable content, and seventeenth-century philosophy a rational justification. Once the idea of an independent, quasi-autonomous order of nature gained a foothold in Catholic theology, it spread to all schools except the Augustinian, including some of Aquinas's commentators such as Sylvester and Cajetan. Thus the medieval synthesis came to an end, and a dualism between nature and a supernatural realm solidly entrenched itself in Catholic theology for four centuries.[23]

An immediate result of the split was the rise of a natural or philosophical theology, that is, a science of God based exclusively on rational arguments. If nature could be understood as an independent entity in its own right, a full understanding also included a proof of the existence of its transcendent cause. No doubt medieval Scholastics, especially Aquinas in the *Summa Contra Gentiles*, had granted a relative autonomy to the mind's natural powers for knowing God. Scripture supported some knowledge of God independently of revelation: "His invisible attributes . . . have been visible, ever since the world began, to the eye of reason, in the things he has made" (Rom. 1:20). Since the early centuries Christians had defended their faith against outsiders by universally admissible arguments based on the course of nature. They had found them in such classical sources as Cicero's *De natura deorum* and Marcus Varro's *Antiquitates rerum divinarum* (reported in Augustine's *City of God*, bks. 6, 7, 8). Boethius had been among the first to do so in a systematic way, but neither he nor his medieval successors had started from a religiously neutral position. Boethius's argument assumes that God is the ultimate reality.[24] Thomas Aquinas, whose proofs were later transformed into the backbone of natural theology, presupposed the monotheist idea of God to be shared by Moslems, Jews, and Christians. In his apologetic *Summa contra Gentiles*, Aquinas devotes little space to the so-called arguments for the existence of God. The knowledge of God through analogy with

nature had always been informed by faith: it served merely as a preambulum to revelation.

What distinguishes the natural theology that emerged in the sixteenth
century is that it brackets all those theological and religious assumptions
and detaches the realms of nature and faith from each other. Even those
who contested the viability of a natural theology did not object to the
separation of two totally independent realms, but to the capacity of one
to support the other. Thus Bacon writes: "Out of the contemplation of
nature, a ground of human knowledges, to induce any verity or persuasion
concerning the points of faith . . . is not safe: *Da fidei quae fidei sunt.*"[25]
Bacon's fideism, based on the idea first formulated by Saint Bonaventure
(to a very different effect) that nature is not an image of God, eliminates
all cosmological speculation from faith. Theology can no longer rely on
the analogy of nature. "Divinity is grounded upon the *placets* of God."[26]
The advocates of natural theology insisted on proving the existence of a
Creator of the cosmos independently of any revelation.

The most one could expect reason to accomplish toward this ambitious purpose consisted in showing that nature, though autonomous,
implies a natural transcendence that could be conceived as conforming to
revealed doctrine or, at least, as not conflicting with it. In the event, the
new philosophical theology attempted a great deal more. First, it derived
the concept of nature integrally from ancient authors—mostly Stoic or
influenced by Stoicism (as Cicero and Seneca were)—for whom it had
been linked to religious conceptions of the cosmos essentially different
from the Christian one. An idea of nature based on a theological foundation could hardly be considered philosophically pure. Second, the conclusions of their arguments for the existence of God claimed to establish
a far more specific kind of transcendence than the premises warranted.
The arguments all concluded with the existence of a typically Judeo-
Christian God: one, personal, perfect. Little in this natural theology could
be called natural in the sense in which philosophers had come to understand nature. One of the earliest and most influential exercises in this
modern natural theology was *De providentia numinis* by the Flemish
Jesuit Leonardus Lessius—a strange mixture of Stoic philosophy, natural
arguments, and hidden theological concepts that was to have many imi-
tators.[27]

Natural theology began as an earnest attempt to restore to a concept
of nature a transcendent orientation that had been severed from it. Its
early proponents may also have been motivated by a religious desire to

remove the discussion from ever-growing theological polemics concerning the interpretation of Scripture and the authority of ecclesiastical tradition. It failed for a number of reasons, of which the presence of alien theological elements—implied in Stoic, Neoplatonic, and Epicurean philosophies— was only one. The fundamental problem was that the new natural theology continued to argue on the basis of God's immanent presence in nature (both human and cosmic) after having defined nature as an independent, self-sufficient entity. Before the end of the sixteenth century many had lost their optimistic trust in the success of such a dubious enterprise.

That loss of confidence is reflected in Montaigne's changed attitude toward one of his earlier projects, the translation of Raymond de Sabonde's *Natural Theology* (1484). The young translator, wary of dogmatic or rational aprioris, had welcomed the gigantic effort to establish religion on an empirical foundation on which all religious parties ought to have been able to agree. By the time Montaigne wrote his "Apology," however, Sabonde's argument had thoroughly ceased to convince him. Montaigne's controversial epilogue, although it questioned much of what was held to be accepted doctrine, must not be read as an expression of religious skepticism, but rather as a defense of a wholly nonfoundational fideism. "It is faith alone that vividly and certainly comprehends the deep mysteries of our religion; but withal, I do not say that it is not a brave and a very laudable attempt to accommodate the natural and human capabilities that God has endowed us with to the service of our faith."[28] Distrusting a reliance on reason that had resulted only in conflicting philosophies, Montaigne abandons natural theology and takes refuge in the authority of custom and tradition. "Since I am not capable of choosing, I take other men's choice, and keep myself in the state wherein God has placed me."

The confidence that had marked the beginning of the sixteenth century had, partly under the impact of the political and religious turmoil, been completely reversed. The sense of failure left by reasonable efforts to reach the object of its natural desire throws reason back upon faith. "'Tis not by meditation or by virtue of our own understanding that we have acquired our religion, but by foreign authority and command". Indeed, Montaigne's initial statement of what he intends to do in his "Apology" reads as a direct attack on natural theology and on much of the religious program of the humanists: "The means that I use, and that I think most proper, to subdue this frenzy [trust in nature], is to crush and spurn underfoot pride and human arrogance; to make them sensible of the inanity, vanity, and nothingness of man; to wrest the wretched arms of their reason out of their hands; to make them bow down and bite the ground, under the authority and reverence of the divine majesty."[29]

Despite its lack of success, natural theology continued its efforts to provide a "foundation" to faith. The arguments developed in the seventeenth century by the Jesuits, the Cartesians, and the Jansenists formed the backbone of the theological rationalism of the modern age. From Lessius, via Descartes, Leibniz, Clarke, and Paley, to the seminary courses in *Theologia Naturalis* taught until the middle of the twentieth century, the approaches differed somewhat and the accents were occasionally replaced, but the basic structure remained solidly in place. In this new religious architecture the upper structure—the so-called supernatural— was assumed to rest on a base of nature, but that base was conceived as detached from the superstructure. Nature had become independent in the sense in which Spinoza defined substance, namely, as "that which is in itself and is conceived through itself, independently of any other conception" (*Ethics* I, Def. 3), while the supernatural order of grace, detached from its concrete base, was relegated to an airless sphere of abstraction. As the concept of nature lost its transcendent orientation, the assumptions on which natural theology came to be based contained the seeds of late-modern atheism.[30] Instead of the expected new integration of the two levels we find religion becoming naturalized, that is, becoming part of that closed universe the new philosophical concept of nature denoted. Thus the neo-Aristotelian Pomponazzi advanced an evolutionary theory that subjects all religions (including Christianity) to the natural law of generation and corruption. Revelations, miracles, and prophecies attain their greatest power at the beginning of a religion and weaken toward its end. The Christian faith, like other religions that preceded it, has already begun to grow frigid and scarce in miracles: it obviously is approaching the end of its allotted term. Pomponazzi's naturalism virtually eliminates transcendence from religion. The same is true in varying degrees of Jean Bodin's *Heptaplomeres* and Guillaume Postel's *Absconditorum a constitutione mundi clavis*. Their views, however, are symptomatic of a future secularism far more than of the mentality of their own time. On the whole, early modern culture remained genuinely religious; in some respects more so than the period immediately preceding it. Few thinkers drew the conclusions from their hazardous theological premises.

Religious Naturalism and Its Alternative

As theologians withdrew from the domain of nature, other thinkers rushed to fill the theological vacuum. They attributed to nature a divine quality independent of the supernatural realm theology had arrogated as its own (and sole) domain. Early Renaissance thought, less inhibited by a dogmatic tradition that was being challenged from various sides, spawned a number of pantheistic and panentheistic mystical philosophies. They drew heavily on Neoplatonic and Stoic sources. These sources had never ceased to feed Christian speculation but had been constrained by a Christian doctrine of creation denying that nature had necessarily emanated from God. For the Stoics, as well as for Plotinus and Proclus, nature had been divine. So when thinkers like Patrizzi, Bruno, and Telesio turned to those ancient sources, they must have been attracted by a position that greatly contrasted with the questionable dualist theologies of their own time. Earlier naturalists, such as the members of the twelfth-century school of Chartres, had appealed to scriptural or theological support for ascribing a divine quality to nature. For pantheistic and panentheistic philosophers of the Renaissance, that divine quality revealed its truth independently of any revealed authority.

Here I shall consider only two forms of this religious naturalism: Bruno's wholly unorthodox one and Cusanus's untraditional but orthodox one. The radicalness of their innovations indicates how seriously Scholastic theology had become discredited in their eyes. At Bruno's trial the comprehensive charge underlying most others was, as it would be in Galileo's case, the assumption that a definitive truth could be gathered from the study of nature independently of Scripture or ecclesiastical authority. The theologian Osiander had understood early on that this would be the crucial issue of all future controversy, and in his preface to Copernicus's *Revolutiones* he tried to circumvent the problem by referring to the heliocentric theory as a mere hypothesis rather than an established truth. Later Galileo was offered the same choice by the Holy Office and eventually accepted it to avoid further difficulties. Bruno paid with his life for adopting a more straightforward strategy.[31]

The Copernican theory had, of course, played a major role in rendering the conception of a self-sufficient nature, and with it that of a definitive truth based on natural evidence alone, acceptable. Bruno immediately understood that once the earth had been dislodged from its central position, the question of causal dependence had to be formulated differently

than it had been in the Ptolemaic world picture. The idea of a divine
power transmitted to the cosmos from a single fixed point ("above")
became meaningless. This was particularly the case if, for other reasons,
the universe had to be conceived as infinite in space and time, as Bruno
thought. Motion, then, could no longer be assumed to come from above
and yet had to be caused continuously. Bruno placed its source within
the cosmos. There had been a few medieval precedents for such a view
of God's causal immanence in the cosmos (among them, David of Dinant,
Amaury de Bène, and William of Auvergne), but Nicholas of Cusa's argument that all points of creation are equally close to God seems to have
provided the immediate occasion for Bruno's concept of a total divine
presence in nature. The divine principle necessarily communicates itself
to all points of nature at once. For Bruno, this necessity coincides with
divine freedom, for the highest freedom consists in acting in accordance
with the demands of one's nature.[32]

Because he expresses himself totally and necessarily, God is as immanent in the universe as he is in himself. He unfolds himself exhaustively in nature. Indeed, nature "is God Himself, or the divine power
manifest in things" (De immenso). Even though the ultimate principle
(Bruno refers to it as the One or as God) remains unknowable in itself, it
reveals all that can be revealed through nature. God hides no secrets
behind his worldly appearance. His manifestation in nature is so total
that it excludes any historical revelation as redundant. The naturally
revealed is the entire revealable. And yet, though "only-born child of
God," nature remains only a shadow, a fragmented image (il gran simu-
lacro) of the divine Absolute. No single part fully expresses the Absolute.
"In the specific mode which we have indicated the universe is all that it
can be, but in an unfolded, dispersed, distinct mode."[33]

Bruno's God undoubtedly dwells more immanently in nature than
any Christian philosophy had ever conceived. At the same time, God's
internal essence surpasses his unfolding in nature so greatly as to remain
closed to human understanding. Bruno borrows Saint Bonaventure's formula for describing the relation between God and nature: "Intra omnia
non inclusus, extra omnia non exclusus . . . in quo sunt omnia, et qui in
nullo." (Within all things, yet not contained; outside all things, yet not
excluded; in whom all things are, and who is none.)[34] Elsewhere he writes:
"He is all in all who gives being to all; and yet he is none of all, for he is
above all, surpassing the singular and the total through essence, nobility,
and power." (Est enim omnia in omnibus, quia dat esse omnibus; et est

nullum omnium quia est super omnia, singula et universa essentia et nobilitate et virtute praetergrediens.)[35]

Bruno distinguishes the *natura naturans* from the *natura naturata* by means of his concept of nothingness that he, reinterpreting Cusanus's principle (Alteritas ex nihilo oritur), understands as an open space between God and nature. Nature, while being *toto infinito* (wholly infinite), is not *totalmente* (in all respects) *infinito*. God remains distinct from nature by an unqualified unity that excludes any kind of mediation with cosmic multiplicity. In order to avoid any pantheistic confusion between the One and the many, Bruno rejected the intra-divine distinctions of the Christian doctrine of the Trinity. In his view, they jeopardize divine unity and weaken its distinctness from nature. He replaced the horizontal relations in God of traditional Christian doctrine by a single vertical one whereby the divine generation of the Son becomes the birth of nature. For Bruno, creation is God's generation of his otherness. At the same time, he attempted to avoid the dualism that such a firm distinction between the one and the many might imply by insisting that God's manifestation in the universe is itself divine. As one, God remains unknown; as manifest, he is totally knowable. But by attributing God's manifestation to his essence Bruno appears to sacrifice with one hand the divine unity he is trying to preserve with the other. Moreover, he qualifies the exhaustive revelation through nature by reserving a special, more intimate revelation to the true lovers of God. He even distinguishes the divine attribute of goodness as consisting either in the law that rules nature and is knowable to all or in a higher order "according to which only some, those to whom it has been revealed, are good" (secundum quam bonitatem quidam tantum, quibus revelavit, boni sunt).[36] Most likely this distinction refers not to any supernatural realm, but to those who in the order of nature are capable of perceiving the hidden divine unity. Bruno's *Eroici furori* (*Heroic Frenzies*) confirms the existence of degrees of religious knowledge in the natural order.

In this poetic work Bruno compares the divine light to Apollo, the sun god. Only the reflection of that light in the beauty of the divine Diana, that is, "the light shining through the obscurity of matter and so resplendent in the darkness," grants the mind a glimpse of Apollo's splendor.[37] Even so, it is given to few to see Diana naked. Nor is the mind capable of seeing the light by its own powers. The intellect desires to know, but true vision is reserved to the great lovers who, driven by a powerful eros, reach the Good that lies beyond knowledge. Only those

raptured beyond themselves by divine love may hope to attain that ultimate vision. Bruno here combines a Platonic eros with a naturalist version
of Christian infused love. In a sublime sonnet he applies Plato's metaphor
of the hunter for truth (*Phaedo* 66-C) to the ascent to the Good. The
mythical hunter Actaeon surprises Diana while she is bathing in a secret
pond in the woods. The goddess punishes his indiscretion by transforming
him into a stag—a prey for his own dogs. Thus the divine lover pursuing
the beautiful quarry is transformed from hunter into hunted—"e'l gran
cacciator dovenne caccia." The sonnet concludes:

> I lift my thoughts to the high prey
> And they sprang back at me
> Devouring me with fierce and cruel bites.

> I allargo i miei pensieri
> Ad alta preda, ed essi a me revolti
> Morte mi dàn con morsi crudi e fieri.[38]

The allegory of an active longing for the infinite unnameable, which
becomes converted into a passive absorption into it, culminates in a
mystical identification of seeing God with being seen by him (veder la
divinità è l'esser visto da quella.)[39] Bruno may have found this transition
from active desire to passive rest in Nicholas of Cusa's mystical work *De
visione dei.* Both echo Eckhart's saying that the eye wherewith I see God
is the eye wherewith God sees himself. To reach a transcendent God, the
active ascent must be transformed into a passive "being drawn." From
the beginning the eros that drives the mind upward consists in a power
that attracts it from beyond. Such a rapture would neither be possible nor
needed unless a clear distinction separated the finite from the *totalmente
infinito.*

Bruno was, of course, not the only thinker of the Renaissance to
construe a new, panentheist religious system. So did Campanella, Pomponazzi, and Bodin, whose achievements we leave to the historians of
Renaissance. But Bruno presents the paradigmatic case of a totally consistent naturalism that did not die with him at the stake on the Campo
dei Fiori. Its main assumption had already found a surprising shelter
within Catholic teaching in the form of the natural theology that preceded
traditional courses on revelation.

Reflecting on the direction religious thought took toward the end of
the Middle Ages, we cannot but wonder whether the extremes of a reli-

gious naturalism such as Bruno's and a supernaturalist philosophy such as that of late Scholasticism could have been avoided. The answer confronts us, once again, in the towering intellectual figure of Nicholas of Cusa. Recapitulating almost the entire past tradition—the Greek as well as the medieval—he adapted it to the demands of the emerging humanist and scientific culture of the modern age. In a comprehensive synthesis the Rhineland cardinal succeeded in bridging the gap that nominalist thought had opened between nature and its transcendent source. Cusanus was probably the last thinker to reunite the theocentric and anthropocentric forces that had begun to pull the medieval synthesis apart. He anticipated and avoided the problems a heliocentric picture would cause to the traditional religious worldview by rethinking the relation between God and nature in such a manner that God is no longer the pinnacle of a cosmic hierarchy but a spiritual center that unfolds itself in the cosmos.

Cusanus understood that a primary condition for restoring the divine immanence in nature consisted in containing the nominalist interpretation of God's *potentia absoluta* within predictable borders. This required redefining the concept of possibility. At a first glance the cardinal appears to concede the nominalist thesis when he declares that possibility, no less than actuality, depends on God's absolute power.[40] Had nominalist theologians not asserted that God's omnipotence enabled him to create whatever held no logical contradiction? By making possibility dependent on God's creative act, then, Cusanus seemed to reassert the unlimitedness of that power. In fact, however, his thesis purposely undermined the more fundamental nominalist dualism between a realm of infinite possibility subject to God's absolute power and one of limited actuality subsequently chosen by God's ordained power. Cusanus reunited possibility with actuality as two complementary elements of one creative act. Possibility cannot be detached from actuality as a vacuum that will be filled in part only by God's actual creation. One originates with the other because creation includes the totality of all that could be realized.[41] The actual world expresses, for Cusanus, divine reason in the only possible way. No Leibnizian choice between possible worlds precedes the act of creation. Whatever is, is *eo ipso* the best possible.

Cusanus removes himself further from the separation of nature and grace into two independent orders of reality by arguing that the act of creation is the very unfolding (*explicatio*) of God's Being. As such, it implies a more intimate union between God and the creature than Christian theology had traditionally supported (or tolerated). Indeed, the universe is, in the mode of multiplicity, the very being which God is in a unified way (*complicatio*). Since it includes all that exists and could exist, the universe may rightly be called infinite. Cusanus did not hesitate to apply the medieval metaphor of God as an infinite circle with an ubiquitous center to the cosmos itself. The world constitutes the otherness of God's Being while God is the non-otherness of created being.

In his theological treatise *On the Not-Other* (*De non-aliud*), Cusanus, like Eckhart, describes God as the principle through which things are identical with themselves. The absolute, though infinitely surpassing the relative, cannot be defined as "other": it must define both itself and the relative. For Cusanus, this meant that God, as ground of the world, constitutes his own essence as well as that of all creatures. Difference limits the identity of a thing with itself. A finite being is defined as much by its relation to others as by its relation to itself, but what constitutes its otherness also separates it from itself. Since self-identity consists in nonseparateness, a finite being can derive it only from its union with the absolute. Cusanus therefore concludes that God is literally more the thing than the thing is itself.[42] To avoid what he perceived as a problem created by the Neoplatonic supremacy of the One—namely, that it is opposed to the many—Cusanus ranks not-otherness as the highest mode of being. Though the created cosmos is indeed distinct from the divine unity, God's immanence in it continues to secure the cosmos's unity. Only insofar as created being coincides with uncreated Being does it attain the unity which conveys its self-identity. The same term, then, which most adequately describes God's Being, also defines the creature's innermost reality.

To uphold a sufficient distinction between Creator and creature Cusanus recurs to the metaphor of one-point perspective with which contemporary painters had begun to experiment. Although infinite in its identity with the absolute, created being is a broken infinity that reflects various but always limited perspectives of the uncreated infinite. Like a mirror, each fragment presents a different view of God's face, though none shows his full countenance. But the analogy needed to be corrected. Unlike the mirror, created being does not exist prior to its reflecting. The mind does not receive the divine illumination as in a preexisting receptacle: its very being partakes in the divine intellect while its otherness is no more than the limit of its mode of participation.[43]

Cusanus also calls God's vision a mirror, but unlike finite knowledge, God's "seeing" does not depend upon what it knows. It establishes the ontological truth of things, which the human mind reflects in images. "When someone looks into this Mirror, he sees his own form in the Form of forms, which the Mirror is. And he judges the form seen in the Mirror to be the image of his own form, because such would be the case with regard to a polished material mirror. However, the contrary thereof is true, because in the Mirror of eternity that which he sees is not an image but is the Truth, of which the beholder is the image."[44] Though grounding all representations, the divine essence remains hidden. Its presence does appear, not in likeness or image but in symbolic ciphers of the human mind's making. With the nominalists, Cusanus denies any sort of analogy between sign and signified, yet, unlike most of them, he holds that finite symbols manifest the *presence* of an invisible infinite.

In the theology of Christ, exposed in the third part of *On Learned Ignorance*, Cusanus fully overcomes the nominalist dualism between a divine and a human order. In the Incarnation the hypostatic union of divine and human nature intrinsically transforms nature as a whole and, with it, the entire creation. Nor must that union be considered the result of God's decision subsequent to or in anticipation of the fall. "Divinity does not exist in different ways according to an earlier and a later time."[45] As divine person Christ ontologically precedes that created nature which he, through his humanity, enables to participate in God's nature. Nature and grace remain indissolubly united in Cusanus's conception, and thought, for him, moves toward and culminates in mystical *visio* or *intuitio*. Cusanus's philosophy, then, unlike early modern school philosophy, cannot be separated from his theology. Karl Jaspers has drawn proper attention to that: "His philosophy does not presuppose particular articles of faith, but it does imply a fundamental attitude of faith, which he explicitly calls Christian. Because Cusanus regards his mind as a copy of the divine original, philosophical faith and revealed faith are for him identical. . . . What we call the duality of his thinking was to him no such thing. He does not recognize multiple sources of faith, but only one, the Christian."[46]

While in many respects correcting the nominalist theology of the late Middle Ages, Cusanus's synthesis contained too many problems to serve as a model for the new age. Aside from depriving philosophy of its autonomy and linking it indissolubly to Christian faith, his synthesis suffers from an internal inconsistency. The Incarnation, he claims, unites the absolute *maximum* of God's Being with the relative, worldly *maximum* of Christ's humanity. But what is a *maximum?* He uncritically assumes that the idea of Christ as "the perfect man" implies an ontological all-inclusiveness. But earlier Cusanus had rejected the idea of absolute perfection in the finite order as an invalid concept: a higher and a different mode of perfection remains always thinkable. Even more important, we might add, is that in many instances one finite perfection often excludes another. The idea of an entire universe reaching absolute perfection in one of its parts is logically inconsistent.[47]

In the end, Cusanus's insight that grace becomes united with nature in a single order of being remains more significant than the actual synthesis in which he incorporated it. This insight led him to the ecumenical idea of a universal religion. According to *De pace fidei* (1453), all religions reveal a part of that truth of which the divine Logos constitutes the totality. No single faith can exhaust the conceptual depth of God's Being. The book contains a fable in which representatives of various faiths gathered around the divine throne are ordered to instruct their respective nations that all true worship is one and that a religious unity of all believers may be reached once they understand how all religions emerge from one source and all rituals relate to that same source.

Cusanus's theology presents the last major alternative (before the twentieth century) to the dualist School theologies of the modern age. After him, theologians either accepted the late Scholastic view of nature and grace as independent entities or they stressed one at the expense of the other. Spiritual theologies alone succeeded in recapturing in the lived experience of devotional practice the synthesis that systematic theology had lost in speculation. These speculative failures and practical successes form the subject of the next two chapters. But they did not succeed in reversing the trend whereby, at the end of the sixteenth century, theology lost its hold on a culture whose substance it had once shaped. It became reduced to a science among others, with a method and object exclusively its own. Other sciences henceforth could freely ignore it. For the most part modern thinkers readily availed themselves of the opportunity to avoid potentially hazardous and always useless theological controversies.

Chapter 8

The Attempted Reunion

In this chapter I will review three major attempts to overcome the theological dualism modern culture inherited from late medieval thought, namely, those of humanist religion, the early Reformation, and Jansenist theology. According to such Christian humanists as Valla, Erasmus, and Ficino, a universal divine attraction sanctifies the natural order and draws it back to its source. Archaic religion, ancient philosophy, Hebrew and Christian revelation—in an order of increasing intensity—all responded to the same divine impulse. Generally speaking, humanism offered more an alternative than an answer to the questions raised by fifteenth-century School theology. Humanists, even when acquainted with the Christian theological tradition, felt reluctant to engage in a serious discussion on the problems of contemporary Scholasticism. The same cannot be said of the Reformation, which confronted the theological questions of the age head-on. Luther and Calvin rejected any theologically neutral concept of nature, the Scholastic as well as the classical one. They perceived how grace, conceived as an addition to nature, deprived culture of its transcendent dimension altogether. But they and their followers stressed the difference between the stages of nature before and after the fall to a point where it threatened to cause an historical dualism within nature. Contrary to the Reformation, Jansenius and his early disciples posited that human nature was intrinsically redeemed. But the objective, historical redemption alone did not suffice to sanctify the individual believer. Actual redemption required a personal election, not granted to all or even to most. By its exclusiveness, Jansenist theology prevented in fact if not in principle a genuine reintegration of nature and grace.

Humanist Religion and Renaissance Theology

Humanist theology seldom receives the attention it deserves. Nineteenth-century thinkers tended to dismiss the whole movement as a return to paganism with a few half-hearted compromises between an undogmatic Christianity and a Neoplatonic philosophy. The French historian Michelet regarded the Renaissance as an anti-religious anticipation of eighteenth-century French rationalism. A secularist assumption also underlies Burckhardt's classic *The Civilization of the Renaissance in Italy*. He and many of his readers considered the condition of the early modern age as totally void of every moral and religious ideal—*die volle Diesseitigkeit*. To be sure, secularist tendencies existed among Italian humanists. Poggio considered classical culture in all respects superior to Christian—including in its moral values. Next to this humanist classicism, there was what the Renaissance scholar Hans Baron has called a "civic humanism," of which Leonardo Bruni was the prototype, deeply concerned with the political models of the Roman republic but indifferent to religious disputes. Yet even in classicist or civic humanists we must not confuse a primary concern for secular matters with what we now call "secularism." The fallacy of holding men and women of a homogeneously Christian culture to standards of consistency considered normative in a religiously pluralistic society continues to distort our assessment of the religious attitudes of the Renaissance. Contemporary scholars, such as Toffanin, Trinkaus, Grassi, Boyle, Camporeale, Mazzotta, have thoroughly discredited the secularist interpretation of Italian humanism. Even Machiavelli, if we may believe a recent study, was a regular churchgoer and today would be regarded as a man of religious habits. Rabelais was no less a believer for parodying ecclesiastical mores and Scholastic theology. Nor was the humanist princess Marguerite of Navarre, sister and cultural mentor of King Francis I of France, a less sincerely devout poet for having also written the ribald *Heptameron*. Montaigne's reputation of being a religious skeptic is even less founded.[1]

Being first and foremost a rhetorical movement, early humanism attached a religious meaning to the poetic word that partakes in the Eternal Word. While Dante and Mussato initiated a religious interpretation of poetry, Petrarch and Salutati developed rhetoric into a *theologia rhetorica*. Scripture, Petrarch claims, consists essentially of poetry, that is, metaphorical speech about God. "I might almost say that theology is the poetry of God, what else is it if not poetry when Christ is called a lion or a lamb or a worm. In Sacred Scripture you will find thousands of such examples too numerous to pursue here. Indeed what else do the parables of the Saviour in the Gospels echo if not a discourse different from ordinary meaning or, to express it briefly, figurative speech, which we call allegory in ordinary language? Yet poetry is woven from this kind of discourse, but with another subject. Who denies it?"[2] Indeed, theology began as poetry. Metric language was the ancient complement to ritual ceremony. All later reflection on the divine originated in that early hymnic language.[3]

We remember how vigorously Salutati argued against the classicist Poggio that the wisdom of Christians surpasses the philosophy of the ancients.[4] Lorenzo Valla took the same position when the older Poggio later resumed his polemics.[5] The *theologia rhetorica* of early Italian humanism prepared Valla's and Erasmus's theology grounded in Scripture and the Latin fathers. But the older humanists did not feel the aversion to Scholasticism characteristic of later humanists and reformers.[6] Nor did Petrarch and Salutati, though critical of Scholastic methods, have any intention of replacing the medieval synthesis. Still, rhetorical theology unquestionably pointed in a new direction, as appeared in its attitude toward pre-Christian, classical literature. Ancient pagan myths, humanists argued, originated in the same religious aspirations to which Scripture had given a definitive, but by no means unique, expression. The key to their common message lay hidden in the *prisca theologia* of hermetic writings that had preceded both biblical and classical literature.[7]

The ancient classics were believed to contain a nobler truth than their blatant polytheism revealed. The many gods merely represented various attributes of the one God. Classical polytheism concealed, in fact, a rigorous monotheism, Coluccio Salutati claimed. "For as they [the Greeks] called one and the same divinity in the heavens Luna, in the forests Diana, and in the underworld Proserpina, they also presupposed this whole complex of gods as a single essence of them all and named it according to the plurality of its possibilities and with the different names of their activities."[8] The assimilation of ancient paganism continued all through the Renaissance. Giordano Bruno captured its meaning in his formula: "The Greeks did not adore Jupiter as if he were the deity; they adored the deity as if it were Jupiter."[9] Each god represented a particular mode in which the one God has manifested himself. The ancient theology preserves its symbolic power in a Christian interpretation.

With Lorenzo Valla began what might be called an alternative theology. He initiated a systematic philological study of Scripture, the fathers, and such ancient documents as the "symbols" of Christian faith. At the same time, he set new standards of historical criticism. How could theology credibly present the message of faith through texts of which it understood neither the meaning nor the historical context? In addition, Valla considered it an urgent theological task to compare how the Christian worldview related to the newly discovered ancient literature. He was the first to fully understood the unprecedented challenge the classical conceptions of human nature presented to the principles of traditional Christian theology. His *De voluptate* (1431), later reissued under the less provocative title *De vero bono* (1433), shows him at an early age prepared to meet the issue head-on. Rather than turning to friendly theories such as the Stoic, the Aristotelian, and the Platonic ones, he tried to accommodate the one system that had consistently been deemed incompatible with Christian doctrine: Epicureanism. Human beings are by nature hedonists, the Epicurean spokesman argues in the first two books of his dialogue. Nature invites us to trust our inclination to pleasure. "All that nature has shaped and formed cannot fail to be saintly and praiseworthy."[10] Even those pleasures that society prohibits are not intrinsically wrong: adultery, promiscuity of unmarried women, and sharing of married ones. Philosophy, especially Stoic philosophy, has perverted our sense of moral values by subjecting humans to a code of prohibitions that go against nature. Christian revelation, on the contrary, if uncontaminated by Stoic thought, positively responds to nature's legitimate aspirations. By offering the highest pleasure, it invites humans to forego the lower ones, however legitimate they are in themselves. The ancients, unacquainted with the highest pleasure, indulged only in the lower ones or developed an inordinate pride in denying them. Epicureanism alone recognizes the true status of human nature without grace.

The notion of a pre-Christian Epicurus, first introduced by Valla, was to stay in modern thought and increasingly to influence Renaissance ethics. Thomas More's utopians uninhibitedly embrace the principle of pleasure. "Nature herself, say they, prescribes to us a joyful life, that is to say, pleasure as the end of all our operations."[11] Medieval Christians had toppled Epicurus, whom late antiquity (including Augustine in *Confessions* VI, 6) had regarded as a saint, from his console. With Valla he reentered theology on the very issue that was to divide early modern theologians, namely, whether nature could be sufficient without grace. In some respects Valla anticipated the negative answer of the Reformation, but the Roman humanist remains ambiguous in his attitude toward ancient naturalism. On balance, however, his fundamental concern was Christian, and there is no doubt that he provided "fertile elements" for a new theological synthesis (Camporeale). Among them stands out his attempt to steer religious thought toward a *theologia sermocinalis* (a theology of the Word), which would soon be adopted and transformed in different ways by Erasmus, Luther, Calvin, and the "devout humanists," whom I shall discuss in the next chapter.[12] Valla presented a new theological agenda, but did he produce a new theology? Salvatore Camporeale, Valla's principal advocate in our time, cautions against inflated expectations. Valla prepared theological renewal but never achieved a new synthesis.[13]

Rather than following chronological order, I will turn first to Erasmus, who in several respects followed in the tracks of the Roman humanist. Confronting this intellectual giant one feels at a loss to define the extraordinary scope of his theological conception. His overall project, so broad and complex as to defy simple description, may well have surpassed that of the more influential accomplishments of Luther and Calvin. They were, at least in the beginning, theological reformers; Erasmus wanted to reform the culture itself of which theology was the heart. His *philosophia Christi* aims at nothing less than a "grandiose synthesis of revelation and reason, of philosophical and celestial truth, of the entire past and present of history."[14] It was at once a cosmic vision of a culture ruled by the message of Christ, a new initiation into the Christian mysteries, and an alternative theology.[15] Some have seen it as a moral religion that, dispensing with dogmas and sacraments, anticipated the Enlightenment. Such a reading, once popular, has now been discredited.[16]

Erasmus's theology, based on Scripture read according to recently acquired philological methods, pursued a theoretically leaner but spiritually richer understanding of the Christian faith. It restored the unique sacramental meaning of the word of revelation. Erasmus pursued a more ambitious theological goal than preparing critical editions and reliable translations of Scripture and the fathers. They constituted only the first phase of a program directed at a religious renovation of the entire culture. To return Christian thinking to its scriptural, evangelical roots required a solid knowledge of its origins, for which Greek, Latin, and Hebrew, as well as an ability to interpret ancient literature were indispensable. The Dutch humanist has rightly been called the father of biblical criticism, yet his work was neither a plea for *sola Scriptura* nor an argument against a spiritual interpretation of the Bible. Quite the contrary! In the *Enchiridion militis christiani* (1501), the first sustained expression of his Christian humanism, Erasmus strongly advocates a spiritual reading of Scripture. He recommends those interpreters "who move farthest away from the letter" (qui a littera quam maxime recedunt), such as Origen, Ambrose, Jerome, and Augustine and criticizes theologians unwilling to penetrate beyond "the flesh" of the letter to the hidden mystery of the spirit.[17] Without a spiritual reading, the biblical accounts of Adam's creation, of David's adultery, or of the incest of Lot's daughters in no way surpasses the myths of Prometheus, of Minerva, or of Circe.[18] It is strange to hear the man who, with Valla, pioneered in restoring access to the original (literal!) meaning of Scripture so strongly supporting a purely symbolic reading of the Old Testament.

For Erasmus, the study of theology began with piety and aimed at spiritually transforming theologians and their readers. To accomplish this renewal, theology had to be stripped of what he regarded as accretions of Scholastic verbiage, superstitious ritual, and unsupportable interpretations of Scripture. Of course, an analysis of the Scriptural message would inevitably lead to larger theoretical questions. Erasmus possessed a solid enough knowledge of Scholastic theology to deal with them and usually preferred the *via moderna* for doing so.[19] But he felt a deep-seated aversion for the Scholastic bent of mind. It had alienated the Gospel from the faithful by burying it under an esoteric language. Moreover, that language was so offensive to the ear as to spoil the attractiveness of the evangelical message. Much of Scholastic theology was a pseudo-science derived from corrupt texts, poor translations, and historical misunderstandings. Erasmus wanted to restore the original proclamation to its pristine clarity and simplicity. The Gospel for him consists of a dramatic story—the *fabula Christi*—and theology has no other purpose but to retell that story. Scripture offers narrative and divine drama, not dialectic and logical dispute. Erasmus accepted that on the basis of the original text a doctrinal tradition had evolved and, when challenged, he stood ready to defend it. But he refused to let the ever subtler *conclusiones theologicae* drawn from the original story obscure its primeval light and beauty.

In the *Enchiridion* Erasmus sums up what he regards as the essence of Christian piety. As central principle he posits the rule to move "from visible things to the invisible reality" (a rebus visibilibus . . . ad invisibilia proficere).[20] The invisible is equated with "the intelligible world" inhabited by God and the blessed spirits. This may seem little more than a slightly Christianized version of Plato's doctrine in *Symposium*, *Phaedrus*, and *Timaeus*. Indeed, the *Enchiridion* recommends "the Platonic writers" since they came closest to the "mode of expression" (*figura*) of the prophets and the Gospels.[21] But the specific christocentric character of Erasmus's piety appears as he elucidates the nature of his principle. Only in Christ, he claims, does the visible become fully symbolic of and conducive to the invisible. As eternal image of God, the God-man carries the entire invisible realm within himself. In his person Christ unifies the two realms and through his word (as recorded in Scripture) he enables humans to move from one to the other. "Even as nothing is more like the Father than the Son, the Father's Word forthcoming from his innermost heart, nothing is more like Christ than the word of Christ expressed from the secret depth of his heart."[22]

Erasmus appears less inclined to apply his principle—from flesh to spirit—to nonverbal symbols of faith. The cult of relics, the veneration of saints, and the institution of monastic life rarely receive his approval. Although he did not advocate an asacramental form of Christianity, as has often been written,[23] his piety shows little patience with popular devotions. It is entirely oriented toward the spirit. "Christi corporea praesentia inutilis ad salutem" (The bodily presence of Christ plays no role in salvation).[24] Nor does he allow Christian truth to be equated with dogmatic formulations. Such formulations never fully express the divine mystery which they intend. Though needed for guidance, they do not warrant the divisive polemics that have so deeply disturbed the faithful. Equally suspicious of speculative theology and of popular devotion, Erasmus all the more stresses the radically Christian quality of his views. "[Your eye] should remain fixed on Christ as the only and the highest good, to the point where you love, admire, or desire nothing but Christ or because of Christ" (Ad solum Christum tanquam ad unicum summum bonum spectet, ut nihil ames, nihil mireris, nihil expetas, nisi aut Christum aut propter Christum).[25] Yet Christ does not merely function as a moral exemplar. Luther's charge of moralism, still repeated by some recent interpreters,[26] overlooks the fact that for Erasmus morality was solidly anchored in a theology of the Holy Spirit. "Christi Spiritus inhabitans cor hominis totam illius imaginem componet" (The Spirit of Christ who inhabits the human heart will fashion the entire image of Christ).[27] But, based on the principle that grace requires cooperation, this theology was primarily practical in orientation. In other respects Erasmus shared Luther's principles of reform.

After Luther had been condemned, Erasmus continued his theological discussion with him,[28] but gradually his admiration for "Eleutherius" (the free one) gave way to an aversion for Luther's strident polemics. In the end he broke with him altogether, considering a controversy about theological formulations not worth the sacrifice of Christian unity. From their debate about freedom it appears doubtful whether Erasmus comprehended the depth of Luther's theological insight. His argument, valid on its own level, fails to come to grips with the substance of Luther's objections. What divides them are two different concepts of nature, an early Augustinian and a late Augustinian, not an opposition between pagan humanism and evangelical piety. Erasmus considered the chasm between the ancient and the Christian worldview as unbridgeable as Luther and criticized those to whom the classics were "dearer than the glory of Christ."[29] But, unlike Luther, he continued to accept the classical conception of nature as "docility and inner propensity *ad res honestas.*"[30] Without a natural inclination toward good and the ability to choose it, the will would cease to be human altogether and become reduced to animal appetite.[31]

Grace fosters this inclination toward virtue and enables it to grow. "What else is the philosophy of Christ, which He himself calls a rebirth, than the restoration of human nature originally well formed?"[32] The continuity between nature's potential for goodness and the gradual transformation of grace invites the Christian to embrace the entire classical culture. Erasmus appears to have held that grace is offered to all (*nulli deest*). "Perhaps the spirit of Christ is more widespread than we understand, and the company of saints includes many not in our calendar."[33] His very conception of Christian virtue induced Erasmus to embrace classical ideals. In Marjorie Boyle's elegant wording: "For Erasmus wisdom does not consist in despoiling a humiliated paganism, but in collaborating pedagogically with its highest expression."[34]

His inclusive spiritual vision inspired doctrinal tolerance. In a letter to Albert of Brandenburg, the archbishop of Mainz, written in the midst of the Lutheran crisis (October 19, 1519), Erasmus criticized theologians who instead of teaching spend their time polemicizing and condemning. Having come under attack for his lenient attitude, Erasmus wrote to the rector of the university of Louvain (October 18, 1520): "I wished him [Luther] to be corrected, not to be lost. If that implies showing favor to Luther, I simply confess that, even now, I do so; even as the Roman Pontiff does, I believe, and as you all would do, if you were theologians, or, at least, Christians."[35] Christian faith was to be lived in practice, not in polemics.

Erasmus's theology surpassed the earlier *theologia rhetorica* by a more comprehensive vision as well as by intellectual superiority. His elegant style, wit, and erudition conquered intellectuals throughout Europe. If theological success can be measured by spiritual vision and intellectual insight, the Dutch humanist probably surpassed all his contemporaries. But if it consists in implementing that vision to a degree where it would substantially change the practice of theology in the modern age, Erasmus succeeded only in part. Why did his genius not bear more lasting fruit? Was it because the fragmentation of the theological worldview begun in late medieval theology had progressed too far to be reversed? Or was it because the Church soon afterward in the Council of Trent reimposed traditional theological methods? Yet his theological influence also waned rapidly among Protestants. The main cause of the decline may well lie in Erasmus's method of doing theology. Certainly a theology need not be systematic as the medieval *Summae* were, but to produce a lasting effect it must be sufficiently comprehensive to deal with the basic problems of human existence and sufficiently structured to do so in a coherent doctrine. What do we find in Erasmus? Insights dispersed over hundreds of letters, *pièces de circonstance,* but relatively few explorations in depth of a single theme (the *De libero arbitrio diatribè* followed by the *Hyperaspistes* being the principal exception). His best theological work consists of commentaries, short treatises (such as the *Enchiridion*) mostly of a practical, spiritual nature.

Theology demands more. Erasmus's writings on such various subjects as catechesis, confession, and counseling of the married and of the dying undoubtedly originated in a single theological vision.[36] That vision, as well as the new method to implement it, held the seeds of an alternative theology, but its elaboration remained too fragmentary to provide the new religious synthesis that was needed. To do more lay beyond his interest and, possibly, his ability. His aversion to Scholastic theology (which he set aside in his two polemical debates with Luther over the freedom of the will) obstructed his efforts toward a decisive theological renewal. Alfons Auer, who contributed much toward restoring Erasmus's theological standing, concludes his study with a very qualified assessment:

> We must admit that his knowledge of medieval theology was inadequate and that he failed to pay sufficient attention to it. Could one, after the thesis of Scholastic Aristotelianism and the antithesis of biblical-patristic humanism, hope for a synthesis that would integrate both extremes? Whatever the answer, the fact remains that Erasmus in his antagonism to the late Scholastic extreme, did not find that measured medium, but yielded to the opposite extreme. A time as theologically fertile as the Middle Ages can, in the end, not simply be shoved aside without paying the price of a heavy loss. Above all, Erasmus ought to have considered that the [divine] Logos has operated not only in classical Antiquity but also in the Christian Middle Ages.[37]

Despite its theological limitations, Erasmus's work continues to fascinate. Theologians critical of the dualist conception of nature and grace have returned to his work. But the attraction of Erasmus's ideal has gone beyond theology. Europeans seeking to regain the unity they lost at the end of the Middle Ages, a unity whose binding force was Christian theology and classical culture, have found in Erasmus, the last great representative of that universality, a model of the future. The extent to which his vision inspires reflection on the future of the West is symbolized by the fact that the most prestigious cultural prize awarded by the European Community has been named after the Dutch humanist.

If, as Paul Kristeller maintains, humanism was neither a philosophy nor philosophical in its approach, then those who considered themselves primarily philosophers, such as Ficino and Pico, ought not to be counted among the humanists. They certainly did not share the humanist ideal of rhetorical elegance. Although Ficino maintained a continuous contact with humanists and dedicated his majestic *Theologia platonica* to Angelo Poliziano, he clearly removed himself from their objectives. Words for him function exclusively as means for conveying ideas. In a more fundamental sense, however, Ficino provided the humanist *theologia rheto-*

rica with fresh theological support. Ficino explored the relation between God's eternal expression in the divine Word and human expressiveness. For this purpose he turned to classical thought, selecting the one philosophy whose central concept was divine expressiveness—namely, Plato's, especially as interpreted by Plotinus.

The Greek scholars who brought their manuscripts as well as their knowledge of Plato and Aristotle to Italy had opened new prospects for integrating Plato's philosophy with the Christian faith. Bessarion, one of the Greek immigrants, argued in his polemical *Against the Calumniators of Plato* (1458 in Greek; 1469 in Latin) that Plato's idea of God, as developed by Plotinus and Iamblichus, was eminently compatible with Christian doctrine. Thus began in the West a systematic and, in scope, unprecedented effort to reconcile Platonic philosophy with theology, an effort that in Greek Christianity had been uninterrupted since its beginning in the fourth century. Marsilio Ficino, who had translated all of Plato's and Plotinus's works, spent much time demonstrating to his classically schooled contemporaries that Plato's thought, far from being based on the idea of a self-sufficient nature, assumed the kind of transcendent openness on which Christian theology ought to be built. Disturbed by the theological dualism of Averrhoist Aristotelians (especially those in nearby Padua), he considered Plato's philosophy ideally suited for overcoming the separation between an order of nature (object of philosophy) and one of grace (object of theology). That philosophy—unlike Aristotle's (at least as interpreted by his Averrhoist followers)—was uniquely suited to lay a natural foundation for a Christian theology of grace.[38] In focusing his *Platonic Theology* (1474) on Plato's theory of immortality, Ficino went to the heart of the controversy on nature and grace; the Averrhoists had sharply distinguished natural knowledge from revelation on the question of the individual soul's survival after death. How far they were willing to separate the two orders appeared soon in Pomponazzi's treatise *On the Immortality of the Soul* (1516), which in its conclusion asserted as theologically true a doctrine of immortal life that his Aristotelian argument had shown to be false.

In his use of Platonic and Neoplatonic philosophy, the Florentine physician went far beyond the church fathers' tactic of "expropriating the spoils of the pagans." Rather than mining ancient texts for spare parts in an exclusively Christian theology, he read them as holy writ, placing Plato and Plotinus on an equal footing with the prophets and assuming a

fundamental continuity from creation to elevation. A true revelation must
be universally accessible, he argued, and hence the religious teachings of
the ancients must be compatible with it. Far from being restrictive, the
truth of revelation acquires the full depth of its meaning only in the light
of other faiths. Religion, for Ficino, is "a natural instinct" common to all
peoples and divinely inspired.[39] It had inspired the magi of Persia and the
priests of Egypt as well as the Hebrew prophets and Platonic philosophers;
the wise and the educated no less than the uneducated. The mind reveres
God as naturally as it loves the good. Rites of worship vary, but a common
divine impulse induces all toward worshipping the same one God ("com-
munem ipsam omnium gentium ad Deum unum religionem" (*Theologia
platonica*, XIII, 10).

To render his concordism compatible with Christian revelation, Ficino had to modify the negative theology of Neoplatonic thought. If God
is totally ineffable, as Plotinus's One is, his nature remains totally unknown and cannot be revealed. Hence Ficino reinterpreted it by means of
Plato's doctrine of form. As perfect form God unites in himself all forms.
"In the highest Being *to be* is to be 'formosus' and bright, indeed to be
form and light."[40] God as supreme form and source of all forms (*formaque
fons formarum*) includes all forms without being fully contained in any.
But, for Ficino, perfection of form coincides with fullness of light. This
divine light enables the mind to see and to see the light reflected in what
it sees. "The intelligence's natural insight, as well as the will's desire, is
a ray infused by the divine light through its direct illumination, and it
naturally reflects this light not resting before it finally restores that light
to its sun." (Ibid., XVIII, 8; also XI, 4).

To avoid the all-too-physical implications of identifying God with
light and perfect form, Ficino somewhat incongruously insists on the
invisibility of both transcendent light and divine form. Its abundant light
renders the divine form unknowable to the intellect ("Deus ob nimiam
lucem est incognitus"), but the warmth of this light makes itself all the
more felt in the will.[41] The divine form directs the act of creation, "not
only of the form but also of the matter in which the origin of the singularity of things lies" (Ibid., XVIII, 8). The theological mission of the artist
consists in rendering the invisible divine form indirectly visible. Ficino's
paradoxical theory of invisible form provided poets, painters, architects,
and sculptors with a spiritual justification for displaying the natural form
as a reflection of the invisible one.[42]

Ficino constantly appeals to Scripture, but his theory remains essentially a natural theology. God discloses himself through nature while Scripture interprets what nature accomplishes. But the human person mediates God's presence to nature. Being spirit, the soul is a direct emanation from God's being and naturally attracted to God, but only divine grace can reunite the soul with God.[43] This natural desire for God enabled Ficino to legitimate the existence of other religions and to consider them indispensable for satisfying that desire. The faith of Israel together with Greek philosophy formed a necessary complement to the Christian revelation. Yet *De religione christiana* justifies all other religions on the basis that no region of the world at any time should remain deprived of worship. The variety of religions results in a cosmic harmony: "It is even possible that such a variety through God's own disposition creates a certain beauty in the world worthy of admiration" (chap. 4).

Pico della Mirandola, Ficino's young disciple, though more Aristotelian than his master, felt similarly inspired to amplify the Christian message into a *philosophia perennis* that would include Platonic philosophy, as well as the Arab commentaries on Aristotle and the Jewish Kabbalah. Underneath the surface of the overt doctrines of Christianity and Judaism he detected an ancient, universal faith esoterically expressed in the mystical Kabbalah. Its secret doctrine not only resolves all doctrinal conflicts between Jews and Christians, but holds the key to those hermetic teachings of ancient religions in which all faiths convene. In these alleged discoveries Pico thought he had found positive proof for the existence of one universal religion. Whereas for Cusa and Ficino other religions found their fulfillment in the Christian faith, Pico regarded that faith a part of the universal religion, not fully intelligible without the hermetic doctrines that combined it with all others. Pico's syncretism earned him a brief excommunication and a short term in a French prison, but he managed to preserve some of its universalism in its famous *Oration*.[44] Such concordist attempts to reintegrate nature with grace based on ancient philosophies—real or fictional—could not solve what was essentially a modern, Christian problem. Pico's and Ficino's syntheses are in essence naturalist theologies couched in Christian terminology and Christian in intention. In fact, soon afterwards this Neoplatonic theology would pave the way to deism.[45] Erasmus, with a much keener sense of the difference between classical thought and Christian theology, avoided this kind of doctrinal concordism while keeping Christian thought open to the natural desire of God.

The Reformation

If the *theologia rhetorica* presented an alternative, albeit a flawed one, to the dualist theology of the modern age, the Reformation constituted the most theologically articulate attempt to overcome that dualism. The early reformers Luther, Zwingli, Calvin—men of religious genius who by sheer spiritual authority turned European culture in a new direction—truly belong to a new age. This deserves to be emphasized in the face of those who, in retrospect, have called the Reformation a reaction against the modern spirit introduced by the Renaissance. Nietzsche considered the Reformation a wild and vulgar counterpart of the Italian Renaissance, a regressive movement whose authors attempted to decant the new wine of modernity into old sacks. In the barbaric North, he claimed, a drive to liberate nature from religious slavery had to disguise itself in religious garb, thus betraying the very principles that had motivated it and returning freedom to the prison from which it had just escaped. Of course, Nietzsche gratuitously assumed that the Renaissance was essentially "the *reversal (Umwertung) of Christian values*, the attempt undertaken with every means, with every instinct, with all genius, to bring the *counter-values*, the *noble* values to victory."[46] Less biased writers, however, have also described the Reformation as an attempt "to solve medieval problems in a new way."[47] Are they right? Does the Reformation belong to the modern age at all, or is it merely the aftermath of problems unsettled in the previous one? It is undeniable that Luther's work displays a strong continuity with medieval spirituality and theology. Roland Bainton refers to Luther's spirituality as "the last great flowering of the Middle Ages."[48] Contemporary scholars have shown in detail how closely Luther's doctrine is linked to the nominalist theology of the late Middle Ages. Luther inherited both the mystical piety and the theological nominalism (despite his outspoken opposition to much of the latter) from the earlier period. The fact that the two conflict with one another conveys an unusual complexity to his thought.

The spiritual-mystical impact appears in the *Theologia Germanica*, a fourteenth-century text that he reedited (in 1516 and 1518) and from which he never dissociated himself. The amazing thing about this work is that it stresses an internal sanctification through grace (the "created light" in the soul), a direct inhabitation of God himself (the "uncreated light") that is incompatible with a mere "forensic" justification. "When God lives in a godly person or in a divinized or sanctified person, there is always something in the human manifestation that is God's own, belongs only to God and not to the created being; it is in God Himself, quite apart from the creature, originally, substantially, not as form or deed."[49]

To the extent that Luther personally appropriated this and similar passages, they shed a different light on his principle that the justice which justifies the believer remains God's own. Indeed, the justifying God is present in the soul! This implies a far more intimate union than is suggested by the term imputation, which is usually interpreted as being justified extrinsically before God's tribunal, but not intrinsically. In his late lectures on the first chapters of Genesis Luther appears to teach a doctrine much closer to a concept of intrinsic sanctification than in his earlier works. There he declares the human person to be an image of God, fully endowed with all the glories of nature, of which the original state of justice was an attribute. "Indeed, let us declare that this justice was not an added gift, separate from human nature and coming to it from without, but that it was truly natural, as it was in Adam's nature to love God, to believe in God, to know God, etc."[50] After the fall the person continues to bear the divine image that calls him to be united with God. At least some theologians in Lutheran orthodoxy remained faithful to this position. Johann Gerhard notes a century later: "The image of God in the first man was natural and constituted the supreme perfection of the whole person."[51]

Elsewhere, however, Luther shows the divisive impact of nominalist theology. God's will is totally sovereign, unfettered by any but his inscrutable law. Natural goodness plays no role in "earning" eternal salvation. Moreover, the corruption of the human will vitiates all acts it performs. God's salvific will is autonomous and inscrutable. Divine justice becomes a substitute for our inability of inner sanctification. Clearly, this aspect of his thought is at variance with the more mystical one. Yet Luther was never a nominalist—in his later years even less than in his earlier ones.[52] Much of his writing, beginning with his early *Disputation against Scholastic Theology* (1517) that consists of one long attack on positions held by leading nominalists (Ockham, d'Ailly, Biel, and . . . Erasmus), polemically confronted nominalist theology. His use of nominalist language serves mostly an anti-nominalist purpose, namely, to assert that God's justifying agency remains at all times exclusively his own and, consequently, that God does not surrender his absolute power to an "ordained" decision of rewarding good works as the nominalist Gabriel Biel had claimed. Nominalist theology here proves to be a two-edged sword. On one side, the separation between God's absolute power and his ordained power could, as it did in the case of Biel, practically result in a semi-Pelagian theory of justification. In the order chosen by God over all others, God rewards good deeds with eternal salvation, not because of their intrinsic merit but merely because of his decision to do so. Once he decides, his choice is definitive, and salvation comes, in fact, to rest in the believer's own hands. On the opposite side, God's absolute sovereignty tolerates no interference with his sanctifying agency, and hence neither natural capacity nor good works prepare a person for the reception of grace.[53]

That a person is justified by grace alone is of course not an exclusively nominalist thesis. One finds it in Saint Thomas as well as in the nominalist Gregory of Rimini, but Luther phrases it in the distinctly nominalist terminology of divine unaccountability, "forensic" justification and the simultaneous presence of sin and justification. All of these concepts were born or had received a new meaning in nominalist theology. In traditional Catholic teaching the two aspects of redemption, the judicial one of justification—the act whereby God declares the sinner justified—and the mystical one—which intrinsically sanctifies the person and actually unites him or her with God—had remained united. For nominalist theologians, "justification" meant that guilt would no longer be imputed while grace became largely an extrinsic addition. At the same time, the mystical tradition had kept the idea of an inner transformation very much alive up to Luther's day and, judging from his attitude toward the *Theologia germanica*, also in his mind.

It is by no means sure that Luther ever held the purely extrinsic imputation that the Council of Trent rejected.[54] Indeed, the reformer attempted to reunite what nominalist thought had sundered. But Luther thinks dialectically: he tends to hold the two terms of an opposition simultaneously present, stressing now one, then the other, rather than intrinsically uniting them. Nowhere does this appear more obvious (and did it create more useless controversy) than in his famous slogan: *simul justus et peccator*. The Christian tradition had unquestionably assumed the coexistence of grace and sinfulness in the same person, as the practice of confession and penance shows. Yet when nominalist theology separated imputation from sanctification, this could be taken to mean that God justifies the sinner by disregarding his sinfulness but without internally sanctifying him. No compelling reason, however, forces us to interpret Luther's theology of justification as excluding inner sanctification as long as both are entirely attributed to God's working. Such a position had been well known in spiritual theology: the belief that God alone justifies and sanctifies had consistently supported the mystics's assertion of God's uncreated presence in the soul (beyond the one mediated through created grace). Whatever Luther's position exactly may have been—a question that will remain difficult to settle because of his habit of alternatively stressing dialectical extremes—he obviously intended to reunite the order of nature with the divine order of grace. In that light I prefer to read his negative pronouncements about nature. What Luther humbles is not nature as such, but the *natura pura* of late nominalist theology.[55] The unmistakably modern quality of Luther's thought lies in his dialectical presentation of unresolved tensions.

This returns us to the original question: does Luther belong to the modern age? It is well known that Luther stood close to the humanist movement and that he drew some of his prominent followers from its ranks. Most humanists, including Erasmus, were strongly reform-minded and a number of French humanists (such as Lefèvre d'Etaples and King Francis's sister Marguerite of Navarre) continued to applaud his efforts long after Rome's excommunication. In Luther they greeted the dawn of a spiritual renewal. Indeed, far beyond the German lands, many bishops, priests, and religious who did not break with Rome listened to the Augustinian's message as to a sound of liberation that announced a new age. Yet, one might object, this need not be a signal of modernity: it could have been a revival of a more ancient Christian past in an attempt to overcome the problems that had been responsible for its decline. The fact of the matter is, however, that Luther did not solve the problems of the past but presented them in a wholly new way, a way that was characteristically modern and that allowed those who followed him to live with the problems rather than being paralyzed by them. Both Luther's theological greatness and his limitation lies in a dialectical style that displays the qualities typical of the early modern mind: opposition rather than synthesis, search rather than acquisition, uncertainty rather than security. There are similar characteristics in the literature of Tasso and Cervantes, in the philosophies of Montaigne and Descartes, and in the political theories of Machiavelli and Hobbes. Luther lived them before he expressed them, and he expressed them before his age had become fully aware of them. His inner struggle between a feeling of spiritual impotence and his forceful assertiveness of the free individual; his insistence on the personal interpretation of Scripture and his authoritative way of imposing his understanding of it; his alternation between a desperate awareness of the infinite distance that separates God from the soul and a peaceful trust in an intimate union with Christ—all those tensions without resolutions make Luther appear as a modern man in medieval garb. His mind exudes freedom and confidence, yet his theology persistently cautions the Christian about the lack of freedom and impotence of human nature.

Luther's debate with Erasmus dealt with a specifically modern theme: the meaning of personal freedom within the context of redemption. Erasmus argued that a freedom incapable of playing an active part in the process of salvation was not worthy of its name and conflicted with the obvious meaning the term *freedom* had also in the New Testament. What disturbed Luther was Erasmus's failure to perceive the distinctive quality of the freedom proclaimed in the New Testament. He felt Erasmus had adopted a Greek idea and applied it uncritically to Paul's teaching on sin and justification. Such a procedure missed the radically novel quality of Paul's message. The New Testament required an unqualified acceptance of its concept, not an adjustment to a different one. The dispute, resulting from two entirely different approaches—one based on some passages of Saint Paul, the other on the classical conception of nature (also present in the New Testament)—ended, not surprisingly, in a methodological impasse. Describing freedom as the power of the will to elicit those acts that lead to eternal salvation, Erasmus, in Luther's eyes, underestimated the fundamental disruption that has taken place in man's natural religious aspirations and capacities. Luther wrote about salvation, which cannot be attained through natural freedom. Advancing different notions of freedom, Luther and Erasmus barely made contact with one another. Their dialogue of the deaf effectively ended the common cause of Reformation and Renaissance humanism.[56]

The disagreement was as fundamental as it could be, but it must not be described as a clash of the modern with the ancient. Luther's position was every bit as modern as Erasmus's. The reformer never questioned the existence of a natural freedom, but he perceived that the concept of freedom introduced by Biel's late nominalist theology, particularly when amplified by the Renaissance idea of unlimited human creativity, posed an unprecedented problem to the Christian doctrine of justification. Not freedom as such, but its particular modern form was the issue. Biel's theology raised the question how far freedom would go if, as he claimed, God's "ordained power" had practically left human salvation to its efforts. The Renaissance exaltation of a creative power moved in a direction

opposite to that of absolute dependence, thus giving the question a specifically modern urgency. Reacting against both, Luther declared a purely
natural freedom totally powerless in the area of justification. With this
claim he really said nothing theologically new, but as he was addressing
a modern problem, he said it in a new and paradoxical manner. The
difference of the specifically Christian freedom with regard to salvation
also forced him to reexamine the nature of Christian morality. Was there
any natural morality left after the fall? If so, how significant were the
precepts of the Gospel and what impact would they make? Would they
transform ethics to a point where it, in fact, ceased to exist?

Luther did not question the person's natural capacity for leading an
ordinary moral life. The voice of conscience is indeed the voice of God
that speaks to all humans. The Mosaic law codified the essential precepts
of natural morality into divine commands. Hence no outward behavior
substantially distinguishes the Christian from the virtuous non-Christian.
The difference lies in the intention with which the Christian follows
these commands. Christian morality transforms natural morality from
within, so to speak. It becomes a matter of inner obligation—a *Gesin-
nungsethik*.[57] External behavior loses its decisive significance for one who
knows that all human efforts are inadequate for achieving the one thing
that really matters. Since all depends on God's saving grace, the Christian
must be primarily concerned with confessing his impotence on the highest level, trusting in God's mercy, and gratefully accepting his redemption.

By the same token, he or she must not deny nature's ordinary inclinations their natural satisfaction, as medieval asceticism demanded. Salvation does not depend on their denial. Three centuries later Kierkegaard
was to attack this "hidden Christianity" as a hypocritical cover for religious inertia and a straight road to secularization. Luther's intention was
precisely the opposite. For the believer, the light of God's graceful mercy
illuminated and inspired all aspects of life. Under its divine guidance
the Christian would not fail to perform good deeds, even though justification cannot be merited by them. Lutheran piety here shows a remarkable similarity with that of the devout humanism to be discussed
in chapter 9.

Luther was among the first fully to perceive the magnitude of the
problem created by the split between nature and grace. His entire theology
addresses it. Did he actually succeed in closing the breach? It seems not.
Precisely the dialectical nature of his thought that makes him so modern
prevented him from doing so. Uncompromising in his refusal to present

as one what in the theology of his time appeared inherently divided, Luther converted the religious tension into the very essence of a new Christian piety. His appears the most religiously authentic of all attempts toward a reintegration. But a theology that fails to overcome the dialectical opposition between a totally corrupt nature and a divine justification must fall short of solving the particular problem afflicting the religious consciousness of the modern age, namely, the separation of nature from grace. The one-sidedness of the concept of a definitively corrupt nature parallels the naturalism of the late Renaissance. How much substance does such a totally negative concept of nature preserve? The unresolved tension between Luther's mysticism and his nominalist dualism leaves the answer ambiguous. For a different response, though based on the same premises, we turn to Calvin.

Calvin belongs clearly to the modern age. William Bouwsma's recent portrait of the French reformer leaves no doubt about the typically modern traits of his psychology: a man torn by anxiety not merely about his election or, like Luther, about God's continued approval of the momentous responsibility he had assumed, but also about his ability to relate to others, to give and receive love, and to find a modicum of human happiness.[58] His authoritarian posture covered much uncertainty, his austere expression hid intense feelings, and his reserved countenance concealed passions controlled yet never definitively subdued. The young Calvin appeared as a rising star among the second generation of French humanists. Formed by outstanding classicists, he had shown early promise of becoming a leading Latinist. At age twenty-two he published a Latin commentary, complete with textual emendations, of Erasmus's edition of Seneca's *De clementia* (1532). This erudite, elegantly written work reveals a logical but by no means rigid mind. Nothing originally distinguished him from such other French humanists as Montaigne, Budé, and Lefèvre d'Etaples except perhaps a greater moral seriousness.

Calvin understood the religious problem of modernity because he experienced it within himself. Once converted, he single-mindedly focused on the issue that concerned religious humanists most seriously, namely, the radical incompleteness of a nature that requires a transcendent dimension yet somehow appears to be deprived of it. Calvin attributes that incompleteness to the fall. Too often his picture of the state of corruption has been caricatured as incapacitating nature altogether. Calvin's participation in the humanist movement makes such a conception of nature apriori improbable. In fact, he leaves no doubt that the *ordo naturae* continues to manifest God's presence and guidance. In his glorification of the natural qualities of the human mind and of the beauty of the cosmos, the true intent of Calvin's theology appears most clearly. Grace enables nature to overcome its existential insufficiency and to attain its final destiny, but nature continues to form the basis of redemption.

Calvin admires the *pietas* of those thinkers who hold that a universal spirit (*universa mens*) animates the world or even that nature itself is divine (*naturam esse Deum*). "I confess, indeed, that the expression that nature is God, may be used in a pious sense by a pious mind; but as it is harsh and inconsistent with strict propriety of speech, nature being rather an order prescribed by God, it is dangerous in matters so momentous, and demanding particular caution, to confound the Deity with the inferior course of his works" (*Inst.* I, 5, 5; *Opera* 2, 45).[59] Nevertheless, the thesis of a totally immanent God is preferable to that of a "lazy" God (*Deus otiosus*) who remains unconcerned about the world (*Inst.* I, 16, 3; *Opera*, 2, 146). The course of nature, even after the fall, continues to symbolize God's abiding presence (*Opera* 31, 102). Nature manifests God's wisdom to all—pagans as well as Christians (*Inst.* I, 5, 2–3; *Opera* 2, 42–43). The order of physical causality expresses the divine will, yet God does not allow himself to be shackled by "the golden chains" of that order (*Opera* 8, 353). Even a symbol as sacred as the Eucharist remains only a sign of the divine presence without fully capturing it (*Opera* 8, 352).

In chapter 5 of the first book of the *Institutes* Calvin extols the beauty and order of the cosmos. "The universe is a mirror, in which we may contemplate the otherwise invisible God" (*Inst.* I, 5, 1; *Opera* 2, 41). On all his works he has inscribed his glory "in clear, unequivocal and striking" characters. But no work reflects God's glory more brightly than the person, who is a mirror of the world and a "microcosm" (*Inst.* I, 5, 3; *Opera* 2, 43). Endowed with wisdom, immortality, and freedom, the person surpasses all other creatures (*Inst.* I, 15, 3; *Opera* 2, 137–38). He alone is an *image* of God. "This term denotes the integrity which Adam possessed, when he was endued with a right understanding, when he had affections regulated by reason, and all his senses governed in proper order, and when, in the excellency of his nature he truly resembled the excellency of his Creator" (*Inst.* I, 15, 3; *Opera* 2, 138).

Most significant, Calvin regards all these qualities as natural, that is, essential attributes of human nature.[60] In a well-known passage of the *Institutes*, he praises the virtues of the ancients in a humanist encomium.

Nor shall we deny the light of truth to ancient lawyers, who have
delivered such just principles of civil order and polity. Shall we say
that the philosophers were blind in their exquisite contemplation
and in their scientific description of nature? . . . On the contrary,
we shall not be able even to read the writings of the ancients on
these subjects without great admiration; we shall admire them, because we shall be constrained to acknowledge them to be truly excellent. And shall we esteem anything laudable or excellent, which
we do not recognize as proceeding from God? Let us, then, be
ashamed of such great ingratitude, which was not to be charged on
the heathen poets, who confessed that philosophy, and legislation,
and useful arts, were the inventions of their gods. Therefore, since
it appears that those whom the Scripture styles "natural men," *psy-
chikous,* have discovered such acuteness and perspicacity in the investigation of sublunary things, let us learn from such examples,
how many good qualities the Lord has left to the nature of man.
(*Inst.* II, 2, 15; *Opera* 2, 198)

Calvin stands farther removed than Luther from the pessimistic mood
that clouded the end of the Middle Ages.

When God's image in the person was "obliterated" (*obliterata fuit
coelestis imago*) (*Inst.* II, 1, 5; *Opera* 2, 179)[61] by the fall, the entire order
of nature became inverted (*In Genesin,* ch. 3, 19; *Opera* 23, 75). Yet human
nature preserved a *residuum* of this divine image. In the elect God restores
it "to true and perfect integrity" (*Inst.* I, 15, 4; *Opera* 2, 138–39). For
Calvin, divine justification transforms the believer from within and
through the witness of the Holy Spirit grants him or her an actual experience of salvation. At this point Calvin's argument confronts the same
dilemma as Luther's: on one side, a nature so irremediably wounded that
even divine justification fails to cure human corruption; on the other, an
intrinsic transformation of the elect that conveys to them the inner
certainty of being chosen. Although a more logical and less dialectical
thinker than Luther, Calvin also hesitates between those alternatives.
The same inversion of nominalist theology found in the German reformer's doctrine appears in the French one. Whereas for a late nominalist like
Biel, God's ordained power neutralizes his absolute power, for Calvin,
after the fall God's absolute power decisively overrules the ordained power
of nature. Salvation depends exclusively on divine election, rather than
on an all-comprehensive assumption of nature in grace. That election

owes nothing to the natural course of creation. No good works prepare it and no natural "cooperation" supports it. God redeems the elect individually, by an inscrutable decision. The natural order has been so thoroughly disturbed in the individual, in the cosmos, and in society, that it provides no basis for grace.

In faith God presents himself to those he chooses. Calvin defines faith as "a steady and certain knowledge of the divine benevolence towards us which, being founded on the truth of the gratuitous promise in Christ, is both revealed to our minds, and confirmed to our hearts, by the Holy Spirit" (*Inst.* III, 2, 7; *Opera* 2, 403). Through the testimony of the Holy Spirit faith acquires an experiential quality that links Calvin's doctrine to the Patristic mystical tradition. The believer does more than mentally receive the word of Scripture: he or she personally encounters God as he reaches out in Christ, God's Word. The Holy Spirit opens believers' hearts to the Word and enables them to participate in that Word. "Christ when He illuminates us with faith by the power of his Spirit, at the same time ingrafts us into his body, that we may become partakers of all his benefits" (*Inst.* III, 2, 35; *Opera* 2, 427). Through this participation a believer becomes "mystically united" (*unio mystica*) with Christ.[62] Much in Calvin's description of God's presence to the believer in his Word is reminiscent of Erasmus.

Calvin's stress on the certainty of faith remains continuous with the earlier spiritual theology of experience, which also influenced Luther's theology. Because God sanctifies the elect without the intermediacy of an "infused habit" of grace, the believer has the certainty of being justified. In another respect, however, Calvin's stress on the need for subjective certainty reveals a particularly modern feature of his teaching. It evokes Descartes's search for a foundation of truth in the feeling of evidence. Without that subjective assurance, faith loses its support. "In short, no man is truly a believer, unless . . . he feels an undoubted expectation of salvation" (*Inst.* III, 2, 16; *Opera* 2, 411; also *Inst.* III, 2, 28; *Opera* 2, 420). Although God's promise in Scripture provides the sole objective basis for faith, that foundation fails to support the individual believer if it fails to develop into a personal, private trust. As for Descartes the objectivity of truth did not fully become established until it rested on the certainty of irrefutable evidence, for Calvin the undoubting confidence in one's personal election forms an essential part of the election itself.

That subjective experience, however, is not a substitute for the divine foundation of faith, for according to Calvinist doctrine, the experience of salvation reaches the elect from a trans-subjective source. "The religious experience both convinces him of certain religious truths and verifies the truths. . . . The same mental event in which he gains his assurance somehow transcends itself and reveals to him God, the source of the event."[63] Faith, then, surpasses a merely subjective certainty insofar as it attaches that certainty to a transcendent source. On this crucial point Calvin abandons the modern concept of the wholly autonomous creative subject. Subjective certainty is itself a grace granted by God. With the divine promise the elect receive the trust and peace of mind that are a token of its fulfillment. "For first we believe in the promises of God. Having done so, we receive the confidence that enables us to be of good, peaceful disposition." Only because of the ultimately receptive attitude of faith can the believer regard his or her own feeling of certainty as unshakable evidence.

Since this transcendent quality emerges in the experience of faith, it cannot be simply transmitted to others. To the nonbeliever, such a transition from subjective certainty to objective truth remains wide open to the objection that faith is a self-authenticating act deprived of any foundation beyond itself. With Calvin's notion of the certainty of faith provided by faith itself, the problem of authority, still implicit in the early Luther, became fully explicit. If on the one hand, Scripture is the objective rule of faith, and on the other, the interpretation of that rule must be left to the inner certainty of the believer, the question arises whether the application does not abolish the rule itself.[64] The objection frequently embarrassed Calvinists in their polemics with Catholics. To the outsider it remains unanswerable, but to the believer it carries little weight. Indeed, it could be turned against those who defend an objective foundation of authority. For on what grounds is ecclesiastical authority founded? It rests itself on an interpretation of Scripture.

While praising the wonderful perfection of nature, Calvin was fighting a battle with a Renaissance naturalism whose strong attraction he had experienced. The more he wanted to acclaim the greatness of nature as derived from God's presence, the more he emphasized its intrinsic corruption. A profound ambiguity affects his view of human nature. The person is both an image of God and a moral degenerate. The same ambiguity also marks Calvin's view of the cosmos. Its beauty and order reflects God's greatness and participates in the person's nobility. Yet standing under God's judgment, it ceases to be a realm of secondary causation. After the fall all its powers depend directly on God and are at any moment subject to God's intervention.[65] The entire order of nature, including the so-called natural law, has been imposed by divine decree. Henceforth only the positive divine law revealed in the Ten Commandments remains. Though still the norm of things, nature no longer conveys a "certain sound, a distinct knowledge" (*Inst.* I, 5, 12; *Opera* 2, 50) to the wounded mind. After human nature has become estranged from its own internal teleology, it must find its direction through obedience to divine commands.

Calvin's conception of the social order displays an equally complex relation between a direct thearchy and a democracy based on the natural order. All power derives from God, yet no natural authority is intrinsically sacred. No ruler, however abusive, can govern without being allowed to do so and hence without serving as an instrument of divine providence. His subjects owe him at least external submission, but if he has acquired his office illegitimately or fails to observe the God-given rules for exercising it, he loses his divine authority. His subjects then may resist or even overthrow him if an alternative with real power of no lesser legitimacy is available. Precisely because he ceased to regard political authority divine in the natural order, Calvin's political theology could, despite his theocratic government, become so influential in the rise of modern democracy. His followers, though respecting royal power as divinely permitted, stood in the front ranks of those who challenged the theory of the divine right of kings. Questioning the divine origin of the throne, they instigated resistance movements in France and England that prepared future republics and constitutional monarchies. For Calvin, natural sovereignty rests with the people, and its exercise requires a secular authority. But that authority is subject to religious restrictions. This restrictive clause allowed the Dutch Calvinists to wage war against their legitimate king, Philip II, and justified an anonymous French Calvinist, author of *Vindiciae contra tyrannos* (1579), to appeal to the sovereign will of God while inciting to revolt.

Basing the right of kings on a divine foundation as King James did in *The True Law of Free Monarchies* (1598) and Filmer did in *Patriarcha* (1680) was a rearguard action in defense of the rapidly disappearing idea of a natural hierarchy of authority. Calvinism spoke with the voice of the future in rejecting any claims for absolute sovereignty derived from an unconditional, divinely instituted order of nature. The political order merely serves as a means to enable human beings to regain their way to God in their lapsed condition. Calvin distinguishes two realms—the spir-

itual and the temporal. The temporal order with the support of civil laws
has as task to facilitate the observation of the moral law directly derived
from God. Although the civil order enjoys a certain degree of autonomy,
on the whole it remains subordinate to the spiritual order. Whichever
political system advances people toward their religious destiny is, in
principle, acceptable. Civil government basically exists for the people,
and the basis of its legitimacy remains with the people from which it
derives its authority. But since the entire political order is a relative one,
it remains at any moment subject to God's decrees.

The Reformation in both its Lutheran and its Calvinist forms made
a fundamental attack upon the theological dualism of nature and grace,
and it did so on a solidly evangelical basis. Still, in the end we must raise
the same question about Calvin as about Luther. Did he truly restore
nature's transcendent dimension or did he rather submit a diminished
nature to God's inscrutable dispensation? By a sad irony (to which Kierkegaard was to draw attention), in downgrading nature as *totaliter cor-
rupta* reformed theology actually weakened the powers to resist the
triumphant march that an unfettered naturalism had already begun
through modern Europe. In Calvin as in Luther we witness the modern
struggle between two principles. The mystical one attributes the entire
process of redemption to the living presence of God who directly sanctifies
and divinizes those whom he chooses. The genius of Protestantism consists in having restated that God alone is holy, with the full force that
principle had in Saint Paul. This principle implies that God is directly
present to the believer, but its theological efficacy was weakened by the
inversion of the nominalist relation between God's *potentia absoluta* and
the "ordained" order, whereby human nature lost the intrinsically normative quality it had had for ancient and medieval thinkers.

Nature is no longer capable of serving as a reliable and sufficient
guide on the journey through life; a person must rely on a divine revelation
for guidance. Even though nature still provides assistance, it has ceased
to do so on its own authority. God must sanction its teleology by a positive
divine decree. To know what God has decreed nature must be studied in
the light of revelation. For the English Puritans, the study of physical
nature guided by biblical readings formed an essential part of godliness.
All natural signs of God's greatness had been planted by divine decision
for the salvation of a fallen world—they no longer are the intrinsic language of nature itself. Since philosophy had assumed that nature, endowed
with its own teleology and acting autonomously, could be understood

through itself, it lost much of its authority among the reformed. Not before the Enlightenment rebelled against the subordination of nature and returned to an outright naturalism would it be restored to its previous authority.

The Jansenist Attempt

Doctrinal battlefronts at the beginning of the modern age ran not only along the line that divided Rome from the Reformation; equally fierce struggles were fought within the opposite camps. Yet the issue remained the same: how to overcome the fateful dualism that had severed nature from its transcendent dimension. The theologies of Baius and Jansenius, both professors at the University of Louvain, had only one objective: to combat an emerging naturalism that descended directly from the concept of "pure nature." In the end they were defeated—not by the Reformation or by their naturalist opponents, but by the Church they had attempted to protect against an ever-widening theological dualism. Their theses were rejected, and the Catholic distinction between nature and the supernatural continued to harden into two separate orders of being. The theological complexity of Jansenism accounts for its singular elusiveness. Although condemned five times, it always succeeded, by one distinction or another, in slipping through the mazes of the censorial net to start again under a new guise. What finally terminated its overt existence was not doctrinal pressure but armed assault. King Louis XIV burned down its main center, the convent of Port-Royal, in 1710. Subterraneously Jansenism survived until the nineteenth century. Today its impact still maintains its hold on the mentality of segments of the Catholic population of France, the Low Countries, and Ireland, as their contemporary literature reveals.

The concept of pure nature was solidly entrenched in Catholic theology by the middle of the sixteenth century when Michel du Bay (Baius) attempted to restore an integrated concept of nature and grace. On the basis of a passage in Augustine, Baius denied that human nature had been fully formed until it received the *forma filiorum Dei*—the original state of justice, which later Scholasticism had come to call "supernatural" in order to stress its gratuitousness. God's grace responded to a demand of nature. Adam's nature reflected God's image in its purity, and his natural powers sufficed to reach his divine destination. Thus Baius with one bold stroke united what centuries had sundered. Yet could what nature demanded still be called "gratuitous"? How did such a position differ from the Pelagianism that Augustine had fought in his later years? Of course, appeals to Augustine, made by all parties, could not decide the outcome of a debate that so substantially had changed the meaning of the terms. Augustine had declared nature a divine gift endowed from the beginning with a trans-natural destiny. But what for Augustine had formed a single, gratuitous reality, Baius interpreted as a juridical entitlement of nature. He thus implicitly reintroduced the very separation he fought. Baius reversed the situation after the fall. Since grace had been the power steering nature toward the good, nature deprived of grace inevitably tended toward evil. Even the virtues of this fallen nature rightly deserve to be called "splendid vices." The opposition between the original state of justice and the present one, which is naturally sinful, once again results in two separate orders of reality and reestablishes a theological dualism as pronounced as the one it attempted to overcome.

The irony that a theory based upon the anti-Pelagian writings of Augustine came under fire for Pelagianism discloses the unresolved ambiguity of Baius's thought. His description of the original condition of the human race shares some of the naturalist assumptions of Renaissance Stoicism, specifically that nature considered in itself cannot but be perfect. If any external cause diminishes its perfection, nature's ability to perform its normal functions will be impaired. Thus Baius's Stoic optimism concerning nature's beginnings turns into a profound pessimism about nature's condition after the fall. The failure of Baius's rather simplistic argument would hardly warrant a discussion had his theory not been assumed into a far more sophisticated theological complex. Baius had been condemned for Pelagianism and had submitted. Yet the admiring Jansenius felt that more than a little of his controversial position deserved saving.

Who was Jansenius? A gifted refugee from Protestant Holland who had become Regius Professor of Scripture and dean of the faculty of theology at the University of Louvain. Later he became rector of the university, and he concluded his eventful life as bishop of Ieper in West-Flanders. He was truly a man of a single book and even of a single idea: the revival of Augustine's theology of grace. Yet despite the single-mindedness with which he pursued a life project that was not even quite completed at the time of his death, he appears to have been an exceedingly complex character. He was ascetic, pious, and religiously submissive, yet vain about his accomplishments, ambitious in seeking ecclesiastical honors, and unscrupulous in furthering his theological objectives; abstemious in food and drink, yet surprisingly concerned about money and quality housing; given to solitude, yet known for political savvy and worldly prudence; polemical to an extreme, dour, and censorious, yet effusively warm in his correspondence with his lifelong friend the abbé de Saint-Cyran; secretive and disingenious in hiding his convictions, yet intolerant of those who even slightly disagreed with them; obsessed with an almost pathological antipathy for the Society of Jesus—the Jesuits claimed that of all the persecutions predicted for their order he incarnated the worst—yet, once a bishop, showing great friendship to the Ieper Jesuits who eagerly responded to his appeal for collaboration.

No such ambivalences cloud what he considered his sole purpose in life: to be a theologian. And a "pure theologian" he became, "obstiné au seul vrai" as Sainte-Beuve once described him, determined to set matters straight once and for all on the relation between grace and nature, whatever the cost of personal sacrifice and divisive polemics. In his voluminous *Augustinus* he left posterity the fruit of a lifetime of meditation and research. The book caused an immediate and violent reaction. The Jesuits saw their own theology of grace directly attacked. Moreover, the publication violated the ban imposed by Pope Paul V in 1607 on the polemics concerning divine grace and free will. In these discussions the Jesuits under Molina's guidance had emphasized the need for free cooperation with a divine grace granted to all, while the Dominicans (with Banez) had stressed the need for a special divine election to receive efficacious grace. Their disputes had rocked the Catholic theological world and, until the Pope's intervention, seriously threatened a doctrinal peace badly needed after the trauma of the Reformation. *Augustinus* had the rare distinction of being condemned several times over. The first was in 1642 on grounds of its appearance without the previous approval required for publications on grace. In 1653, five specific propositions culled from Jansenius's book were declared heretical; among them, that Christ had not died for all people but only for some and that interior grace is irresistible. Then, in one of the most curious episodes in the history of dogma, two of his most gifted followers—Antoine Arnauld and Nicole (the same men who had first presented the five controverted propositions)—recognized Rome's sentence in principle (*de droit*) but denied the fact (*de fait*) that the five propositions were actually contained in *Augustinus*. Pope Alexander VII vainly attempted to settle the matter once and for all by formally declaring in 1656 that the propositions did appear in *Augustinus*.

Adam's state, Jansenius explains in *Augustinus*, could not be called
a state of grace. Although he did not merit nature's orientation toward a
beatific union with God, God morally owed it to his own perfection to
call an intellectual creature to the highest form of spiritual life. In the
original state of justice, nature itself had been grace. Adam needed no
grace (symptomatically defined as what is added to nature) to be properly
disposed for willing (*velle*) this divine union. All his nature required was
a divine assistance for being able (*posse*) to act rightly toward its attainment.[66] We, after the fall, require grace both for the *velle* (disposition) and
the *posse* (the ability to act). The general redemption of the human race
does not suffice for its individual members to overcome efficaciously the
irresistible inclination to evil consequent upon the fall—and hence to be
saved. That efficacious grace reaches only those whom God has predestined for it.

Combining Baius's rigorous logic about a nature wounded in its very
essence with a pessimism of his own, Jansenius concluded his system by
consigning the great majority of the human race to damnation while
preserving a few for salvation. Grace in the elect takes a most peculiar
relation to nature. Rather than assisting or healing nature, it turns into a
substitute for it. Jansenius assumes that the will, once vitiated by *cupi-
ditas*, can be redeemed only by losing its *liberum arbitrium*, that means,
by ceasing to function naturally. In de Lubac's dramatic expression: "C'est
sur les ruines de la nature, autrefois maitresse d'elle-meme, que règne
aujourd'hui la grâce de Dieu."[67] Jansenius successively eliminated either
one of the two components of the synthesis: first nature exists without
grace, then grace without nature. An opposition in time has replaced the
Catholic juxtaposition in space.

More than any other theological system Jansenism has consistently
drawn the theological conclusions from the modern premises. At the same
time it discloses how the beginnings of a dualism that had never ceased
to inhere in Latin Christianity must be sought in the later Augustine.
The tradition initiated by the Latin father with its profound pessimism
about nature carries within itself an internal tension that, mixed with
the right ingredient, would rend the Christian synthesis apart. Nominalist
philosophy put the fuse to the keg, thus causing the actual split. The self-
assertiveness of the modern mind provided that separate nature with a
content of its own. The same Augustine whom Jansenius claimed to
follow was actually the remote ancestor of the naturalists he fought. The
significance of Jansenius's attempt to combat a modern theology in the

name of an earlier tradition consists in having unintentionally revealed the ancient origins of a modern problem. To say so is not simply to attribute the responsibility for the exact form in which that problem actually came to haunt modern theology to Augustine or to Paul. Without a specifically modern factor the ancient tension would never have resulted in a separation. In Jansenius, the presence of such a factor appears in a conception of grace identified with a conscious intention—the *motivum caritatis*—that needs to be actualized ever anew. What for the Scholastics had been a *habitus* implanted in nature and ennobling it, became for the Flemish theologian a separate entity detached from the nature it was meant to heal and redeem. The equation of moral reality with actual intention, independent of ontological context, follows directly from the modern primacy of the conscious self as the sole and ever-active source of meaning. The principle, here only implied, will culminate in Kant's ethical system.

The moral grandeur involved in Jansenius's call to abandon the security of one's given nature in order to confront alone a distant God did not resolve the religious predicament of the age. But it inspired some of its greatest minds. In Pascal and Racine, and also indirectly in Corneille and Bossuet, this heroic antinaturalism unexpectedly blossomed into a new moral humanism. Its refinement of the moral sensitivity opened up unknown depths in the soul that enhanced not only the literature of seventeenth-century France but the inner perceptiveness of an entire culture.

Chapter 9

A Provisional Synthesis

In this final chapter I shall consider three responses to the religious predicament that, at least temporarily, succeeded in reuniting modern culture with its transcendent component.

We can hardly speak of a single movement since a variety of individuals and groups belonging to different camps worked, for often opposite reasons, toward the goal of restoring an all-inclusive religious vision to their world. The pursuit of that common vision gave birth to a new Christian humanism in the Reformation as well as in the Counter-Reformation. It included Catholics and Protestants, mystics and Baroque artists. In differing degrees and by different methods they accomplished in spiritual, moral, and aesthetic practice what theologians had failed to attain in theory.

Turning from the momentous changes in the cosmic, anthropological, and theological conceptions of the modern age to the devout life as it was actually lived, one cannot but be struck by the continuity with the past. The remote sources of modern spirituality sprang up in twelfth-century Christian humanism; its more recent ones in Rhineland mysticism. Eckhart's idea that God (equated with Being) constitutes the natural ground of all beings found its way, via Nicholas of Cusa and the Brothers of the Common Life, into much Renaissance piety. It indirectly supported Ficino's natural desire of God as well as Erasmus's "natural Christianity" and influenced even Lutheran piety. Scholars who defend a total originality of Renaissance culture fail to account for its spiritual continuity, a continuity that does not consist in returning theological patterns thinly disguised under a secular surface—a thesis rightly refuted by Hans Blumenberg—but rather in the persistence of a spiritual tradition. Nor must this persistent tradition be dismissed as a stagnant backwater bypassed by more secular waves of renewal. Quite the contrary, the mystical currents of the twelfth century were the very sources of that early humanism that marked the birth of modern culture. Notwithstanding its continuity with late medieval piety, however, spiritual life in the early modern stage adopted a different attitude: instead of withdrawing from public life it inspired the culture at large with a spiritual vision.

In stressing continuity we need not deny the innovations—occasionally watersheds—that separate modern from past piety. But the fact remains: spiritual attitudes change at a slower pace than most cultural transformations do. Nor do those changes parallel other epochal divisions. An historian of the late Middle Ages writes: "The life of the mind and the life of spirit seem at certain times in history to go their own ways and to draw on different sources; and in the fourteenth and fifteenth centuries, when men were finding new ideas and mental attitudes in the works of classical antiquity, their religious sentiments remained true to medieval themes and were nourished by traditional works of spirituality, especially those written in the twelfth century."[1] Ignatius of Loyola, who may have influenced the spiritual direction of the early modern Church more than any other Catholic, derived much of his inspiration from that medieval humanism introduced by the early Franciscans. Ludolf of Saxony's *Life of Christ*, based on Pseudo-Bonaventure's *Meditations on the Life of Christ*, was one of the two books that converted him during a convalescence.

Whence then the obvious difference in tone and orientation of the new spirituality? To a major extent it stemmed from the clearcut separation between spiritual doctrine and School theology. This isolation, in the end fatal to both, freed spiritual life from the burden of an incompatible theology and rendered it more congenial to the modern age. Theology's severance from the religious experience, once an integral part of *contemplatio*, had marginalized it with respect to culture as well as to piety. Mysticism became relegated to the back pages of texts in systematic theology, as an appendix that dealt with private, somewhat marginal phenomena. But spirituality's removal from a theology in full decline initially strengthened its cultural potential. Precisely because they offered an alternative to School theology, the spiritual writers of the age—Ignatius, Teresa, Francis de Sales, and their followers—succeeded in gaining an access to their contemporaries that had been denied to theologians.

Increasingly separated from systematic theology, spiritual life was forced to coin a language of its own. The independence it thereby acquired accounts both for its strength in the beginning and for its decline in the latter half of the seventeenth century. Having adopted the language of its time it allowed spiritual men and women, however traditional in their piety, to dialogue with their contemporaries and eventually to collaborate on the religious synthesis of the Baroque. Later, when the rupture between theology and the new conception of nature began to undermine the doctrinal and institutional foundation of religion itself, the language of piety became a specialized discourse, remote from the main concerns of modern life. The very creation of the noun "mysticism" (or *mystique*) was symptomatic of this isolation, conveying as it did a quasi-independent status to an exclusive, private experience. By means of a specialized language doctrinal schools and movements acquired a relative autonomy with respect to cultural or even ecclesiastical structures.

The degeneration set in after the period I am here considering. At its origin the new spirituality accomplished a religious renewal and mightily contributed toward the cultural reintegration of the Baroque. It did so particularly by restoring to human nature a transcendent orientation. Expressing the reunion of nature and grace in the voluntarist language of the Renaissance, it directly appealed to the men and women of its time and succeeded in creating a veritable spiritual humanism. Only in few instances, however, did that humanism produce a cosmic reintegration.

Devout Humanism

The ambiguity inherent in the term *Christian humanism* extends well beyond the limits admissible by a meaningful use of it. Some have granted the name Christian humanist to all writers who, in whatever capacity, shed light on the religious quality of Renaissance culture, including such dubious candidates as Rabelais.[2] Others have defined Christian humanism as an exclusively spiritual movement that, with or without connections with humanism proper, combined a traditional religious piety with a modern commitment to secular duties. So-called devout humanism originally referred to the school of Francis de Sales and his followers, as a particular kind of this Christian humanism.[3] Later the term occasionally denoted all spiritual movements of the early modern age inspired by a similar confidence in the powers of redeemed nature. In the present section I have often followed this enlarged usage of the term *devout humanism* in order to avoid confusion with the more comprehensive meanings of Christian humanism. The two figures discussed here, Ignatius and Francis de Sales, are by no means its sole representatives, but they undoubtedly fulfilled a paradigmatic function in the spiritual life of the Counter-Reformation.

The most original Catholic response to the religious challenge of the modern age was unquestionably the one given by Ignatius of Loyola. In truly modern fashion (despite his medieval sources) Ignatius places the person at the center of his universe. No fixed place or established life style constrained him or his followers. Like Pico's Adam, they must shape themselves under the guidance of God's spirit. In his *Spiritual Exercises*, Ignatius assumes that persons ought to control their own lives and that they can do so only by a methodic, systematic training of their will power. The *Exercises* are arranged in an order that forces the exercitant at each stage to keep a clear eye on a self-determined goal—*id quod volo*. Now, the idea of using a method for spiritual advancement—a system of rules and maxims designed to steer a person toward a well-defined goal—is, of course, intrinsically modern. Descartes, perhaps influenced by his Jesuit masters, later adopted a comparable method for conducting the mind along paths of rigorous rationality.[4] The *Exercises* emphasize the primary importance of spiritual discernment, that is, the ability to distinguish effective from ineffective strategies. Moreover, they betray a typically modern awareness of the limited time available for effective action. Their insistence on making the most effective use of one's spiritual potential resembles so closely contemporary secular attitudes as to cast suspicion on its religious nature. What does it mean to trust God as if the result depended exclusively on your own work and to commit yourself to your work as if nothing depended on you? Is this more than a naturalist axiom varnished with a light coat of Christian piety? Does Ignatius's trust in nature not hide a secret naturalism which merely aggravates a condition that had reduced grace to a supplement of an autonomous natural order?

In fact, the *Exercises* present a uniquely modern synthesis of freedom and grace, far superior to the one achieved by the theology of the time. Ignatius does more than methodically direct nature's potential toward a transcendent goal. In his case, the goal—the glory of God (*ut laudet Deum*)—intrinsically transforms the very method for attaining it. He inverts the modern ideal of self-realization. Grace must first liberate nature from a state of unfreedom in order to enable it to reach its natural potential. The underlying conception of freedom stands closer to Luther than to Erasmus! In the central meditations—"On the Kingdom" ("De regno") and "On Two Standards" ("De duobus vexillis")—Ignatius redefines freedom from being a capacity for self-realization (here presented as the pursuit of wealth and glory) to a divinely inspired surrender within which action itself becomes grounded in passivity. The age-old emblem of the person at the fork in the road leading to virtue and to vice here assumes the new meaning of a choice between freedom raised to transcend the self or freedom enclosed within the range of self-centered objectives. Ignatius narrows the traditional choice between good and evil down to the subtler distinction between a good that fully liberates and one that only partially does so. Freedom, for him, consists in acting under the motion of grace. He therefore attaches a particular significance to the capacity to perceive the delicate, highly personal touches of grace and instructs his followers to learn how to distinguish "the various motions that present themselves in our heart." Ignatius's method is planned to result in an attitude of total passivity toward grace. In his devout humanism a movement descending from God precedes the one ascending from man. "The love that moves and causes one to choose *must descend from above*, that is, from the love of God."[5]

Ignatius's spiritual vision, although articulated in the anthropocentric language of modern culture, subverts, in fact, the anthropocentric attitude. The *Exercises* present God as the foundation of human nature and the goal of its accomplishments: "Man is created to praise, reverence, and serve God our Lord. . . ." Starting from a theocentric *Fundamentum*, they conclude with a contemplation of God's active presence in all things and an invitation to view "all blessings and gifts as descending from above" (*Omnia bona descendunt desursum*) (# 237). The metaphor of descent and return dominates the two cardinal visions that shaped Ignatius's spirituality. In Manresa he saw the entire creation proceeding from God the Father and, via the Son, returning to its divine origin. The world became transparent of God in the light flooding from above.[6] Fifteen years later another vision near Rome transformed that contemplative vision into one of action. Or, more correctly, it converted the apostolic action upon which Ignatius was ready to engage into contemplation. He perceived that action itself as participating in the "outgoing" movement of God's trinitarian life. Humans are called not to rest in divine quiet but to descend with the Son into the created world for the purpose of sanctifying it. That extrovert movement at the core of spiritual life sanctioned the worldly mission of Ignatius and his followers. Such a vocation required a different kind of asceticism than monastic piety had practiced. Ignatius urged his followers to seek self-denial primarily through total devotion to their work and submission to those whose task it is to guide them in accomplishing it.[7] Thus a contemplative spirituality based on medieval sources results in a typically modern worldliness. Ignatius transforms the anthropocentric ideal of creative self-development by placing it within a radically theocentric perspective.

The vision of humans continuing God's creative act and thereby becoming God's representatives provided the main inspiration of the Catholic Baroque. On the domes of Baroque churches artists portrayed this vision of God's love descending from the divine throne through hosts of angels and saints and filling the universe below. Retranslating Dionysius's celestial harmony into the language of an anthropocentric world picture, they sacralized Renaissance naturalism from within. In presenting human creativity as descended from above, Ignatius inverted the naturalist view of the person, but that inversion would not have been possible without the modern tension between a divine and a human order conceived as separate centers of power. The harmonious medieval synthesis did not allow this kind of dynamic theocentrism based on a dialectical opposition between two centers. The Basque mystic did the exact opposite of what Blumenberg considered characteristic of modern culture, namely, to fill traditional religious forms with a modern content. He conveyed to the modern worldview a traditional spiritual content.

While the Reformation rebuilt the synthesis of nature and grace along the lines of Augustine's later theology, the Christian humanists discussed in chapter 8 attempted to recast the synthesis by means of early Augustinian, Neoplatonic principles. Tensions remained present in both, pulling the latter toward a superficial optimistic naturalism and the former toward a pessimistic view of nature. Ignatius's complex spiritual vision succeeded in keeping the centrifugal forces united. With the Reformation Loyola opted uncompromisingly for the primacy of grace. But, contrary to a major strand in Protestant thinking, he insisted on the intrinsic restoration of nature in grace. With early Christian humanism he fully accepted the divine presence in nature, but for him that presence resulted entirely from a divine descent not from a self-directed human ascent.

During the Counter-Reformation the classical ideal of perfect form, revived in the Renaissance, acquired a new spiritual meaning. Devout men and women strove to express spiritual nobility through grace in demeanor and manners. The French model of the *honnête homme* originated in the attempt to find a balance between pious inwardness and social acceptance. In the final chapters of his *Courtier* (*Il Cortegiano*), Baldassare Castiglione had already drawn an aristocratic code based on a religious ideal. Francis de Sales, bishop of Genève, presented a less elitist but theologically more substantial directive in his *Introduction to the Devout Life*. It may seem frivolous to compare the French bishop's manual to the Italian courtier's mundane guide on courtly etiquette, yet both flow from the same source. While Castiglione moves from the graceful appearance to what he considers its inner condition—divine grace—Francis seeks in graciousness of manners outwardly to express that inner grace. In their concern with form devout humanists showed the seriousness of their intent to reintegrate the divine and human components of culture.

Francis's *Introduction* rarely discloses its theological foundation. For that we must turn to his more theoretical *Treatise on Divine Love*, in which he describes human nature as dynamically oriented toward the love of God. "We have been created to the image and likeness of God. What does that mean but that we stand in a relation of extreme correspondence [*convenance*] with his divine majesty? Even as the person cannot become perfect except through God's goodness, that goodness itself can nowhere better activate its external perfection than in our humanity."[8] Grace transforms nature from within, resulting in a single reality that is both human and divine. Charity, the sanctifying agent, is "infused," but since it is also a "virtue," it requires the active cooperation of those natural inclinations that are "the wild branches on which we must graft the loots of God's eternal love."[9]

Grace rules spiritual life, but it does so by attracting rather than forcing the will. "When the will follows the attraction and consents to the divine motion, it follows freely, just as it freely resists when it resists—even though our consent to grace depends much more on grace than on the will" (II, 12). Francis never succeeded in bringing the relation between free will and grace to theoretical clarity. His formulation that God grants his grace to those who will respond, appears to depend on Molina's questionable assumption of a divine foreknowledge in accor-

dance with which God, in a second moment, grants grace. Yet he is not
committed to any branch of School theology and simply wants to assert
that supernatural grace appeals to natural inclination. "It operates in us
without us, because it is God's favor which thus comes to our encounter
[la faveur divine qui nous prévient]" (II, 13). Francis avoided becoming
embroiled in School disputes, rightly feeling that those were in large part
responsible for the spiritual poverty of theology. Instead, he concentrated
on practical piety wherein de facto grace appeared united with nature.

Sin, which casts such a long shadow across the spiritual literature of
the time, does not stunt the divine impulse of nature for Francis, although
nature's dynamism needs assistance to do what in its original state it
could do normally.

> Our poor nature, wounded by sin, acts like the palm trees we have
> on this side [of the Alps]: they display some imperfect products,
> some attempts at fruit. But for them to bear full-grown dates [sic] is
> reserved to warmer regions. Similarly, the human heart naturally
> produces certain beginnings of the love of God, but to arrive at that
> love of God beyond all things in which a truly mature love derived
> from divine goodness consists, belongs only to hearts animated and
> assisted by heavenly grace and remaining in a state of holy charity
> (XVII, 2).

God's assistance may be called "supernatural," but the love practiced by
means of that divine support remains natural, Francis insists, because
"this love would go only to God as He is recognized as Creator, Lord, and
sovereign end of all creatures by the *natural* light—and hence is esteemed
lovable and estimable above all things by *natural* inclination and propensity" (XVI, 3, emphasis added).[10] The idea of pure nature, however, is
absent from Francis's writings: nature never appears self-sufficient. His
constant references to Stoic moralists—so common in the French Renaissance—are in this respect quite misleading. The Stoic idea serves as a
model not of pure nature, but of what nature, already included within a
divine vocation, is able to accomplish without the final grace of revelation. Its response remains imperfect, but its virtue is real and continuous
with grace.

It comes as a surprise to a reader of the world-wise *Introduction* to
find the spiritual theory exposed in the *Treatise* strongly advocating internal withdrawal from the world. While Francis succeeded in restyling

the modern synthesis of nature and grace in accordance with the new type of personhood, he utterly fails to do the same for either cosmos or society. The Salesian synthesis remains a strictly interior one, between God and the soul. This may seem an implausible conclusion to all who have undergone the spell of Francis's analogies with natural "events," as improbable as Pliny's "observations" but described with a good deal more charm. The saint obviously "accepts the physical world"[11] —but that does not mean that he theologically integrates it. In a memorable example of pachidermic modesty he admonishes married Christians: "The elephant, not only the largest but the most intelligent of animals . . . is faithful and tenderly loving to the female of its choice, mating only every third year and then no more than five days, and so secretly as never to be seen, until, on the sixth day, it appears and goes at once to wash its whole body in the river, unwilling to return to the herd until thus purified. Such good and modest habits are an example to husband and wife."[12] The equally modest, though less faithful, lioness serves as a model for frequent confession: having been defiled by a leopard, she hastens to cleanse herself before the return of her mate "lest the odor offend him" (II, 19). The salamander that puts out the fire in which it takes refuge, reminds us that sin ruins friendship (III, 22).[13] Yet this affectionate interest in the natural world, anticipating the mood of La Fontaine's fables, remains outside the compass of the spiritual universe that, in the *Treatise* as much as in Augustine's *Confessions*, remains restricted to the relation between God and the individual soul.

Salesian humanism succeeded in incorporating the new image of the person within its spiritual vision but failed to accommodate the new cosmology. Ignatius's vision had been more cosmically oriented. This allowed it to play a leading part in the aesthetic culture of the Baroque and to partake actively in the scientific conquest of the cosmos. It is ironic that just when Galileo was bringing the scientific world view in line with what had already been established aesthetically, philosophically, and in part religiously, the Papacy forced the reluctantly obedient Jesuits, whose teaching at their Roman College had actively contributed to the formation of a new scientific world picture, to fight a rearguard battle against it.

Later spiritual masters, especially Jansenists and Quietists, assimilated much of Francis's theological unworldliness without possessing his human warmth. In fact, aside from a few exceptions, Catholic spirituality never fully reestablished the link with cosmos or society. (The Capuchin

Yves de Paris with his "contemplation naturelle" was one of the few who did.) Christian spirituality remained mostly an affair between God and the soul, and substantially differed from that comprehensive vision that from Origen to the High Middle Ages had inspired a cosmic liturgy. The consequences of this acosmic piety became visible in the seventeenth century when spiritual life definitely withdrew into a separate culture, isolated from all scientific and social renewal. The language of devotion became ever more disincarnated and self-absorbed. Nature mysticism, wherever present, tended to adopt unorthodox or highly untraditional forms as in the alchemical systems of Weigel and Boehme (to be discussed in the next section). What did emerge, however, was a spiritual vision of nature that with increasing power inspired the founders of modern science from Copernicus to Newton. For Kepler, the sensuous as well as the spiritual originate in God and hence natural instinct and sense experience enable the devout searcher to detect a spiritual ground in natural processes. Nature's divine quality appeared in the harmony that linked its diversity to the fundamental unity constituted by God's own presence.

Ignatius and Francis de Sales rethought spiritual life in modern terms. For others, no less influential in the century, the medieval, fully integrated cosmos had never broken down. Teresa of Avila, as perceptively introspective as Montaigne, and John of the Cross, a model poet of the Spanish Renaissance, thought within the earlier synthesis. Certainly, their affective, subjective language substantially differs from the objective, Neoplatonic one of Eckhart, Ruusbroec, and their fifteenth century disciples. Yet their worldview remains unaltered, and they illustrate spiritual life's independence of the new cultural environment. Neither Teresa nor John had to confront the full challenge of modernity. For that reason I shall not discuss them here.

The Religion of the Heart in the Reformation

The early reformers incorporated the principle of subjectivity while avoiding the extremes of theological supernaturalism and Renaissance naturalism. Yet they allowed fallen nature no active part in the process of salvation. In the next generation some Lutheran and Calvinist churchmen began to reassert the need for some mode of cooperation. In fact, the assumption of such a cooperation had never been absent from reformed practice. When Philip Melanchton insisted on the necessity of saintly living and irreproachable conduct in the believer's response to God's grace, he was accused of "innovating." But he mainly translated practical norms into theoretical principles. The Formula of Concord (1580) softened the ethical emphasis of the Philippists, but it also restrained the theory of total passivity held by their theological adversaries. The mystical under-current of the Reformation, obvious in Luther's personal piety but less so in some of his early followers, also resurfaced. Wherever it was allowed a free course, the idea of Christ's transforming power prevailed over that of forensic justification. As those ethical and mystical currents became stronger, they resulted in a reformed variety of Christian humanism.[14]

In Calvinist Holland this humanism took the form of a surprising religious ecumenism. Although Calvinism had become de facto a state religion that after the Synod of Dordrecht occasionally repressed dissi-dents, Holland remained for the most part a safe haven for the unorthodox. In some instances humanist toleration threatened the ecclesiastical foun-dations of the Calvinist confession. Thus to Dirk Volkertszoon Coornhert who proclaimed living in accordance with the moral precepts of the Gospel to be the only test of Christianity, doctrinal differences lost their decisive significance. Grace coincided with the very effort to respond to God's salvific will. Others, such as the radical Dirk Rafelson Camphuy-sen, rejected all doctrinal definition, theological speculation, and even ecclesiastical organization. The impulse to the devout life originates within the heart: there alone does God's grace meet the human will. Camphuysen and like-minded dissenters carried the Protestant principle of interiority to a paradoxical extreme where it coincided with good works and pious dispositions. In them the Reformation rejoins Erasmus's pious humanism and exceeds it in dogmatic tolerance.[15] Reason, internally enlightened by faith—not by Church authority—now serves as final rule of piety and conduct.

Reactions against restrictive doctrinal rules appeared also elsewhere in Calvinism. Calvin's early collaborator and later his vociferous critic, Sebastian Castellio, writes: "Righteousness is learned and known as much by nature as by teaching. Nature endowed man with reason, by which he can discern the true from the false, the good from the evil, the just from the unjust. And teaching which is guided by reason [*ratione duce*] con-firms nature and teaches that man is to live according to nature, pro-nouncing those who do so 'just' and those who do not 'unjust.'"[16] In fact, Erasmus's ideal of Christian humanism and interior piety had persisted even in increasingly intolerant Catholic countries. The *alumbrados* in Spain and the *spirituali* in Italy privately continued to advocate the cen-

trality of Scripture and the justification by faith alone. Reacting positively
to the challenge of Protestantism yet opposed to a break with the Church,
they continued to hope for a reconciliation between Rome and the Reformation at the coming council (of Trent).[17] Their theological proposals
never exceeded the level of inconsistent compromises. They emphasized
(one-sidedly, it seems) the mystical element in Luther's position which
led them in various degrees to embrace the Protestant understanding of
justification by faith without abandoning the Catholic idea of an intrinsic
sanctification of human nature.

A search for inwardness also inspired Lutherans, especially in Germany, to a "religion of the heart." Of course, late medieval piety continued to link it in often unpredictable ways with the Catholic tradition. In
the preface to his 1518 edition of the *Theologia deutsch* Luther himself
had recognized his loyalty to this spiritual tradition: "It is now brought
home to me how false it is when many learned people speak disparagingly
about us Wittenberg theologians, alleging that we are disseminating nov-
elties. They speak as though there would not have been people in the
past and in other places who said what we say."[18]

That same work continued to direct many of his followers to an
earlier mysticism. Rather than dismissing the *Theologia deutsch* as a
sentimental relic of Luther's monastic past, they reissued, paraphrased,
and never stopped recommending this medieval treatise. We find the
names of the most prominent Protestant dissenters connected with it.
Hans Denck produced a revised edition, Sebastian Franck a Latin para-
phrase, Castellio a French and a Latin translation, Valentin Weigel a
summary of its content. All base their support on a theme that had been
essential in all Rhenish and Flemish mysticism of the fourteenth century,
namely, that the soul as image of God enjoys God's permanent presence
which instructs and sanctifies her from within. Even during Luther's
lifetime Thomas Müntzer had preached that God's grace may touch the
hearts of those who never heard the biblical message. God's voice speaks
inwardly and receives outward support from the order of nature.[19] Indeed,
according to the Saxon pastor Valentin Weigel, the only cognitive experience we may hope to obtain of God in this life comes from God's inner
presence. Scripture fulfills merely an instrumental role. It awakens the
truth that, after the fall, lies dormant in the soul.

> Because the Word of God is already present in us, it does not follow
> that one ought not preach, teach, and study it. And conversely, be-

cause it is preached, taught, and heard in church, it does not follow
that it was not previously present in us. Indeed, one should preach,
read, hear, pray, and strive for the Word of God precisely because it
is already there. For were it not, then there would be no book, no
Scripture, and all writing, preaching, reading, and hearing would be
in vain.[20]

Such pronouncements, surprising in the mouth of an active Lutheran
pastor, were a far cry from the *sola Scriptura*, yet they were derived from
the same inward piety that had been an inspiring force behind Luther's
thought. The Reformation held an objective message—to return to the
word of Scripture—as well as a subjective one—to restore the direct
contact of the soul with God through Christ. Their different orientation
had often caused tension. Religious inwardness assumed that God's image
in the soul had been preserved, while the New Testament proclamation
of the (Pauline) doctrine of sin and justification stressed the corruption of
human nature. By and large the two tendencies had managed to coexist
in a somewhat uneasy balance. In the religion of the heart the first
tendency clearly gained the upper hand.

Those mystical movements within the Reformation removed a major
roadblock that had previously obstructed the way toward a new cultural
synthesis. Reacting against the naturalism implicit in the idea of pure
nature, Luther had declared nature after the fall incapable of attaining
genuine goodness. The simultaneous presence of God's justice and human
sinfulness (*simul justus et peccator*) juxtaposed fallen nature with grace,
rather than restoring their unity. The spiritual dissenters overcame this
separation. For them, God was actually present in the soul, even after the
fall, and before the reception of Scripture or baptism. Nor did they simply
return to medieval mystical piety. Their notion of the *self* is a modern
one: an independent center of meaning.

The religion of the heart often suffers from the acosmism characteristic of devout humanism. Although it supports no monasticism, it
strongly encourages an inner withdrawal. Valentin Weigel, a visionary
Lutheran pastor, eventually came to experience this as a defect. While he
had derived the inspiration for his early mystical writings from medieval
spirituality, he later developed a religious cosmology wherein God's direct
presence filled the entire universe. At first his cosmic speculations merely
prefaced an exhortation to move beyond the earth, insignificant "against
the infinity in which it hangs suspended," in order to enter the infinite

world of the soul. But in his last great work, a *Postille* of Sunday sermons (1579), he developed a complete mystical cosmology. True believers partook in Christ's body—a body that, conceived through the Holy Spirit, was divine. By doing so, the faithful extended this divine body over the entire cosmos while anticipating in their earthly community the celestial Jerusalem of the future. "The new Jerusalem must take flesh just as Christ went bodily upon the earth and was not only spiritually among us. . . . [It] must dwell on earth, and Christ must still come to pass on earth— not that he must come physically and visibly in person as before, but rather that he dwell bodily in his own in the house of Jacob, so that we all, under him, are taught by God, needing no longer preachers and prophets, for Christ is everything in us."[21] In Weigel's eschatological vision, God's mystical presence reaches beyond the confines of the spiritual. But his attempt to rebuild a triadic religious synthesis remained an exception. On the whole, Lutheran piety—no less than devout humanism—rarely surpassed an ideal of personal holiness. German Pietism was to raise this flight from worldly involvement into a religious virtue.

An even more radical and less orthodox reunion of nature with its transcendent source was attempted by the Lutheran theosophist Jacob Boehme (1575–1624). Having been influenced by the writings of both Paracelsus and Valentin Weigel, Boehme built a wholly untraditional theological cosmology on alchemical principles. At first we may feel inclined to consider him one of the panentheist or pantheist humanists discussed in the previous chapter. In fact, Boehme's position is decidedly antipantheist, perhaps more clearly so in his later than in his early work. The powers interacting in nature are divine in origin because God animates nature just as the soul animates the body. But they do not coincide with God, even though the entire structure of creation, both the macrocosmos and the microcosmos, is derived from a development in God's inner life. Boehme's interpretation required that he rid the doctrine of creation of those arbitrary, voluntarist, and exclusively causal connotations it had acquired in late medieval theology. God creates freely, yet divine freedom coincides with the necessity essential to God's nature. In creating God brings his nature to its fullest possible expression. To be for him consists in manifesting his essence. Without such a manifestation God would not be the living God of whom Scripture speaks. He would remain the *Ungrund*, the *ewig Nichts*,[22] the Absolute without determination and even without essence. This nameless, essenceless Absolute constitutes indeed a "moment" in divine life. But the deity needs an "other" in which it can mirror itself and thereby acquire full knowledge of itself.

Boehme formulates the divine urge toward expression in trinitarian language but avoids the usual reference to "persons." For him the traditional doctrine of the Father names God's indeterminate will, while that of the Son intends both the determinate will and the divine light as it becomes manifest. The third principle, the Spirit, drives the divine ground to express itself *ad extra*. The divine wisdom therefrom derived is still coeternal with God, but in the order of necessity posterior to the Trinity. Wisdom functions as the model of nature but does not yet constitute the actual world in which God fully knows himself. Creation, then, has its origin in God's innermost essence. No idea appears more repugnant to Boehme than that of a *creatio ex nihilo.* In order to differentiate the organic cosmos from God's own being from which it emerges, the Saxon visionary ascribes to the Creator a body acquired in the very act of creating.[23] Only by means of an organic body can God give birth to an organic nature. Space must be filled with divine presence, and space is for Boehme the primary condition for the existence of a cosmos. In the human mind, however, God's spirit dwells with its own light, and through that mind it enlightens the entire cosmos. The idea of a microcosmos, so central in alchemical thought, here receives a mystical interpretation. The meaning of Boehme's daring metaphors often eludes a firm grasp. One careful interpreter laments that Boehme's doctrine is no doctrine but a vision expressed in symbols.[24]

The crucial challenge to Boehme's attempt to reunify God and nature came with the event of the fall, so decisive to Lutheran theology. How could he explain the opposition it caused between God and nature without disrupting the newly found unity altogether? If nature was necessarily united to a divine source, how could God avoid being responsible for evil? Boehme's entire work may be read as one elaborate theodicy construed to protect his thesis of a primeval unity between nature and its transcendent source. But his interpretation of the origin of evil underwent considerable developments in the course of the years. In his early *Aurora* he held the archangel Lucifer's fall, an event unforeseen by God, responsible for the disturbance of the cosmos. The present world is a poor substitute for the original one, in which humans replace the rebellious angels. Yet God's nature never ceased to remain within the cosmos and his divine light, now rekindled, appeases the tumultuous powers released by Lucifer's fall. In later works Adam rather than Lucifer appears as the cause of disharmony in the present world. His fall had been foreseen but, given his free will, could not have been divinely prevented. Here the question of divine responsibility becomes particularly urgent. If God created beings capable of committing evil, at least their potential for doing so had to be attributed to the Creator, and since creation itself had proceeded from an internal necessity in the divine nature, the sources of evil in some way lay in God himself.

Rather than qualify in his position on the union between God and creation, Boehme appeals to the dialectical oppositions within the divine nature introduced by Luther's theology: God's mercy balanced by God's wrath, his love by his anger. In a most unconventional manner Boehme identifies these contrasts with the distinctions within the Trinity. The Father stands for wrath, the Son for mercy. Fallen nature one-sidedly develops into conflicts what in divine nature remains harmoniously enfolded. The mystic's task consists in reducing these oppositions to their original unity and thereby restore the harmony of the cosmos. The redemption of the cosmos as envisioned by Boehme rests on the idea, totally contrasting with Gnostic and even Neoplatonic doctrines, that the material world, directly created by God, is and remains an image of God's own body. Purifying the earth from the contaminations caused by the fall sublimates evil to a divine sphere: it does not extinguish it.[25] The German mystic understood that attributing all goodness to God and all evil to creation would decisively separate Creator from creature. Redemption in that case would be either added or imputed to a corrupt nature. Rather than thus jeopardize the initial state of union, Boehme preferred to reinterpret traditional doctrines—Lutheran as well as Catholic—in order to keep the transcendent and immanent factors united. There, despite the hermetic obscurity of his concepts and the inconsistency of his claims, lies the modern significance of his message.

Around the middle of the seventeenth century Lutheran as well as Catholic spirituality became increasingly estranged from the social and scientific revolutions of the modern age. Spiritual life withdrew from culture at the very time when its principles had begun to permeate the Baroque attempt to develop an expansionist cultural synthesis. Derivatives of "world," such as "worldly," "mondain," and "weltlich," received a negative religious connotation. By the time the term *secular* adopted its present meaning, the breach had become complete. Spiritual men and women attempted to reunite the fragments of their divided world within a purely internal synthesis. But before the spiritual withdrawal that began in the late seventeenth century, European culture rallied its disparate forces for one last short period into the comprehensive unity of Baroque culture. Glorious as it was, it did not fully succeed in reintegrating the three components of the ancient synthesis. Its assertive rhetoric hid a discrepancy between public word and private feeling. Its declamatory character covered a fear of silence—the fear of not being able to express the fundamental truth within the modern context. The Baroque confronts us with a Janus face: one side torn by tension and insecurity; the other, serene and glowing with confidence.

The Last Comprehensive Synthesis: The Baroque

It may appear preposterous to present the culture of the Baroque as having realized, however provisionally, the ideal of an integral Christian human-ism. For one thing, the Baroque was far from being homogeneously reli-gious. It had its critics, its libertines, even its agnostics. But, more fundamentally, the overall demeanor of Baroque society—as disclosed in its sensuous poetry and ribald novels, in its *mondain* court and licentious public life, in its rising class barriers and indifference to the plight of the poor, in its constant warfare and inhuman cruelty toward defenseless populations, in its ruthless exploitation of the colonies and murderous policies toward the indigenous—hardly corresponds to what one normally associates with religious virtue. We tend to remember the period as glam-orously superficial, grandiloquent more than substantial, fecund in pre-senting new problems but sterile in solving them. With its unprecedented tensions, social as well as religious, the Baroque appears a dubious model of an integrated culture. My justification for introducing it here is that, despite tensions and inconsistencies, a comprehensive spiritual vision united Baroque culture. At the center of it stands the person, confident in the ability to give form and structure to a nascent world. But—and here lies its religious significance—that center remains vertically linked to a transcendent source from which, via a descending scale of mediating bodies, the human creator draws his power. This dual center—human and divine—distinguishes the Baroque world picture from the vertical one of the Middle Ages, in which reality descends from a single transcendent point, as well as from the unproblematically horizontal one of later mod-ern culture, prefigured in some features of the Renaissance. The tension between the two centers conveys to the Baroque a complex, restless, and dynamic quality.

It also accounts for the expansionist impulse that so strongly motivated the Baroque mind. It was the time when colonization continued to
extend the limits of the European world and when, within Europe, newly
developed national states coalesced into such supranational power blocks
as the Hapsburg Empire or the confederation of Protestant states. One
may be inclined to look upon the politics of the early seventeenth century,
which caused the largest devastation of Europe before the present century,
as being no more than a cynical display of raw personal and national
ambitions. But, as Carl Friedrich in *The Age of the Baroque, 1610–1660*
argues, such a view erroneously abstracts politics from what, incompre-
hensibly to us, inspired it:

> Liberal historians found it difficult to perceive that for baroque man
> religion and politics were cut from the same cloth, indeed that the
> most intensely political issues were precisely the religious ones.
> Gone was the neopaganism of the renaissance, with its preoccupa-
> tion with self-fulfillment here and now. Once again, and for the last
> time, life was seen as meaningful in religious, even theological,
> terms, and the greater insight into power which the renaissance had
> brought served merely to deepen the political passion brought to
> the struggle over religious faiths.[26]

Ambitious political and military leaders believed that they were serving
a higher cause, however dubious the means for achieving it may appear
to us. A typical Baroque hero like Wallenstein combined religious faith
with a limitless greed for power and an unfailing sense of the spectacular.
The Baroque hero "was forever walking on a stage . . . and the beauty of
a performance was enhanced by a dramatic exit".[27]

But it is in its aesthetic achievements that the concluding period of
early modernity fully displays its complexity. Significantly, the period
owes its name to a sobriquet given to its artistic expression. The oddly
nondescriptive term *Baroque* suggests the elusiveness of a movement
that could not be captured in a single concept. Even in art history the
term refers not to a clearly definable style but to a number of styles linked
only by a complex aesthetic vision. For all its striking innovation, Baroque
art does not constitute a break with the Renaissance. The quest for form
continues to dominate artistic creation, and it amplifies Renaissance
techniques more than it rejects them. Yet the ideal of form has shifted
from simple harmony to dramatic tension. Great artists of the early

Renaissance such as Brunelleschi, Donatello, and Mino da Fiesole had translated spiritual vision into formal perfection. But the older Michelangelo became dissatisfied with an aesthetics of self-enclosed form. Seeking a more intense spiritual expressiveness he developed a less confining ideal of form. Artists everywhere followed his quest for an open-ended, dynamic representation. Painters broke through the visual enclosure of the framed space by means of an upward surging, outward moving, diagonal line. Sculptors favored expressive form over formal harmony. Architects abandoned the Renaissance ideal of a building that in a single impression of completeness reveals all its parts at once, and by means of a more complex totality invited ever-further exploration of its parts. The developmental quality of Baroque art symbolizes an expanding world permanently in a state of being created and refusing to be confined within established forms. The endless openness of its style—more than the nature of its subjects or the feelings that inspired them—conveys a spiritual quality to Baroque art.

In its symbolic expressiveness Baroque art continued a trend that had been initiated by the so-called mannerist style. The derogatory name "mannerism" fails to capture the spiritual impulse behind the movement. Mannerists, rebelling against the constraints imposed by a narrow form purism, had turned their interest toward the mysterious, the cryptic, even the disharmonious. (One need think only of Tintoretto's weird perspectives, Palladio's illusionistic depths, El Greco's elongated bodies, or Giovanni da Bologna's weightless sculptures.) Baroque art incorporated this trend within a more comprehensive synthesis. In particular, the Baroque tightened the link with language, indispensable for conveying a complex spiritual meaning through a visible image. Compared with the oblique and intricate symbolism of Baroque representations, those of Renaissance iconography, though mostly based on classical sources, appear relatively straightforward to one basically acquainted with the mythical background. The emblems of Baroque representation, although faithful to the fundamental axiom of Renaissance art that meaning must be conveyed in and through material form, rarely yield their full meaning at once.

The tension between spiritual reference and aesthetic symbolization in visual or auditory form evoked stylistic innovations. Even when desiring to convey a clearly transcendent meaning, the Baroque artist avoids a direct presentation of the divine. Instead he symbolizes it through a cascade of earthly mediations. Karsten Harries has rightly drawn attention to this mediative quality in the late Baroque architecture of Bavaria:

"The gap that has opened up between the visible and the spiritual, between picture and reality, makes it impossible for the Church of the Counter-Reformation to simply return to the medieval understanding of the church as a more or less literal representation of the divinely established order of the Heavenly City or the Cosmos."[28] But the mediators that link the higher to the lower realm differ from the Dionysian hierarchs in the older Christian worldview. In the Baroque each one actively prepares the position of the next, rather than serving as a mere channel through which, unfiltered, a divine power passes. Angels and saints actively link God with the human world while the person mediates the divine presence with the cosmos. Painting and sculpture support architecture in mediating an enclosed space with the unlimited one beyond the building.

This mediating quality makes Baroque culture essentially representational.[29] Each aspect of it may be considered both as it is in itself and as it refers to a higher, spiritual reality. In its successful achievements, the horizons of immanence and transcendence become totally fused. The theatre serves as a metaphor of the entire culture. The stage represents the *theatrum mundi.* Its heroes constantly remind the spectator that they are on stage. Theatrical ostentation covers the self with what a French critic has called "un moi de parade, une âme spectaculaire."[30] The splendor and glitter of Baroque society form part of that spectacular representation. To an amazing degree its members realize that their pomp and ostentation present no more than an image, doomed to vanish soon and to make room for new re-presentations. The sense of transiency is as intense as the love of pageantry. Humans are called to play a short part on the world's stage, and this part—half written, half improvised—contains the true meaning of their existence.[31] Occupying a position between the absolute (which they represent) and the relative (which they are), they can allow themselves a great deal of posturing without confusing appearance with reality. A deep-seated awareness of their representational role prohibit them from fully appropriating the dignity of the represented. Where theatre is the metaphor of life, the idea lies near that life itself may not be more than a representation. The human vocation—half tragic, half comic—consists in performing a spectacle that involves the entire cosmos and in bringing it to its divine destiny.

Of course, the stage had already been a leading metaphor of life in the Renaissance and theatre had become, especially in Elizabethan England, a favorite art form. Thriving on disguises, mistaken identities, magical transformations, and illusions of all kind, Renaissance drama had stressed the ever-deceptive quality of appearances. In its more serious mood it had explored the gap between what humans appear to be and what they are. Similarly, in Baroque drama the possibility of deception inheres in the very concept of representation. In the final scene of Corneille's early comedy *L'illusion comique*, the actors depose their gowns and each takes his share of the receipts. Here the playwright unmasks the unmaskers, but in real life the deception may continue forever. For representation tends to feed on itself, turning reality into an endless play of mutually reflecting mirrors—especially when life itself comes to be viewed as a representation.

Still, the basic insight of Baroque drama differs from that of the Renaissance: it deals less with the contrast between truth and illusion than with the fact that life constantly oscillates between the two. Both what the person represents and what he or she privately is, are true. The two never coincide, but they complement each other in constituting the dual human reality. Baroque culture constantly questions the validity of appearance while expressing an obsessive concern with appearance.[32] Appearance belongs to the very core of existence. Even the indubitable awareness of reality in the present loses its substance as soon as that present turns into remembrance. Prince Sigismund, the hero of Calderon's *Life Is a Dream*, wonders:

> What past bliss is not a dream?
> Who has had his happy fortunes
> Who has said not to himself
> As his memory ran o'er them,
> 'All I saw, beyond a doubt
> Was a dream?'
>
> . . . . . .
>
> Is there then twixt one and the other
> Such slight difference, that a question
> May arise at any moment
> Which is true or which is false?[33]

To refer to the Baroque consciousness as being essentially representational or theatrical is to assert that it knows itself to belong to both spheres of reality and appearance.

The playwright exalts human greatness only to warn the audience of the ultimate vanity of a glory that inevitably ends in decay—and often does so on the stage. He relishes in surrounding royal and aristocratic heroes with majestic ceremony while at the same time exposing the vanity of noble titles and courtly pomp. Shakespeare anticipated a fundamental Baroque theme in often choosing as subject a king who either loses his throne or is in imminent danger of doing so: King John, Richard II, Richard III, Henry IV. Like no other, the tragedy of *King Lear* directly relates the honor of the office to the depth of its bearer's humiliation. Calderon de la Barca, the Baroque dramatist par excellence, delights in contrasting what the hero represents with what he or she truly is. *The Great World Theatre* contains a scene in which the king, divested of his regalia, appears as what he is by himself—a poor naked man. Human greatness arises from a greater-than-human mission. That mission may call the hero to the battlefield or it may summon the heroine to subdue passions that threaten her moral vocation. Whether fought with inner or with outer enemies, the struggle to excel in a superhuman task stands at the center of Baroque drama.

Significantly, Baroque drama in the strict sense displays a surprising absence of character development. It contains, to be sure, plenty of movement but little internal action. Often the adventures and vicissitudes that form the warp and woof of a Baroque play—especially a German or Spanish one—do little more than expose the alternation of delusion and reality through which its heroes pass, without intrinsically transforming their character.[34] Even Corneille's psychologically more searching dramas lay the entire moral issue out in the first act, to resolve it in the next twenty-four hours with much struggle but little inner growth.

In the Baroque era the church functions as a theatre for humans to act in more than as a shrine for God to dwell in. The choir provides a stage for dramatic action—open, well lit, and highly visible to spectators. The hieratic motion of an elaborate liturgy symbolizes the majestic dignity of an action at once human and divine. That action moves beyond the choir and into the nave where the statues of saints deliver their timeless messages from pillar to pillar, and beyond the space of the building where through windows, cupolas, and balconies—real or painted—it integrates the entire world within a cosmic liturgy. Bernini's window in the apse of the Vatican basilica floods Saint Peter's chair with mysterious light, suggesting the transcendent setting for the superhuman drama to be performed under the supervision of the church's patron saint. Painting and sculpture merge with Baroque architecture in creating perspectives that extend the sacred realm far beyond the church's dimensions and incorporate the entire visible world.[35] Protestant temples for "hearing the Word" underwent an even more dramatic transformation. The sacred center no longer lies in the eastern apse—formerly the locus of God's sacramental presence—but in the middle of the building where the congregation, seated around the pulpit, waits to hear the word and to respond to it in hymns and prayers.[36]

Baroque culture views creation as pervaded by a natural desire of God. To bring the world to its sacred destiny, it brightens forms and shapes with the transcendent glow of nature redeemed. Such an ideal of religious restoration may seem to have its roots in a strictly Catholic concept of redemption. In fact, however, the Protestant lands of central and northern Europe created a Baroque culture of their own, more inwardly oriented but no less comprehensive in scope. It attained a depth of emotion—primarily in poetry and music—seldom equaled by the more extroverted Catholic Baroque. For the reformed artist, the source of symbolic representation lies within the soul touched by God's grace, and from that inner sanctum it radiates its light over the visible world. While Catholics primarily (though by no means exclusively) perceived God's presence in the cosmos, for Protestants that presence appeared more manifest in history. Thus the French Calvinist Agrippa d'Aubigné in his immense poem *Les Tragiques* narrates the story of God's vindication over his enemies across the centuries. The great German poet Andreas Gryphius saw God glorified in the events of the Thirty Years' War. Dutch Calvinists expressed their theocratic vision of history in painting and sculpture, as well as in poetry. In numerous sketches Rembrandt interiorized the biblical story into a symbol of the intimate relation between God and the soul.[37] Nothing more convincingly refutes the once conventional and still not quite vanquished opinion that Protestant piety erected an insurmountable barrier between a corrupt nature and divine grace than its artistic and poetic achievements of the Baroque. German music and religious poetry, English metaphysical poetry, Dutch painting and poetry—all attained an intensity of religious feeling that was anything but forensic. In unsurpassed masterworks Gryphius, Donne, Herbert, Revius, Rembrandt, and, somewhat later, Buxtehude symbolized a sacralization of nature that, although different from that of the Catholic Baroque, rivaled it in expressiveness.

But the religious culture of the Baroque also shows a darker side. Religious conflicts and the political upheavals they caused introduced a period of continuous warfare and unprecedented terror. Tasso, whose work still belonged to the Renaissance, forefelt this sadder mood. More than glorifying its heroes, his great epic laments the transitoriness and futility of even the greatest human accomplishments. In the end only forgetfulness—*tacita e nera*—awaits the heroic deeds of the past. The poet's song merely succeeds in temporarily rescuing them from the annihilation of time. Tasso's brooding awareness of the instability of all things marks a clear departure from the optimistic confidence of the Renaissance. The worm of corruption inhabits all human enterprises. As they approach their actual realization, the high ideals that inspired them rapidly disintegrate. The long-awaited conquest of Jerusalem—after so many heroic deeds and sacrifices—ended in a rampage of plunder, rape, and slaughter of innocents. Even religion, our ultimate solace, often intensifies the sadness of life. Tasso felt abandoned by God, and the uncertainty of ultimate salvation tortured him even while it inspired his sublime poetry. Few artists expressed the somber mood of the Baroque epoch more poignantly than those who stood at its beginning: Tasso and Michelangelo (especially in his later sonnets). Nevertheless, throughout the period poets and artists succeeded in sublimating their religious anxiety into a deeper, more comprehensive harmony.

Others expressed that anxiety in a less sublimated manner. Witch hunts, progroms, and heresy trials at the end of the sixteenth and the beginning of the seventeenth centuries exposed the cracks developing in what, despite confessional divisions, had remained a homogeneously Christian civilization. Galileo's problems with the Holy Office, the burnings of Bruno and Servet, unprecedented outbreaks of antisemitism in Poland and the German lands, the terror of the Spanish Inquisition in the Low Countries—all of these were symptoms of a religious tradition under siege that was at pains to defend itself while attempting to retighten its already slipping hold on European culture.[38] Doctrinal discipline began to take priority over living faith. Especially after the Council of Trent, theology became regimented, homogenized into a single form of orthodoxy. Its precise, quasi-technical language gave it the appearance of a rigorous science supported by an endless stream of arguments for the existence of God. A "science" of contemplation began to define the stages of spiritual life. Professional exorcists placed evil on public trial, enjoining devils—labeled and classified in hierarchies and subclasses—to respond (in Latin) to precise theological questions. Amazingly, they always complied! The possessions at the Ursuline convent at Loudun at regular intervals transformed the peaceful lives of the nuns into a witches' sabbath. Its violent eruptions announced the end of a religious era. As Michel de Certeau noted, the sacred was becoming marginalized in its mystical as well as in its demonic forms: "They join each other at the same place of society: on the sidelines."[39]

But where theologies failed, political disasters struck, and churches were embroiled in polemics, the pursuit of formalized expression and aesthetic harmony assisted men and women in finding their way back to an orderly universe. Precisely the tragic conflicts of the time gave Baroque culture its depth and complexity. If war and religious upheavals had not challenged its artists to create harmony out of conflict, the art of the Baroque would soon have degenerated into formalism, and its poetry into empty rhetoric—as they eventually did. Instead, at the high point of Baroque culture, poets like Gryphius and Vondel converted the sorrows of life into symbols of eternity through majestic verse. Among their dominant themes was the evanescence of time and the imminence of death.[40] The unique dramatic power of Baroque poetry consists in holding existential extremes together without reducing one to the other. In metaphysical poetry the opposition conveys an internal tension that deepens the meaning of existence. Conflict becomes a metaphor of life. We tend to read the wide-ranging contrasts in the symbolic register of Baroque poets as successive swings of mood, from the erotic to the devotional, due to religious conversion, misfortune, or purely formal differences in poetic genre. Such factors were undoubtedly present—Donne's conversion obviously transformed the mood of his poetry—but far more significant is the underlying unity that integrated those contrasts into a single symbolic meaning. Conversion alone fails to explain how the author of sensuous love poetry could also write this poignant lament on the soul's fate of having to dwell within an ill-suited body:

> Think that no stubborn, sullen anchorit
> Which, fix'd t' a pillar or a grave, doth sit
> Bedded and bath'd in all his ordures, dwells
> So foully as our souls in their first-built cells.
> Think in how poor a prison thou didst lie
> After, enabled but to suck and cry.

Think, when twas grown to most, twas a poor inn
A province park'd up in two yards of skin.[41]

Such contrasts, abundant in Baroque poetry, are inspired by more
than conversions from worldly moods to sober-minded ones. Indeed,
faith's main struggle at the time was with despair not with sensuousness.
Sometimes both faith and despair appear in the same poem, as in Johann
Christian Guenther's disconcerting "Geduld, Gelassenheit." This uncompromising display of contrasting extremes, written a few years after the
period here considered, typifies the amazing range of Baroque sensitivity.

Geduld, Gelassenheit, treu, fromm und redlich sein,
Und wie ihr Tugenden euch sonst noch alle nennet,
Verzeiht es, doch nicht mir, nein, sondern meiner Pein,
Die unaufhörlich tobt und bis zum Marke brennet,
Ich gebe euch mit Vernunft und reifem Wohlbedacht,
Merkt dieses Wort nur wohl, von nun an gute Nacht.

(Patience, abandon, being faithful, pious, reasonable
And what else you care to name your virtues all,
Forgive, not me, no, but my pain,
Which rages on and burns me to the end,
That, knowingly and after ripe reflection, I bid you,
Please, note my word, henceforth good night.)

Systematically, through six long strophes, the poet elaborates his rejection
of virtue as pure sham, only to conclude with the following aspiration:

Ach Jesu, sage selbst, weil ich nicht fähig bin,
Die Beichte meiner Reu; ich weisz nicht mehr wohin
Und sinke dir allein vor Ohnmacht in die Armen.

(Oh Jesus, say you, for me no longer capable,
The confession of my repentance; I know not whither
And you alone I sink, powerless, in the arms.)[42]

The poet juxtaposes two incompatible spiritual worlds, seeking neither
to reconcile them nor to reduce them to one another. "For the metaphys-
icals it [the impulse toward unity] resides in a tenuous balance of contradictions, a dramatization of the conflict between appearance and reality
which requires as its instruments metaphor and conceit, paradox and
irony."[43]

No literary form proved more appropriate for bringing such contrasts to a head and for aesthetically bridging them than drama. Baroque drama forced the chaos created by the inner conflicts of the age into a pattern of order. Even the restrictive interpretation (especially in France) of the space and time limits Aristotle set to dramatic action and the rigid division into acts and scenes assisted in regimenting the unpredictable forces of the irrational that played such havoc in real life. The drama projected those contrasts onto a higher ground where they might be viewed as patterns of a providential design. It resolved no conflicts but showed how a transcendent power controls those conflicting forces and reconciles them on a higher level. Whether religious or secular, its theatrical and moral effect presupposed a transcendent governance of human affairs.

The Baroque achieved this balance of harshly contrasting yet interacting forces by means of a more inclusive conception of harmonious form than the Renaissance had possessed. Its complex form could grant the warring components a great deal of independence. This enabled poetry and art to thrive in the midst of religious dissent, endless wars, and profound spiritual tensions. France, Spain, and the Netherlands refer to this century, the first half of which must be counted among the cruelest and most unsettled periods in Western history, as their "classical" or "golden" one. The awareness of an all-embracing transcendence kept the conflicting elements of the Baroque synthesis together.

Remarkably enough, theology proper played no major role in establishing or maintaining this religious synthesis. Having failed to incorporate the world picture presented by modern science, theological doctrine withdrew from one bastion after another without making new intellectual conquests. The Council of Trent may have stimulated the initial impetus, and it certainly rallied some of the forces for rebuilding a Catholic culture. But it supplied no adequate theological principles for supporting the structure it had helped to create. The decree on justification, though admirably phrased, did not answer the fundamental question raised by the Reformation and contributed little toward closing the widening gap between the two orders—natural and supernatural. The theology formed in its wake was dogmatically too restrictive to assimilate the emerging modern cosmology. Indeed, in the next decades that theology held the front line of the forces resisting the acceptance of the new cosmology, despite the efforts of enlightened prelates (like de Bérulle and Francis de Sales), Jesuit astronomers, and such prominent Catholic scientists as Descartes, Pascal, and, indeed, Galileo. As a result, theology missed the dynamic strength indispensable for shaping a culture in which science had begun to speak with the voice of authority. It would have required an extraordinary speculative and practical effort fully to assimilate the modern creations of science, art, poetry, education, and even spiritual life into a new theological synthesis. That effort was not made or even seriously tried. For many years theology continued to reason as if humanity dwelled at the bottom of an inverted celestial pyramid, the end of a downward causal chain. At the critical junction when a new culture was ready to take off, Scholastic theology and Protestant orthodoxy settled in for a long sleep. The first signs of deism and atheism around the middle of the seventeenth century failed to waken them.

Lacking the firm yet flexible theological base it needed, the complex Baroque synthesis began to unravel. Without such a base the transcendent component, already removed from the center, lost its capacity to function as an integrative power. Thus began the definitive withdrawal of the transcendent dimension from Western culture. The pursuit of form degenerated into formalism. Isolated from existential concerns, the vigorous art of the Baroque turned into one of decoration. An overgrowth of auxiliary forms crowded into the place of a single guiding form. Rococo style rarely created more than form without soul, parts without a center.

Around 1660, the last comprehensive integration of our culture began to break down into the fragmentary syntheses of a mechanist world picture, a classicist aesthetics, and a theological scholasticism. Soon a flat utilitarianism would be ready to serve as midwife to the birth of what Nietzsche called modern man's small soul. Regions where the Baroque lingered on fell out of step with the crude but efficient forces in pursuit of more immediate goals. Only the autumnal glow of what once had been a radiant culture but had now lost its creative impulse continued to embellish these relics of a greater past. Christopher Dawson wrote: "With the passing of the Baroque culture, a vital element went out of Western civilization. Where its traditions survived into the 19th century, as in Austria and Spain and parts of Italy and South Germany, one still feels that life has a richer savour and a more vital rhythm than in lands where the bourgeois spirit is triumphant."[44] Indeed, but the more valuable heritage of the past consists in the vital promises it holds for the future. Obviously, those remnants hold no promise.

Conclusion

Modernity is an *event* that has transformed the relation between the cosmos, its transcendent source, and its human interpreter. To explain this as the outcome of historical precedents is to ignore its most significant quality—namely, its success in rendering all rival views of the real obsolete. Its innovative power made modernity, which began as a local Western phenomenon, a universal project capable of forcing its theoretical and practical principles on all but the most isolated civilizations. "Modern" has become the predicate of a unified world culture.

The West could not have exercised such a global influence if other civilizations, however different, had not been receptive to innovation. The dynamic tension between the components of a cultural synthesis enables them at any time to assume a greater independence with respect to the whole. The more dynamic and complex the original synthesis, the more likely its constituents will become emancipated. The vitality of medieval civilization predisposed it toward granting its component factors a great deal of independence. Yet as the analyses of early humanism and the Baroque have shown, an increased autonomy of the parts need not undermine the balance of the whole. What does follow from such an emancipation, however, is a shift in the overall structure of the synthesis. Thus

249

when early humanists placed a new and strong emphasis on human creativity, they added a secondary center to the one traditionally reserved to the transcendent source of power. The philosophy of the subject converted this center into a primary one. Except for the short-lived balance achieved during the Baroque period, that model prevailed and in the course of time succeeded in affecting every aspect of culture with its theoretical and practical benefits and liabilities.

The constrictiveness of an anthropocentric model of culture has provoked strong reactions. The recent self-destruction of the Marxist social systems that dominated half of Europe can be seen as the latest explosion of a revolt against the modernist dogma, from which Marxism drew the most extreme conclusions. Still, as suggested in the Introduction, the various reactions generally referred to as "post-modern" remain for the most part faithful to the fundamental principle of subjectivity. To be sure, basic changes have taken place since the early modern period. The form principle that has determined Western culture since the beginning—and with renewed force during the early modern age—appears to be receding in our time. It has come under increasing attacks for veiling both the openness of existence and the indeterminacy of Being itself.

Some traditional societies feeling threatened by modernity have attempted to defend themselves against it by often violent reversals to the past. Such rearguard actions are not likely to prevail. Science and technology have become inevitable and practically indispensable for survival, even for those who reject the ideologies that made them possible. Their methods and principles are by nature universal, however particular (and, to some, questionable) their origins may be. Nor can any region close itself definitively to the impact of modern culture. For one of that culture's remarkable achievements consists in having created an all-encompassing system of communications. The downfall of the communist regimes was due in major part to an inability to screen their radical experiments in social engineering from outside influences. A modern society cannot permanently withhold information from its members. Open communication forms an integral part of its make-up. With respect to science and technology we can expect the culture of the future to be global and homogeneous.

But in another, perhaps more fundamental sense the future may hold a far greater diversity than modernized societies now display. Thus far the one-sidedness of its achievement has unduly narrowed the scope of the revolution's original potential. The development sketched in this

essay began with a change in the relation of the components of the
traditional synthesis, not with the exclusive dominion of any single one.
As early humanism intimated and Baroque culture showed, this change
held a richer and more complex potential than its later accomplishments
realized. From that perspective the modern program appears not so much
obsolete as unfinished. Its completion will require a more equitable recognition of the meaning-and-value-giving function of all three of the
component factors than the absolute dominance of the subject has hitherto admitted. The physical cosmos contains more meaning than a reduction to pure objectivity reveals. Nor can the transcendent factor be
omitted from the meaning-giving process: transcendence is not merely
what lies beyond the world, but first and foremost what supports its
givenness. The achievement of such a more comprehensive synthesis
remains part of the program of the modern age. In that sense at least, our
present and future project remains modern. Nor ought the one-sidedness
of its past realizations discourage us about its future prospects. That one-
sidedness may in the end matter less than the autonomy modernity
has gained for the three components of culture: the spontaneity of a
freedom recognized as an ontological principle, the sufficiency of a self-
supporting cosmos, and the distinctness of a transcendence perceived
as wholly encompassing the finite realm while intrinsically sustaining
its autonomy.

At this point we must return to the question raised in the Introduction: What, if any, is the ontological import of the new cultural symbols,
different conceptions, and other mental attitudes that emerged in the
wake of contingent changes, random events, and fortuitous discoveries?
Have they affected the nature of what metaphysicians used to call the
ultimately real? Inevitably a reflection on modern culture must move
beyond hermeneutic questions to ontological ones. Today even the hard-
nosed empiricist can no longer dismiss them as nonsensical. How can we
fail to perceive a relation between cultural change and a transformation
of the cosmos? Ecological concerns as well as scientific theories have
forced us to take seriously the idea that reality does not remain indifferent
to modes of thinking and feeling. Their correlation appeared less obvious
during the early modern period. Yet mental life is as essential a component of the real as neutrons and Milky Ways—and far more powerful in
imposing its effect upon other forms of reality. The nature of the real is
determined by the nature of the relations among its components, of which
mind is the primary one. Ever since Aristotle, categories of being have

been structures of relatedness. How then could the real remain unchanged when its determining relations become transformed? Any change in these relations affects the status of the whole. Spiritual revolutions transform reality as much as physical changes do. To the physicist no less than to the philosopher, the real consists of more than objects. The Ionian speculation with which Western reflection on the nature of reality began assumed the presence of a mental force.

When modern thought distinguished the real as it is in itself from the real as it exists for itself, it initiated a new epoch in being as much as a new stage of reflection. Indeed, it opened a gap in the very nature of the real that will never be closed again. Despite the erroneous assumption that the meaning of the former depends entirely upon the latter, implied by the modern distinction between object and subject, the more fundamental view that mind stands in a creative relation to that physical reality on which it in other respects depends, is definitive. All Greek thinkers from Plato to Plotinus had declared mind a reality in its own right. But the spiritual discovery of the moderns consists in understanding the active relationship of mind to cosmos as one that changes the nature of the real. As it directly affects the constituent relations of the real, this insight is itself transformative. When Descartes contrasted the physical universe as *res extensa* to the mental one as *res cogitans*, he did more than repeating a distinction as old as philosophy itself: he defined an active relatedness that early humanist speculations on art and poetry had prepared.

The rethinking of the idea of transcendence, even as that of self and cosmos begun in the fifteenth century, has not come to rest in our time. A continuing effort to redefine the meaning of contingency and necessity, of autonomy and dependence has thoroughly destabilized the traditional modes of conceiving the ontological limits of the real. If the change had consisted merely in an attempt to adjust medieval theology to a heliocentric cosmology, it would have caused no serious crisis. But, more fundamental, modern thinkers, even before the advent of the new cosmology, had begun to revise the accepted idea of transcendence in a way that transformed the concept of a power hierarchically transmitted from *beyond* into a source of power *within* the universe whereby God's presence permeated all parts at once. For such panentheistic philosophers as Cusanus, Telesio, Bruno, and, later, Spinoza, the being of the cosmos is no less than a disclosure of God's Being. (One must not too easily call them pantheists since even for Spinoza the relation between the *natura naturans* and the *natura naturata* remains irreversible.) Their views on transcendence never entered the mainstream of modern religious thought, but their ideas have resurfaced in major thinkers of recent times—from Hegel to Whitehead. The search for an adequate conception of transcendence appears far from finished. How does the necessary allow genuine contingency? How does the contingent affect the nature of necessity? These questions remain unanswered, as do so many others introduced by modern culture.

The development analyzed in this book does not suffice to explain the cultural physiognomy of the present age. To do so, it would have to include the second modern revolution, broadly referred to as the Enlightenment. Much of its effect consisted in hardening what had remained fluid and in canonizing what had been no more than open options in the early modern period. Yet that second, less fundamental transformation continues to give the present much of its spiritual outlook. The current critique of the dogmatic certainties of the Enlightenment urges us to return to an earlier stage of modern culture when questions had not yet become principles. Once again we pass through a period of profound insecurity. Critical reflection calls for change. But we have not yet succeeded in grasping the meaning of that past, which constitutes our present self. While anxiously seeking a new wholeness we must nevertheless carefully protect those fragments of meaning that we possess, knowing that they may be the bricks of a future synthesis. As Emerson admonished: "We must hold hard to this poverty, however scandalous, and by more vigorous self-recoveries, after the sallies of action, possess our axis more fully."

Notes

Introduction

1 Paul Oskar Kristeller, "Humanism and Scholasticism in the Italian Renaissance," in *Renaissance Thought: The Classic, Scholastic, and Humanist Strains* (New York: Harper & Row, 1961). The term *middle ages* did not become current until the seventeenth century, though Vergerius Andreas de Buxis, the Vatican librarian, mentions the "intermediate age" in his dedication to Pope Nicholas II of an incunabulum containing some works by Apuleius he published in 1469.

2 Johan Huizinga, *The Waning of the Middle Ages* (1924), trans. F. Hopman (New York: Doubleday, 1956), pp. 324–31.

3 Karl Jaspers, *Vom Ursprung und Ziel der Geschichte* (Frankfurt: Fischer Bucherei, 1955), p. 233.

4 Ernst Cassirer, *The Philosophy of Symbolic Forms*, trans. Ralph Manheim (New Haven: Yale University Press, 1954), vol. 1, p. 84.

5 I have made a modest effort at defining the problem in an essay, "Philosophy and Its History," *Review of Metaphysics* 42 (1989): 463–82.

6 For an intelligent argument on the relation between social structures and cultural life in the early modern age, see Lauro Martines,

Power and Imagination (New York: Alfred A. Knopf, 1979). I have discussed the problem in a more general way in *Marx's Social Critique of Culture* (New Haven: Yale University Press, 1983), chap. 5.

7 Will-Erich Peuckert, *Die grosse Wende: das apokalyptische Saeculum und Luther* (Hamburg: Claassen & Goverts, 1948; rpt. 1966), pp. 415–16. A host of other authorities (specifically with respect to the early modern age), such as Thorndike, Panofsky, Kristeller, and Trinkaus, have confirmed this conclusion.

8 Karl Popper and John Eccles, *The Self and Its Brain* (Berlin: Springer International, 1977), p. 61.

9 Human activity stands in a dialectical relation to the material world which it transforms and by which it is conditioned. See Dupré, *Marx's Social Critique of Culture*, esp. the introduction and conclusion.

10 Henri Daniel-Rops, *The Church in the Seventeenth Century* (*Le grand siècle des âmes* [l963]), trans. J. J. Buckingham (Garden City, N.Y.: Doubleday, 1965), vol. 1, pp. 200–201.

Chapter 1

1 Leslie Stephen, *Hobbes* (1904; rpt. Ann Arbor: University of Michigan Press, 1961),

p. 173. See also Arthur Lovejoy, "Nature as Aesthetic Norm," *Modern Language Notes* (1927): 444; rpt. in *Essays in the History of Ideas* (Baltimore: Johns Hopkins University Press, 1948), p. 69.

2 The popular etymology that traces *physis* to the verb *phyesthai* (to grow), accepted by Heidegger (e.g., "On the Essence of Truth," in *Basic Writings* [New York: Harper & Row, 1976], p. 129], may be hard to support. John Burnet consistently rejected the connection with "emerging" and instead derived *physis* from the root *phy* which, even as the Latin *fui,* relates to *being. Early Greek Philosophy,* 4th ed. ([1982]; London: Macmillan, 1930; rpt. 1957), pp. 363–64.

3 Proclus, *Elements of Theology,* 2d ed., trans. E. R. Dodds (Oxford: Clarendon Press, 1977), # 21, corrolary.

4 Aristotle, *Physics* II, 1, 192b, 21–23. On the meaning of *nature* in Aristotle, see Joseph Owens, *A History of Ancient Western Philosophy* (New York: Appleton, Century, Crofts, 1957), pp. 311–12. On the shifts of meaning in *physis* one may consult, besides the older works by Felix Heinimann (*Nomos und Physis* [Basel, 1945]) and Paul Joos (*Tuchè, Phusis, und Technè* [Winterthur, 1955]), Mihai Spariosu, *God of Many Names: Play, Art, and Power in Hellenic Thought* (Durham, N.C.: Duke University Press, 1991), chap. 2, esp. pp. 75–87.

5 This is a highly simplified summary of a complex development that in successive stages, from Aeschylus to Euripides, reflected various intellectual currents. For a recent study of this development and of the changing ethical attitudes it reflects, see Martha Nussbaum's masterly analysis of tragedies by each of these playwrights in *The Fragility of Goodness: Luck and Ethics in Greek Tragedy and Philosophy* (Cambridge: Cambridge University Press, 1986), chaps. 2, 3, and 13.

6 J. S. Kirk, J. C. Raven, and M. Schofield, *The Presocratic Philosophers.* Fr 110 Simplicius in *Phys,* 24, 7 (Cambridge: Cambridge University Press, 1957, 1983), p. 118.

7 Plato, Letter VII (341C).

8 Plato, *Gorgias,* 508a, trans. W. D. Woodhead, in *Plato: Collected Dialogues,* ed. Edith Hamilton and Huntington Cairns, Bollinger Series 71 (Princeton: Princeton University Press. 1961), p. 290.

9 Plotinus, *Enneads,* trans. A. H. Armstrong (Cambridge: Harvard University Press, 1984), V, 8, 7. Cf., Hans Urs von Balthasar's illuminating discussion on the subject of form in Plotinus, in *Herrlichkeit,* vol. 3, 1, *Im Raum der Metaphysik* (Einsiedeln: Johannes Verlag, 1965), pp. 252–62.

10 Richard Lattimore, *The Odes of Pindaros* (Chicago: University of Chicago Press, 1976), p. 116.

11 R. G. Collingwood, *The Idea of Nature* (Oxford: Clarendon Press, 1945), p. 3.

12 *Heracliti Ephesii Reliquiae,* as arranged by Ingram Bywater, 1, 2, trans. John Burnet, in *Early Greek Philosophy,* pp. 132–33.

13 Hans-Georg Gadamer, "The Relevance of Greek Philosophy for Modern Thought," *Philosophy/Wijsbegeerte* (South Africa), 6, no.2 (1987): 40.

14 Cf. Nussbaum, *Fragility of Goodness,* p. 402. The author rightly denies that the basic issue is relativism (which was not a necessary consequence of the distinction) but the origin of *nomos.* Are conventions preestablished in a divine order, or do they develop under human impulse? In the latter interpretation, adopted by at least some Sophists, the social factor increases enormously in significance. Yet I wonder whether the origins of this position may be traced back as far as Pindarus.

15 Plato, *Gorgias,* 483e, in *Collected Dialogues,* pp. 266–67.

16 Plato, *Protagoras,* 323c-326c, trans. W. K. C. Guthrie, in *Collected Dialogues,* pp. 320–22. See also Hermann Diels, *Fragmente der Vorsokratiker,* rev. by Walter Kranz (Berlin, 1964), sec. 74.

17 In *The Moral Economy of Labor* (New Haven: Yale University Press, 1993) James Bernard Murphy attributes it to a loss or weakening of the principle of *ethos,* which previously had mediated between the two. For various degrees of support, cf., W. A. Heidel, "The *Peri Physeos:* A Study of the Conception of Nature Among the Presocratics," *Proceedings of the American Academy* 45 (1910); Martin Oswald, *Nomos in the Beginning of the Athenian Democracy* (Oxford: Oxford University Press, 1969); C. E. R. Lloyd, *Magic,*

Reason and Experience (Cambridge: Cambridge University Press, 1979).

18 Nussbaum, *Fragility of Goodness*, p. 258.

19 Cf., Aristotle, *Metaphysics* 12.5, 1074 b 1–14. Also, *Met.* 1.2, 982 b 18; and *Eud. Ethics* 1.6, 1216 b 27. Professor Gerard Verbeke (University of Leuven) drew my attention to the significance of this position.

20 On context and teleology in Stoic ethics, see A. A. Long, "Greek Ethics after MacIntyre and the Stoic Community of Reason," *Ancient Philosophy* 3 (1983): 184–97. The reference to Chrysippus appears on p. 192.

21 Robert Warrand Carlyle, *History of Medieval Political Theory in the West,* vol. 1 (Edinburgh and London: W. Blackwood, 1903). Cf., for instance, Cicero's attack upon the necessity of some injustice in government in *De republica* 2, 44.

22 Robert Spaemann, "Natur," in *Philosophische Essays* (Stuttgart: Reclam, 1983), p. 21. In fact, Cicero applies the juridical term *res* (that over which one legally disposes) to nature itself, thereby indirectly indicating that nature becomes subject to active human intervention. Ernesto Grassi, *Rhetoric as Philosophy* (University Park: Pennsylvania State University Press, 1980), p. 9.

23 Ernesto Grassi, *Renaissance Humanism: Studies in Philosophy and Poetics* (Binghamton, N.Y.: Medieval and Renaissance Texts and Studies, 1988), pp. 68–70.

24 Michael B. Foster, "The Christian Doctrine of Creation and the Rise of Modern Natural Science," *Mind* 43 (1934): 464.

25 Cornelia De Vogel, "'Ego sum qui sum' et sa signification pour une philosophic chrétienne," *Revue des Sciences Religieuses* 35 (1961): 346–54.

26 Georg Picht, *Der Begriff der Natur und seine Geschichte* (Stuttgart: Klett-Cotta, 1989), p. 85.

27 Gregory of Nyssa developed this theory in *De Hominis Opificio* and in *De Anima et Resurrectione.*

28 Their religious concern appears clearly in the statement issued by the ecclesiastical Council of Hieria in 754: "He [the painter] makes an image and calls it Christ. The name *Christ* signifies *God and man.* Consequently it

is an image of God and man, and consequently he has in his foolish mind, in his representation of the created flesh, depicted the Godhead which cannot be represented, and thus mingled what should not be mingled." (Trans. H. R. Percival, in *The Seven Ecumenical Councils of the Undivided Church,* ed. P. Schaff and H. Wace, vol. 14 of *A Select Library of Nicene and Post-Nicene Fathers of the Christian Church* [Grand Rapids: Eerdmans, 1955], p. 543.)

29 On this significance of the dogma of the Incarnation, see Hans Urs von Balthasar, *The Glory of the Lord A Theological Aesthetics,* vol. 1, *Seeing the Form,* trans. Erasom Leiva-Merikakis (San Francisco: Ignatius Press, 1982), passim, esp. p. 151. On the continuance of the need for a cosmology: *Herrlichkeit* III/1 (volume as yet untranslated), pp. 286–88.

30 How all-pervasive this realistic conception of knowledge was before the twelfth century and how much it differs from the modern symbolic one, Edward Cranz has shown in two unpublished papers to which I owe a considerable debt.

31 Bernardus Sylvestris, *Cosmographia.* That some gnostic elements remain appears from occasional pronouncements such as the following: Below the midpoint of the teaming air wander "evil spirits and agents of the lord of cruelty" that have been cleansed only slightly "of the ancient evil of matter" (p. 108).

32 Bonaventure, *In Hexaemeron, Visio III, Coll.* 4. Cf., Max Wildiers, *The Theologian and His Universe* (New York: Seabury Press, 1981), pp. 43–48.

33 Such was already Johan Huizinga's conclusion in *The Waning of the Middle Ages* (1924), trans. F. Hopman (New York: Doubleday, 1956).

34 Etienne Gilson, "Le moyen age et le naturalisme antique," *Archives d'histoire doctrinale et littéraire du Moyen Age* 7 (1932): 25. Also, Winthrop Wetherbee, "The Function of Poetry in the *De planctu nature* of Alain de Lille," *Traditio* 25 (1969): 117–19, and M-D. Chenu, *Nature, Man, and Society in the Twelfth Century* (Chicago: University of Chicago Press, 1968). Medieval naturalism did not always remain in harmony with grace, and this was decreasingly so toward the end of the Middle Ages. In the long second part of the *Roman* *de la rose* (1273) Jean de Meung defends an unmitigated naturalism, the supreme law of which is to follow the love instinct—wherever it may lead. Social structures and institutions, customs, classes, laws are all artificial and must yield to the higher law of reason, namely, instinct. Monastic life with its vow of chastity goes against nature and ought to be abolished. Nature is set up as an anti-pope, "vicaire et connétable de l'empereur éternel." Yet the poet claims to do no more than restore the Gospel of charity to its original purity!

35 See Jesse Gellrich, *The Idea of the Book in the Middle Ages: Language Theory, Mythology, and Fiction* (Ithaca: Cornell University Press, 1985).

36 Bonaventure, *In Hexaemeron* XII, 14.

37 For William of St. Thierry, the contemplative life culminates in a "loving understanding" that surpasses human understanding. "When the object of thought is God and the things which relate to God, and the will reaches the stage at which it becomes love, the Holy Spirit, the Spirit of life, at once infuses himself by way of love." (*The Golden Epistle*, trans. Theodore Berkeley O.C.S.O. [Kalamazoo, Mich., Cistercian Publications, 1980], # 249, p. 92.)

38 Michel Foucault, *The Order of Things*, anon. trans. from *Les mots et les choses* (1966; New York: Vintage Books, 1973), p. 40.

39 "Through the truth God comes to be present to the soul and the understanding, and hence we need no abstract concept in order to know Him. Still, the mind that knows Him receives the form of a cognitive image, some sort of likeness—this, however, is not an abstraction, but something impressed." (Bonaventure, *In Sententias* I d.3 I q.1 ad 5.) Hans Urs von Balthasar paraphrases this text: "[Christ] alone, as the total expression of God, gives expression in himself to all that can be created in its infinite multiplicity—and not only in general, but in the smallest particular details (*singulare*), in a *distinctissima expressio*, just as the one unique light, for example, gives expression to many different colors." (Hans Urs von Balthasar, "Bonaventure," in *The Glory of the Lord: A Theological Aesthetics*, vol. 2, *Studies in Theological Style: Clerical Styles*, trans. Andrew Louth, Francis McDonagh, Brian McNeil [San Francisco: Ignatius Press - Crossroad, 1984], p. 295.)

40 Durandus a S. Porciano, *Sent.* II, d.3, q.6 n. Ockham, *Sent.* I, d. 27, q. 2K and 3J; II, q. 14 and 15. Erich Hochstetter, *Studien zur Metaphysik und Erkenntnislehre Wilhelms von Ockham* (Berlin: W. de Gruyter, 1927), pp. 35–46. I remain, of course, aware of the distinctions between Durandus and Ockham on the one side and between Ockham and the nominalists on the other.

Chapter 2

1 Marsilius Ficinus, *Opera Omnia* (Basel, 1576; photographic repro. Turin: Bottega d'Erasmo, 1959), vol. 2, pp. 1325–26.

2 The first statement appears in *The Science of Logic*, trans. A. V. Miller (New York: Humanities Press, 1969), pp. 825–26; the second in *The Philosophy of Spirit*, trans. William Wallace (Oxford: Clarendon Press, 1971), § 133.

3 Johan Huizinga, *The Waning of the Middle Ages* (1924), trans. F. Hopman (New York: Doubleday, 1956), p. 323. A recent study of the subject shows how intimately form continues to be connected with language. "The discipline that has been responsible for educating a person to form by educating him *through* form . . . is rhetoric." John H. Smith, *The Spirit and Its Letter: Traces of Rhetoric in Hegel's Philosophy of Bildung* (Ithaca: Cornell University Press, 1988), p. 51.

4 Paul Oskar Kristeller, *Renaissance Thought: The Classic, Scholastic, and Humanist Strains.* (New York: Harper & Row, 1961), pp. 98–99.

5 Jacob Burckhardt, *The Civilization of the Renaissance in Italy*, trans. S. G. C. Middlemore (New York: Harper & Row, 1929, 1958), p. 294. For Dante's portrayal of the individual person, see Erich Auerbach, *Dante, Poet of the Secular World* (1929), trans. Ralph Mannheim (Chicago: University of Chicago Press, 1969).

6 Petrarch, "The Ascent of Mont Ventoux," in *The Renaissance Philosophy of Man*, trans. Hans Nachod, ed. Ernst Cassirer, Paul O. Kristeller, and John Randall (Chicago: Chicago University Press, 1948), p. 44.

7 That future becomes visible in Petrarch's later letters, as when he informs his correspondent "quanta voluptate solivagus ac liber, inter montes et nemora, inter fontes et flumina, inter libros et maximorum hominum ingenium respiro." *Rerum familiarium* VII, 4, ed. Francassetti, I, 367.

8 *Memoirs of a Renaissance Pope: The Commentaries of Pius II,* trans. Florence A. Gragg, ed. Leona C. Gabel (London: Allen and Unwin, 1960), pp. 154–55. I remember only one comparable earlier description. In a letter to a friend, St. Bruno transforms the inhospitable solitude of his hermitage in the Calabrian wilderness into a garden of earthly delights: "What words can describe the delights of this place—the mildness and wholesomeness of the air—the wide and fertile plain between the mountains, green with meadows and flowering pastures—the hills gently rising all around— the shady valleys with their grateful abundance of rivers, streams and fountains, or the well-watered gardens and useful growth of various trees? But why should I linger over these things? The delights of the thoughtful man are dearer and more profitable than these, for they are of God. Yet the weak spirit, which has been tired by the harder discipline of spiritual endeavour, is often refreshed and renewed by such things." (A. Wilmart, "Deux lettres concernant Raoul le Verd, l'ami de saint Bruno," *Revue Bénédictine* 51 (1939): 257– 74, trans. in R. W. Southern, *The Making of the Middle Ages* [New Haven: Yale University Press, 1953], p. 168.)

9 MS British Museum 153 r.

10 Huizinga, *Waning of the Middle Ages,* p. 264.

11 I found this point clearly stated by Clifton Olds in "Aspect and Perspective in Renaissance Thought," a paper read at the 1990 meeting of the Cusanus Society. Olds defines Jan Van Eyck's technique as follows: "Jan understood intuitively the phenomenon of convergence, and in all of his paintings in which linear perspective is called for, parallel lines running perpendicular to the picture plane recede toward a vanishing area if not a specific point. . . . Jan seems intent upon establishing an irrational space in which God or references to God exist apart from the mathematical calculation of optical reality."

12 Leonardo da Vinci, *The Literary Works,* ed. J. P. Richter (Oxford, 1939), vol. 1, p. 372, cf., Michael Baxandall, *Painting and Experience in Fifteenth Century Italy* (Oxford: Clarendon Press, 1972), pp. 119–21.

13 Leon Battista Alberti, *On Painting,* trans. John R. Spencer (New Haven: Yale University Press, 1956), p. 72.

14 Marsilius Ficinus, *Theologia platonica* bk. XIII, chap. 3. Théologie platonicienne de l'immortalité des âmes. Texte critique établi et traduit par Raymond Marcel (Paris : Les Belles Lettres, 1964–70), vol. 2, p. 223.

15 Lauro Martines, *Power and Imagination: City States in Renaissance Italy* (New York: Alfred A. Knopf, 1979), p. 259.

16 Leonardo da Vinci, *Trattato della pittura,* Ludwig edition (Vienna, 1882), Trat. 27.

17 Leonardo, *Trattato della pittura,* Trat. 8. See also Trat. 39 and the theoretical foundation in the *Paragone* (ibid.). I owe the references to these remarkable texts to Robert Zwynenberg: "Leonardo da Vinci en de eenheid van kunst en wetenschap," *De uil van Minerva* 5, no. 2 (Winter 1988): 89–91.

18 There was, however, a lively interest in mathematics for its own sake. See P. L. Rose: *The Italian Renaissance of Mathematics: Studies on Humanists and Mathematics from Petrarch to Galileo* (Geneva: Droz, 1978, 1975).

19 Cusanus, *De coniecturis* I, 4; *De mente,* chap. 6; *De possest,* chap. 8. In his last great work, Cusanus attributes to numbers that proceed from the human mind the same clarity as God has with respect to the real beings that proceed from the divine mind. *De venatione sapientiae,* chap. 21.

Only theological contemplation conveys, albeit in a negative way, some intuitional evidence of God's Being. For that reason Cusanus claims a greater certainty for it. "Patet quod in theologicis debet esse maior certitudo quam in mathematicis; et non est verum quod prima certitudo est in mathematicis nisi addamus ad quam rationem attingimus. Contemplatio vera certitudo est, quia visio intellectualis, illa enim nihil praesupponit nec arguit aut inquirit, sed est simplex intuitio." (*Cod. Cusanus* 184, fol. 12, in Paul Wilpert, *Anmerkungen zu,* Nicholas von Kues, *Vom Nichtanderem* (Hamburg: Meiner, 1976), p. 198.)

20 See Ernst Cassirer's insightful discussion in *Individuum and Kosmos in der Philosophie der Renaissance,* (Darmstadt: Wissenschaftliche Buchgesellschaft, 1963), pp. 161–68.

21 George Berkeley, *A Treatise Concerning the Principles of Human Knowledge* (1710), sec. 109. In support of this view, however, he strangely invokes the authority of "a treatise of mechanics demonstrated and applied to nature by a philosopher of a neighboring nation [Newton!]." (Sec. 110.) On Van Helmont, see Allen Debus, *The Chemical Philosophy: Paracelsian Science and Medicine in the Sixteenth and Seventeenth Centuries*, 2 vols. (New York: Science History Publications, 1977), I:295–379.

22 William James, *Principles of Psychology* (1890; New York: Dover, 1950), vol 2., pp. 665–66.

23 Cf., Allen G. Debus: "The Scientific Revolution: A Chemist's Reappraisal," in *Science, Pseudo-Science, and Utopianism in Early Modern Thought*, ed. Stephen A. McKnight (Columbia: University of Missouri Press, 1992), pp. 37–54.

24 Mircea Eliade traces its beginning to the old conception of the Earth-Mother, bearer of embryo-ores. "But above all it was the experimental discovery of the *living* substance, such as it was felt by the artisans, which must have played the decisive role. Indeed, it is the conception of a *complex and dramatic Life of Matter* which constitutes the originality of alchemy as opposed to classical Greek science." (Mircea Eliade, *The Forge and the Crucible*, trans. Stephen Corrin [New York: Harper & Brothers, 1962], pp. 148–49.)

25 Arthur Lovejoy, *The Great Chain of Being* (Cambridge: Harvard University Press, 1936), chap. 2. For a different view, see Francis Oakley, *Omnipotence, Covenant and Order* (Ithaca: Cornell University Press, 1984), and Amos Funkenstein, *Theology and the Scientific Imagination* (Princeton: Princeton University Press, 1986).

26 B. J. T. Dobbs, "Alchemical Death and Resurrection: The Significance of Alchemy in the Age of Newton," in *Science, Pseudo-Science and Utopianism*, ed. McKnight, pp. 55–87. On Neoplatonic influences on Renaissance hermeticism, see Eugenio Garin, *Testi umanistici su l'ermeticismo* (Rome: Fratelli Bocca, 1955). Also, Stephen McKnight, ed. *The Modern Age and the Recovery of Ancient Wisdom* (Columbia: University of Missouri Press, 1991).
    A few Renaissance thinkers sought in the Jewish *kabbalah* the secret communication that Neoplatonic philosophy promised but failed to deliver. According to the *Zohar*, the

gnostic text written in the fifteenth century but disguised as a much earlier work, each word—indeed, each letter of Scripture—contains a hidden meaning capable of disclosing the mystery of ultimate reality. Pico della Mirandola appears to have been the first Christian to use the *kabbalah* in support of the modern idea of the person as endowed with powers to restore the perfect harmony of the cosmos. Among those spurred on by Pico to study the *kabbalah*, the German humanist Reuchlin stands out with two remarkable studies—*De verbo mirifico* (1504) and *De arte cabalistica* (1517). Yet Pico and his followers sharply distanced themselves from astrology and alchemy.

27 Charles Whitney, "Bacon's *Instauratio*," *Journal of the History of Ideas* 50 (1989): 371–90.

28 M. Caron and S. Huttin, *The Alchemists*, trans. Helen R. Lane (New York: Grove Press, 1961), p. 132.

29 Dobbs, "Alchemical Death and Resurrection," pp. 60–62.

30 Ivor Leclerc, *The Nature of Physical Existence* (New York: Humanities Press, 1972), chap. 11.

31 Giovanni Pontano, *De rebus coelestibus* (Naples, 1512), lib. II, sig. D7. I owe this text, as well as much of the translation to Charles Trinkaus, "The Astrological Cosmos and Rhetorical Culture of Giovanni Gioviano Pontano," *Renaissance Quarterly XXXVIII* 3 (1985): 462–63.

32 Marsilio Ficino, *De vita triplici libri tres* [1489] (Basel, 1576; rpt. Turin: Bottega d'Erasmo, 1959), *Three Books on Life: A Critical Edition and Translation with Introduction and Notes*, Medieval and Renaissance Texts and Studies, vol. 57, trans. Carol Kaske and John Clark (Binghamton, N.Y.: Renaissance Society of America, 1989), bk. 3. Cf., McKnight, *Modern Age*, chap. 3; also, S. Klibansky, E. Panofsky, and F. Saxl, *Saturn and Melancholy* (New York: Basic Books, 1964).

33 Pietro Pomponazzi, *De naturalium effectuum admirandorum causis seu de incantationibus liber* (Basel, 1567), pp. 134, 223, 245, 306–07.

34 Ernst Cassirer, *The individual and the Cosmos in Renaissance Philosophy*, trans. Mario

Domandi (Philadelphia: University of Pennsylvania Press, 1963), p. 118.

35 Will-Erich Peuckert, *Nikolaus Kopernikus*
(Leipzig: Paul List, 1943), pp. 130ff. On Luther's views, see *Tischreden*, 678, 855, 1480,
2541 b. Cf. Will-Erich Peuckert, *Die grosse
Wende; das apokalyptische Saeculum und Luther*, (Hamburg: Claassen & Goverts, 1948;
rpt. 1966), p. 722. Calvin himself writes:
"Truly we may call astrology an alphabet of
theology." (*Works* [Edinburgh, 1844–56], vol.
38, pp. 58–59.) But the term probably refers
to astronomy (also called *astrologia* at the
time) since elsewhere he firmly rejects astrology.

36 Giordano Bruno, *Eroici furori* II, 1, 4, in
Dialoghi italiani, ed. Giovanni Gentile (Bari,
1907; Florence: Sansoni, 1957). *The Heroic
Frenzies*, trans. Paul Eugene Memmo (Chapel
Hill: University of North Carolina Press, 1964),
p. 193.

37 Giordano Bruno, *Spaccio della bestia trionfante (The Expulsion of the Triumphant
Beast)*, in *Dialoghi italiani*, ed. Gentile.

38 Thomas S. Kuhn, *The Structure of Scientific Revolutions* (Chicago: University of Chicago Press, 1962, 1970). Hans Blumenberg,
The Genesis of the Copernican World, trans.
Robert Wallace (Cambridge: MIT Press, 1991).

39 On this, see Oakley, *Omnipotence, Covenant and Order*, and Funkenstein, *Theology
and the Scientific Imagination*.

40 Cusanus supports his position by the following consideration: "For since the center is a
part equidistant from the circumference and
since there cannot exist a sphere or a circle so
completely true that a truer one could not be
posited, it is obvious that there cannot be posited a center [which is so true and precise] that
a still truer and more precise center could not
be posited." (*Nicholas of Cusa on Learned Ignorance*, trans. Jasper Hopkins [Minneapolis:
Arthur J. Banning Press, 1981, 1985], II, 11, #
157; henceforth abridged as *DI*, followed by
Roman numeral for the book and number for
the chapter.)

41 This is Alexandre Koyré's claim in: *From
the Closed World to the Infinite Universe*
(New York: Harper Torchbooks, 1958), p. 18.

42 The idea of an unlimited universe also
proved consonant with the form-creative aes-

thetics of the Renaissance. The absence of limits leaves a vacuum of indeterminacy to be
filled by human creativity. On the significance
of this view and possible link with the one-
point perspective, which at that time was
emerging in Italian painting, see Karsten Harries, "The Infinite Sphere," *Journal of History
of Philosophy* 13 (1975): 5–15.

43 Originally it was mainly the Stoic concept
of an all-penetrating *logos* that, as *ratio Dei*,
found its way into such early Christian writers
as Tertullian, Minucius Felix, and Novatianus,
but after Augustine the idea of a world soul
would be exclusively Neoplatonic.

44 Cardanus, *De subtilitate* (Basel, 1554). Cf.
Frank Dawson Adams, *The Bible and the Development of the Geological Sciences* (Baltimore: Williams & Wilkins, 1938), chap. 4, "On
the Generation of Stones." Allen G. Debus,
Man and Nature in the Renaissance (New
York: Cambridge University Press, 1978),
p. 34. It was, of course, a traditional tenet of
alchemical theories that metals grow in the
earth, even as plants grow on its surface.

45 Ficino, *Theologia platonica*. I have used
the photographic reproduction of the 1576
Basel edition (Turin: Bottega d'Erasmo 1959),
bk. XVIII, chap. 8; bk. IV, chap. 1, as well as
the critical edition by Raymond Marcel.

46 *Nicholas of Cusa On Learned Ignorance*,
trans. Hopkins, II, 9, # 142–146.

47 Giordano Bruno, *De l'infinito* in *Dialoghi
italiani*, ed. Gentile, p. 377.

48 Giordano Bruno, *De immenso* VI, 10, in
Opera latina, ed. F. Fiorentino e.a. (Naples,
Florence, 1879–91; rpt. Stuttgart: Friedrich
Frommann Verslag, 1962), vol. I/2.

49 On the relation between immanence and
transcendence in Bruno, see Werner Beier-
waltes's introduction to the German translation
(by Adolf Lasson) of *De la causa, Von der Ur-
sache, dem Prinzip, und dem Einen* (Hamburg:
Felix Meiner, Philosophische Bibliothek, 1982),
esp. pp. xxii–xxvi.

50 Giordano Bruno, *Concerning the Cause,
Principle and One*, ed. and trans. Sidney
Thomas Greenberg (New York: Octagon
Books, 1978), p. 119. This is a translation of
De la causa, principio ed uno. At times Bruno
presents the world soul as Aristotle's *agent in-
tellect* "which endows all with understanding

and through which they are intelligent in act."
(Bruno, *Cabala del cavallo Pegaseo* in *Dialoghi italiani*, ed. Gentile, p. 889.)

51 Giordano Bruno, *De la causa, principio ed uno*, in *Dialoghi italiani*, ed. Gentile, p. 230. Cf. the entire passage, pp. 230–48.

52 Ibid., p. 234. That forms are present in matter and must be extracted from it is a thesis already held by Albert the Great. See also Leclerc, *Nature of Physical Existence*, p. 134.

53 On the later religious interpretation of the principle, esp. in the deeply Christian Richard Hooker, see Samuel Leslie Bethell, *The Cultural Revolution of the XVIIth Century*, (New York: Roy Publishers, 1951), pp. 44, 54.

Chapter 3

1 The whole relation between the physical and the spiritual centers is splendidly developed in Hans Blumenberg, *The Genesis of the Copernican World*, trans. Robert Wallace (Cambridge: MIT Press, 1991).

2 Robert Lenoble, *Equisse d'une histoire de l'idée de nature* (Paris: Albin Michel, 1969), pp. 309–13.

3 Robert Hooke, *Micrographia* (1665), preface.

4 Richard S. Westfall, *Never at Rest: A Biography of Isaac Newton* (New York: Cambridge University Press, 1980), p. 14.

5 Galileo, *Dialogue on Two Chief World Systems*, trans. Stillman Drake (Berkeley: University of California Press, 1967), p. 207. My discussion of Galileo's "Platonism" and mathematical idealization owes much to two excellent articles: Ernan McMullin, "Galilean Idealization," *Studies in History and Philosophy of Science* 16, no. 3 (1985): 247–73, and Thomas P. McTighe, "Galileo's Platonism: A Reconsideration," in *Galileo: Man of Science*, ed. Ernan McMullin (New York: Basic Books, 1967), pp. 365–87.

6 Ernan McMullin, *The Concept of Matter in Modern Philosophy* (Notre Dame, Ind.: University of Notre Dame Press, 1978), p. 13.

7 Michael Buckley, *Motion and Motion's God* (Princeton: Princeton University Press, 1971).

8 Hans Jonas, *The Phenomenon of Life* (Chicago: Chicago University Press, 1966), pp. 69–70. This shift from aesthetic intelligibility to empirical rationality initiates a disenchantment of nature that will continue until the twentieth century when, in the face of new mysteries unexplainable in mechanistic terms, such notions as the "probable," the "aesthestically acceptable," and so on have become current again.

9 Nicholas of Cusa anticipated some of this when he allowed the mind to supply (from without) an intelligibility that finite essences do not possess in themselves. Thomas P. McTighe, "Nicholas of Cusa's Theory of Science and Its Metaphysical Background," in *Nicolo Cusano agli inizi del mondo moderno: Atti del congresso internazionale in occasione del V centenario della morte di Nicolo Cusano* (Florence: Sansoni, 1964), pp. 317–38.

10 See Ivor Leclerc, *The Nature of Physical Existence* (New York: Humanities Press, 1972), pp. 31–32.

11 Bacon does, however, admit in *The New Organon* (bk. II, #8) that inquiries into nature "have the best result when they begin with physics and end in mathematics." Peter Urbach concludes from this and a few other passages that mathematics played a considerable role in Bacon's method. "Francis Bacon as a Precursor to Popper," *British Journal for the Philosophy of Science* 33 (1982): 113–32. But such statements conflict with what he wrote elsewhere and, especially, with the way he practiced science. Nor was Bacon alone in his anti-mathematical bias. Konrad Celtis, a German Renaissance genius, declared in his inaugural lecture at the University of Ingolstadt: "Whoever attempts to decipher the work of nature and the wisdom of its Creator through mathematical truth, whoever raises himself ever so little above the viewpoint of the common people, gains esteem. But those whose hands have ground the majestic beauty of nature into disembodied concepts, horrible abstractions, and empty subtleties, have terribly flattened and diluted philosophy." (Quoted in Will-Erich Peuckert, *Die grosse Wende* (Hamburg: Claassen & Goverts, 1948), p. 378.)

12 Francis Bacon, *The New Organon*, trans. R. L. Ellis in *The Works*, ed. James Spelling, Robert Leslie Eddis, and Douglas Denon Heath (London, 1858–74), vol. 8, bk. I, 24–28 (arabic numbers refer to the aphorisms).

13 Basil Willey, *The Seventeenth Century Background* (1934; New York: Doubleday, s.d.), p. 44.

14 Mary Horton, "In Defence of Francis Bacon," *Studies in the History and Philosophy of Science* 4 (1973): 241–78. Ernan McMullin, "Conceptions of Science in the Scientific Revolution," in *Reappraisals of the Scientific Revolution*, ed. by David C. Lindberg and Robert S. Westman (New York: Cambridge University Press, 1991), pp. 27–92, esp. pp. 45–54. Urbach, "Francis Bacon as a Precursor."

15 Francis Bacon, *Valerius Terminus,* in *Works,* bk. III, 233. Cf., Charles Webster, *The Great Instauration: Science, Medicine, and Reform 1626–1660* (London: Duckworth, 1975), p. 24. Also, J. Mouton, "The Masculine Birth of Time: Interpreting Francis Bacon's Discourse on Scientific Progress," *Philosophy/Wijsbegeerte* 6, no. 2 (1987): 43–50.

16 Francis Bacon, *Silva Silvarum,* in *Works* II, 602.

17 Robert Boyle, *Certain Physiological Essays* (1661).

18 Richard Foster Jones, *Ancients and Moderns: A Study of the Rise of the Scientific Movement in Seventeenth-Century England* (St. Louis: Washington University Press, 1961; New York: Dover Publications, 1982), pp. 178–80. Obviously for the purposes of chemistry a purely mechanistic theory that equates the essence of physical being with quantity is not very helpful, and Boyle hastens to qualify what he nevertheless claims to embrace right from the start of "The Origin of Forms and Qualities to the Corpuscular Philosophy," in *The Works of the Honourable Robert Boyle* (London, 1772), pp. 23–26.

19 That few technical innovations accompanied the insistent proclamations of the "usefulness" of science should not be held against the practical effectiveness of the new concept. The sixteenth and seventeenth centuries could do no more than prepare the methods and the attitudes that would make an unprecedented technical development possible. Its realization had to wait for the proper social-economic conditions to create both the demand and the means for producing major technical innovations at the time of the industrial revolution.

20 Aristotle, *Metaphysics* Z (7) 1032 a. Augustine, *In Johannis Evangelium* XXXVII, 8,

P.L. 35, 1674. See Edward Cranz, "St. Paul and Ancient Modes of Thought," address delivered at Connecticut College, New London, Conn., April 24, 1984. On *technē,* see André Malet, "Le croyant en face de la technique," *Revue d'histoire et de philosophie religieuses* 55, no. 3 (1975): 417–30, trans. in *Theology and Technology,* ed. Carl Mitcham and Jim Grote (Lanham, Md.: University Press of America, 1984), pp. 91–105. Also, Heidegger's still provocative essay, "Die Frage nach der Technik," in *Vorträge und Aufsatze* (1954), pp. 13ff, trans. as "The Question Concerning Technology" by William Lovitt in a collection that appeared under the same title (New York: Harper & Row, 1977), pp. 3–35. The Prometheus myth indicates that for the Greeks the fabrication of tools had to be revealed by the gods. The furtive way in which Prometheus transferred its secret to the human race suggests the ambivalent feeling that continued to linger in the Greek mind concerning its legitimacy.

21 R. G. Collingwood, *The Idea of Nature,* (Oxford: Clarendon Press, 1945), p. 16.

22 Isaac Newton, *Principia Mathematica,* bk. 1, prop. 69, theorem 29 Scholia.

23 Cf., Richard J. Blackwell, "Descartes' Concept of Matter" in *The Concept of Matter in Modern Philosophy,* ed. Ernan McMullin (Notre Dame, Ind.: University of Notre Dame Press, 1978), pp. 66–69.

24 Newton, *Principia Mathematica,* bk. 3, rule 3, "The qualities of bodies, which admit neither intensification nor remission of degrees, and which are found to belong to all bodies within the reach of our experiments, are to be esteemed the universal qualities of all bodies whatsoever." Those qualities include in the first place extension, but also hardness, impenetrability, mobility, and inertia. Newton does not call them "essential" qualities, being suspicious of metaphysical essences. But he felt that some qualities had to be universally present, and he chose the ones he considered stable, that is, the ones that do not allow matter to change without continuity. For the difficulties caused by Newton's universalization of observed qualities to all bodies, see Ernan McMullin, *Newton on Matter and Activity* (Notre Dame, Ind.: University of Notre Dame Press, 1978), pp. 13–27. Newton falls, of course, beyond the limits set to this study, but he brings earlier developments to sometimes unexpected conclusions.

25 F. H. Bradley, *Appearance and Reality* (1893; London: George Allen and Unwin, 1916), p. 435. Also, for a more critical view of spatial abstraction, Max Horkheimer and Theodor Adorno, *Dialectic of the Enlightenment*, trans. John Cumming (New York: Herder and Herder, 1972), p. 26.

26 Giordano Bruno, *De immenso* III, 1, in *Opera latina*, vol. I/1, p. 318. My translation.

27 Ibid., II, 10, in *Opera latina*, vol. I/1, p. 299.

28 Alfred North Whitehead, *Science and the Modern World* (New York: Macmillan, 1925). John Dewey, *The Quest for Certainty* (1929; New York: G. P. Putnam, 1960), p. 28.

29 Lenoble, *Esquisse d'une histoire de l'idée de nature*, p. 325.

30 Brian Ellis, "The Origin and Nature of Newton's Laws of Motion," in *Beyond the Edge of Certainty: Essays in Contemporary Science and Philosophy*, ed. Robert G. Colodny (Englewood Cliffs, N.J.: Prentice Hall, 1965), p. 65. Also, Gerald Galgan, *The Logic of Modernity* (New York: New York University Press, 1982), pp. 76–78, who refers to Ellis's text.

31 Descartes, letter to Mersenne of December 18, 1629, in *Oeuvres,* ed. Adam-Tannery (Paris: Vrin, 1964), I, 100 (henceforth abridged as AT).

32 See the excellent pages of Donald Crosby, *The Specter of the Absurd* (Albany, N.Y.: SUNY Press, 1988), pp. 187–97, and Leclerc, *The Nature of Physical Existence*, pp. 226–27.

33 Montaigne, *Essais* I, 26 ("On the Education of Children").

34 Francis Bacon, *Valerius Terminus*, in *Works* III, 220.

35 Descartes, Fifth set of Objections to the *Meditations*, AT VII, 292; *The Philosophical Writings of Descartes*, trans. John Cottingham, Robert Stoothoff, and Dugald Murdoch (Cambridge: Cambridge University Press, 1984), II, 203 (henceforth abridged as CSM and volume). Surprisingly, Richard Rorty does not refer to this text in *Philosophy and the Mirror of Nature*.

36 Alexander of Aphrodisias, *De anima*, in *Alexandri Aphrodisiensis . . . Commentaria in*

Aristotelem Graeca, ed. Ivo Bruns, pt. I, vol. 2, 89, 21. Athanasios P. Fotinis, *The De Anima of Alexander of Aphrodisias: A Translation and Commentary* (Washington: University Press of America, 1971), p. 118. For Aristotle, see, inter alia, *De anima* III, 8, 431, 621–23; III, 4, 429b30. I owe the references to Alexander to Professor Edward Cranz, but my debt to him extends well beyond them because his (unpublished) essays convinced me that the earliest opposition between knower and known is not the one between subject and object of the seventeenth century (prepared in the sixteenth), but the one initiated by St. Anselm's distinction between meanings and things and completed in twelfth-century Scholasticism.

37 God's absolute power could convey an intuitive notion of what does not exist—"if the divine power were to conserve a perfect intuitive cognition of a thing no longer existent . . . the intellect would know evidently that this thing does not exist." (William of Ockham, *Ordinatio* q 1, N., in *Philosophical Writings*, ed. and trans. Philotheus Boehner, O.F.M. [New York: Thomas Nelson, 1957]; trans. rev. by Stephen Brown [Indianapolis: Hacket, 1990], p. 23.) Thus the mind may have intuitive cognition of nonexisting things.

38 Descartes, *Meditations* (VI), AT VII, 78; CSM II, 54. The consequences of nominalist thought upon Descartes's philosophy are carefully explained in André de Muralt, *L'enjeu de la philosophie médievale* (Leiden: E. J. Brill, 1991), esp. Etudes II, III, VIII.

39 Nicolaus von Autrecourt, *Briefe*, ed. and trans. R. Imbach and D. Perler (Hamburg: Felix Meiner, 1988), p. 44.

40 Descartes, AT VII, 78; CSM II, 54.

41 Descartes, AT VII, 41; CSM II, 28.

42 Montaigne, *Essais* I, 13: The term *essai* with its emphasis on the provisional, experimental quality indicates Montaigne's attempt to retrace experience itself while abstaining from any kind of rational universalization. One translator correctly defines *essai* as *experience*: "All this medley that I am scribbling here is but a record of my life's experiences (*essais*)." Montaigne, *Essays*, III, 13, trans. J. M. Cohen (Baltimore: Penguin Books, 1958), p. 361.

43 Just before this text went to press I became acquainted with Dan Garber's recent *Descartes's Metaphysical Physics* (Chicago:

University of Chicago Press, 1992). Contrary to Toulmin's *Cosmopolis*, he downplays the significance of skepticism in Descartes's thought. According to Garber, Descartes's primary concern was to find an adequate foundation for a physical science. I hope to deal with this thesis at some future time.

44 Descartes's *cogito* had already been foreshadowed by Ockham's *"ego intelligo,"* which the praeceptor declares to be "simpliciter prima, et ita non potest evidenter cognosci per aliam priorem" (*Ordinatio. Prologue* q. 1. *Opera Theologica* [New York: Editiones Instituti Franciscani Universitatis S. Bonaventurae, 1967–84],vol. 1, pp. 40–41.) Yet Ockham had more cautiously rejected the criterion of intuitive clarity as a reliable basis for truth. "Maybe when something is known intuitively clearly and perfectly, it can be discerned from another specifically distinct thing that is known by an intuitive, perfect, and clear knowledge; yet when something is known intuitively obscurely and imperfectly, this may not be the case. But in our present condition the intellect knows nothing intuitively clearly and perfectly, and hence it is not in a position to discern that thing from any other thing." (*Prol.* Ibid., vol. 1, p. 68. Cf., Arthur Stephen McGrade, "Some Varieties of Skeptical Experience: Ockham's Case," in *Die Philosophie im 14. and 15. Jahrhundert: In Memoriam Konstanty Michalski, 1879–1947*, ed. Olaf Pluta (Amsterdam: Gurner, s.d.), pp. 424–42.

45 Descartes, AT X, 420; CSM I, 42. On the controversial matter of "simple natures" another interpretation is possible. Rather than being simple "real" existents, they may have been no more than objects of the mind as they exist in the mind, hence modes of thought. But such a reading (to which Thomas P. McTighe drew my attention) would only reinforce Descartes's problem of representation as an idea-object called to mediate thought with external reality.

46 Descartes, *The Fifth Set of Objections*, AT VII, 278; CSM II, 194.

47 Descartes, *The Seventh Set of Objections*, AT VII, 528; CSM II, 359.

48 On the universalization of the mathematical criterion, see Martin Heidegger, *What Is a Thing?* (1962), trans. W. B. Barton and Vera Deutsch (Chicago: Henry Regnery, 1967), p. 275. Heidegger's point becomes highly questionable, however, if it implies that Descartes equates metaphysics with mathematics. Metaphysics, though even as mathematics, a science of foundations, is far more fundamental, as Descartes indicates in his letter of April 15, 1630, to Mersenne: "On peut démontrer les vérités métaphysiques d'une façon qui est plus évidente que les démonstrations de géometrie."

49 The problems connected with Descartes's "foundationalism" have been discussed by Frederick L. Will, *Induction and Justification* (Ithaca: Cornell University Press, 1974); William P. Alston, "Has Foundationalism Been Refuted?" *Philosophical Studies* 29 (1976): 287–305 (a critique of Will's thesis); Jeffrey Stout, *The Flight from Authority* (Notre Dame, Ind.: University of Notre Dame Press, 1981), esp. chaps. 1 and 2; and most recently, Garber, *Descartes's Metaphysical Physics.*

50 Descartes, AT IX, pt. 2, 20. *Principles of Philosophy*, "Preface to the French edition," trans. V. R. Miller and R. P. Miller (Dordrecht: Reidel, 1983), p. xxviii. This work is only excerpted in CSM, but the present text appears in CSM I, 189.

51 Maurice Merleau-Ponty, *The Visible and the Invisible* (Evanston, Ill.: Northwestern University Press, 1968), pp. 36–37.

52 Ian Hacking, *The Emergence of Probability* (Cambridge: Cambridge University Press, 1975).

53 Pascal, *Pensées*, trans. A. J. Krailsheimer, #170 Lafuma edition (London: Penguin Books, 1966).

54 Stout, *Flight from Authority*, p. 56.

55 Descartes, of course, does not hold the idealist thesis that the real exists solely as idea. The objective reality of ideas is not constituted by the mind (the argument for the existence of God is precisely based on the presence of an objective idea which the mind alone could not have constituted), yet the mind alone conveys the ideal form, which enables that objective reality to qualify for truth.

56 Hegel, realizing the gravity of the problem caused by a philosophy of consciousness, devoted his first great work, the *Phenomenology of Spirit*, to an attempt to bridge certainty with truth. His solution, the dialectical process of Spirit from its subjective beginnings to the Absolute that grounds this subjectivity, undermines the very basis on which the Cartesian project had been erected.

Others in our own time have attempted to preserve Descartes's starting point in the subject by giving it a different interpretation. Thus Edmund Husserl in his *Cartesian Meditations* redefined the Cartesian project in the light of Kant's *Critique:* "The aim of the *Meditations* is a complete reforming of philosophy into a science grounded on an absolute foundation." (*Cartesian Meditations,* trans. Dorian Cairns [The Hague: M. Nyhoff, 1960], p. 1.) For him, the *ego* is known only as transcendental subject, not as a substance. This reading takes the principle of subjectivity out of the world altogether, turning Descartes's *ego cogito* into an atom of meaning, separate from the world and isolated from all similar atoms.

57 Jean-Luc Marion, *Sur le prisme métaphysique de Descartes* (Paris: Presses Universitaires de France, 1986).

58 Marion, *Sur le prisme métaphysique de Descartes,* p. 110.

59 Descartes, *Meditations* (III), AT VII, 37; CSM II, 26.

60 Descartes, AT VII, 110; CSM II, 79.

61 Descartes, *Discourse on Method,* AT VI, 45; CSM I, 133–34.

62 George Louis Leclerc, Comte de Buffon, *Histoire naturelle,* in *Oeuvres complètes* (Paris, 1774–78), vol. 13, p. 32.

63 Ibid., p. 39.

Chapter 4

1 Charles Taylor, *Sources of the Self: The Making of the Modern Identity* (Cambridge: Harvard University Press, 1989), pp. 123, 131. Plotinus's idea of interiority was prepared by the ethical-religious struggle of the Stoa that resulted in the concept of *conscientia.*

2 See, also the evocative pages of Heinz Heimsoeth, *Die sechs groszen Themen der abendländischen Metaphysik und der Ausgang des Mittelalters* (Berlin, 1922), pp. 125–41.

3 Even when Hippias in Plato's *Protagoras* declares all present to be "of one kin—by nature (*physei*), not by convention (*nomoi*)" (337c-3), he merely refers to the natural kinship of people who think and act alike not to a uni-

versal humanity. See Eric Voegelin, *The World of the Polis* (Baton Rouge: Louisiana State University, 1957), p. 282. On *humanitas* in Greek thought, Bruno Snell, *The Discovery of Mind,* trans. T. G. Rosenmeyer (New York: Harper Torchbooks, 1960), chap. 11.

4 Augustine, *Confessions,* bk. III, chap. 10, trans. F. J. Sheed (London: Sheed and Ward, 1944).

5 Early Italian humanists chose their models of ideal humanity from different periods of Roman antiquity in accordance with their political aspirations. Thus in Florence the imperial figures (Augustus, and even Caesar) who had dominated the fourteenth century gradually yielded to republican heroes (Cicero or Brutus) as political circumstances changed. Hans Baron, *The Crisis of the Early Italian Renaissance: Civic Humanism and Republican Liberty in an Age of Classicism and Tyranny* (Princeton: Princeton University Press, 1966).

6 Charles Trinkaus, "Il pensiero antropologico-religioso nel Rinascimento" in *Il Rinascimento: Interpretazioni e problemi,* festschrift for Eugenio Garin (Bari: Laterza, 1979), pp. 111–12.

7 Juan Luis Vives, *De Tradendis* I, 1. See Ernesto Grassi, *Renaissance Humanism,* (Binghamton, N.Y.: Medieval and Renaissance Texts and Studies, 1988),pp. 65–67. Also Charles Trinkaus, *In Our Image and Likeness,* (Chicago: University of Chicago Press, 1970), vol. 1, pp. 3–50, and Trinkaus, "Il pensiero," pp. 116–32.

8 Gregory of Nazianze, *Second Theological Oration* PG 36, 58. The expression also appears in Nemesius of Emesa (*De natura hominis* PG 532), as well as in Macrobius (*De Somnio Scipionis,* chap. 12) and in Gregory of Nyssa (*In Psalmos* I, PG 44, 441 and *De hominis opificio* PG 44, 177). It probably originated in Plato's discussion of the cosmos as "ensouled" (*Tim.* 30b) in analogy with the human person. In the Renaissance we find it in Cusanus, Pico (who may have taken it from Ficino), Paracelsus, and Calvin (*Institutes,* bk. I, chap. 5, 3). A classical study on the subject is Rudolf Allers, "Microcosmos: From Anaxagoras to Paracelsus," *Traditio* 2 (1944): 319–407. (Republished in *The Philosophical Work of Rudolf Allers,* ed. Jesse A. Mann [Washington: Georgetown University Press, 1965] pp. 123–191).

9 Nicholas of Cusa, *De coniecturis*, bk. II, 14. I translated *homo* by the inclusive "person" or "human" rather than by "man."

10 A speculative humanist theory is generally absent from Renaissance writers and artists and is explicitly rejected by some (Montaigne foremost among them). Ernest Cassirer, *Individuum und Kosmos in der Renaissance,* (Darmstadt: Wissenschaftliche Buchgesellschaft, 1963), p. 89.

11 Giovanni Gentile, *Giordano Bruno e il pensiero del Rinascimento* (Florence: Vallechi, 1925), p. 29. Some of this naturalism was anticipated by Jean de Meung, the amazing thirteenth-century author of the second part of the *Roman de la rose*, who, in a bold inversion of accepted moral norms, supports his invitation to unbridled sensuousness by appealing to the "law of nature."

12 On Ariosto's ambiguity, see Bartlett Giamatti, *The Earthly Paradise and the Renaissance Epic* (Princeton: Princeton University Press, 1966), pp. 137–64.

13 Of course, reflection has always distrusted appearances. That is how philosophy started! But while formerly its objective had been "to save the appearances" after having subjected them to a critical investigation, in the modern epoch it mostly resulted in a permanent distrust of the phenomenal as such. See Hannah Arendt, *The Life of the Mind. I. Thinking* (New York: Harcourt Brace, 1978), p. 53.

14 Jacques Claes (*De wieg van het verdriet* [Antwerp: De Nederlandse Boekhandel, 1983]) directly relates this feeling to the modern separation between man and world. Panofsky's study on Dürer (Erwin Panofsky, *Das Leben und die Kunst Albrecht Dürers* [München, 1977], pp. 224–25) links the artist's famous etching of Melancholy (1514) to an emerging geometrical vision of the world symbolized by the quadrant, the sandglass, and the geometrically shaped rock.

15 Montaigne, *Essays* II, 18, trans. Charles Cotton, ed. W. Carew Hazlitt (Chicago: University of Chicago Press, 1952).

16 Sainte-Beuve, *Port-Royal* (1866) III, chap. 2.

17 Trouillogan represents Pyrrhonism in bk. III, chap. 36.

18 Emile Male, *The Gothic Image* (New York: Harper Torchbooks, 1958), p. 32.

19 Augustine, *Sermons*, Migne P.L. 126, 6. Marcia Colish, *The Mirror of Language: A Study in Medieval Theory of Knowledge* (New Haven: Yale University Press, 1969). The section on Augustine richly develops this idea.

20 Abaelardus, *Logica Ingredientibus*, p. 315. Once again, credit for the theory of the epistemological and linguistic break of the twelfth century, as well as for the location of this particular passage must go to Edward Cranz.

21 Bernard Lonergan, *Verbum: World and Idea in Aquinas*, ed. David Burrell, C.S.C. (Notre Dame, Ind.: University of Notre Dame Press, 1967), p. 33. My translation of Aquinas is taken from *On the Truth of the Catholic Faith*, trans. with intro. and notes by Anton C. Pegis (Garden City, N.Y.: Doubleday, 1955). vol. 1.

22 Boethius, *De interpretatione* P.L. 64, 297ff.

23 Ockham, *Summa totius logicae* I, chap. 1. *Philosophical Writings*, ed. and trans. Philotheus Boehner, rev. Stephen F. Brown (Indianapolis, Ind.: Hacket, 1990), p. 48. See Philotheus Boehner, "Ockham's Theory of Signification," *Franciscan Studies* 6 (1946): 143–69.

24 Jacques Derrida, *Of Grammatology*, trans. Gayatri Chakravorty (Baltimore: Johns Hopkins Univerity Press 1976), pp. 13–14.

25 Though Petrarch was strongly influenced by Augustinians (Dionigi di Borgo S. Sepolcro, Bartolomeo da Urbino, Luigi Marsigli)—all of whom must have had connections with the "modern" theology. One person who clearly belonged to both camps—the humanist and the nominalist—was the Dutch Brother of Common Life Wessel Gansfort. See Heiko A. Oberman, "Headwaters of the Reformation," in *Luther and the Dawn of the Modern Era*, ed. Heiko A. Oberman (Leiden: E. J. Brill, 1974), pp. 40–88, esp. p. 70. The relation between nominalism and the humanist movement, mostly subterranean, remains far from clear, as is evident from Karl-Otto Apel's searching explorations in *Die Idee der Sprache in der Tradition des Humanismus von Dante bis Vico* (*Archiv fur Begriffsgeschichte*, 8 [1953]).

26 Cicero, *De oratore* III, 16. See J. Lohman, "Das Verhältnis des abendländischen Menschen zur Sprache," *Lexis* 3:30.

27 Nevertheless Christian philosophers often still adopt ancient philosophical descriptions of language, as Scottus Eriugena does when writing, "The rational soul is able to pursue knowledge *in itself,* away from the sound of the articulate voice and the broken speech" (*De divisione naturae* V, 4, in Migne P.L. 122, 860). See Ernesto Grassi, "The Claim of the Word and the Religious Significance of Poetry: A Humanistic Problem," *Dionysius* 8 (1984): 135–39.

28 Johan Huizinga, *Erasmus and the Age of Reformation,* trans. F. Hopman (1924; New York: Harper and Brothers, 1957), p. 115.

29 Giovanni Pontano, *De sermone libri sex,* ed. S. Lupi and A. Riscato (Lugano 1954), I, 1 (p. 3).

30 Coluccio Salutati, *De laboribus Herculis* I, 13, 9.

31 Ibid., I, 1, 19.

32 Albertino Musato, Letter VII, 44B, in *Tragoediae, Eclogae et Fragmenta, Epistolae* (Venice, 1636). See also Ernesto Grassi, *Heidegger and the Question of Renaissance Humanism* (Binghamton, N.Y.: Medieval and Renaissance Texts and Studies, 1983), p. 60.

33 Boccaccio, *De genealogia deorum* (Bari, 1951), p. 706. See also Grassi, "Claim of the Word," p. 146.

34 "The traditional idea of a *theologia poetica* seems . . . to have led straight into the later conception of *theologia platonica,* thus providing another link between the humanists and the Platonists." Charles Trinkaus, *In His Image,* vol. 1, chap. 17.

35 Torquato Tasso, *Discorsi del Poema Eroico* 89 and 90. My reading was supported by Erminia Ardissino, "Le lacerazioni della storia: Sacro e poesia in Tasso," Ph.D. diss., Yale University, 1993.

36 "Transumanar—significar *per verba* non si poria; pero l'esemplo basti a cui esperienza grazia serba." In Canto XIX Dante invokes Apollo to make him a vase of divine power and to transform him into a god. On the "eccesso del Verbo," see Rubina Giorgi, *Dante e Meister Eckhart: Letture per il tempo della fine* (Salerno-Rome: Ripostes, 1987), pp. 5–52.

37 Philip Sidney, *Defence of Poecy,* in *Works,* ed. Feuillerat, vol. 3. See J. P. McIntyre, "Sidney's Golden World," *Comparative Literature* 14 (1904): 356.

38 "[S]ubtile quoddam et acutum loquendi artificium." Giannozzo Manetti, *De excellentia et praestantia hominis* (1448), Lib. III, p. 152.

39 Lorenzo di Medici, *Commento* 20. On the entire development of the *vulgare* of civilized Florentine society to standard language of the northern Italian cities, see Edward Stankiewicz, "The 'Genius' of Language in Sixteenth-Century Linguistics," in *Logos Semantikos: Studia linguistica in honorem Eugenio Coseriu, 1921–1981* (Berlin, 1981), vol. 1, p. 177. Also, Lauro Martines, *The Power and the Imagination,* (New York: Alfred A. Knopf, 1979), pp. 318–21.

40 "[F]rustra fieret per plura quod per pauciora fieri potest" (Guillaume Postel, *De originibus, seu de varia et potissimum orbis Latin . . . historia* [Basel 1553], p. 20).

41 Arturo B. Fallico and Herman Shapiro, eds. and trans., *Renaissance Philosophy,* vol. 1, *The Italian Philosophers: Selected Readings from Petrarch to Bruno* (New York: Modern Library, 1967), pp. 114–15. That Ficino and Pico can be regarded as humanists in their own right was the position held by the classicist Moses Hadas. See *Old Wine, New Bottles* (New York: Simon and Schuster, 1962), p. 70.

42 Fallico and Shapiro, eds. and trans., *Renaissance Philosophy* 1:107–08.

43 Galileo, *Il Saggiatore,* in *Opere* (Rome: Edizione nazionale, 1890), VI, p. 332. *The Assayer,* in *The Controversy of the Comets of 1618,* trans. Stillman Drake, (Philadelphia: University of Pennsylvania Press, 1960), pp. 183–84.

44 Richard Foster Jones, *Ancients and Moderns: A Study of the Rise of the Scientific Movement in Seventeenth Century England* (New York: Dover, 1982), p. 99.

45 With characteristic bluntness Hobbes declares: "To him that thinketh not himself upon the things whereof, but upon the words wherewith he speaketh, and taketh those words on trust from puzzled schoolmen, it is not only hard, but impossible to be known" (Thomas Hobbes, *Questions Concerning Liberty, Necessity, and Chance,* in *The English Works of*

Thomas Hobbes, ed. William Molesworth [London: J. Bohn, 1839–1845], vol. 5, p. 359).

46 Heidegger, however, completely failed to appreciate the unique contribution of what he dismissed as a naive anthropomorphism. Ernesto Grassi has rightly argued that Stefan George's verse "where word breaks off no thing may be," quoted by Heidegger as the very principle by which man gains access to Being, constitutes the essence of Italian humanism. See Grassi, *Heidegger,* pp. 12, 17, and passim.

47 Heidegger all too simplistically attributes this reversal to Descartes. See "The Origin of the Work of Art," in *Poetry, Language, Thought,* trans. Albert Hofstadter (New York: Harper & Row, 1979), pp. 23–24.

48 See, for instance, Scotus, I *Sent.* dist. 36, q. un., no. 45–47. *Opera omnia* (Civitas Vaticana, 1950), vol. 6, pp. 288–89. Cf., André de Muralt, "La doctrine médievale de l'*esse objectivum,*" *L'enjeu de la philosophie médiévale* (Leiden: E. J. Brill, 1991), pp. 90–127.

49 Kenneth Schmitz, "Toward a Metaphysical Restoration of Natural Things," in *An Etienne Gilson Tribute,* ed. Charles O'Neill (Milwaukee: Marquette University Press, 1959), pp. 245–62, espec. 252, 256.

50 Thomas Campanella, *De sensu rerum,* chap. 2.

51 On the development of the Prometheus myth in antiquity see Hans Blumenberg, *Work on Myth,* trans. Robert Wallace (Cambridge: MIT Press, 1985), pp. 299–349. Here we learn also how a later restorer of the Prometheus myth, the emperor Julian, felt the need to deprive it of its God-challenging aspect. Prometheus did not have to steal the fire: the gods generously granted it to the human race. Blumenberg also writes about the myth of Prometheus during the Renaissance (pp. 362–67).

52 William J. Bouwsma, *John Calvin: A Sixteenth Century Portrait* (New York: Oxford University Press, 1988), p. 101. On the general presence of anxiety in the sixteenth century, see Bouwsma's valuable essay, "Anxiety and the Formation of Early Modern Culture," in *After the Reformation: Essays in Honor of J. H. Hexter,* Barbara Malament, ed. (Philadelphia: University of Pennsylvania Press, 1980), pp. 215–46.

53 Richard H. Popkin, *The History of Skepticism from Erasmus to Spinoza* (Berkeley: University of California Press, 1979).

54 Pierre Charron, *La Sagesse,* bk. II, chap. 1–2, in *Toutes les oeuvres de Pierre Charron* (Paris, 1635), pp. 10–32. Cf., Richard H. Popkin, "Charron and Descartes: The Fruits of Systematic Doubt," *Journal of Philosophy* 51 (1954): 832.

55 Stephen Toulmin, *Cosmopolis* (Chicago: University of Chicago Press, 1992).

56 Pierre-Silvain Régis, *Réponse au livre qui a pour titre P. D. Huet: Censura philosophiae cartesianae* (Paris 1691), p. 106. I take this quote as well as the distinction between epistemic and moral doubt from Henri Gouhier's remarkable essay, "Le malin génie et le bon Dieu," in *Descartes: Essais* (Paris: Vrin, 1949), esp. pp. 176–96.

57 Descartes AT V, 224.

58 Thus Descartes dismisses a nominalist objection: "What is it to us that someone may make out that the perception whose truth we are so firmly convinced of may appear false to God or an angel, so that it is absolutely speaking false? Why should this alleged 'absolute falsity' bother us, since we neither believe in it nor have even the smallest suspicion of it?" (AT VII, 145; CSM, II, 103).

59 Descartes, AT VI, 3–4; CSM, I, 112. On the relation between Descartes and Montaigne, Léon Brunschvicg has written well in his *Descartes et Pascal, lecteurs de Montaigne* (Paris, 1944).

60 Descartes, AT VII, 52; CSM, II, 36. Cf., Karl Jaspers's comments in *Descartes und die Philosophie* (Berlin, 1937), p. 21.

61 Gerhard Kruger, "Die Herkunft des Selbstbewusteins," in *Freiheit und Weltverwaltung* (Freiburg: Karl Alber, 1958), pp. 12–17.

62 Eberhard Juengel, *God as the Mystery of the World,* trans. Darrell L. Guder (Grand Rapids, Mich.: Eerdmans, 1983). Jean-Luc Marion, *Sur la théologie blanche de Descartes* (Paris: Presses Universitaires de France, 1981), passim, and *Sur le prisme métaphysique de Descartes* (Paris: Presses Universitaires de France, 1986), pt. 4 ("Dieu").

63 Descartes, *Meditations* III, AT IX, 40.

64 Descartes, *Meditations* IV, AT IX, 42; CSM, II, 53.

65 Marion, *Sur le prisme métaphysique*, p. 79. Heidegger's question appears in *Being and Time*, trans. John Macquarrie and Edward Robinson (New York: Harper & Row, 1962), pp. 44–46.

66 Descartes, *Meditations* II, AT VII, 31; CSM, II, 20–21.

67 Such has been the reading of respected interpreters from Hamelin and Brunschvicg to Marion. Nevertheless, with characteristic elusiveness Descartes also provides some counterindications. Thus in a letter to Regius (May 1641) he declares intellection to be "truly the passion (*passio*) of the mind while volition is its action" (AT III, 372). I see no other way of reconciling this with the "active" statements but by distinguishing between the *passio mentis* with respect to its ideal object (which he accepts) and the mind's receptivity with respect to the senses (which he rejects).

68 Cf., Jean-Luc Marion, "La solitude de l'ego," in *Questions Cartésiennes*, pp. 189–219.

69 Friedrich Nietzsche, *Die fröhliche Wissenschaft (The Gay Science)* (1882), in *Werke*, ed. Karl Schlechta (Berlin, 1954) §377.

Chapter 5

1 Georg Wilhelm Friedrich Hegel, *Phänomenologie des Geistes* (Hamburg: Philosophische Bibliothek, 1952), pp. 151–54.

2 Klaus Bannach, *Die Lehre von der doppelten Macht Gottes bei Wilhelm von Ockham* (Wiesbaden: Franz Steiner Verlag GMBH, 1975), pp. 248–75. Some of Bannach's conclusions would have to be qualified by William J. Courtenay, *Capacity and Volition: A History of the Distinction of Absolute and Ordained Power* (Bergamo: Pierluigi Lubrina Editore, 1990), esp. pp. 119–23.

3 See the illuminating pages of André de Muralt, *L'enjeu de la philosophie médiévale* (Leiden: E. J. Brill, 1991), pp. 64–75.

4 Cusanus, *De coniecturis* II, 14. See also *De ludo globi: The Game of Spheres*, trans. Pauline Watts (New York: Abaris Books, 1986), p. 71; *De beryllo*, chap. 5; *De venatione sap-*

ientiae, chap. 17. Already Ernst Cassirer drew attention to Cusanus's idea of *humanitas* in this respect (*Individuum und Kosmos in der Renaissance,* p. 94). Later the humanist Bovillus, a follower of Lefévre d'Etaples (who published Cusanus's works), emphasized that the formation of *humanitas* does not come with human nature itself—which is still given.

5 Marsilio Ficino, *Theologia platonica* XIII, 3. See Charles Trinkaus, "Marsilio Ficino and the Ideal of Human Autonomy," in *Marsilio Ficino e il ritorno di Platone,* ed. Gian Carlo Garfagnini (Florence: Leo Olschki, 1986), pp. 197–210.

6 Pico della Mirandola, "Oration on the Dignity of Man," trans. Elisabeth Forbes (translation changed), in *The Renaissance Philosophy of Man,* ed. Ernst Cassirer, Paul O. Kristeller, and John Herman Randall (Chicago: University of Chicago Press, 1948), p. 255. Beside Ficino and Pico, Gianozzo Manetti (*De dignitate et excellentia hominis*), Bartolomeo Fazio (*De excellentia et praestantia hominis*), and Leon-Battista Alberti (*Della famiglia*) immediately come to mind.

7 See Hans Blumenberg, *Work on Myth,* trans. Robert Wallace (Cambridge: MIT Press, 1985).

8 Giordano Bruno, *Lo Spaccio della bestia trionfante* III, *Dialoghi italiani,* ed. Giovanni Gentile, 3d ed. (Florence: Sansoni, 1957), pp. 732–33.

9 Bruno, *De immenso* I, 11, *Opera latina* I/I p. 243.

10 Mikhail Bakhtin, *The Dialogic Imagination: Four Essays,* ed. Michael Holquist, trans. Caryl Emerson and Michael Holquist (Austin: University of Texas Press, 1981), p. 39. The idea is developed by Robert Anchor, "Bakhtin's Truths of Laughter," *CLIO* 14:3 (1985): 237–57.

11 Pauline Watts has drawn attention to the important role eschatological speculations and prophecies played in the Spanish project of discovering and christianizing the new world. "Many of his [Columbus's] contemporaries . . . were convinced that, with the victory over the Moors at Granada, the time when the Spanish monarchy would play a special role in history had arrived. Phelan [*The Millennial Kingdom of the Franciscans in the New World* (1970)] demonstrated how the ancient emperor-messiah myth, which was an essential part of medieval apocalypticism, was applied to the Spanish monarchy by early Franciscan missionaries." ("Prophecy and Discovery: On the Spiritual Origins of Christopher Columbus's 'Enterprise of the Indies,'" *The American Historical Review* 90, no. 1 [1985]: 73–102. Quote on p. 99.)

12 Salvador de Madariaga, *Englishmen, Frenchmen, Spaniards* (Oxford: Oxford University Press, 1929), p. 176.

13 Aristotle, *Politics* 1332 a 40. *Complete Works of Aristotle*, ed. Jonathan Barnes (Princeton: Princeton University Press, 1984).

14 Cicero, *De legibus* I, 7, 18. Also Marcus Aurelius: "To a rational creature the same act is at once according to nature and according to reason" (*Meditations* VII, 11). On the classical origins of natural law, one may consult Frederick Crosson, "Religion and Natural Law," *Liberty and Law: Civil and Religious. Catholic Commission on Intellectual and Cultural Affairs Annual,* 8 (1989): 80. See also Helmut Koester, "Nomos Physeos: The Concept of Natural Law in Greek Thought," in *Religions in Antiquity* (The Hague: Nyhoff, 1977).

15 The argument on the command to hate God appears in Ockham II, *Sent.* q. 19, art. 1 ad 30. As Philoteus Boehner has shown, it does not question the absoluteness of ethical commands but stresses the absoluteness of God's power and of his supremacy over his creation (*Collected Articles on Ockham*, ed. E. M. Buytaert [New York: St. Bonaventure, 1958], pp. 22ff). See also Heiko Oberman, *The Harvest of Medieval Theology* (Cambridge: Harvard University Press, 1963), pp. 92–93. On the shift from natural appropriateness to divine authority, see André de Muralt, "La structure de la philosophie politique moderne," in *Souveraineté et pouvoir. Cahiers de la Revue de Théologie et de Philosophie* 2 (Genève-Lausanne, 1978), p. 22. On the role of community and tradition in the Middle Ages, see Alasdair McIntyre, *After Virtue,* 2d ed. (Notre Dame, Ind.: University of Notre Dame Press, 1984) and *Whose Right? Which Rationality?* (Notre Dame, Ind.: University of Notre Dame Press, 1988).

16 Charles Taylor, *Sources of the Self: The Making of Modern Identity,* (Cambridge: Harvard University Press, 1989), p. 79.

17 Justus Lipsius, *De constantia* I, 19–20. Are we justified in attributing to the Stoic studies of Calvin's early years some influence upon his later predestinationism? At age twenty-three he published, with critical commentary, Seneca's *De clementia* (1532).

18 Campanella, *De sensu rerum et magia* (Frankfurt 1620). See Robert Spaemann's remarkable essay, "Bürgerliche Ethik und nicht-teleologische Ontologie," in *Subjectivität und Selbsterhaltung: Beiträge zur Diagnose der Moderne,* ed. Hans Ebeling (Frankfurt: Suhrkamp Verlag, 1976), p. 81.

19 Spinoza, *Ethics,* bk. I, definitions, and proposition XI (note).

20 Descartes, letter to Mesland AT IV, 173. Ferdinand Alquié, *La découverte métaphysique de l'homme chez Descartes* (Paris: Presses Universitaires, 1950), chap. 14. In this voluntarist interpretation we recognize once again the lingering influence of nominalist thought. Ockham had already claimed that the cause of a true proposition rather than a false one, or of an affirmative rather than a negative one, is the will which "wills to form one and not the other (*Quaestiones variae,* q. 5; *Opera theologica* VIII, p. 170). For inconsistencies in Ockham's description of the role of the will in the act of judgment, see Marilyn McCord Adams, *William Ockham* (Notre Dame, Ind.: University of Notre Dame Press, 1987), pp. 500, 531–32.

21 Descartes, *Meditations* (IV) AT VII, 57; CSM II, 40.

22 Other elements of Cartesian morality, such as the letters to Queen Christina and to Chanut or the *Treatise of the Passions* do not fill this gap. See Henri Gouhier, "L'itinéraire moral de Descartes," in *Descartes: Essais* (Paris: Vrin, 1949), pp. 197–252.

23 Paul Bénichou, *Morales du Grand Siècle* (Paris: Gallimard, 1948), p. 23.

24 Hannah Arendt, "What is Freedom," in *Between Past and Future* (1961; New York: Penguin Books, 1977), esp. p. 147.

25 Aristotle, *Nichomachean Ethics,* bk. I, chap. 2 (1094-b-10).

26 Diogenes Laertius, *Vitae philosophorum,* ed. H. S. Long (Oxford: Clarendon Press, 1965), 7, 87.

27 Cicero, *De finibus* III, 73. On the meaning of nature in Stoic ethics, see John Finnis, *Natural Law and Natural Right* (Oxford: Oxford University Press, 1980), pp. 374–76.

28 Thomas Aquinas, *Summa Theologiae* I-II, Quest. 58, arts. 6 and 7; Quest. 90, art. 2.

29 Remigio de'Girolami, *De bono communi*, ed. and with intro. by Maria Consiglia De Matteis, *La teologia politica communale di Remigio de'Girolami* (Bologna: Patron, 1977), p. 42.

30 See Hans Baron, *The Crisis of the Early Italian Renaissance* (Princeton: Princeton University Press), esp. chap. 18. Nancy Struever portrays Bruni's ideal of freedom. "In Bruni there is no Petrarchan or Romantic connection of privacy and freedom, of an inner freedom where one escapes from the world and feels 'free', but the classical connection of publicity and freedom." Nancy Struever, *The Language of History in the Renaissance* (Princeton: Princeton University Press), p. 111.

31 What Michael Oakeshott describes as a characteristically late-modern view of social responsibility began much earlier. "Almost all modern writing about moral conduct begins with the hypothesis of an individual human being choosing and pursuing his own direction of activity. What appeared to require explanation was not the existence of such individuals, but how they could come to have duties to others of their kind and what was the nature of those duties." Michael Oakeshott, "The Masses in Representation Democracy," in *The Politicization of Society*, ed. Kenneth S. Templeton, Jr. (Indianapolis, Ind.: Liberty Press, 1979), p. 321. The nominalist sources of modern political theories are well explained by de Muralt, *L'enjeu de la philosophie médiévale*, esp. pp. 80–81.

32 Ernst Cassirer, *The Myth of the State* (New Haven: Yale Univeristy Press, 1954), p. 135.

33 Machiavelli, *The Discourses* I, 39, trans. Christian E. Detmold (New York: Random House, 1950), p. 216.

34 Machiavelli, *Discourses* I, 41. See the pertinent commentary of Harvey Mansfield, Jr., *Machiavelli's New Modes and Orders* (Ithaca: Cornell University Press, 1979), p. 132. In the next two chapters (42, 43) Machiavelli urges that a person may advantageously change the qualities with which nature has endowed him,

provided he does it by degrees. Moral considerations do not enter into this political operation: pride is as good as humility.

35 Machiavelli, *The Prince*, trans. Luigi Ricci, rev. E. R. P. Vincent (New York: Random House, 1950), p. 29.

36 Machiavelli, *Discourses* II, 2, p. 285.

37 Cicero, *De legibus* II, 4, 8; and *De republica* III, 22.

38 Recent literature on the subject includes: A. P. d'Entrèves, *Natural Law* (New York: Harper, 1951, 1965); Finnis, *Natural Law and Natural Rights;* Leo Strauss, *Natural Right and History* (Chicago: University of Chicago Press, 1953, 1968); and James Bernard Murphy, "Nature, Custom, and Stipulation in Law and Jurisprudence," *Review of Metaphysics* no. 43 (1990): 751–90.

39 Aquinas, *Summa Theologiae* I-II, Q. 91 a2c; Q. 95 a2c, and the entire questions I-II, 93–95. On Aquinas's conception of natural law, see Dom Odon Lottin, O.S.B., *Le droit naturel chez St. Thomas* (Bruges, 1931); Bernard Roland-Gosselin, *La doctrine politique de St. Thomas d'Aquin* (Paris, 1928); and John Finnis, *Natural Law and Natural Rights.*

40 John Calvin, *Institutes of the Christian Religion*, trans. John Allen (1813) (Philadelphia, 1844), bk. IV, chap. 20, # 16. On Calvin's theory of natural law, see Günther Gloede, *Theologia Naturalis bei Calvin*, Tübinger Studien zur systematischen Theologie (Stuttgart-Berlin: W. Kohlhammer, 1935), esp. pp. 102–10; John T. McNeill, "Natural Law in the Teaching of the Reformers" *Journal of Religion* 26 (1946): 168–82. In Luther we find a great deal of concern for the common good, but law is, to the best of my knowledge, always discussed as positive law, even when God-given.

41 Calvin, *Opera*, vol. 8, 354, ed. G. Baum, E. Cunitz, E. Rensz in *Corpus Reformatorum* (1863–1900).

42 Francesco Suarez, *De legibus ac Deo legislatore* (1612), trans. James B. Scott in *Selections From Three Works*, in *The Classics of International Law* (Oxford: Oxford University Press, 1944), bk. II, chaps. 5, 6 and bk. I, chap. 5. On the natural law as law of reason in Suarez, see Otto Gierke, *Natural Law and the Theory of Society, 1500 to 1800*, trans.

with intro. by Ernest Barker (Boston: Beacon Press, 1960), pp. 26–40, 242–43, 264.

43 Suarez, De legibus, bk. III, chap. 2, # 3.

44 Ibid., bk. III, chap. 2, # 4.

45 De Muralt, "La structure de la philosophie politique moderne," in Souveraineté et pouvoir, p. 61. In his incisive probe of the nominalist sources of early modern political theory, de Muralt suggests that Suarez harks back to Scotus's materia that already possesses through itself a quasi forma endowing it with some kind of independent existence before its formal constitution. Historically this interpretation may be specious but as comparison it is convincing.

46 On the various religious theories that fed the resistance against the absolute monarchy, see J. W. Allen, A History of Political Thought in the Sixteenth Century (1928; New York: Barnes and Noble, 1960), pts. 2(ENDASH)3. On the doctrine of the Jesuit thinkers, see the same work, pp. 353–66.

47 De Muralt, "La structure de la philosophie politique moderne," pp. 48–49. Another source of Hobbes's theory may have been the passage in Cicero's De inventione in which the eloquent orator is said to rally an anarchical mob into a social order. But the philosophical argument is nominalist.

48 Thomas Hobbes, Leviathan, pt. I, chap. 14 (New York: Penguin English Library, 1983), p. 189. Henceforth quoted in text by part, chapter, and page of the Penguin edition.

49 See Leo Strauss, The Political Philosophy of Thomas Hobbes (Oxford: Oxford University Press, 1936), esp. p. 156.

50 Aquinas, Summa Theologiae, I, Q. 95, a2c.

51 Ibid., I-II, Q. 96, a1c.

52 See, e.g., Grotius, The Law of War and Peace (De jure belli ac pacis) (1625), bk. I, chap. 1, secs. 4–10. Richard Tuck, Natural Rights Theories (Cambridge: Cambridge University Press, 1979).

53 Allen, History of Political Thought in the Sixteenth Century, pp. 199–331.

54 Gierke, Natural Law and the Theory of Society, p. 234, n.29.

55 Recently John Finnis in Natural Law and Natural Rights has attempted to incorporate the modern conception of rights within a traditional theory of natural law. He considers recognition of values basic for human fulfilment prior to any specific social structures indispensable. This interesting interpretation, though different from the traditional one, escapes, I believe, the problems inherent in the one introduced by Hobbes and Locke. For even if human rights here unquestionably precede positive law and concrete social structures, Finnis reintegrates them with that higher law of nature through which the person partakes in the eternal order of things. Through their participation in that order these rights have a concrete contextual quality within the whole of creation that the modern, abstract ones do not possess. For a critical evaluation see Ernest Fortin, "The New Rights Theory and the Natural Law," Review of Politics 44 (1982): 590–612.

56 Raymond Polin, Politique et philosophie chez Hobbes (Paris: 1951), p. 126.

57 Proclus, The Elements of Theology, trans. E. R. Dodds (Oxford: Clarendon Press, 1933), prop. 25, p. 29.

Chapter 6

1 Schelling, Die Zeitälter der Welt (The Ages of the World), Werke, vol. 8, p. 259.

2 Blumenberg put it concisely: "It is true that a sense of history is not yet a resolve to bring about a particular future; but there is simply no other way of gaining sensitivity to a future than through insight into the uniqueness and irretrievability of what is past. The fact that the future is composed neither of the wax figures of the past nor of the imagines of utopian wishes is something that one can learn only from the specific futures of the past times that already make up our past." Hans Blumenberg, Work on Myth, trans. Robert Wallace (Cambridge: MIT Press, 1985), p. 99.

3 The French revolution with its concomitant wars and the subsequent rise and fall of Napoleon entailed a mass experience of history. (See Georg Lukacs, The Historical Novel, trans. Hannah and Stanley Mitchell [London: Merlin Press, 1964], p. 23.) Apocalyptic movements such as that of the spiritual Franciscans or of Thomas Münzer's Anabaptists had introduced a future that broke with the entire past. To them the present was the decisive epoch. It

was different from other times, not one historical epoch among others. See Norman Cohn, *The Pursuit of the Millennium* (New York: Essential Books, 1957), chaps. 7 and 12.

4 Eric Voegelin, *The Ecumenic Age*, vol. 4 of *Order and History* (Baton Rouge: Louisiana State University Press, 1974), p. 7.

5 Erich Auerbach writes about Dante: "He remodelled Virgil as though Augustan Rome were separated from his own epoch only by the passage of time, as though certain events had taken place and a certain amount of knowledge had been amassed in the meantime, but not as though man's whole form of life and thought had changed. Virgil the ancestor speaks the language of his descendant." (*Dante, Poet of the Secular World* [1929], trans. Ralph Manheim [University of Chicago Press, 1961], p. 158.) On the absence of a developed sense of historical difference in medieval culture, see Ricardo Quinones, *The Renaissance Discovery of Time* (Cambridge: Harvard University Press, 1972), p. 7 and Peter Burke, *The Renaissance Sense of the Past* (London: Arnold, 1969), pp. 2–3.

6 Thomas M. Greene, *The Light in Troy: Imitation and Discovery in Renaissance Poetry* (New Haven: Yale University Press, 1982), p. 90. I owe much to this beautiful book and even more to its kind author. Theodor Mommsen, "Petrarch's Concept of the Dark Ages," *Speculum* 17 (1942): 226–43. Petrarch's metaphor of standing astride two epochs appears in *Res memorandae, Studi Petrarcheschi I* (1931) (Arezzo: Accademia Petrarca di lettere, arti e scienze, 1931 ff.). Ricardo Quinones's work contains an insightful discussion of Petrarch's strong awareness of the transiency of time.

7 Walter Pater, *The Renaissance*, (1873; London: Macmillan, 1912), p. 51.

8 See A. J. Parel, "The Question of Machiavelli's Modernity," *The Review of Politics* 53, no. 2 (Spring 1991): 320–39. The idea of the past as teacher of the present also underlies Bacon's *De sapientia veterum* (1609), which seeks new political wisdom in ancient fables and myths, and appears in Vico's *De antiquissima italorum sapientia* (1710).

9 Nancy Struever, *The Language of History in the Renaissance* (Princeton: Princeton University Press, 1970), See also Hans Baron, *The Crisis of the Early Italian Renaissance* (Princeton: Princeton University Press, 1966), passim.

10 Wilhelm Humboldt, "On the Historian's Task" ("Ueber die Aufgabe des Geschichtschreibers") [1820], in *Wilhelm von Humboldts Gesammelte Schriften* (Berlin, 1903), vol. 4, pp. 35–56, trans. in *History and Theory*, 6, pp. 57–71.

11 See Quinones, *Renaissance Discovery of Time*, chap. 5. Also M. Seidlmayer, "Petrarca das Urbild des Humanisten," in *Wege und Wandlungen des Humanismus* (Goettingen, 1965), pp. 125–73.

12 Bernard McGinn, *Visions of the End: Apocalyptic Traditions in the Middle Ages* (New York: Crossroad, 1979). Apocalyptic thinking continued well beyond the Middle Ages and regularly resurfaced in ever new form, as is shown by Thomas J. J. Altizer, *History as Apocalypse* (Albany: SUNY Press, 1985).

13 Juergen Habermas, *Theory and Practice*, trans. John Viertel (Boston: Beacon Press, 1973), p. 54.

14 Thomas More, *Utopia*, trans. Peter K. Marshall (New York: Washington Square Press, 1965), p. 124.

15 Tomasso Campanella, *La Città del Sole: Dialogo Poetico* (*The City of the Sun: A Poetical Dialogue*), trans. with intro. by Daniel J. Donno (Berkeley: University of California Press, 1981). Cf. Frank Emmanuel and Fritzie Prigalizy, eds., *Utopian Thought in the Western World* (Cambridge: Harvard University Press, 1979).

16 Descartes, AT VII 596; also VII 580.

17 In a letter written on July 13, 1379, to Giovanni Bartolomei, *Epistolario*, F. Novati, ed., 4 vol. (Rome, 1891–1911) 1:334–42.

18 *Epistolario* 4:134. See Charles Trinkaus, "Humanistic Dissidence: Florence versus Milan, or Poggio versus Valla?" in *Florence and Milan: Comparisons and Relations*, ed. Sergio Bertelli, Nicolai Rubinstein, and Craig Hugh Smyth (Florence: La Nuova Italia Editrice, 1989), pp. 17–40.

19 *Epistolario* 4:136.

20 Baron, *Crisis of the Early Italian Renaissance*, chap. 3.

21 In the prefaces and introductions of Etienne Pasquier's *Recherches de la France* (1560), Nicolas Vignier's *Bibliothèque historiale* (1588), and Jean Bodin's *Methodus ad facilem historiarum cognitionem* (1566), the authors take position both against past methods of historiography and against the cult of the past. See George Huppert, *The Idea of Perfect History: Historical Erudition and Historical Philosophy in Renaissance France* (Urbana: University of Illinois Press, 1970).

22 Jean Bodin, *Method for the Easy Comprehension of History*, trans. Beatrice Reynolds (New York: Octagon Books, 1966), p. 226.

23 Bacon, *Valerius Terminus*, in *Works*, ed. Spelling, Eddis, and Heater (London, 1857–74), vol. 3, pp. 220–21. Charles Webster in *The Great Instauration: Science, Medicine, and Reform, 1626–1660* (London: Duckworth, 1974) links Bacon's belief in progress to a millennial eschatology, which would account for its success among the Puritans.

24 See Charles Whitney, *Francis Bacon and Modernity* (New Haven: Yale University Press, 1986); Stephen McKnight, *The Modern Age and the Recovery of Ancient Wisdom*, chap. 7, "Francis Bacon: Ancient Wisdom and Utopian Reform" (Columbia: University of Missouri Press, 1991), pp. 127–44; Sharon Achinstein, "How To Be a Progressive without Looking Like One: History and Knowledge in Bacon's *New Atlantis*," *Clio* 17/3 (1988): 248–64.

25 See Harry Levin, *The Myth of the Golden Age in the Renaissance* (New York: Oxford University Press, 1969), p. 17.

26 Bacon, *Works*, vol. 4, p. 82.

27 Bacon, *Works*, vol. 4, p. 311. See Richard Foster Jones, *Ancients and Moderns*, (1936; rpt. New York: Dover, 1982), pp. 44–47 and Hans Blumenberg, *The Legitimacy of the Modern Age* (Cambridge: MIT Press, 1983), p. 340.

28 A more moderate version of this opinion appears in George Hakewill's *Apologie* (1627). On these and similar odd comparisons, no work has yet surpassed J. B. Bury's erudite and witty classic, *The Idea of Progress: An Inquiry into Its Growth and Origin* (1932; New York: Dover, 1955), chap. 4.

29 Peter Berger, *Facing Up to Modernity* (New York: Basic Books, 1977), p. 73.

30 The fifteenth-century Angelo Poliziano shows some vague forefeeling of it in the conclusion of the first part of his Latin oration on Quintilian and Statius, two writers who came after the great classical epoch: "There is no part of life, no time, no fortune, no age, no nation, in which rhetorical skill has not gained access to the highest dignities and to supreme honors." Angelo Poliziano, "Oratio super Fabio Quintiliano et Statii Sylvis," in *Prosatori Latini del Quattrocento*, ed. Eugenio Garin (Milano: Riccardo Ricciardi, s.d.), p. 884.

31 Descartes, *Discourse on Method* AT VI, 6; CSM I, 113–14.

32 Descartes, *Rules* AT X, 367; CSM I, 13. Malebranche, *Recherche de la vérité*, in *Oeuvres*, ed. Adam-Tannery X 502.

33 David Lachterman, "Descartes and the Philosophy of History," *Independent Journal of Philosophy* 4 (1983): 38.

34 See Guido Maertens, "Augustine's Image of Man," in *Images of Man in Ancient and Medieval Thought. Studia Gerardo Verbeke dicata*, ed. F. Bossier et al. (Leuven: Leuven University Press, 1976), pp. 175–98. Also, Jean-Marie Le Blond, *Les conversions de saint Augustin* (Paris, 1950) and Jean Guitton's classical study *Le temps et l'éternité chez Plotin et Saint Augustin* (Paris, 1933).

35 Descartes, *Discourse* AT VI, 4; CSM I, 112.

36 M. G. Cohen, *Ecrivains français en Hollande dans la première moitié du XVII siècle* (Paris, 1920), pp. 417–18.

37 For an analysis of this attitude, see Emile Durkheim's classic *Le suicide* (Paris, 1897).

38 I have devoted an essay to that problem: "The Absolute Spirit and the Religious Legitimation of Modernity," in *Hegels Logik der Philosophie: Religion und Philosophie in der Theorie des absoluten Geistes*, ed. Dieter Henrich and Rolf-Peter Horstmann, *Veroeffentlichungen der Internationalen Hegel-Vereinigung* (Stuttgart: Klett Verlag, 1984), pp. 224–33.

39 G. E. Lessing, *Lessings Werke*, ed. Lachmann-Muncker, 23 vols. (1886–1924), vol. 13, pp. 1–8. "On the Proof of the Spirit and of Power," in *Lessing's Theological Writings*, trans. Henry Chadwick (Stanford: Stanford University Press, 1957), pp. 51–56.

40 Keiji Nishitani, *Religion and Nothingness*, trans. Jan Van Bragt (Berkeley: University of California Press, 1983), p. 234.

41 Maurice Blondel, *L'action* (Paris, 1893). In English: *Action*, trans. Oliva Blanchette (Notre Dame, Ind.: University of Notre Dame Press, 1984). Karl Jaspers's even more fundamental analysis of freedom has appeared in *Philosophie* (Berlin: Julius Springer, 1932), vol. 2, pts. 2 and 3. Paul Ricoeur, *Finitude et culpabilité*, pt. 1, *L'homme faillible*, pt, 2, *La symbolique du mal* (Paris: Aubier, 1960). In English: *Fallible Man*, trans. Charles Kelbley (Chicago: Henry Regnery, 1965), and *The Symbolism of Evil*, trans. Emerson Buchanan (Boston: Beacon Press, 1967). See also Martin Heidegger, *Being and Time*, trans. John Macquarrie and Edward Robinson (New York: Harper & Row, 1962), pts. 5 and 6, and Martin Heidegger, "The Essence of Truth," in *Basic Writings*, trans. John Sallis (New York: Harper & Row, 1976), esp. pp. 129–33.

Chapter 7

1 W. D. Ross, *Aristotle* (1923; New York: Meridian Books, 1959), p. 147. The crucial passage is in *De anima*, bk. III, 430 a (10–25). Professor Martin Moors has rightly drawn attention to this and related texts in a paper, "Naming 'He Who Is,'" read at the centennial celebration of the Higher Institute of Philosophy at Leuven (Belgium) in 1991.

2 Irenaeus, *Adversus Haereses* IV, 34, 1; also III, 18, 7.

3 Maximus Confessor, *Ambigua*, P.G. 91:1084.

4 Vladimir Lossky, *The Mystical Theology of the Eastern Church* (Crestwood, N.Y.: St. Vladimir's Seminary Press, 1976), p. 101.

5 Thomas Aquinas, *Summa Theologiae* I-II, Quest. 62–63.

6 Karl Rahner, *Theological Investigations*, vol. I (London: Barton, Longman, Todd, 1968), p. 302. On the symbolic function of nature in the Christian vision, see Bernhard Stoeckle, *Gratia supponit naturam. Geschichte und Analyse eines theologischen Axioms*, vol. 49 of *Studia Anselmiana*, vol. 49 (Rome: Pontificium Institutum S. Anselmi, 1962), p. 206. Rahner justifies this theological subordination of na-

ture philosophically: "Certainly the philosopher has his own well-grounded concept of the nature of man: the irreducible substance of human being, established by recourse to human experience independently of verbal revelation. This concept may largely coincide with the theological concept of man's nature, insofar as without Revelation the greater part of what goes beyond this theological 'nature' is not experienced, and at any rate is not recognized *as* supernatural without the help of Revelation to interpret it."

7 Henri de Lubac, *Surnaturel* (Paris: Aubier, 1946), chap. 5. The classical passage (cited by de Lubac) reads: "Opportet quod homini superaddatur aliqua supernaturalis forma et perfectio, per quam convenienter ordinetur in finem" (Some supernatural form and perfection must be super added to man whereby he may be ordered suitably to the aforesaid end). Aquinas, *Summa contra Gentiles* III chap. 150, §5. See also chap. 152, §3.

8 Sylvester Ferrariensis, *Opera* (Venice, 1535), vol. 1, pp. 39–41.

9 Aquinas, *Summa Theologiae* III, Q. 1, a 3. This statement is counterbalanced, however, by the preceding articles which describe the fitness of the Incarnation on the basis of God's goodness and of man's "full participation in the divine nature" (*Summa Theologiae* III, Q. 1, a 2). The connection with sin appears to rest on a scriptural basis, the *modus loquendi Sacrae Scripturae*.

10 On the relation between motion and transcendence in Aristotle, see William Buckley, *Motion and Motion's God* (Princeton: Princeton University Press, 1971), pt. 1.

11 In a mechanistic system of reality, God could not be truly immanent in the finite without being a part of the system, as Spinoza perceived, or, since this would conflict with the definition of an infinite Being, without constituting the totality itself as its originating principle. In Spinoza's terms: *Deus, sive natura*, that is, *natura naturans*.

12 See Cornelio Fabro, *La nozione metafisica di partecipazione secondo S. Tomasso d'Aquino* (Brescia, 1939) and L. B. Geiger, *La participation dans la philosophie de St. Thomas* (Paris, 1942).

13 Aquinas *Summa Theologiae* I, Q. 8, a 1.

14 William J. Bouwsma, "Renaissance and Reformation," in *Luther and the Dawn of the Modern Era,* ed. Heiko A. Oberman (Leiden: E. J. Brill, 1974), p. 136.

15 Aquinas, *Summa contra Gentiles,* bk. IV, chap. 43.

16 John Duns Scotus, *God and Creatures: The Quotlibetal Questions,* trans. with intro. and notes by Felix Alluntis and Allan Wolter (Princeton: Princeton University Press, 1975), pp. 434–35. Scotus's position on humanity obeyed his general principle that being as being is neutral with respect to theological implications. On the fourteenth-century reaction against Aristotelian rationalism, the primacy of the will, and the new emphasis on religious experience instead of theological speculation, see K. Michalski, *Le problème de la volonté à Oxford et à Paris au XIVe siècle* (Lwow: Studia Philosophica, 1937), esp. chaps. 2 and 3. Also Stefan Swiezawski, "La crise du rationalisme au 15e siècle," in *Images of Man in Ancient and Medieval Thought,* ed. Carlos Laga et al. (Leuven: Louvain University Press, 1976), pp. 357–368.

17 See Alfred Freddoso, "Human Nature, Potency and Incarnation," *Faith and Philosophy* 3, no. 1 (1986): 27–53.

18 Ockham, III *Sent.* d1q1G. Heiko Oberman refuted the charge long ago in *The Harvest of Medieval Theology: Gabriel Biel and Late Medieval Nominalism.* (Cambridge: Harvard University Press, 1963; rpt. Durham, N.C.: Labyrinth Press, 1983), pp. 256–58. Yet it continues to reappear for different reasons as, for instance, in Peter Geach, "Nominalism," *Sophia* 3, no. 2 (1964): 1–14. Meanwhile Marilyn McCord Adams in *William Ockham* (Notre Dame, Ind.: University of Notre Dame Press, 1987) has refuted it once again.

19 This theory of two distinct powers can definitely not be attributed to Ockham who explicitly rejects it in *Quodlibeta Septem* VI, q. 1. *Opera theologica* IX (New York: St. Bonaventure, 1980), pp. 585–86. William Courtenay's recent substantial study, *Capacity and Volition: A History of the Distinction of Absolute and Ordained Power* (Bergamo: Pierluigi Lubrina, 1990), came too late to my attention to fully profit from it. But he convincingly argues the traditionality of Ockham's position. This work will force scholars to revise substantially the traditional presentation of the distinction

between *potentia absoluta* and *potentia ordinata* among nominalists. It clearly removes Ockham from the nominalist flock.

20 Oberman, *Harvest of Medieval Theology,* pp. 38–48. See also William J. Courtenay, "Nominalism and Late Medieval Religion," in *The Pursuit of Holiness in Late Medieval and Renaissance Religion,* ed. Charles Trinkaus and Heiko A. Oberman (Leiden: E. J. Brill, 1974), pp. 26–59.

21 Aquinas, *Summa contra Gentiles* P. III, chap. 70, trans. Anton C. Pegis in *Basic Writings of Saint Thomas Aquinas* (New York: Random House, 1945), vol. 2, p. 130. See Kathryn Tanner's lucid analysis of this confused development: Kathryn Tanner, *God and Creation in Christian Theology* (Oxford: Basil Blackwell, 1988), pp. 97–99.

22 Thus the influential spiritual theologian of the fifteenth century Dionysius the Carthusian is as clear in his distinction as firm in his resistance to any separation when he writes: "If the human person had been created only for a natural beatitude, as philosophers thought, he certainly would have needed neither divine law nor grace, but the natural law and natural powers would have sufficed. For a natural happiness and end natural means suffice. But since we have been created for a supernatural beatitude which transcends even the happiness of angels, it is certain that we need a supernatural law and a gratuitous grace. There is a twofold grace or human perfection, then, namely, a natural one of which the philosophers speak and a supernatural one which Scripture teaches." Dionysius Carthusianus, *De donis Spiritus Sancti, Tractatus* I, art. VII, in *Opera Omnia* 35, p. 164 (Tournai, 1908) (my translation). See also *Tractatus* II, ibid., p. 200.

23 On the modern history of the concept, see Josef Fuchs S.J., *Natural Law: A Theological Investigation* (New York: Sheed and Ward, 1965), chap. 3.

24 See Wendy Raudenbush Olmsted, "Philosophical Inquiry and Religious Transformation in Boethius's *The Consolation of Philosophy* and Augustine's *Confessions,*" *The Journal of Religion* 69 (1989): 14–35.

25 Francis Bacon, *The Advancement of Learning,* bk. II, 6, 1.

26 Bacon, *Advancement,* bk. II, 25, 3.

27 On this work, its early successes, and later contribution toward deist and atheist trends in modern thought, see the remarkable study of Michael Buckley, *The Origins of Modern Atheism* (New Haven: Yale University Press, 1987), pp. 42–55.

28 Montaigne, *Essays* II, 12. Charles Cotton trans. (Chicago: University of Chicago Press, 1952), p. 209A.

29 Ibid., p. 213A.

30 On the relation between natural theology and atheism, see Buckley, *Origins of Modern Atheism.*

31 See Ernst Cassirer, *The Philosophy of the Enlightenment*, trans. Fritz Koelln and James P. Pettegrove (Princeton: Princeton University Press (1951), 1968), pp. 39–40.

32 Giordano Bruno, *De immenso*, in *Opera latine conscripta*, ed. Fiorentino, Tocco, et al. (Naples, 1879–1891; facsimile Stuttgart: Friedrich Fromann, 1962), I, 1, p. 243.

33 Giordano Bruno, *De la causa*, in *Dialoghi italiani*, p. 668.

34 Giordano Bruno, *De triplici minimo et mensura*, in *Opera latine conscripta* I, 3, p. 147.

35 Giordano Bruno, *Summa terminorum metaphysicorum,*in *Opera latine conscripta* I, 4, p. 86.

36 Ibid., I, 4, p. 75.

37 Giordano Bruno, *Eroici Furori*, in *Dialoghi italiani*, p. 1123.

38 Ibid., p. 1006.

39 Ibid., p. 1092.

40 In *De venatione sapientiae* (1463), chap. 3, Cusanus distinguishes a first moment of possible creation (*posse fieri*) from the actual creation in time (*posse factum*).

41 It is true that in *De venatione sapientiae* (chap. 27) Cusanus claims that God could have created another world than the present one. But this discrepant statement implies no return to the unrestricted *potentia absoluta* of nominalism, as Blumenberg maintains (*The Legitimacy of the Modern Age* [Cambridge: MIT Press, 1983], p. 528), but rather, I think, emphasizes the total dependence of the world upon a rational Creator who, though his rea-

son surpasses human intelligence, for Cusanus never acts inconsistently.

42 Nicholas of Cusa, *De docta ignorantia*, bk. I, chap. 11, in *Nicholas of Cusa on Learned Ignorance*, trans. Jasper Hopkins (Minneapolis: Arthur J. Banning Press, 1981; 1985).

43 Nicholas of Cusa, *De coniecturis*, bk. I, chap. 13.

44 Nicholas of Cusa, *De visione Dei*, chap. 16, # 67, in *Nicholas of Cusa's Dialectical Mysticism: Text, Translation and Interpretive Study of De visione Dei*, trans. Jasper Hopkins (Minneapolis, Minn.: Arthur J. Banning Press, 1985), pp. 194–95.

45 Nicholas of Cusa, *De docta ignorantia*, bk. III, chap. 2 (# 193), in *Learned Ignorance*, trans. Hopkins, p. 129.

46 Karl Jaspers, *Anselm and Nicholas of Cusa*, vol. 2 of *The Great Philosophers*, trans. Ralph Manheim (New York: Harcourt, Brace, Jovanovich, 1974), p. 58.

47 It ought to be noted in Cusanus's defense that his synthesis does not exclusively depend on the idea of the maximum. In *De filiatione Dei* he outlines a different but still christocentric argument.

Chapter 8

1 Readings of this kind, made in the autumnal glow of the Enlightenment, were refuted in monographs such as Lucien Febvre, *Le problème de l'incroyance au XVIe siècle: La religion de Rabelais* (Paris, 1942) and *Amour sacré, amour profane: Autour de l'Heptameron* (Paris, 1944). Also, on Montaigne and Rabelais, by Francis Hermans, *Histoire doctrinale de l'humanisme chrétien* (Tournai, 1948), vol. 2. On Machiavelli, Sebastian de Grazia, *Machiavelli in Hell* (Princeton: Princeton University Press, 1989). Giuseppe Toffanin, in *Il secolo senza Roma* and *Storia del Umanesimo*, presents the humanist movement as a theologically inspired attack upon the naturalism unleashed by the averroistic philosophy of the thirteenth century, a thesis that lacks sufficient support to be convincing.

2 Petrarch, *Letters on Familiar Matters (Rerum familiarium libri IX–XVI)*, trans. Aldo S. Bernardo (Baltimore: Johns Hopkins University Press, 1982), X 4, p. 69. See also *Invective* *contra medicum*, bk. III, and, indirectly, *De vita solitaria* and *De otio religioso*. The idea of a *theologia poetica* attained through rhetoric and poetry as an alternative to scholastic theology in the Renaissance was first clearly presented in E. R. Curtius, *European Literature and the Latin Middle Ages*, trans. W. R. Trask (New York: Pantheon, 1953). Charles Trinkaus developed it for Petrarch in *The Poet as Philosopher: Petrarch and the Formation of Renaissance Consciousness* (New Haven: Yale University Press, 1976), pp. 90–113. A particularly strong and overall convincing defense of Petrarch's theology is Marjorie O'Rourke Boyle, *Petrarch's Genius: Pentimento and Prophecy* (Berkeley: University of California Press, 1991). See also Giuseppe Mazzotta, "Humanism and Monastic Spirituality," *Stanford Literature Review* 5, nos.1–2 (1988): 57–74, and *The Worlds of Petrarch* (Durham, N.C.: Duke University Press, 1993). For a quite different, more secular reading, however, see Thomas M. Greene's *The Light in Troy: Imitation and Discovery in Renaissance Poetry* (New Haven: Yale University Press, 1982), pp. 81–146.

3 Petrarch, *Rerum familiarium* X 4 (3–5).

4 Coluccio Salutati, *Epistolario*, 4 vols., ed. F. Novati (Rome, 1891–1911), 4:134–36. See Ronald Witt, "Coluccio Salutati and the Conception of the *Poeta Theologus* in the Fourteenth Century," *Renaissance Quarterly* 30 (1977): 538–63.

5 Charles Trinkaus, "Humanistic Dissidence: Florence versus Milan, or Poggio versus Valla?" in *Florence and Milan: Comparisons and Relations*, ed. Sergio Bertelli, Nicolai Rubinstein, and Craig Hugh Smyth (Florence: La Nuova Italia Editrice, 1989), pp. 17–40. Salvatore I. Camporeale, *Lorenzo Valla: Umanesimo e Teologia* (Florence: Istituto Nazionale di Studi sul Rinascimento, 1972). Ronald Witt, *Hercules at the Crossroads: The Life, Works, and Thought of Coluccio Salutati* (Durham, N.C.: Duke University Press, 1983), pp. 266–67, 402–06.

6 Still, Valla and Erasmus possessed a detailed knowledge of Scholastic theology and Aristotelian philosophy. Valla's discussions of Aristotle's logic in his *Dialecticae disputationes* (1439) show him to be a formidable logician while his *De vero bono* (1433) reveals a clear understanding of the principles of Scholastic ethics. Erasmus's *Hyperaspistes* (1527), espe-

cially in the last part, continues much of the discussion on "merit" toward salvation that was taking place in the nominalist schools of theology of the preceding century.

7 On the *prisca theologia* in the Renaissance, especially in Ficino who translated the *Corpus hermeticum*, see Stephen McKnight, *The Modern Age and the Recovery of Ancient Wisdom* (Columbia: University of Missouri Press, 1991).

8 Colluccio Salutati, *De laboribus Herculis* II, chap. 2.12; also chaps. 4, 5, 6. See Ernesto Grassi, *Heidegger and the Question of Renaissance Humanism* (Binghamton, N.Y.: Center for Medieval and Early Renaissance Studies, 1983), pp. 57ff.

9 Giordano Bruno, *Lo spaccio della bestia trionfante*, dial. 3, in *Dialoghi italiani*, ed. Gentile, Aquilecchia (Florence: Jansoni, 1957), p. 779.

10 Lorenzo Valla, *De voluptate*, bk. I, chap. 10, in *Opera omnia* (Basel 1540; photoreproduced Torino: Bottega d'Erasmo, 1962), p. 906.

11 Thomas More, *The Utopia* (Princeton: Van Nostrand, 1947), pp. 110–11.

12 See Charles Trinkaus, "The Religious Thought of the Italian Humanists and the Reformers: Anticipation or Autonomy?" in *The Pursuit of Holiness in Late Medieval and Renaissance Religion*, ed. Charles Trinkaus and Heiko A. Oberman (Leiden: E. J. Brill, 1974), p. 361. Charles Trinkaus's *In Our Image and Likeness* (Chicago: University of Chicago Press, 1970) has done much to restore Valla's discredited religious reputation. I have followed his interpretation but remain aware that a more cynical reading is possible.

13 Camporeale, *Lorenzo Valla*. The author's assessment of Valla's lack of originality in treating the Trinity, "the central mystery" of Christian faith (pp. 248–49), may be extended to other topics of theology. In his later *Lorenzo Valla: Tra Medioevo e Rinascimento, Encomium Sancti Thomae* (Pistoia: s.n.l., 1977), Camporeale expresses a higher appreciation for Valla's overall theological significance.

14 P. Imbart de la Tour, *Les origines de la Réforme*, vol. 2 of *L'Eglise catholique* (Melun, 1944), p. 413.

15 Among them, E.-W. Kohls, *Die Theologie des Erasmus*, 2 vols. (Basel: Reinhardt Verlag,

1966); Charles Béné, *Erasme et Saint Augustin, ou l'influence de Saint Augustin sur l'humanisme d'Erasme* (Geneva, 1969); Georges Chantraine, S.J., *"Mystère" et "Philosophie du Christ" selon Erasme* (Gembloux: Duculot, 1971); Marjorie O'Rourke Boyle, *Christening Pagan Mysteries: Erasmus in Pursuit of Wisdom* (Toronto: University of Toronto Press, 1981); Marjorie O'Rourke Boyle, *Erasmus on Language and Method in Theology* (Toronto: University of Toronto Press, 1977). Charles Trinkaus, "Introduction to Erasmus's Debate with Luther Over Free Will," to the forthcoming trans. of De libero arbitrio and Hyperaspistes, in vols. 76 and 77 of the *Complete Works of Erasmus* (CWE). Jean-Pierre Massaut, "Humanisme et spiritualité chez Erasme," in *Dictionnaire de Spiritualité* 7/1, 1006–028.

16 The modernist interpretation of Erasmus, clearly expressed in Augustin Renaudet, *Etudes érasmiennes, 1521–1529; Erasme: Sa penseé religieuse et son action d'après sa correspondance* (Paris, 1939) but also present in Febvre, *Le problème de l'incroyance,* has been effectively refuted by Chantraine, *"Mystère" et "Philosophie du Christ,"* a study that has perceptively caught the spirit of Erasmus's theology while going well beyond the letter.

17 Erasmus, *Enchiridion,* in *Opera Omnia,* LB V, 8D. The Amsterdam edition (Amsterdam: North-Holland, begun 1969) (ASD) is still in progress and has to be complemented by the Leiden edition of 1703–6 (10 vols.), ed. Jean Le Clerc (LB) or by the Basel edition of 1540 (9 vols.), ed. Beatus Rhenanus and, for Erasmus's Letters, by the *Opus epistolarum,* 11 vols., ed. P. S. Allen (Oxford 1906–47).

18 Erasmus, LB V, 29 B-D.

19 John B. Payne, *Erasmus, His Theology of the Sacraments* (Richmond, Va.: John Knox Press, 1970), sums up his argument: "We have noticed that, far from repudiating scholasticism, however much he may have detested the subtleties of scholastic argument, Erasmus had considerable knowledge of and appreciation for some of the scholastics, especially the late medieval nominalistic tradition. He enlists the support especially of Gerson and Durandus, but also of Biel, for his views on [the sacraments]" (pp. 228–29). See also Christian Dolfen, *Die Stellung des Erasmus von Rotterdam zur scholastischen Methode* (Osnabrück, 1936). Erasmus's critique of Scholasticism was

often harsh, but he never outright rejected it; he denied it a monopoly in the practice of theology.

20 Erasmus, LB V, 27 D.

21 Erasmus, LB V, 7 F.

22 Erasmus, LB V, 32 A.

23 A number of recent critics have refuted the charge. Beside Chantraine's *"Mystère" et "Philosophie du Christ,"* selon Erasme, see Alfons Auer, *Die vollkommene Frömmigheit des Christen: Nach dem Enchiridion militis Christiani des Erasmus von Rotterdam* (Dusseldorf: Patmos Verlag, 1954), esp. chap. 7. I owe much to this erudite, beautifully balanced commentary on the *Enchiridion.*

24 Erasmus, LB V, 32 C.

25 Erasmus, LB V, 25 B.

26 Thus, for instance, J. Lortz, "Erasmus-kirchengeschichtlich," in *Aus Theologie und Philosophie: Festschrift für F. Tillmann,* ed. Th. Steinbüchel and Th. Müncker (Düsseldorf, 1950), pp. 271–326, esp. 310. And, more radically, Augustin Renaudet, *Etudes érasmiennes; Erasme: Sa penseé religieuse et son action d'après sa correspondance* (Paris, 1926). In defense of Erasmus, Auer, *Die vollkommene Frömmigkeit,* pp. 116–19.

27 Erasmus, *In Ecclesiastem,* in *Opera,* LB V, 849; A. Auer, *Die vollkommene Frömmigkeit,* pp. 103–08.

28 His *De libero arbitrio diatribè sive collatio* (1524) came after Luther's condemnation of 1520. See Marjorie O'Rourke Boyle, *Rhetoric and Reform: Erasmus' Civil Dispute with Luther* (Cambridge: Harvard University Press, 1983) and "Erasmus and the 'Modern' Question: Was He Semi-Pelagian?" *Archiv für Reformationsgeschichte* 75 (1984): 59–78.

29 In a letter to Franciscus Vergara, professor in Alcala (October 13, 1527). *Opus epistolarum Des. Erasmi Roterodami,* ed. P. S. Allen, vol. 7 (Oxford: Clarendon Press, 1928), p. 194.

30 Erasmus, *De pueris instituendis,* ed. Jean-Claude Margolin, in *Opera Omnia,* ASD I-2, p. 39.

31 Erasmus, *Hyperaspistes diatribae adversus servum arbitrium Martini Lutheri* (1526, 1527), in *Opera Omnia,* ed. Le Clerc (Leiden,

1706), LB X, pp. 1522–24. Cf. Charles Trinkaus, "Erasmus, Augustine, and the Nominalists," *Archive for Reformation History* 67 (1976): 5–32.

32 Erasmus, *Paraclesis*, trans. John Olin, in *Christian Humanism and the Reformation: Selected Writings of Erasmus*, 2d ed. (New York: Fordham University Press, 1975), p. 100. Also, *Hyperaspistes*, LB X, p. 1527.

33 First quote from *Enarratio in psalmos*, ASD V-2, p. 48. Second from "Convivium religiosum," in *Colloquia*, ASD, I-3 p. 251. Marjorie O'Rourke Boyle, who quotes the passage in *Christening Pagan Mysteries*, p. 86, shows how Erasmus vacillated on this point. The text on "the universal gift of Christ" appears in *Hyperaspistes*, LB X 1534.

34 Boyle, *Christening Pagan Mysteries*, p. 63.

35 Erasmus, *Opus epistolarum*, vol. 4, pp. 362–63. On Erasmus's tolerance, see Joseph Lecler, S.J., *Toleration and the Reformation*, trans. T. L. Westow (New York: Association Press, 1960), pp. 114–42. Erasmus believed that the search for theological truth could proceed only within a Christian consensus or concord. See J. K. McConica, "Erasmus and the Grammar of Consent," in *Scrinium Erasmianum*, J. Coppens, ed. (Leiden: E. J. Brill, 1969).

36 See Payne, *Erasmus* and, on Ecclesiology, Willi Hentze, *Kirche und kirchliche Einheit bei Desiderius Erasmus von Rotterdam* (Paderborn: Bonifacius Drückerei, 1974).

37 Auer, *Die vollkommene Frömmigkeit*, p. 137. Others, especially E.-W. Kohls, would undoubtedly disagree with my assessment that Erasmus's theology lacks comprehensiveness and even a sufficient unity. But Kohls's own *Die theologie des Erasmus* oversystematizes its subject.

38 Ardis B. Collins, *The Secular Is Sacred: Platonism and Thomism in Marsilio Ficino's Platonic Theology* (The Hague: Nyhoff, 1974) shows Ficino's ardent anti-Averrhoism but tends to overstress his Thomism.

39 Marsilio Ficino, *Theologia platonica* (Basel, 1532), bk. XIII, chap. 9.

40 Marsilio Ficino, "Argumentum in Platonicam Theologiam ad Laurentium Medicem," in *Prosatori Latini del Quatrocento*, ed. Eugenio Garin (Milan: Ricciardi, 1952), p. 342. Garin

translates *formosus* as *bello*, and *forma* as *bellezza*, thereby sidestepping the ambiguity but forcing the meaning.

41 "Deus ergo in summa intellectus cognitione quodammodo nox quaedam est intellectui. In summo voluntatis amore certe dies est voluntati." ("Argumentum," in *Prosatori*, ed. Garin, p. 344.)

42 Ernst Cassirer, *Individuum und Kosmos in der Renaissance* (1927; Darmstadt, 1963), p. 142.

43 Walter Dress, *Die Mystik des Marsilio Ficino* (Berlin, 1929), pp. 48- 60.

44 "Oration on the Dignity of Man," in *The Renaissance Philosophy of Man*, ed. Ernst Cassirer, Paul O. Kristeller, and John Randall (Chicago: University of Chicago Press, 1948), pp. 282–83. See David Ruderman, "The Hebrew Book in a Christian World," in *A Sign and a Witness: 2000 Years of Hebrew Books and Illuminated Manuscripts*, ed. Leonard Singer Gold (Oxford: Oxford University Press, 1988), pp. 101–13.

45 This transition occurred in Herbert of Cherbury. See Hans Urs von Balthasar, *Glaubhaft ist nur Liebe* (Einsiedeln: Johannes Verlag, 1963), p. 15.

46 Nietzsche, *The Antichrist*, bk. 1, § 61, in *The Portable Nietzsche*, trans. Walter Kaufmann (New York: Viking Press, 1954), p. 653. I translate *Umwertung* as "reversal" rather than "revaluation."

47 John Herman Randall, *The Making of the Modern Mind* (1926; New York: Columbia University Press, 1976), p. 144.

48 Roland Bainton, *Here I Stand* (New York: Abington Press, 1950). Luther's resistance to the secularization of the Renaissance is defended by Gerhard Ritter, *Luther: Gestalt und Tat* (München: Bruckmann Verlag, 1959). Will-Erich Peuckert calls Lutheranism "a reborn medieval Church," *Die grosse Wende* (1968; Hamburg: Claassen and Goverts, 1966), p. 585. Cf. Lewis W. Spitz, "Headwaters of the Reformation," in *Luther and the Dawn of the Modern Era*, ed. Heiko Oberman (Leiden: E. J. Brill, 1974), pp. 89–116.

49 *The Theologia Germanica of Martin Luther*, trans. Bengt Hoffmann, in *The Classics of Western Spirituality* (New York: Paulist Press, 1980), chap. 29, p. 101.

50 "Qui hoc statuamus justitiam non fuisse quoddam donum, quod ab extra accederet, separatum a natura hominis: sed fuisse vere naturalem, ut natura Adae esset diligere Deum, credere Deo, cognoscere Deum etc." Luther, *Genesis Vorlesung,* in *Werke* (Weimar, 1911), vol. 42, p. 124.

51 Johann Gerhard, *Werke,* ed. Fridericus Cotta, (Tübingen, 1762–89), vol. 4, p. 293. I owe this reference to Robert Spaemann, *Philosophische Essays* (Stuttgart: Reclam, 1983), p. 27, who speaks of a "naturalism" of grace.

52 See Heiko Oberman, "Nominalism and Luther," in *Luther and the Dawn of the Modern Era,* ed. Oberman, esp. pp. 65–68. The thesis defended by Denifle and Lortz that Luther's theology was basically nominalist has been generally abandoned. Even more so Bouyer's claim that the Reformation consisted of nothing more than traditional Christian piety couched in nominalist philosophy. It certainly does not apply to such early reformers as John Wyclif and Jan Hus, who both followed the *via antiqua* rather than the *via moderna.* Even their new theology of the sacraments and of the Eucharistic presence relies on a medieval, somewhat Platonizing scholastic realism.

53 On Luther's opposition to Biel concerning the question of justification, see Heiko A. Oberman, *The Harvest of Medieval Theology* (Cambridge: Harvard University Press, 1963; Durham, N.C.: Labyrinth Press, 1983), chap. 5, esp. pp. 139–45. In fact, St. Thomas in his *Summa Theologiae* had already denied that humans possess a natural capacity for preparing the reception of grace, a position Luther attributed to the extreme nominalist Gregory of Rimini (Oberman, pp. 143–44).

54 See the very instructive pages of Hans Küng in *Justification,* trans. Thomas Collins, Edmund E. Tolk, and David Granskou (New York: Thomas Nelson, 1964), pp. 208–21. According to the Lutheran theologian H. Rückert, *Die Rechtfertigungslehre auf dem Tridentinischen Konzil* (Bonn, 1925), the condemnation of Trent would have affected not Luther but Melanchton who alone had explicitly taught that God's declaration of justice does not render the person just.

55 The term *natura pura* was not used before Robert Bellarmine (1542–1621)—hence long after Luther. See H. Rondet, "Le problème de la nature pure en la théologie du XVIe siècle,"

Recherches de science religieuse 35 (1948): 481–522; Piet Smulders, "De oorsprong van de theorie der zuivere natuur," *Bijdragen* 10 (1949): 105–27. Yet the concept of the person (*in puris naturalibus*) had been around for well over a century, as is clear from Oberman, *Harvest of Medieval Theology* and Henry de Lubac, *Surnaturel* (Paris: Aubier, 1946).

56 Roland Bainton, *The Reformation of the XVIth Century* (Boston: Beacon Press, 1952), p. 69. How Luther and Erasmus argued at cross purposes appears in two essays by Marjorie O'Rourke Boyle, "The Chimera and the Spirit," *Michigan Germanic Studies* 10, nos. 1–2 (1984): 17–31; "Erasmus and the 'Modern' Question," *Archiv für Reformationsgeschichte* 75 (1984): 59–77 (elaborated in her *Rhetoric and Reform*). On the general relation between Luther and Erasmus, see Peuckert, *Die grosse Wende,* pp. 598–627.

57 Ritter, *Luther,* chap. 9. One understands why Kant has been called the philosopher of Protestantism.

58 William J. Bouwsma, *Calvin* (Berkeley: University of California Press, 1988).

59 I refer to the *Opera quae supersunt omnia,* 59 vols. (Brunswick, 1863–1900), *Corpus Reformatorum* series. For the *Institutes of Christian Religion,* I prefer to quote from John Allen's still excellent translation of 1813, which went through many editions.

60 Thomas F. Torrance, *Calvin's Doctrine of Man* (London: Lutterworth Press, 1949), pp. 61, 80.

61 In *Inst.* I, 15, 4 (*Opera* 2, p. 139) Calvin qualifies this to "almost obliterated."

62 C. Graafland, *De zekerheid von het geloof* (Wageningen, 1961), p. 35, and the entire section, pp. 29–44. Also, S. P. Dee, *Het geloofsbegrip van Calvijn* (Kampen, 1918), pp. 193ff.

63 Richard Popkin, *The History of Scepticism from Erasmus to Spinoza* (Berkeley: University of California Press, 1979), p. 190.

64 Cf. Paul Feyerabend, "Classical Empiricism," in *The Methodological Heritage of Newton,* ed. Robert Butts and John W. Davis (Toronto: University of Toronto Press, 1970), pp. 151–55. Cf., Jeffrey Stout, *The Flight from Authority* (Notre Dame, Ind.: University of Notre Dame Press, 1981), chap. 2.

65 Michael Walzer, *The Revolution of the Saints: A Study in the Origins of Radical Politics* (Cambridge: Harvard University Press, 1965), pp. 35, 152.

66 Jansenius supported this naturalist interpretation of Adam's condition by an amazing interpretation of Augustine's expression of wonder at the even greater abundance of grace granted to the elect after the fall.

67 De Lubac, *Surnaturel*, p. 69.

Chapter 9

1 Giles Constable, "The Popularity of Twelfth Century Spiritual Writers in the Late Middle Ages," in *Renaissance Studies in Honor of Hans Baron*, ed. Anthony Molho and John A. Tedeschi (DeKalb: Northern Illinois University Press, 1971), p. 5. Johan Huizinga had already made a similar claim: "The Renaissance exercised hardly any influence on the conception of saintly life. The saint and the mystic remain almost wholly untouched by the changing of times" (*The Waning of the Middle Ages* [1924; New York: Doubleday, 1956], p. 183).

2 Francis Hermans in his four-volume *Histoire doctrinale de l'humanisme chrétien* (Tournai: Casterman, 1947) holds this position.

3 The term *Christian humanism* appears in its spiritual sense in Henry Bremond, *Histoire littéraire du sentiment religieux en France* (Paris: Bloud et Gay, 1916–33), vol. 1, intro. chap. The term *devout humanism*, in Julien-Eymard d'Angers, O.F.M. Cap., *L'humanisme chrétien au XVIIe siécle: S. Francois de Sales et Yves de Paris* (The Hague: Martinus Nijhoff, 1970).

4 Even those medieval writers who influenced Ignatius, such as Gerson, Thomas a Kempis, and Pseudo-Bonaventure, did not leave rules for prayer. The twelfth-century *Scala Claustralium* presents an early attempt, but its counsels lack the conciseness and precision of the *Exercises*. Cf., Alexandre Brou, S.J., *S. Ignace, Maitre d'oraison* (1925). Only Garcia de Cisneros's *Exercitatorio* (1492) anticipated Ignatius's work with his developmental concept of the three "ways," but Ignatius alone succeeded in combining disparate rules into a practical guide for an undeviating, goal-directed progression.

5 Ignatius of Loyola, *The Spiritual Exercises of St. Ignatius*, trans. Louis J. Puhl (Westminster,

Md.: Newman Press, 1954), # 184 (henceforth referred to by paragraph number only). In the Constitutions Ignatius in even more explicit terms prescribes for his followers: "Let them seek God in all things, freed as much as possible from the love of creatures in order to refer all their love to the Creator, loving Him in all his creatures *and all creatures in Him*, according to His holy and divine will" (pt. III, chap. 1, # 26; rule 17 of the *Summarium Constitutionum*).

6 Transparencia was the distinctive trait of Ignatius's spirituality according to Ignacio Iparraguirre, *Espiritu de San Ignacio de Loyola* (Bilbao, 1958).

7 In the *Letter on Obedience*, § 7, Ignatius claims that such a submission, far from diminishing freedom, augments and perfects it.

8 Francis de Sales, *Traité de l'amour de Dieu*, in *Oeuvres de Saint Francois de Sales* (Annecy: Niérat, 1892–1964), vol. 5, bk. I, chap. 15 (henceforth referred to by Roman numeral [book] and number [chapter]).

9 Francis de Sales, *Oeuvres*, vol. 20, *Lettres*, p. 281.

10 The manner in which Francis streamlines the dual causality of God and man bears the nominalist marks of the disputes on nature and grace as pursued in the theology of his time. Lacking the speculative ability to sail between the cliffs of either human effort or divine predestination as the principal agent of salvation or reprobation, he ended up embracing Molina's theory. God grants efficacious grace to those whom he foresees will respond to it, thus assuming a time sequence in God who first wants to save all people, then, in a second moment, grants grace only to those who will adequately respond to it (VIII, 3).

11 Imbric Buffum, *Studies in the Baroque from Montaigne to Rotrou* (New Haven: Yale University Press, 1957), pp. 77–114.

12 Francis de Sales, *Introduction to the Devout Life*, trans. Michael Day (Westminster, Md.: Newman Press, 1955), bk. III, chap. 39, p. 197.

13 De Sales, *Introduction*, pp. 77 and 148.

14 Eric Lund, "Protestant Spirituality. Second Age of the Reformation: Lutheran and Reformed Spirituality," in *Christian Spirituality: Post-Reformation and Modern*, ed. Louis

Dupré and Don E. Saliers, vol. 18 of *World Spirituality* (New York: Crossroad, 1989), pp. 213–39.

15 On Coornhert, Camphuysen, and other dissidents in the Dutch Reformed Church, see Leszek Kolakowski, *Chrétiens sans Eglise* (Paris: Gallimard, 1969).

16 Sebastian Castellio, *De arte dubitandi*, in *Per la storia degli eretici italiani del secolo XVI in Europa*, ed. D. Cantimori and F. Feist, vol. 7 of *Studi e documenti* (Roma: Reale Academia d'Italia, 1937), p. 314, trans. in Steven E. Ozment, *Mysticism and Dissent* (New Haven: Yale University Press, 1973), pp. 190–91. Steven Ozment has shown how far removed this religion of "reason" stood from the rationalism of the Enlightenment. Castellio found it most satisfactorily expressed in mystical writings. He himself edited the *Theologia germanica* in Latin and in French. Grace united the soul with God, inspiring contemplation as well as good works.

17 P. McNair, *Peter Martyr in Italy: An Anatomy of Apostasy* (Oxford: Oxford University Press, 1967), p. 8. On the entire movement viewed from the perspective of its main representative in Italy, Cardinal Pole and his Viterbo circle, see Dermot Fenlon, *Heresy and Obedience in Tridentine Italy: Cardinal Pole and the Counter Reformation* (Cambridge: Cambridge University Press, 1972). Also, the classical text, D. Cantimori, *Eretici italiani del Cinquecento* (Florence, 1939).

18 *The Theologia Germanica of Martin Luther*, trans. Bengt Hoffman, *The Classics of Western Spirituality* (New York: Paulist Press, 1980), p. 54.

19 Thomas Müntzer, *Thomas Müntzer: Schriften und Briefe. Kritische Gesamtausgabe*, ed. Guenther Franz (Gütersloh, 1968), p. 425.

20 Valentin Weigel, *Gnothi seauton* (1615), bk. I, p. 54. Quoted in Ozment, *Mysticism and Dissent*, p. 219.

21 Valentin Weigel, *Kirchen-oder Hauss-Postill* (s.l., 1700), bk. III, pp. 39–41, trans. in Ozment, *Mysticism and Dissent*, p. 236.

22 Jacob Boehme, *Mysterium magnum* (1623), in *Werke*, ed. Johann Wilhelm Ueberfeldt (Leiden, 1730), vol. 1, 2.

23 Boehme, *De signatura rerum*, in *Werke*, ed. Ueberdeldt, vol. 9, 1.

24 Alexandre Koyré, *La philosophie de Jacob Boehme* (Paris, 1929), p. 393.

25 Heinz Heimsoeth, *Die sechs groszen Themen der abendländischen Metaphysik und der Ausgang des Mittelalters* (Berlin: Georg Stilke, 1922), pp. 54–81.

26 Carl S. Friedrich, *The Age of the Baroque, 1610–1660* (New York: Harper and Brothers, 1952), p. 161. One may compare this view with D. J. Gordon's concordant judgment on the politicized iconography in the art of Rubens's time: "This was a world where the 'real,' the 'historical,' could cohabit with the feigned, where the hard political programme could, without distortion, undergo translation into symbol. . . . If we persist, in a later mode, in being scandalized about boundaries between the sacred and profane, or the 'real' and the 'feigned,' we can never understand or feel the power of such great public images." J. D. Gordon, *The Renaissance Imagination*, ed. Stephen Orgel (Berkeley: University of California Press, 1975), p. 32.

27 Friedrich, Ibid., p. 186.

28 Karsten Harries, *The Bavarian Baroque Church: Between Faith and Aesthetics.* (New Haven: Yale University Press, 1983), p. 179.

29 This is the leading idea of Hans Urs von Balthasar's discussion of the Baroque in *Herrlichkeit*, pt. III, vol. 1 (Einsiedeln: Johannes Verlag, 1965), pp. 459–63 and of the Baroque theatre in *Theodramatik* (Einsiedeln: Johannes Verlag, 1973), vol. 1, pp. 147–160. Cf., Peter Casarella, "Representation: Zum Barockverständnis bei Hans Urs von Balthasar (1905–1988)," in *Reisen des Barok: Selbst-und Fremderfahrungen und ihre Darstellung*, ed. Regina Pleithner, *Abhandlungen zur Sprache und Literatur*, ed. Richard Baum (Bonn: Romanistischer Verlag, 1991), pp. 1–24.

30 Jean Rousset, *Le baroque*, vol. 2 of *Histoire des littératures* (Paris: Gallimard, 1956), p. 217.

31 John Donne links the theatre metaphor to man's religious destiny in a sermon: "Hath God made this World his Theatre, *ut exhibeatur ludus deorum*, that man may represent God in his conversation; and wilt thou play no part?" *The Sermons of John Donne*, ed. George R. Potter and Evelyn M. Simpson (Berkeley: University of California Press, 1962), p. 206. I owe this reference to Peter Casarella's rich article. On the *theatrum mundi,* see Richard Alewyn, *Das grosze Welttheater: Die Epoche der höfischen Feste in Dokument und Deutung* (Hamburg: Rowohlt, 1959), pp. 9–70. On Baroque drama itself, see Hans Urs von Balthasar, "Theologie und Metaphysik des Welttheaters im Barock," in *Theodramatik,* vol. 1, pp. 147–60. The role is all that matters, yet the actor must actively interpret it, and he remains aware of the fact that he represents only what he plays. Nowhere does the contrast between the meaning represented and the means of representation appear more evidently than in drama.

32 See Frank J. Warnke, *European Metaphysical Poetry* (New Haven: Yale University Press, 1961; 1974), p. 2.

33 Calderon de la Barca, *Life Is a Dream,* trans. Denis Florence MacCarthy, in *The Chief European Dramatists,* ed. Brander Matthews (New York: Houghton Mifflin, 1944).

34 Von Balthasar observed: "The moment, the now, is the ever and never returning occasion for moral decision. Baroque life is thus at once static, void of development, and dramatically propelled." Hans Urs von Balthasar, ed., *Deutsche Barock Lyrik* (Basel: Benno Schwabe, 1945), "Nachwort, p. 202.

35 Harries, *The Bavarian Baroque Church,* esp. chaps. 1–3.

36 See the beautiful study of C. A. van Swigchem, T. Brouwer, and W. van Os, *Een huis voor het woord* (s'Gravenhage: Staatsuitgeverij, 1984), on reformed church architecture in the northern Netherlands since the sixteenth century.

37 C. E. Hooykaas, *Christus bij Rembrandt* (Huis ter Heide, 1925); also, R. Miedema, *De Bijbel in de beeldende kunst* (The Hague: Servire, 1947), chap. 9.

38 See the revealing chapters on anti-semitism (9), witch hunting (11), and heresy trials (13) interpreted as expressions of fear in Jean Delumeau, *La Peur en Occident* (XIVe siècles) (Paris: Fayard, 1978).

39 Michel de Certeau, *La possession de Loudun* (Paris: Julliard, 1970; 1990), p. 12.

40 See Walter Benjamin, *The Origin of German Tragic Drama,* trans. John Osborne (London: NLB, 1977). (The original *Ursprung des deutschen Trauerspiels* was published in

1928.) On Gryphius: Hans Küng and Walter Jens, *Dichtung und Religion* (München: Kindler, 1985), the entire chapter on Gryphius.

41 John Donne, "The Second Anniversary" (of Elisabeth Drury's death), in *The Poems of John Donne,* ed. Herbert J. C. Grierson (Oxford: Clarendon Press, 1912, 1968), vs. 169–76.

42 Von Balthasar, ed., *Deutsche Barock Lyrik,* pp. 88–90 (my translation).

43 See Warnke, *European Metaphysical Poetry,* p. 23. I do not find it necessary to distinguish metaphysical from High Baroque poetry as he does. The former contains the quintessence, the deeper meaning, of the latter.

44 Christopher Dawson, "Catholicism and the Bourgeois Mind," in *Dynamics of World History,* ed. John J. Mulloy (La Salle, Ill.: Sherwood Sugden, 1978), p. 209.

Index

In some larger entries the subentries are in historically chronological order.